D0014030

I Saw the Light

I Saw the Light

The Story of Hank Williams

COLIN ESCOTT

with George Merritt
and William MacEwen

BACK BAY BOOKS
Little, Brown and Company
New York   Boston   London

Copyright © 2004 by Colin Escott

All rights reserved. In accordance with the U.S. Copyright Act of 1976, the scan-
ning, uploading, and electronic sharing of any part of this book without the permission of the publisher constitute unlawful piracy and theft of the author's intellectual
property. If you would like to use material from the book (other than for review purposes), prior written permission must be obtained by contacting the publisher at
permissions@hbgusa.com. Thank you for your support of the author's rights.

Back Bay Books / Little, Brown and Company
Hachette Book Group
1290 Avenue of the Americas, New York, NY 10104
littlebrown.com

Revised edition originally published in trade paperback by Back Bay Books under the
title *Hank Williams: The Biography,* April 2004
Back Bay paperback media tie-in edition, November 2015

Back Bay Books is an imprint of Little, Brown and Company, a division of Hachette
Book Group, Inc. The Back Bay Books name and logo are trademarks of Hachette
Book Group, Inc.

The publisher is not responsible for websites (or their content) that are not owned by
the publisher.

The Hachette Speakers Bureau provides a wide range of authors for speaking events.
To find out more, go to hachettespeakersbureau.com or call (866) 376-6591.

ISBN 978-0-316-73497-4 (rev. ed.) / 978-0-316-31505-0 (media tie-in ed.)
Library of Congress Control Number 2003026510

10 9 8 7 6 5 4 3 2 1

RRD-C

Printed in the United States of America

CONTENTS

TO A HILLBILLY SINGER DYING YOUNG

*H*ANK Williams has been dead for fifty years. In fact, it was fifty years ago the night of this writing that he began his last journey. Knowing all that we now know about the precise route, it's tempting to look at the clock and imagine where he was. It's equally tempting to wonder if *he* knew where he was. Midnight struck for Hank Williams somewhere on that last eerie road trip. But where? Born in the oppressive heat and humidity of south Alabama, he almost certainly died with snow in his headlights.

Ten years ago, I was finishing the first edition of this book. I clearly remember working on New Year's Eve 1992, having much the same thoughts as I have now. Where was he forty years ago tonight? If asked, I wouldn't have bet on too much new information turning up between the fortieth and fiftieth anniversaries of his death. Perhaps a couple of interviewees who'd eluded us would emerge; perhaps one or two who'd avoided us would cooperate; perhaps a few recordings would turn up. I thought our little book would otherwise stand unchallenged and unchanged. But I was wrong. Several of Hank's former bandmembers, long thought lost, have indeed come forward. Many new recordings have been uncovered. Hank's sister, Irene, died, leaving a trove of photos, papers, and memorabilia that no one knew she possessed. Another trove of legal correspondence has surfaced, and beneath the lawyers' dry concision there's a sense of the bitter conflict that drove one legal action after another, year upon year. Crucial information has emerged on the blues musician, "Tee-Tot," who taught Hank. Even more information has surfaced on the long car ride during which Hank died and the bogus doctor who treated Hank with such disastrous results over his last weeks.

As early as New Year's Day 1953, Hank Williams became an object. Parties wrestled over him, not only as if he wasn't there (which, of course, he wasn't), but as if he'd *never* been there. He was like an antique to which several family members laid claim. Yet the reason that the legal actions continue year after year is that the small body of work left to us grows in importance. Every year, several hundred thousand people buy a Hank Williams CD. Surely longtime fans aren't buying these records. Thanks to the record companies, longtime fans have every hit several times over. Those several hundred thousand new sales must, for the greater part, represent a new audience discovering the truths that we discovered all those years ago. It seems as though the sterner stuff survives. Both Frank Sinatra and Perry Como sold millions of records, yet it's Sinatra's dark soliloquies that have lasted while Como's records remain trapped in their place and time. Bruce Springsteen's bleakly minimalist *Nebraska* dismayed the stadium rock crowd on release in 1982, but now sounds better with every passing year. The fierce, insurgent music of Hank Williams still reaches us in a way that the cheerier music of Eddy Arnold and Red Foley does not. Yet, in the late 1940s and early 1950s, Arnold and Foley comfortably outsold Hank Williams.

Hank Williams had the great fortune to come and go at exactly the right time. Most of his contemporaries lived long enough to make some very bad records; Hank didn't. Most of his contemporaries had to come to terms first with rock 'n' roll, then with the Nashville Sound; Hank didn't. Several of his contemporaries found themselves hawking remakes of their greatest hits on cable television; Hank didn't. Death is a good career move if it can be timed right, and no one ever timed it better than Hank Williams. In terms of forging a legend, he could have done no better than burn out at twenty-nine before his fire grew dim and the face of country music changed. His death left what is still the most important body of work in country music; in fact, one of the defining caches of American music. It also left the tantalizing promise of what might have been.

Perhaps the next ten years will see as much new information emerge as has emerged in the last ten years, but that's no reason to hold off this revision. For a few weeks in 1994, we flattered ourselves into believing that our old work was definitive. That's no longer the case. Enough new information has surfaced to warrant a complete rewrite, and so many new photos have been found that Kira Florita and I coproduced a photo-essay, *Hank Williams: Snapshots from the Lost Highway* (DaCapo Press, 2001), which serves as a companion piece to this work.

Thinking about Hank Williams, I return endlessly to a poem I learned back in England when I was a child, A. E. Housman's "To an Athlete Dying Young." Housman says much that I've struggled to say when called upon to explain the iconic power of Hank Williams. Here it is, in part.

> *Smart lad, to slip betimes away*
> *From fields where glory does not stay*
> *And early though the laurel grows*
> *It withers quicker than the rose.*
>
> *Eyes the shady night has shut*
> *Cannot see the record cut,*
> *And silence sounds no worse than cheers*
> *After earth has stopped the ears;*
>
> *Now you will not swell the rout*
> *Of lads that wore their honours out,*
> *Runners whom renown outran*
> *And the name died before the man.*

Colin Escott
New Year's Eve 2002

I Saw the Light

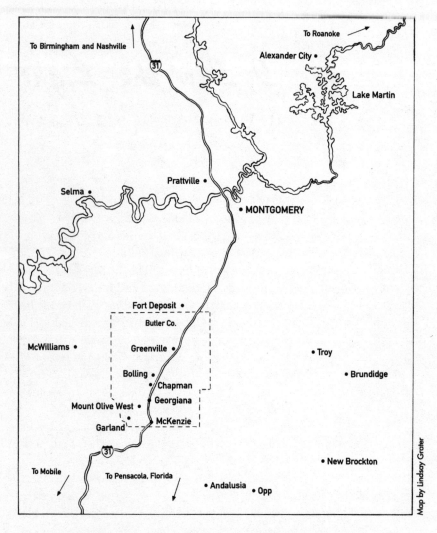

South Central Alabama

The road to that bright happy region
Is narrow and twisted, they say
But the broad one that leads to perdition
Is posted and blazed all the way.
"The Drifting Cowboy's Dream" (unknown)

• •

THE DRIFTING COWBOY'S DREAM

• • • • • • • • • • • • • • • • • • • •

*T*HE Mount of Olives, which overlooks Jerusalem from the east, will, according to the Book of Matthew, be the gathering place when the dead rise upon the Messiah's return. Those buried on the Mount will be the first to rise, and will have pride of place at the Messiah's side. As a child, Hank Williams would not go to sleep unless a Bible lay beside him in bed, so he inevitably learned about the Mount of Olives, but had he returned to his birthplace in Mount Olive, Alabama, he would have seen a red-dirt settlement of half a dozen houses strung desultorily along an unpaved road. Not even a crossroads. The few souls that resided there eked out a living as farmers or as indentured employees of the lumber companies opening up the dark, coniferous forests of south Alabama.

Hank was the third and last child of Elonzo "Lon" Huble Williams and his wife Jessie Lillybelle "Lilly" Skipper Williams. Their first child was alive at birth but died soon after; it's unknown if he or she was even named. Lon and Lilly's second child, Irene, was born on August 8, 1922; Hank followed on September 17, 1923. According to Lon, Hank was to be christened Hiram, after King Hiram of Tyre in the Book of Kings, but when he was belatedly registered with the Bureau of Vital Statistics at the age of ten, it was as "Hiriam." Friends, family, and neighbors called the boy "Harm" or "Skeets." He was born at home in a double-pen log house known as the Kendrick Place because it had been built in the late 1800s by Mr. Wiley Kendrick and his wife, Fanny. Lon proudly told Hank's first biographer, Roger Williams, that he paid thirty-five dollars to have a doctor in attendance, and had enough money set aside to hire a black nanny.

Lon Williams was thirty-one years old when Hank arrived. Lon was born on December 23, 1891, in Macedonia in Lowndes County, Alabama. His family came from North Carolina, and the surviving photo of his grandmother shows a woman with high Indian cheekbones and deep-set eyes. Hank always said he was part Indian, and there was probably some Creek or Cherokee on his father's side. Lon's mother, Martha Ann Autrey Williams, committed suicide when he was six. Lon would tell his children about the time he found his mother dead; sometimes he said she drank rat poison, other times he said she hanged herself. Never did he say why. His father, Irvin, moved the family to McWilliams, Alabama, a lumber company town some thirty miles from Greenville. Irvin died in 1909 when Lon was seventeen, but from the time he was twelve, Lon drifted, working as a water boy, ox driver, or anything else he could get. He grew up without a father just as Hank would, just as Hank Jr. would. Hank Jr.'s children might have wished he was around more, too.

Jessie Lillybelle Skipper was a delicate name for a woman who, had she been a canary, would have sung bass. Born in Butler County on August 12, 1898, Lilly was a large, broad-boned woman, and the one thing that everyone agrees upon is that she didn't take no crap. Quite what Lon saw in her, or she saw in Lon, is unclear; later in life, neither could mention the other's name without a curse. Lilly ruled every one of her roosts with a steely sense of purpose, hardened by having to deal with one feckless, useless man after another. She could be funny, even tender, but always formidably strong willed, and not much given to self-doubt.

The Skippers lived for a while around Chapman, Alabama, and Lon was probably working near there on a lumber train crew when he met Lilly. She was eighteen, almost a spinster, when they married on November 12, 1916. On July 9, 1918, as the First World War was drawing to a close, Lon was sent to Camp Shelby in Mississippi, then on to France with the 113th Regiment of Engineers, 42nd Division. Shortly after arriving, he suffered an injury, but not one sustained in combat. He later told his family that he'd fallen from a truck while hauling rocks, although others in the family heard that he'd gotten into a fight with another soldier, reportedly over a French girl. He either fell from the truck onto his head or was struck on the side of his head in the fight. He spent about a week in the base hospital before being shipped back to the front. He seemed to have recovered, but it was an injury that would come back to haunt him.

On June 26, 1919, Lon was discharged from Camp Gordon, Georgia, returned to Alabama, and began working for the lumber companies. The company crews ran narrow-gauge railroad tracks up to the logging sites, and entire families lived on-site in boxcars for weeks or months at a stretch. Lon drove the log trains, and worked, as he was fond of saying, "from can to cain't."

When Irene and Hank arrived, though, Lon and Lilly were renting the old Kendrick place for eighty dollars a year, and running a small strawberry farm with a country store on one end of their house. Then a late frost hit, probably in the spring of 1924, and Lon was forced back to work for the lumber companies. He started with Ray Lumber in Atmore, then moved to W. T. Smith. By the time Lilly finally got around to registering Hank's birth in 1934, she stated that Lon was working as an engineer for the lumber companies when Hank was born, which was a few months shy of the truth.

Hank later said that his first recollection was of living in the W. T. Smith boxcar at the McKenzie camp near Chapman. Soon after that, Lon bought a house a mile and a half out of Georgiana and worked on the Ruthven job. Then, in 1927, he sold up and bought a house and ten acres in McWilliams, continuing on the Ruthven job for W. T. Smith until 1929. It was in McWilliams that Hank attended first and second grade. McWilliams was another tiny settlement almost entirely dependent upon the lumber business. Every house, every business was built of pine, and every man worked either for the lumber companies or for a business that depended on them. The Louisville and Nashville (L&N) Railroad opened up the town around 1900, and it was as bustling as it ever was when Lon and Lilly moved there. It was insular and self-contained in the way that communities were when the mule was more commonly seen on the roads than an automobile.

Hank was his parents' child in every respect. Whether through propinquity or some mystery of DNA, Hank had Lilly's driving ambition, but it would be repeatedly subverted by Lon's tendency to backslide. Later, when he was berated for his drinking, Hank was fond of saying, "If you think I'm a drunk, you shoulda seen my old man" (although as Hank knew well, Lon had ceased drinking by then). For her part, Lilly saw some of Lon's lack of willpower and damnable sloth in Hank and cursed them both, telling her son that he was no better than his wastrel of a father.

Writing about Hank in a notoriously unreliable memoir called *Life Story of Our Hank Williams,* Lilly said that he always liked to sing, but so do most children. Looking now down the wrong end of the telescope, it's hard to tell if Hank was the wunderkind in whom talent was innate, or if he simply had a bent for music that he nurtured until it became the easiest way he knew of making a living. Between Lon and Lilly there was some musical talent. Lon played the Jew's harp, and Lilly played the organ at the Mount Olive Baptist Church and at other churches they attended. Her father, John, wrote folk hymns. She sang in her strong, resonant voice, which some said could make the skin tingle on your neck. She loved to tell how Hank always sat beside her and sang too, and Hank certainly seemed to view those Sundays at his mother's side as the beginning of it all. "My earliest memory," he told journalist Ralph J. Gleason, "is sittin' on that organ stool by her and hollerin'. I must have been five, six years old, and louder 'n anybody else."

One reason that Hank might have been drawn to music is that he knew from an early age that he wasn't as physically strong as most kids, and was unsuited to logging or farming. Lon told a couple of interviewers that there was a raised spot on the boy's spine, but neither he nor Lilly understood what it was. In all likelihood, it was the first sign of spina bifida occulta, a condition in which the vertebral arches of the spine fail to unite, allowing the spinal cord to herniate or protrude through the spinal column. That birth defect would determine the outcome of Hank's life every bit as much as his love of music. From the beginning, he was frail and spindly, and much as he wanted to join in sports, he lacked the physical coordination and stamina. He grew up in a community with strong shared values, chief among them pride in physical strength. His apartness stemmed in great measure from his physical affliction. One of his earliest published songs was "Back Ache Blues," and it would be the one kind of blues he knew all too well throughout his life.

In 1928 or 1929, shortly after moving back to McWilliams, Lon's face slowly became paralyzed; he couldn't blink and couldn't smile. As his condition worsened, he quit W. T. Smith to take a lighter job with Ralph Lumber in Bolling, and in September 1929, he ceased work altogether. The following January, Lilly took him to the Veterans Administration hospital in Pensacola, Florida. From there, he was transferred to the V.A. hospital in Alexandria, Louisiana. Lilly wrote later that he had been gassed and shell-shocked, but Lon told his family that he had a brain aneurysm, probably as a result of the injury in France. He stayed in Alexandria until January 1937. Hank was six when Lon left, and while Lilly was more than up to the task of raising her children by herself, Lon's absence only heightened Hank's isolation. Perhaps the most heartwrenching unpublished song in his early notebooks is one titled "I Wish I Had a Dad":

> When he said, "What do you want that 'til now you haven't
>   had?"
> I said, "You was it once. Could you be again? I want a full-time
>   Dad."

After Lon left, Lilly's brother-in-law, Walter McNeil, moved the family into Garland to live with them and Lilly's mother. Lilly then scrimped and saved enough to move her brood into Georgiana, the first town of any size Hank had ever lived in. It had been founded in 1855 by Pitts Milner, a preacher with a capitalistic streak. He got into the sawmill business and named the town Pittsville in his honor. Then his daughter, Georgiana, fell into a bog and suffocated, so he renamed the settlement in her memory. The Williamses joined fifteen hundred others in Georgiana, 30 percent of them black. The Louisville and Nashville Railroad bisected the town's stores, gins, and other businesses.

The first house Lilly, Irene, and Hank lived in was a dilapidated wooden shack on old Highway 31 (the major north-south route through the South), but it burned down a few months later. Lilly and the children ran out wearing only their nightgowns. Lilly grabbed Lon's shotgun as she was leaving. They moved back with the McNeils for a while, and then, as Irene wrote in the *Washington Post,* "Mother found a small house to rent near the railroad tracks, and she put Hank, me and our few belongings on a wagon and started toward that little house. On the way she stopped to mail a letter. A man walked up to her in the post office and asked if she was the lady whose house had burned. 'I am Thaddeus B. Rose,' he told her. 'I have a house you are welcome to rent free until you can get on your feet.'"

It was an imposing house, by far the finest dwelling Lilly, Irene, or Hank had ever been inside. These days, it's numbered 127 Rose Street, the street that Thaddeus B. Rose named for himself. He excavated the soil from beneath the house for another project, and ordered that the house be built on stilts, raising it six feet off the ground. Rose was one of Georgiana's grandees, a bachelor who lived away from the tracks. He later founded the Georgiana library, and local wisdom has it that he got the idea for the house on stilts from traveling in the swampland around New Orleans. A long hallway ran through the center of the house, the toilet was in an outhouse, and there was one faucet.

Lilly's possessions were few when she moved in. She stuffed feed sacks with corn shucks for beds, used apple boxes for her dresser, and cooked in the fireplace. Local families gave her what they could spare, but Lilly was determined that she would accept charity no longer than she had to. The Simses lived across the street, and Lilly gave them the impression that Lon was dead. "They had no money," said Harold Sims, who was four years older than Hank. "Most Sundays after church, my mother would ask me to take a platter of roast chicken, pork chops, rice and gravy, pie to them. They acted like they were counting on it."

Shortly after the Williamses moved into Rose's house, Lilly took on two more charges, her nieces Marie and Bernice McNeil, the daughters of her sister Annie Skipper and Annie's husband, Grover McNeil. After Annie died of typhoid fever, Grover paid for Lilly to care for Marie and Bernice, and they all became part of Hank's extended family. From time to time, Lilly looked after her mother too, all the while working as a practical nurse at what was called Tippins Hospital. The hospital was a large house that looked like a convalescent home, run by Dr. H. K. Tippins and his brother. Overnight care was offered, and Lilly was on night duty. She later prevailed upon Dr. Tippins to sign Hank's birth certificate. To supplement her income, she lobbied a local politician to collect Lon's full disability pension, and took in a couple of boarders, which gave her the idea of getting into the rooming house business.

Lilly fostered Hank's interest in singing, but she was determined that if he was to sing, it would be in praise of the Lord. She scraped together a few dollars and sent him to a shape-note singing school in Avant, near Georgiana. The hymns Hank learned there and in church every Sunday colored his approach to music as nothing else ever would. Black church music entered his life, too. "Wednesday evenings, me and

Hiram would sit on a board fence around their house and listen to the Negro church," said his neighbor Harold Sims. "It was about a mile away. It was prayer meetin' night. The most beautiful music in the world. The breeze came from the south and it would undulate the sound. One minute soft, next minute loud, like it was orchestrated. One night, Hiram looked up at me and said, 'One day, I'm gonna write songs like that.'" Years later, Hank told his first wife, Audrey, that his favorite song was "Death Is Only a Dream"; its morbidity and superstition resonated within him in a way that the era's popular songs never did.

> Sadly we sing and with tremulous breath
> As we stand by the mystical stream,
> In the valley and by the dark river of death,
> And yet 'tis no more than a dream.

Much else informed Hank Williams' music, but the essence of it is there. From the holy songs, Hank learned how to express profound sentiments in words that an unlettered farmer could understand, and he came to appreciate music's spiritual component. He also loved the warm glow of recognition that the simple melodies elicited, and their effect was so profound that his own melodies would rarely be more complicated than the hymns and folk songs he heard as a child. On his radio shows later in life, he would almost always sing an old hymn, remembering every line of every verse. Hank was a believer, but not, in later life, a churchgoer. Perhaps he felt unworthy, perhaps his schedule didn't permit it, but even in beer joints he would sometimes throw everyone off guard with a hymn. Knowing himself to be a backslider, and knowing that he had been weighed in the balance and found wanting in so many ways, he seemed to find rare peace in the hymns of his childhood.

Another craft that Hank learned early in life was hawking. Lilly and Irene would roast peanuts and Hank would go out onto the streets of Georgiana and sell them. "The first day," wrote Lilly in a booklet not always given to accuracy, "he made thirty cents, and I remember how proud he was when he brought home the thirty cents' worth of stew meat, tomatoes and rice he bought with it. 'Mama,' he shouted, 'fix us some gumbo stew. We're gonna eat tonight!'" A more believable coda to the story came from Oscar Vickery, a neighbor of the Williamses after they moved to Greenville. He remembered Lilly counting the bags of peanuts before Hank left the house and counting the nickels that came back in. Even then, she didn't trust him, but even then Hank was outwitting her by taking a few peanuts from every bag and making up another bag and keeping a nickel for himself. Low cunning to get the better of a grasping woman was a skill that Hank would use the rest of his life.

At the beginning of the September 1933 school year, Hank moved to Fountain, Alabama, to live with his cousins, the McNeils. There was a high school in Georgiana, but not in Fountain, and the McNeils' daughter, Opal, was high school age. Hank was going to grammar school then, so he lived with the McNeils while Opal lived with Lilly and went to high school. For twenty-one years, Hank's uncle, Walter McNeil, was an engineer with W. T. Smith, moving the family from settlement to settlement. In Fountain, they lived in three boxcars, and Hank attended the single-room schoolhouse. His aunt Alice taught him some of the rudiments of music, and his cousin J.C. showed him what growing up in the woods was all about. "We'd fish, hunt," said J.C. "Hell, there was nothin' else to do. Every dog we'd find, we'd try and make it into a hunting dog. We hunted squirrels, rabbits." In interviews and in song, Hank would rhapsodize about rural life, but the year he spent with the McNeils was the last time he lived it. From the time he returned to Georgiana, he was a city boy, and the cities kept getting bigger.

The year with the McNeils also marked the beginning of Hank's drinking. He was eleven at the time. J.C.'s father, Walter, hid his liquor under his mattress, and Hank and J.C. would pour some out, then fill up Walter's bottle with water. Later, Hank and J.C. would watch to see where the loggers hid their hooch when they went to a social, then they'd sneak over, steal it, and make off into the woods. They'd drink, as the saying went around there, 'til they could have laid on the ground and fallen off it.

Hank returned to Georgiana in 1934. By now, he was performing on the streets and at the railroad station, taking requests and learning how to hold an audience. He pestered the town's old-time fiddlers to show him what they knew. Cade Durham was a cobbler who walked with a stick, smoking a stogie jammed into a cigar holder; Jim Warren owned a jewelry and instruments store. Both showed Hank the rudiments of hoedown fiddling and some major chords on the guitar. Late in life, Hank would play the fiddle only when he was in his cups, but throughout his early career he was a half-proficient hoedown fiddler. Where and when he got his first guitar has long been a matter of conjecture; he could have lined a wall with all the first guitars people claimed to have given him. Talking to Ralph Gleason, though, Hank said the first one came from his mother when he was eight, which more or less backs up what Lilly always said. Several people remember him practicing under the house on Rose Street. He would sit on an old car seat, pick out his chords, and sing. Lilly, who was trying to catch some sleep above, would lean out of the window and yell, "Harm, hush up that fuss."

It was probably in Georgiana that Hank met his first acknowledged musical influence, a black street musician, Rufus Payne. Because Payne was rarely found without a home-brewed mix of alcohol and tea, Payne's nickname was "Tee-Tot," a pun on teetotaler. Details about him are not only sketchy, but contradictory as well. According to researcher Alice Harp, Rufus was born in 1884 on the Payne Plantation in Sandy Ridge, Lowndes County, Alabama. His parents had been slaves there, but they moved to New Orleans around 1890, giving Rufus a front-row seat for the birth of jazz. After his parents died, Rufus settled in Greenville, Alabama. Harp insists that Payne became a society musician, playing white functions, learning all the pop hits of the day. The musician that Hank's cousins J. C. and Walter McNeil Jr. remembered was quite different. Payne, said J. C. McNeil, lived down by the tracks in Greenville and worked part-time at Peagler's Drug Store as a cleaner and delivery person. Both McNeils remember that he had a hunched back and long arms that extended almost to his knees. "He would play the guitar and the cymbals," said Walter McNeil. "He had the cymbals tied between his legs, and he had this thing around his neck with the jazz horn, I think he called it, and the Jew's harp. And he could play all those things with the guitar and called himself a one-man band. He had a cigar box in front of him where you'd throw the money." Tee-Tot, sometimes in the company of other musicians, went out into the surrounding towns to play on the sidewalks. Although Hank probably met him on the streets of Georgiana, he later told one of his band members, Lum York, that Tee-Tot was a janitor at the school in Greenville, implying that Hank met Tee-Tot after the Williamses moved to Greenville.

A crowd of kids followed Tee-Tot around, but Hank was the only one who wanted to do more than listen. He wanted to learn. Exactly what passed between Hank Williams and Rufus Payne will never be known. If, as has often been said, Payne gave Hank lessons, it's hard to know what he imparted. Hank probably already knew most of the chords that Payne knew, so perhaps the lessons involved broader strokes. J. C. McNeil, who insisted he also took lessons from Payne, said that Payne always stressed the importance of keeping time and getting a good rhythm going. Later, one of the elements that would set Hank apart from his contemporaries was the irresistible drive to his music. He was never an accomplished guitarist, but his bands would always take their cue from his forceful rhythm guitar playing. He whanged the E chord in a way that any blues singer would recognize. Rufus Payne almost certainly taught Hank some songs, and while Hank probably forgot most of them, he never lost the lazy swing and sock rhythm. The blues feel that permeates all but the goofiest of Hank's songs is another thing that Rufus Payne probably brought out.

Lilly says she fed Payne in exchange for Hank's lessons, but memories of him are otherwise vague. Some say he played the blues alone, others say that he led a little combo that played pop songs and hokum numbers. Irene said that Payne once came to Lilly's house and told her that Hank was going to get both of them into trouble by following him around, which seems to imply that Hank was quite determined in his pursuit. "More than anything," said Walter McNeil, "I think Tee-Tot helped Hank get beyond his shyness, and helped him project himself a little, little more, 'cause Hank was a shy person really. He had to lose that somehow, and I think Tee-Tot was a big help to him in doing that."

As unfashionable as it was to acknowledge the influence of black musicians, Hank later went out of his way to give Payne full credit. "All the music training I ever had was from him," he told the *Montgomery Advertiser* at the time of his 1951 Homecoming. Talking to jazz journalist Ralph J. Gleason the following year, he said, "I learned to play the gitar from an old colored man. . . . He . . . played in a colored street band. . . . I was shinin' shoes, sellin' newspapers and followin' this old Nigrah around to get him to teach me to play the guitar. I'd give him fifteen cents, or whatever I could get a hold of for the lesson." Hank acknowledged Payne again during his Greenville Homecoming and apparently searched for him, but Payne had died in a charity hospital in Montgomery on March 17, 1939. He was on relief at the time, and his trade or profession was marked "unknown" on the death certificate.

Local musicians like Payne would have made a much bigger impression on Hank when he was growing up than the stars of the day. Lilly didn't have a radio or phonograph, although Hank would try to listen to the radio at the Simses' house or in the local stores. Unlike many of his contemporaries, Hank was barely influenced by country music's first superstar, Jimmie Rodgers, who succumbed to tuberculosis in 1933. Rodgers was the original kid with a guitar. Raised in Mississippi, he didn't draw on folk ballads so much as jazz, blues, Hawaiian music, and vaudeville. Like Hank, he turned to music in part because of a physical affliction. In place of Appalachian music's piety and grim resignation, Rodgers' music was populated by good-time pals one step ahead of the law, but still ready to shed a tear for mother and home. He sang with an insouciant, almost insolent drawl, and his sentimental parlor ballads were offset by rowdier songs, such as "In the Jailhouse Now," "Waiting for a Train," "Travelin' Blues," and "T for Texas." Many of the biggest country stars of the 1940s and 1950s, notably Gene Autry, Ernest Tubb, Floyd Tillman, Lefty Frizzell, and Hank Snow, began as Rodgers disciples and recorded his songs. Hank was a few years younger, just nine years old when Rodgers died. Jimmie Rodgers' influence on Hank was less direct. Rodgers brought the barroom culture to country music, and inasmuch as Hank's music came from the honky-tonk, he was a Rodgers disciple. Hank learned to yodel like Rodgers, but usually did no more than break occasionally into falsetto, and he probably learned that from blues singers.

It was probably after Lilly moved to Greenville that she acquired a radio, broadening Hank's horizons. Greenville was fifteen miles further up the L&N tracks toward Montgomery and was four times bigger than Georgiana. As the seat of Butler County, the focal point of the town was the courthouse square rather than the railroad station. Lilly moved her family there in time for Hank and Irene to start school in September 1934. Several of Hank's contemporaries remember him bringing his guitar to school. He would play during the lunch break and tell people that to play and sing was his "highest ambition." The ditty he sang repeatedly was as follows:

> *I had an old goat*
> *She ate tin cans*
> *When the little goats came out*
> *They were Ford sedans*

Lilly set up a boardinghouse by the cotton gin and worked in a sauerkraut cannery known locally as "The Smell of Success." It was the rooming house business that ideally suited her "take no crap" temperament, though. "She'd just as soon knock you in the head as look at you if you made her mad," said J. C. McNeil. "She had to be tough. She'd bounce them suckers out of there if they gave her any crap." One of Lilly's boardinghouse tenants later characterized her as mean and violent with a short fuse. Perhaps in emulation of her, Hank never shied away from a fight, particularly when drunk. He would pitch in with a wild-eyed fury, even knowing he was going to be thrashed. Later, he told a band member that all he needed in a fight was his mother standing behind him with a broken bottle.

For all her shortcomings, Lilly had a singleminded desire to better the lot of herself and her family, and, with the help of Lon's disability pension that she fought hard to get, the family wasn't as badly off as many during the depth of the Depression. In Greenville, Lilly performed charity work rather than being a recipient of it.

What happened to Lon is the subject of some dispute. He later told his second family that his aneurysm burst. He was sitting under a tree, he said, and it was as if a .22 gun went off in his head. Fluid ran from his nose, ears, eyes, and mouth, but instead of being pronounced cured he was diagnosed with dementia praecox and kept in the hospital system against his will. He told Hank's first biographer, Roger Williams, that he was detained on account of Lilly, who tried to get a commitment order against him. Others have a different account, insisting that — for a while at least — Lon was happy to be in the hospital. In January 1937, he was moved to the V.A. hospital in Biloxi, Mississippi, and he stayed there until August 1938. The V.A. in Biloxi is situated on several acres of parkland within walking distance of the beach. Three square meals a day were served, making it a very alluring proposition during the late years of the Depression. "He didn't particularly want to get out," said J. C. McNeil. "He would pull all kinds of tricks. One time they came into his room and they looked everywhere — he had crawled up under the bed, pulled himself up to the springs and held himself there until they had left."

At some point, though, Lon decided that he wanted to leave, and found that he couldn't. He rarely spoke about it in later years, although he spat every time the word *psychiatrist* was mentioned, giving some indication of what happened. The records have been lost, but Lon said that Lilly had told his family that he was dead, and had told the V.A. that he had no family except for her and the kids. Lon insisted that he tried to tell the doctors that he had a brother and sister, but no one would believe him. Finally, he persuaded the kin of another patient to mail a letter to his sister, Bertha, who handed it to Lon's brother, Mack. Bertha detested Lilly, and it's through Bertha that much of the story was handed down, but Bertha insisted that Mack went to the V.A. hospital with affidavits attesting to the fact that he was Lon's brother, securing his release.

Nobody remembers Lilly going to visit Lon very often, so it's unlikely that Hank saw his father more than once or twice during the 1930s. Lon said that Hank came once when he was fourteen, which would have been in 1937 or '38. Perhaps Lon's disappearance meant that Hank, now a spindly kid with steel-rimmed glasses, retreated into himself while perfecting his public mask. Working the streets and having almost limitless access to Rufus Payne, he learned how to be conversational — even confidential — with people he hardly knew. This was a critical skill for someone in the line of work he proposed to take up, but it meant that from an early age the core of Hank Williams became a thing known only to himself, masked by the molassified haw-haw that led people to think that they were his closest friends.

By the time Lilly, Hank, and Irene left Greenville after school finished in 1937, Hank already had a pretty clear idea what he wanted to do in life. He told his cousin Clara Skipper, "I ain't goin' to school always. I'll sing my song and make more money than any of you."

"A Hill-Billie is a free and untrammeled white citizen of Alabama who lives in the hills, has no means to speak of, talks as he pleases, drinks whiskey when he gets it, and fires off his revolver as the fancy takes him."

New York Journal, April 23, 1900

• •

"ROY ACUFF, THEN GOD!"

• •

*L*ILLY, whose recollections after Hank died were often purposely vague, stated with uncommon authority that she, Hank, Irene, Bernice McNeil, and Marie McNeil arrived in Montgomery on July 10, 1937. Walter McNeil, who had settled in Montgomery a year earlier, moved Lilly and her extended family up from Greenville on a logging truck. He laid planks across the joists, and loaded her stove and all the family possessions onto the makeshift trailer. Lilly was trying to better her lot and that of her children. The rooming house business looked more promising in Montgomery; the schools were better, and there were talent shows, more populous street corners, and a radio station for little Harm.

Montgomery was uptown as far as you could get in Alabama. It was the state capital and had been the first capital of the Confederacy until the heat, humidity, and mosquitoes had driven the secessionists to Virginia. In 1937, some seventy-two thousand people lived there. Lilly moved into 114 South Perry Street, which she converted into a rooming house. Hank, then thirteen, was sent out to shine shoes and sell peanuts on the street; Irene sold packed lunches at the fire hall, the police station, and the Montgomery Curb Market. From 1937 until 1939, Lilly had Hank working weekends as a painter for the Heath Decorating Company. In September 1937, she enrolled him at the Abraham Baldwin Junior High School, although he arrived with the attitude that learning interfered with the important things in life, chief among them music. He took eighth and ninth grade at Baldwin, and then transferred to Sidney Lanier High School in 1938, quitting in October 1939, shortly after his sixteenth birthday.

The situation on South Perry Street was complicated when Lon arrived home in August 1938. Lon later told his second family that when he returned to Georgiana and McWilliams, he found people staring at him as if he were a ghost. He would imitate a black man he'd known, who had backed away from him: "Oh, Mistuh Lon, I never done anything to you while you was alive. Why are you comin' back to haunt me?" Lilly had, said Lon, told everyone that he was dead. Clearly feeling unwelcome and perhaps ill at ease after being so long out of circulation, he returned to the V.A. hospital that October. He said that he spent Christmas with Lilly and the kids, although he might not have had his boots off very long. By his own account, he returned once more to the V.A. hospital, finally leaving in April 1939. He went back to his old hometown, McWilliams, and when he filled out his application for Social Security on October 16, 1941, he described himself as "separated." One of the apocryphal stories surrounding his return home is that he arrived to find Lilly in bed with another man, but even if that tale is untrue, Lon would have discovered that Lilly had not been missing him. Although she was acid tongued and built like a logger, she seemed to have no trouble attracting men. "She could be charming when she wanted," said Walter McNeil Jr., and that seems to be the best explanation anyone can offer. She also had a rotating cast of predominantly male boarders at the rooming house.

The female boarders have been the subject of some dispute through the years. Some say that Lilly was running a call-girl business, and toward the end of his life, Hank told a fellow performer that he had started entertaining as a shill for Lilly's racket. Others, though, say they saw no evidence that Lilly was running a bordello, and several of the musicians who lodged at the boarding house insist that they would have been regular customers if Lilly had indeed been running a brothel. The only person to state authoritatively that the boarding house doubled as a bawdy house was Marie McNeil's son, Butch, who said later that Lilly had a sideline running girls.

Immediately after arriving in Montgomery, Hank set about getting noticed, although many of the specifics have been lost to time. In 1946, WSFA program director Caldwell Stewart wrote an introduction to one of Hank's songbooks in which he stated that Hank had been on the station since 1936 — the year before Lilly said she moved to Montgomery. When Hank came back to Montgomery for his Homecoming in 1951 he said he had been on WSFA "eleven years, nine days, and six months," which, if we take him at his word, would place his radio debut in the late months of 1936, six months or more before Lilly says she moved to Montgomery. An article in the *Greenville Advocate* written to coincide with Hank's Montgomery Homecoming also seemed to imply that Hank was on the radio in Montgomery while the family was still living in Greenville. Confusing the issue still further, some around Montgomery swear that Hank was on a rival station, WCOV, before he was on WSFA, but WCOV wasn't launched until 1939.

WSFA was the only game in town when Hank moved to Montgomery. The partnership of two local businessmen, Gordon Persons (later the governor of Alabama) and Howard Pill, the station went on the air in March 1930 and broadcast with one thousand watts from studios in the Jefferson Davis Hotel, within easy walking distance of 114 South Perry Street. In addition to its own programming, the station picked up feeds from NBC and small southern networks. Several former employees of WSFA take credit for bringing Hank to the station, but E. Caldwell Stewart had a better claim than most. Stewart had been hired by WSFA as its staff pianist in 1931 and became the music director several years later. His widow insists that Stewart discovered Hank singing on the street and selling peanuts, and put him on the air. Leaborne Eads, later a performer on WSFA, says that Stewart always told him that he found Hank outside WSFA and ran a remote down so that Hank could broadcast live from his patch on the sidewalk.

Hank certainly knew what he was doing when he set up shop outside the radio station. Bill Hunt, then the advertising manager at WSFA, remembered that Hank used to bug anyone he thought might work at the station. He would sing a song, then hawk the peanuts that Lilly had bagged. "Peanuts, Mister, only five cents, and believe me, Mister, I need the dough. One bag? Two bags?" Hunt said that he put Hank on the air in a sustaining (that is, noncommercial) slot, adding that Lilly would arrange for people to phone the station demanding more of "The Singing Kid."

Chronicling Hank's career on WSFA is made no easier by the fact that he was continually on and off the station, and the program sched-

ules published in the local papers were often sketchy on local programming. Hank might have appeared on other people's shows, but he wasn't
listed as the star of his own sponsored show until 1941. When he spoke
of his eleven years on the station, he seemed to be implying that they
were eleven blissfully uninterrupted years, but he was rarely on the air
for more than three or four months at a stretch until 1947, his last full
year in Montgomery. Between 1937 and 1941 he was off the air more
often than he was on.

If Hank's early career is hazy, his life outside music as he desultorily
attended school is even harder to piece together. Two sisters who lived
near him remember that he would be out on the streets playing cowboys
and Indians, but when the time came for the other children to go in,
Hank would stay outside by himself. Later, he would call the early
evening the lonesomest time of the day, perhaps echoing back to those
years when Lilly was serving and clearing up supper in the boardinghouse and no one had time for little Harm.

Lilly's ambitions for Hank were fairly clear. Christmas 1937 brought
a new guitar, a Gibson with a sunburst finish. This was a major investment, quite probably the most expensive item in the Williams household. Lilly bought it from Art Freehling's Music Store around the time of
Hank's first major public appearance at the Empire Theater's Friday
night talent show. She always spoke of Hank's appearance at the Empire
as if it was just one show, but others remember him appearing and winning so regularly that the management requested that he not appear any
more. Talent shows were the entry level of the entertainment business
then, and Hank seems to have gone for them all. Members of Lon's family remember him entering talent shows at the Wilby Theater in Selma,
fifty miles away.

At one or more of the Empire shows Hank sang a self-composed
song, "WPA Blues." Other than the ditty he'd sung in school, it is generally reckoned to be Hank's first song. As Lilly remembered it, one verse
went as follows:

> I got a home in Montgomery,
> A place I like to stay,
> But I have to work for the WPA
> And I'm dissatisfied — I'm dissatisfied.

There were a couple of tunes kicking around called "WPA Blues," one of them by Casey Bill Weldon, who later wrote Louis Jordan's hit "I'm Gonna Move to the Outskirts of Town," but if the words Hank sang were as Lilly remembered them, they had, for the greater part, been cloned from a record called "Dissatisfied" by string band veteran Riley Puckett. The one part of Lilly's account that is almost certainly true is that Hank partied away the first fifteen-dollar prize he won at the Empire. "When Hank was in the chips, so were his friends — as long as the money held out — always," wrote Lilly in a confused thought that barely disguised her lifelong contempt for the way money ran through Hank's fingers.

Early on in Montgomery, Hank met fiddle player Freddy Beach. Born in Leakesville, Mississippi, in 1916, Beach was the closest to a seasoned musician Hank had met to that point. Beach had toured as a fiddler with Curly Fox and Texas Ruby and had worked as a traveling evangelist. Freddy and another local musician, Dad Crysel, organized a talent show at a hall on Commerce Street. Hank appeared there in 1937 or '38, chaperoned by Lilly. He got up and sang a train song, then started appearing every week. When Hank assembled his first band, Beach was the fiddle player.

It was also around this time, 1937 or '38, that Hank met Braxton Schuffert, who remains the most voluble source for Hank's early career. Born near Montgomery in 1916, Braxton had an early morning radio show on WSFA when Hank was living in Greenville. Lilly later told Braxton that she couldn't get Hank away from the radio when he was on, so Braxton was a bona fide star in Hank's eyes when they met. Braxton was a delivery man for Hormel Meats, and made a regular delivery to the boardinghouse on South Perry Street. One day, he saw the guitar and played a few songs, then Hank played a few. Hank was fourteen or fifteen, but his voice, Braxton noted, was as strong and clear as a man's. The following day, Braxton had to make a delivery to the CCC camps in south Alabama, and Hank went along. Hormel didn't allow riders, but Braxton told his boss that Hank was his little brother. Hank, said Braxton, wouldn't lift more than approximately ten pounds. "Some way or another," concluded Braxton, "I took a likin' to him."

Braxton worked in tandem with a harmonica player, Smith Adair, who called himself "Hezzy." There was a cornball group, the Hoosier Hotshots, on the *National Barn Dance* in Chicago, who'd introduce most songs with "Are you ready, Hezzy?" They were so popular that "Are you ready, Hezzy?" became a national catchphrase, and perhaps that's how Smith Adair became Hezzy. Originally from Birmingham, he moved to Montgomery from Sylacauga when he was sixteen. Braxton met him one morning when he was coming back from the station. Hezzy was walking down Bell Street playing his harmonica. "I said, 'Boy, can you play with a guitar?'" remembered Braxton, "and he said, 'Hell yes, I can play with a guitar,' so I said he should come up to the house and we'd play some. His mother was dead and his dad was a roving sign painter, rode a bicycle. Smith was on his own. We'd go down and play all the cafés. I'd sing, Smith would play the harp, pass the hat around." Braxton and Hezzy figured out when the firefighters got paid, then they'd set up and busk outside the fire halls. They played small theaters, restaurants — anywhere they could draw a crowd and pick up a few nickels and dimes.

By the time Hank arrived in Montgomery, he had decided to drop his given name, Hiram, in favor of Hank. He developed a little set piece to explain how this came about. According to one of his first steel guitarists, Boots Harris, he'd say that "there was a fence outside his house and he'd sleep with the window open, and there was an old cat walking up and down that fence yowling 'H-a-r-r-m-m, h-a-r-r-m-m.' He said he thought the cat was calling him so he changed his name to Hank." The truth, of course, was that "Hank" sounded more like the name of a hillbilly and western music star than "Hiram." That's why Clarence Eugene Snow became Hank Snow, Hubert Penny became Hank Penny, and Lawrence Locklin became Hank Locklin.

In 1938, when Hank was starting out with Braxton Schuffert, Freddy Beach, and Hezzy Adair, he heard the performer who, more than any other, would shape his music. Roy Acuff was twenty years older than Hank, and outlived him by almost forty years. Born on a tenant farm near Knoxville, Tennessee, Acuff grew up in the foothills of the Smoky Mountains. A baseball career seemed likely until he was sidelined by a debilitating bout of sunstroke. During the layoff, he honed his skill on the fiddle and formed a band called the Crazy Tennesseans. Later in life, Acuff tried to gloss over this period, but the Crazy Tennesseans put on a vaudeville show that included several smutty songs. Two of them, "When Lulu's Gone" (better known as "Bang, Bang Lulu") and "Doin' It the Old-Fashioned Way," even got onto disc. Acuff then paid fifty cents to someone he remembered only as "Charlie" for a song called "Great Speckle [sic] Bird." In the Book of Jeremiah, the speckled bird was a metaphor for the church assailed by evil ("Mine heritage is unto me as a speckled bird, the birds round about are against her"). The song was strange and elliptical, unusually rich in metaphor for a country song, and Acuff performed it on the *Grand Ole Opry* on February 5, 1938. The overwhelming response led to an invitation to join the cast.

Once on the *Opry,* Acuff dropped the smutty songs, and the Crazy Tennesseans became the not-so-crazy Smoky Mountain Boys. Acuff sang in a full-throated, emotional style that sounded good crackling through the ether on Saturday night. He hired a Dobro player, and the instrument's tremulous sound perfectly echoed his style. He appeared in movies, toured the country, and twice ran for governor of Tennessee. During the war years, enlisted men would request more songs by Acuff than by anyone else, even Sinatra, and he reportedly earned an astonishing $200,000 in 1942. In Acuff's hands, country music was just that: music for the country people of the South and Southeast. He bridged the gulf between ancient string band music and the modern era, and came to epitomize country music's innate conservatism.

Roy Acuff's Appalachian music resonated with Hank Williams in a way that no western song or parlor ballad ever did. There were no electrified instruments, and no songs of liquor or sin that didn't end in death or perdition. It was highly charged, emotional music, and Hank Williams was riveted. Talking to Ralph Gleason in 1952, after his star had eclipsed Acuff's, Hank was still in the thrall of the older singer. "Roy Acuff is the best example [of sincerity in singing]," he said. "He's the biggest singer this music ever knew. You booked him and you didn't worry about crowds. For drawing power in the South, it was Roy Acuff, then God. He'd stand up there singing, tears running down his cheeks." Acuff became Hank's benchmark, both of success and of heart-on-the-sleeve sincerity.

Acuff met Hank in the late 1930s or early 1940s and would eventually become Hank's music publisher. When Acuff recorded a complete LP of Hank's songs in 1966, he stated on the liner notes that Hank was working with Pappy Neil McCormick, a country bandleader based in the Florida panhandle, when they first met, which would place the meeting in 1940 or 1941. Acuff later told Hank's first biographer, Roger Williams, that Hank would come by his dressing room whenever he played Montgomery. "[Hank] would sit around, sing songs and play the guitar," Acuff said. "He was just a little fellow [Hank at age nine was already taller than Acuff, so quite what Acuff meant by this is unclear], and he just hunkered around in the corner waiting for a chance to sing." Later, Acuff claimed to have gone out to see Hank in the honky-tonks, even going so far as to get up and sing with him. "I wasn't as big then as I am now," he explained. "We both had a type of cry in our voice, and we sang with a lot of energy and feeling."

One of Hank's band members, Paul Dennis, remembered an altogether different encounter. Hank was half tanked, and Acuff admonished him: "You got a million-dollar voice," he told him, "and a ten-cent brain." For all the crocodile tears he shed over Hank's casket, Acuff's opinion never changed much. He later disinherited one of his grandsons who had been busted for drug possession, and his attitude toward Hank's transgressions was never marked by much compassion. Hank, though, never lost his respect for Acuff, and from the late 1930s until his death, he would introduce Acuff's songs in his shows. One of his first recordings, an acetate that ended up in his father's hands, featured an Acuff song, "(Beneath That) Lonely Mound of Clay."

By the time Hank started listening to Roy Acuff in 1938, he was already determined to carve out a career in music, but Acuff became a beacon. On a commercial level, Acuff's success proved that hillbilly music could sell nationwide; on an artistic level, Hank gravitated toward Acuff's full-throated, emotional style. Hank would have played music without Acuff, but whether it would have sounded the way it did or whether the market would have been as ready for him is doubtful.

Hank's first taste of touring was probably in support of Juan Lobo, aka Jack Wolf, a cowboy performer who claimed to have been in Westerns with Ken Maynard. No one named "Lobo" or "Wolf" is listed as one of Maynard's costars, but a ropin', wranglin' extra who could spin a few tales of Hollywood would have impressed Hank Williams in 1938. Hank and Juan Lobo went out on a brief tour supported by Hezzy Adair, Braxton Schuffert, and Freddy Beach. Lobo sold handmade bat-wing chaps and belts, and performed standard cowboy shtick, like whipping a cigarette out of someone's mouth with a sixteen-foot bullwhip, or dancing through twirling lariats. Hank was in his element. School couldn't hold a candle to this, and Hank's teachers knew it. "Aw, don't wake him," they'd say when he fell asleep in class. "He isn't going to learn anything anyway." After Juan Lobo left, Hank recruited Irene for the act and took a steady date at a theater in Roanoke, Alabama, ten miles from the Georgia state line. Braxton remembers that they drove up in Lilly's Ford station wagon, and played three shows a night at 3:00 p.m., 6:00 p.m., and 9:00 p.m. for around one hundred dollars. Everyone came away with fifteen dollars, excellent money for that time.

Braxton fell out of the picture around 1938, but Hank continued with Hezzy Adair, and Braxton remembers hearing them on WSFA's Saturday night barn dance. Accordionist Pee Wee Moultrie joined in 1939. He said:

> I went in Montgomery with another band We went up to WCOV, played a radio program, and while we were playing I saw a couple of guys watching us from outside the studio. So when we got through, they came out. We went outside and they introduced themselves as Hank Williams and Hezzy Adair. They said that they were putting a band together to be called Hank and Hezzy and the Drifting Cowboys, and they wanted to know if the fiddle player, Charlie Mays, would like to have a job with them. So we had been on the road awhile and we were all broke and hungry and so we accepted. We moved our stuff into his mother's boardinghouse and started a radio program five days a week on WCOV. For some reason, Hezzy's name was dropped, but he continued playing bass.
>
> I moved into the boardinghouse on South Perry Street. It was just an old white frame, two-story house, one or two blocks off the main drag. Mizz Williams gave us a room on the second floor. Hezzy lived someplace else. I doubt if Mizz Williams had over three or four people, regular boarders. She had some young girls going to college. Hank took an interest in one of 'em.

Late that year, 1939, Hank and the Drifting Cowboys signed up for a tour of theaters in Georgia, Alabama, and Florida. It was common at the time to bracket a live performance with a movie, and many of Hank's performances were in support of Paul Muni and Bette Davis in *Juarez*. The promoter wanted a girl singer, so Hank and Pee Wee hired a young, fresh-faced cowgirl named Sue Taylor. As Pee Wee remembered:

Hank was on his best behavior the first two weeks. The third week, we pulled into Georgiana and went to the theater. The owner pulled out a bottle of peach brandy. We offloaded the car and Hank and Hezzy went off in search of some more booze. They both got loaded. Hank started the show and told the people that he wished he'd been born in their town and if it happened again, he'd make sure it happened there. He lost his pick and was strumming his guitar with his knuckles. Hezzy walked off to the west wing and vomited. People sitting on the left side could see him, and started walking out. I figured they would run us out of town, but the manager was laughing his head off. He said it was the funniest thing he'd ever seen.

Hank's early career is largely available to us only as an accretion of fragments, and the picture doesn't begin to sharpen for several years. Those who knew him and worked with him say that he never expressed interest in any career other than music, but music was barely getting him by. The money would be gone before it was made, and he'd borrow more. He drank whenever he could, and started to write songs by setting his own words to established melodies. Lilly was seldom out of the picture; she drove the station wagon to dates, collected the money, paid the band members, often housed and fed them too. She put up handbills, encouraged Hank, chided him, and cussed him out when he screwed up. Not even family members got into the shows for free with Lilly on the door.

One of the few surviving artifacts from Hank's early years is a brief audition acetate from the late 1930s. Acetates date back to the pretape era. They were recordings made directly onto ten-inch aluminum discs coated with acetate. Hank and Pee Wee's acetate was clearly intended to land a steady radio job because it was formatted like a radio show. Hank made up call letters for an imaginary station in Fort Deposit, Alabama, and he and Pee Wee kicked off with an instrumental version of Irving Berlin's "Marie" (although written in 1928, "Marie" was a big hit for Tommy Dorsey in 1937). Then there was some chatter before Hank turned to the Sons of the Pioneers' 1935 tune, "Happy Roving Cowboy," which seems to have been his theme song from earliest times. Like most of the Pioneers' best songs, it was written by Bob Nolan. Born in eastern Canada, Nolan captured the outsider's wide-eyed wonder at the untamed vastness of the West, a wonder that filled Hank with ambivalence. The cowboy was never more popular than during the late years of the Depression, and life in the bunkhouse must have looked more appealing than life in the boardinghouse, but Hank got no further than naming his band the Drifting Cowboys and singing a couple of Nolan's songs. The western makeover didn't go very deep.

Pee Wee Moultrie doesn't have altogether charitable memories of his two years as a Drifting Cowboy.

Mr. J. L. Frank [country star Pee Wee King's father-in-law and manager] would frequently come to town representing the *Opry* Artist Service Bureau. He'd rent the city auditorium for a Sunday show, and use us to do his legwork. Then he'd bring in *Opry* stars, like Roy Acuff, and let us do the show with them. We usually got a better response than his *Opry* folks. Drunk or sober, Hank had the uncanny ability to hold an audience's attention, [but] by 1940, Hank's drinking problem was getting worse. All we were getting was three meals a day and most of the money was going to Hank's mother.

It was Lilly, not Hank, who was the driving force, he said. "She owned the car, and by the time she took a cut for the car and the gas and oil, we usually came up on the short end of the stick. She rode herd on Hank and dished him out just enough to keep him from buying booze." For a very short period Hank, Pee Wee Moultrie, and their fiddler, Charlie Mays, relocated to WBHP in Huntsville, but they soon returned to WSFA and a regular Saturday night job at the Fort Dixie Graves Armory.

The original Drifting Cowboys broke up in 1940. "A small group of people stayed at the boardinghouse on the way to a rodeo or carnival [in Texas and Mexico]," Moultrie said later. "Hank took off with them, and left his band sitting there cooling their heels, so we started working with another local band led by Dad Crysel."

Writing to his mother from what is now the Fort Worth suburb of Handley, Texas, on November 18, 1940, Hank apologized for not sending any money. Someone he identifies only as "Jack" had just bought six hundred dollars' worth of western suits for the band, and Jack had also bought a ranch where the band lived, so there would be no money heading east. The identity of "Jack" is unclear. It could have been Juan Lobo

(Jack Wolf), but after Hank's death, someone named Jack Hughes came forward with information about him, and Irene told her attorney that Hughes had bounced checks at the local five-and-dime in 1939 or 1940, then skipped town.

Hank's letter was full of instructions. He asked Irene to go see Pee Wee and give him his address. "Tell Pee Wee I said to be ready to come at any time," he wrote. "This is the greates [sic] country in the world, Texas." He said that he hoped to be home in seven months with a "real band and pleanty [sic] of money to run one on." When he applied for shipyard work two years later, Hank stated that he'd toured Mexico as a musician in 1940, presumably with "Jack." The months in Texas are otherwise blank, except that Hank probably met Ernest Tubb, who'd just moved to Fort Worth to broadcast over KGKO, and was little better known than Hank at the time. Tubb, though, broke through in 1941 with "Walking the Floor over You," and became the preeminent country star of the war years.

According to Pee Wee, Hank returned long before the seven months were up, claiming that he had back trouble. Lilly said later that he fell from a horse in a rodeo, worsening his already serious back problems. Hank was anxious to reassemble his old band; in fact, more anxious than they were to work with him again. He had no problem finding work, though, and quickly assembled a new group of Drifting Cowboys. The Texas dream would resurface when he drank. He'd pack his suitcase — britches and shirtsleeves sticking out — and tell everyone he was off to Texas. Then he'd sober up somewhere around the Alabama state line and hitch his way back home or wire for money. Soon after Hank returned, Lilly pressured him into taking a bookkeeping course at Draughon's College, and, according to Hank, he attended for seven months (others, though, say this is unlikely, as a high school diploma was a prerequisite and Hank hadn't graduated). Lilly, meanwhile, had leased a bigger boardinghouse at 236 Catoma Street, and this would be Hank's permanent address for the next six years.

After Lon's brief reappearance in 1938, he went back to the hospital. Upon his release in 1939, he returned to McWilliams. He divorced Lilly on July 1, 1942, and married Ola Till on September 12 that same year. They had a daughter, Hank's half-sister, Leila, on June 19, 1943. Lon never again took regular employment. He had a full disability check from the Veterans Administration, and he made his way doing odd jobs, occasionally running a country store with Ola. From the time Lon returned to McWilliams, Hank saw him on a fairly regular basis. Whenever Hank was appearing in the neighborhood, he and his band would descend on Lon's house in the middle of the afternoon and then stay for dinner. Hank and Lon's relationship wasn't close: Lon had been gone for too long for that, and Hank wasn't much given to intimacy anyway.

One week after her divorce from Lon, Lilly married Hank's guitarist, Homer H. Haatchett, who played in the band as "Indian" Joe Hatcher. Apparently, Indian Joe died of appendicitis shortly after their marriage. Lilly kept feeding him oil to flush out his system, instead of taking him to the hospital. Two months later, on September 10, 1942, she married a Cajun serviceman, James C. Bozard, and they remained together until May 1, 1946. The one surviving photo of Bozard is of a smiling, gregarious, overweight man in uniform. Those who remember him say that he wasn't around very much.

One of Hank's surrogate fathers was Pappy Neal McCormick, a Creek Indian who led a band variously called the Barn Dance Troubadours or the Hawaiian Troubadours. McCormick was based 150 miles south of Montgomery, in and around Pensacola in the Florida panhandle. He played steel guitar; in fact, he had invented a four-head steel guitar. Four guitars in different tunings were mounted on a railroad tie that turned on a barbecue spit. McCormick's band played for dancing, and although none of his music has survived, Hank almost certainly acquired some ideas about showmanship from McCormick. He might also have dated McCormick's daughter, Juanealya; there's a photo of them together dated April 24, 1941. Hank worked a few weeks at a time with McCormick for several years. Whenever his relationship with Lilly reached boiling point, he would take off for Pensacola, sometimes to work, sometimes to hole up in the San Carlos Hotel and drink. WCOA, where McCormick worked, was also in the San Carlos, so work and play were no more than an elevator ride apart.

A few surviving fragments give us some idea of what Hank was up to as war loomed. Three guys fresh out of high school in Hayneville, Alabama (about twenty miles from Montgomery), heard Hank on WSFA and decided to present him at the local courthouse. They wrote to him in care of the station at the end of March, and several days later Hank wrote back in pencil on lined paper saying he'd work for 60 percent of the gate. The promoters made up thirty signs and posted them around

Hayneville. Hank and three pickers led by guitarist Zeke Crittenden arrived during the afternoon of Friday, April 4. Hank seemed shy and very unlike the outgoing performer the promoters had expected from his WSFA shows. He was shown the courthouse where he'd be playing, and he saw the jail cell. "Awright boys," he said, "they're ready for us. Ever'body on their best behavior tonight." Hank went over well that night, and the following morning the three promoters went over to the courthouse to move back the benches and divide what was left of the thirty dollars they'd taken in.

Two weeks later, Hank worked his bread-and-butter gig at Thigpen's Log Cabin. Perhaps he was working his way south, because he was photographed with Juanealya McCormick shortly after. Thigpen's had opened in 1931 just off old Highway 31 in Georgiana. Fred Thigpen, at six feet four inches and 230 pounds, made a formidable combination with Lilly for anyone who threatened trouble. Hank played for dancing in a walled-in skating pavilion behind the main dining room. The pavilion was roofed, but open to the air with canvas curtains that had to be lowered when it rained. Admission was a quarter, and Hank and his new Drifting Cowboys would play from 8:00 p.m. until midnight or 1:00 a.m. Butler County was still dry, so Thigpen sold ice and setups, and the dancers would retire discreetly to fill their glasses with hooch. Playing every second week, Hank quickly became Thigpen's major draw between 1940 and 1942. Hank alternated with a full dance band led by Cecil Mackey, and even outgrossed name dance bands like Wayne King. He mixed up his set, and did a square dance interlude when he would play fiddle tunes. He couldn't call a square dance, but knew enough hoe-downs to get the crowd on the floor. If Hank served any kind of apprenticeship, it was at Thigpen's and at Pappy Neil McCormick's show dates.

The 1941 Drifting Cowboys included Shorty Seals, who had worked in the McCormick band. Shorty played the bass and did the comedy routines that were expected of bass players back then. Pee Wee Moultrie's buddy, "Mexican" Charlie Mays, played the fiddle (the "swing fiddler," he was called in the band's announcements). Lilly's future husband, "Indian" Joe Hatcher, played guitar and fiddle (he was dubbed the "wrong shoulder fiddler"). Clyde "Boots" Harris played the "singing steel guitar." They gave themselves nicknames to sound like outlaws. Many others dropped in and out of the lineup. Paul Dennis played bass and rhythm guitar; Paul Compton played guitar; and Millard "M.C."

Jarrett and Jimmy Porter played steel guitar. No one stayed long, and playing with Hank wasn't considered a plum job. On most schoolhouse dates, Hank sang without amplification, accounting in part for the forcefulness of his singing style: he was literally struggling to be heard. When Dennis played, the band had a portable public address system that comprised two twelve-inch speakers mounted in a box that could accommodate eight input jacks. The entire band used it until it was smashed in a traffic accident on the outskirts of Montgomery in late November 1941. The same accident permanently crippled Compton when a sun visor bracket penetrated his skull.

Steel guitarist Clyde "Boots" Harris was from Opp, Alabama. As a kid, he coveted a pair of boots in a Sears catalog, but when they arrived, he was disappointed to discover that they were both the same color, not one black and one white as they had appeared in the catalog. Boots led a band with his brothers, but decided to try for a job where he could play three or four nights a week, so he caught the bus to Montgomery in September 1941. First he went to WCOV, then WSFA, where the program director told him that their only hillbilly act, Hank Williams, played solo. Boots went to Lilly's boardinghouse and found Hank lying on the couch. They played a few songs together, and Hank became friendlier.

He said, "Let's go get a cup of coffee," so we went out the front door, and there was a little café right there and I started in it and he said, "Naw, their coffee ain't no good," so we went on down a ways to a little restaurant and they had whiskey lined up on the wall. I had just quit the mill in Opp and I had maybe a week's salary in my pocket. Hank said, "Have you got any money on you?" I said, "Yeah." He said, "Have you got enough for a half-pint?" I said, "I guess so." I didn't drink at all then, so I hadn't been knowing him but thirty minutes and I bought him a half-pint of whiskey.

Lilly put up Harris and other band members at the boardinghouse, docking their pay accordingly. When they were out on a job, Hank used to tell the audience that he paid his band $21.50 a week: "Twenty-one hamburgers and fifty cents." It got a lot of laughs, but it was too close to the truth for the band to find it really funny. They joined him on WSFA from time to time, but the sponsorship fees didn't stretch to cover a band. Joints like Thigpen's together with schoolhouse or courthouse dates were their bread and butter. They played for dancing at the joints, but worked a little comedy into the schoolhouse dates. The latter worked on a split of the gate. Lilly would book a schoolhouse for an evening, and then she, sometimes in conjunction with Leaborne Eads, would put up flyposters all around the neighborhood. On the posters, Hank billed his act as "one-and-a-half hours of good clean comedy, songs and music," and he would announce the show on the radio every morning. After the show date, Lilly would share the door money with the school on a seventy-thirty or sixty-forty split.

Those who paid the twenty-five or thirty cents Lilly charged for admission heard a show comprising, for the most part, other people's songs and traditional favorites. Hank didn't make any commercial recordings during the early 1940s, but he cut several acetates. The problem with acetates is that they can be played only a few times before the acetate coating begins to break up, and that's what happened to a record Hank left with his father. It coupled Roy Acuff's "(Beneath That) Lonely Mound of Clay" with the very appropriate "Mother, Guide Me" (possibly derived from the same root as the Stanley Brothers' "Mother's Footsteps Guide Me On"). The acetate was recorded at Sears, but after Lon hauled it out and played it too many times, the grooves simply wore away.

One set of recordings from Hank's earliest days has survived, though it is not in much better shape than Lon's acetate. The owner of Griffin's Radio Shop in Montgomery recorded Hank off the air at some point in the spring of 1942. As usual, Hank kicked off with "Happy Roving Cowboy," then tackled a sentimental pop song, Bob Miller's "Rockin' Alone in an Old Rockin' Chair," followed by Red Foley's hymn to his dying dog, "Old Shep." An unknown female vocalist joined Hank on the black spiritual "Jesus Walked That Lonesome Valley." Then came Acuff's "(Beneath That) Lonely Mound of Clay" and Ernest Tubb's "I Ain't Gonna Love You Any More." The latter is intriguing because it was recorded *before* Tubb's breakthrough hit, "Walking the Floor over You," lending credence to the idea that Hank had met Tubb in Fort Worth a few months earlier. Next came Rex Griffin's "The Last Letter." Griffin was another Alabamian, and again it's entirely possible that Hank knew him. Griffin traveled throughout the South and Southwest, but was back in Gadsden, Alabama, in 1941 with a band that included Pee Wee Moultrie. Griffin's big hit, "The Last Letter," was the suicide note of an older man besotted with a younger woman. The depth of personal feeling that Griffin invested in his songwriting would inspire Hank to share more of himself in his songs, and Griffin's version of an old pop song, "Lovesick Blues," provided Hank with his breakthrough seven years later.

The radio shop acetates also included a 1912 pop song, "Aunt Dinah's Quilting Party," that had crept into country music in the 1930s, but the most interesting song was "I'm Not Coming Home Any More" because it was the first known recording of one of Hank's own songs. Boots Harris insists that Hank had yet to find his own style. Hank would, said Harris, sing Ernest Tubb songs like Tubb, and Acuff songs like Acuff. "We'd get after him all the time," says Harris. "'Hank, why don't you sing like Hank?' Because we drew better crowds when he did. But he'd sing like Acuff and Tubb, and he'd do recitations like a guy on the border stations called the Texas Drifter." Perhaps Hank sang like Hank on "I'm Not Coming Home Any More" because it was his own song, but, on the skimpy evidence of that one song, his style was intact very early. Backed by a steel guitar and bass, he sings a little higher than he would in later life, but the timbre of his voice and his phrasing are remarkably similar to his first professional recordings five years later. The song, too, is identifiably a Hank Williams song.

Shortly after "I'm Not Coming Home Any More" was recorded, Boots Harris left the Drifting Cowboys to join Curley Williams' Georgia Peach Pickers. The rift came when Hank was on a short tour backing folk and western singer Tex Ritter. They reached Albany, Georgia, where they played a date with Curley Williams. Curley was hopeful of landing a spot on the *Opry,* which was still a pipe dream for Hank. Boots recalled:

> We'd hear records on the jukebox, and Hank'd say, "Someday, I'm gonna be doing that — they're gonna be playing my records." But I didn't see it coming any time soon the way he was going. He was pretty bad into the drink then. I was having to play guitar, emcee the show, do the jokes, and it was just more than I could put up with. I'd already quit him once because of the drinking. I told him if he'd quit the drinking and we'd get on with it, we'd get somewhere. I said, "If you keep drinkin' ain't nobody in the business gonna pay us no attention."

It was an admonition Hank would hear countless more times in the decade or so he had left.

The middle months of 1942 seem to mark one of Hank's periodic troughs. War had been declared in December 1941, but Hank was unfit for service because of his back. Even so, the war took its toll on him. The pool of musicians in Montgomery was depleted, and then gas rationing was introduced. Hank was on WSFA consistently for a little more than a year, from July 1941 until August 1942, but then he was kicked off the station for habitual drunkenness. He moved to WCOV, but by September or October he had quit music altogether.

Hank went to Portland, Oregon, to work in the shipyards. It's unclear why he chose Portland when there were shipyards 170 miles away in Mobile. Perhaps he was trying to get as far as possible from Lilly; perhaps he simply wanted the adventure. The incentive was provided by Kaiser Shipbuilding, which offered free tickets to Portland, free training, free accommodation, and good wages. Paul Dennis says that Hank was drunk on the day he left, so it might have been an impetuous decision made under the influence. He was probably there no more than a few weeks before he wired Lilly for the money to come home, although he later stated that he was there for two months.

In November 1942, Hank moved in with his uncle Bob Skipper in Mobile and applied at the Alabama Dry Dock and Shipbuilding Company. He was there on and off until mid-1944, never for very long at a stretch. Lilly later recalled the end of the first stint: "I believed in Hank," she wrote in *Life Story of Our Hank Williams.* "I knew he had what it took, so I rented a car and went to every schoolhouse and nightclub in the Montgomery area. I booked Hank solid for sixty days. Then, the third week he had been out of the music business, I went to Mobile and got him and put him back in it. When Hank saw the datebook for those shows, he gave me the sweetest smile I've ever seen."

"Thank God, Mother," Hank is supposed to have said in one of the most uncharacteristic remarks ever attributed to him. "You've made me the happiest boy in the world."

Long Ike and sweet Betsy attended a dance
Where Ike wore a pair of his Pike County pants,
Sweet Betsy was covered in ribbons and rings,
Said Ike, "You're an angel, but where are your wings?"

(Trad.)

· ·

SWEET AUDREY FROM PIKE

· · · · · · · · · · · · · · · · · · · ·

*A*UDREY Mae Sheppard Williams spoke often of her late husband. In her revisionist view of their life together, they were young star-crossed lovers. Disturbingly quickly — within days of Hank's death, in fact — Audrey began finding it hard to distinguish between the Hank Williams she'd married and the Hank Williams she wished she'd married.

"I met Hank in Banks, Alabama," Audrey told journalist Dorothy Horstman.

> He was working a medicine show. My dad's only sister was with me and it was her idea to stop and see what was going on. I said, "I never heard of Hank Williams before," but I learned later that a lot of people in the area *had* heard of him. I said, "This guy will be number one on the *Grand Ole Opry* one of these days." I had that feeling very strongly. Anyway, after the show was over, Hank and these other people were going around selling herbs. Little vials. He came up to the car. I'll never forget how country he talked. He said, "Ma'am, don't you think you need some of these herbs?" then he quickly looked back, and he said, "No, I don't believe you do." My aunt asked him what he was gonna do after the show, and he said, "Well, I have no plans." She said, "Well, would you like to go with us?" So he went with us after the show that night, and we went to a little club. I just seemed to be with him from then on. I just wanted to

help him. Though I had no experience in the business, I felt this guy had a tremendous talent.

I'm kinda psychic. I had a brother who was ten years old and I was twelve. He was disgustingly healthy, but I knew for months he was gonna die. Then he went hunting with my dad one afternoon and came in and took double pneumonia. They were bringing in doctors and nurses, and I was thinking to myself, "You can bring Jesus Christ himself, and he will not live." That's how strong I believed it. That's how strong I believed in Hank. He was lucky with a God-given talent, and I was lucky with a few brains, so I used to go out and book shows. I was on the door. I took up money on the door, then I'd go up onstage with him. He used to do a blackface act that was just outasight. He'd sing a little bit, then do a few funnies.

Audrey Mae Sheppard was born near Banks, Alabama, on February 28, 1923, some seven months before Hank. She was a prize; surely the loveliest woman in Pike County. Fine clothes sat well upon her. She once said that her family owned half of Pike County, and true or not, she thought she belonged with the old-money crowd. She characterized herself as independent, although her family probably had another word for it. As early as age eleven or twelve she had learned how to drive and was taking herself off on trips. "I knew what I wanted and I went after it," she said. Her independent streak led her to run off one day with a neighbor's son, James Erskine Guy. She was seventeen years old. They lived in Gadsden for a while, but a year or so later Guy went to work one day and didn't return. Audrey returned to Banks, heavy with Guy's child. Lycrecia Ann Guy was born on August 13, 1941. When Audrey met Hank in the late summer of 1943, she was working in Brundidge as a drugstore clerk, and looking for a way out.

After their date, Hank asked Audrey to meet him the next day. It would be the first of his Bloody Mary mornings in store for her. He was unshaven, and he greeted her in the doorway of his trailer with no shirt on his back and the stench of last night's whiskey on his breath. They went for a drive that afternoon. Hank told Audrey a little about himself, confessed that his drinking had got him kicked off WSFA, and then, after the show that night, he asked her to marry him. "I told my aunt, 'This boy's crazy,'" said Audrey.

What did Audrey see in Hank? The only rung on the show business ladder lower than south Alabama hillbilly music was itinerant blues singing, but Hank and his music still had a vestige of glamour that the Brundidge Drug Store didn't. Audrey also had her gift. She couldn't see her own lack of talent, believing herself to be a singer until the day she died, but she could see talent in others. Early on, she saw something in Hank Williams, something that Hank probably had trouble seeing in himself. What did Hank see in Audrey? She was lovely, and that was enough to secure his interest. But it was more than that. His two wives were feisty, sharp-tongued, and ambitious. Lilly, of course, was precisely that, so the pop-Freudian conclusion is obvious.

Audrey's daughter, Lycrecia, was around two years old when Hank entered their lives, but throughout the years there have been persistent rumors that Hank and Audrey were both parents when they met. Hank's cousin, Marie, was some two years older than Hank, born in Garland on May 8, 1921. She'd lived with Lilly's family since she was twelve. Her father had never let her go to school because she had a withered arm and a prominent strawberry birthmark. The other kids, he thought, would make fun of her. Marie helped Lilly at the boardinghouses, cooking and cleaning, and, by some accounts, running the girls. The two women argued often, and Marie would sometimes pack her bags and move in with Hank's cousins, the McNeils. In 1942, she became pregnant, and at some point the following year, she married a serviceman named Conrad Fitzgerald but, by all accounts, never lived with him. Dr. Stokes at St. Margaret's Hospital delivered the boy child on June 24, 1943. Hank nicknamed him Butch. "[From what I'm told]," said Butch, "when I come home from the hospital, he come in and he said, 'There's my Butch.'" And the nickname stuck. What has never been resolved is whether Hank imparted more than a nickname. From the time Butch, or Lewis, as he was christened, could first remember, he insists that people put the word in his ear that Hank was in fact his father. "When you get a little older in life, you kind of see the light," said Butch. "A lot of people walk up, and start telling you this, that, and the other. Momma had told a lot of people, [and] she hinted to me a lot of times, but she never would just come out and say it. She'd say little things like, 'You such like your daddy, and you walk like him . . . and you got a dropped shoulder like him.'" Butch asserts that Lilly caught Hank and Marie in bed together on more than one occasion, although no one else saw them together in that way.

The musicians who lived with Lilly heard the rumors, but Hank neither confirmed nor denied them. He acted in a caring, paternal way toward Butch, which could of course mean no more than the fact that he was looking out for a fatherless child. There were toys and trips to the movies. Hank, thought Butch, seemed overprotective. Some say that Hank had all the women he wanted and would not have fooled around with Marie, but that was less true in 1942 than later.

Hank almost certainly met Audrey within weeks of Butch's birth. He probably worked in music throughout most of 1943. In all likelihood, the medicine show fell victim to gasoline rationing, but by Labor Day 1943, Hank was back in Montgomery, appearing as a supporting act on a show hosted by Birmingham-based hillbilly singer Hardrock Gunter. The show's headliners were to be Pete Cassell, the Sunshine Boys, and Gunter himself. Gunter remembers Hank hanging around backstage drinking. Someone figured it would be a good idea if Hank introduced Gunter, so Hank grabbed Gunter's guitar, went out, and started singing. The crowd apparently recognized him and he went over well. When he got off, Gunter bawled him out, but Hank took no notice and sauntered off out the door, still with Gunter's guitar slung around his neck. "The guitar's neck and body hit the doorway," remembered Gunter. "He tried twice more to get through the door before I pulled him round. He was belligerent and said, 'You just don't want me to play your guitar.'"

Later that year, Hank played some dates as a local added attraction on a tour led by *Grand Ole Opry* star Pee Wee King. Born Frank Kuczynski in Wisconsin, Pee Wee was leading a polka band in Green Bay when Gene Autry came to town in 1934, trying to replace a couple of his band members who had been injured in a car wreck. Kuczynski signed on, quickly changing his name to Pee Wee King ("Pee Wee" because he was short, and "King" in emulation of another Polish band leader, Wayne King). A few years later, Pee Wee lit out on his own, taking his western-and-polka band to the *Opry* in 1937. He brought drums to the *Opry* stage for the first time, and joined Roy Acuff and Bill Monroe among the show's new headliners.

Another *Grand Ole Opry* headliner, Minnie Pearl, was on that tour. She later said:

I met Hank in Dothan, Alabama. Always, when we went into a town, we'd go to the radio station to plug the show. Well, in the lobby of the radio station, we saw this man and woman sitting there. The man had on a disheveled suit, a cowboy suit but no sequins. And a very dirty cowboy hat, which showed a lot of wear and a lot of use. He was sort of crumpled up, like a stick man, on the sofa. The girl was very, very pretty. We were introduced to them as Hank Williams and his wife, Audrey. They were obviously in very straitened circumstances.

While Hank toured south Alabama with Pee Wee King and his Golden West Cowboys, he sold him one of his original songs, "(I'm Praying for the Day That) Peace Will Come." King said that Hank first pitched the song to him in Montgomery when the band's girl singer, Becky Barfield, said she needed a patriotic number. Hank was hanging around the dressing room between shows and made his pitch. "Hey, King," he said, "listen to this." Hank ran it down, but Pee Wee was dubious, so Hank suggested that he try the song onstage. "He got a pretty good hand with a brand-new song, which is hard to do," said Pee Wee. "He said, 'Now, what do you think?' I said, 'Let's wait.'" On December 13, 1943, the transaction was completed. Hank received twenty-five dollars, and although his name was to appear on the composer credit, he signed away all rights. The agreement was witnessed by Honey Wilds, half of the *Opry*'s blackface comedy act, Jamup and Honey. When King got back to Nashville, he placed the song with Acuff-Rose Publications, which registered it with the Library of Congress on December 20, 1943. As it turned out, the few dollars Hank got for the song was the most anyone made off it. By the time King landed his first recording contract with the Nashville-based Bullet label in 1945, peace had come, and the song languished until the Korean War, when Esco Hankins (recording as Roscoe Hankins) cut it without much success for Mercury.

Hank seems to have returned to the Mobile shipyards immediately after the tour, but, as before, didn't make a significant contribution to the war effort. The McNeils had moved to Mobile in 1943, and Hank's aunt Alice and his cousins Opal and J.C. helped build Liberty Ships. Hank was a welder by day and hung out with musicians at night. "He would hit the joints," said J. C. McNeil. "He tried to get a band together when he was in the shipyards. It was in his blood. I would venture to say that he didn't work more than two or three months all told. He probably slept on the job more than anything else. It was encouraged by the foreman so that he could stretch the hours he could bill."

Audrey always insisted that she joined Hank in Mobile:

> We worked side by side in these pit things [with a blowtorch]. I had never seen [them] before. We'd go back to the little old hotel room, which was terrible, in the evening. I'd wash out our clothes. We didn't do this too long — but we did do it. I knew he had something, and me or someone had to get it out of him. One day I said, "This is just not it, Hank. I want to go back to Montgomery, get a band together for you, and get you back on the radio station and start working shows." And that's exactly what I did.

If true, Audrey had come to Hank's rescue, just as Lilly had done a year earlier.

We know very little of what Hank was up to in 1944. He probably spent part of the year in Mobile before settling back in Montgomery around August. He assembled another group of Drifting Cowboys, this one including Don Helms and Sammy Pruett, who would later work with him in Nashville. Helms was eighteen years old when he joined Hank. He was from a farming family in New Brockton, Alabama. In 1943, he went to Panama City, Florida, to work in the shipyards. He had an aunt in Montgomery who had studied music and had a Hawaiian guitar, and his father played fiddle, but even after his aunt had given him the steel guitar he still had no thought of a career in music. Pappy Neal McCormick was the one who finally sold Helms on the idea of becoming a steel guitar player. "I saw him in a vocational building," said Helms. "He was playing that thing, and I thought, 'Man what a way to have fun. What a way to make a living.'" The only steel guitarist to teach Helms some licks was Boots Harris. When Harris would come back to Opp from Nashville, where he still worked with Curley Williams, Helms would go see him and learn Curley's steel guitar parts.

Very quickly, the steel guitar became the driving force in Helms' life. Every Sunday he tuned in a short-wave program called *Hawaii Calls,* and he listened to all the steel and slide guitar players on the *Opry.* And there were some great ones. Bashful Brother Oswald worked with Roy Acuff and Little Roy Wiggins with Eddy Arnold. The tremulousness in

Oswald's playing complemented Acuff, and Wiggins' dulcet tone complemented Arnold. Don Helms' simple, hard-edged, bluesy playing would soon complement Hank Williams. Helms bought his first electric steel guitar, a Silvertone, from Sears, but, because he had no electricity on the farm, he had to play it on an upended washtub, which resonated just enough for him to practice. Eventually, he took over the steel guitar chair in McCormick's band when McCormick felt like taking some time off.

Back in New Brockton, Helms assembled a band with two cousins and two friends, one of whom was Sammy Pruett. Helms and Pruett had met in Panama City at a Neal McCormick gig, and they stayed in touch. Their band was called the Alabama Rhythm Boys, and they played the honky-tonks around southern Alabama from Wednesday through Saturday. One of the guys in the band knew Hank and went to Montgomery to meet him. Helms recalled:

> He came back and said, "Hank Williams is putting a band together. Y'all wanna go work for him?" We said, "Aw hell, it's probably better 'n this," so we gave three or four days' notice and rode the bus up to Montgomery. We were supposed to meet Hank at Art Freehling's music store, but he wasn't there. We went outside and I saw this real long-legged guy coming. He walked up, and he said, "Y'all the group?" We said, "Yeah." He said, "Well, I'm Hank Williams, follow me." We walked round the corner and down the block to a hock shop. He said, "Jake, you got any more of them blackjacks in there?" and there was a tray of 'em. He passed 'em out, he said, "Boys, if y'all gonna play with me, by God you're gonna need these." He wasn't kiddin' either.

Hank lined up Monday, Wednesday, and Saturday nights at the Riverside Club in Andalusia, and Tuesday and Thursday in nearby Opp. The Riverside was one of the biggest dance halls in Alabama, and there would often be six hundred people there on the weekend. Hank rented a trailer and moved to Andalusia. Helms and the band didn't live far away, so they drove in from New Brockton in Helms' fiancée's car, then went home after the show.

Audrey was with Hank much of the time. It was understood that they would get married at the same time as Helms and his fiancée, Hazel, and another group member and his fiancée. Hank and Audrey jumped the gun, though. He pestered her constantly to marry him, but there were several hoops to jump first. Audrey was still married to Erskine Guy, who by now was an enlisted man. Divorcing a serviceman who was serving overseas was not easy, and both Hank and Audrey had grown attached to the eighty-dollar-a-month allotment check that Audrey received from the military while Guy was away. It didn't help that Audrey's father was bitterly opposed to her relationship with Hank. Audrey also insisted that she never liked the name Williams. "I told my aunt after I started dating Hank, 'I cannot imagine "Audrey Williams," ' " she said. As always, though, the biggest problem was Hank's drinking, but during those late months of 1944, he made a concerted effort to stay sober, and as the year came to a close, sobriety drew its reward.

Audrey always portrayed her decision to marry Hank as a spur-of-the-moment act, but she had to take the first step of divorcing Erskine Guy, a divorce that became final on December 5, 1944, on the grounds of voluntary abandonment. Hank then went to see a Dr. Parker, who declared him free of venereal disease, and then a notary public, who swore out the marriage license. The last stop was a justice of the peace, M. A. Boyett, who operated a filling station near Andalusia and pronounced them man and wife on December 15, 1944. Technically, it was an illegitimate marriage because they hadn't sat out the sixty-day waiting period necessary after a divorce.

Audrey said she was cooking for the band in the trailer, but Paul Dennis, who came down to play with Hank, remembers only one meal — and that was inedible. The honeymoon didn't last long. On the weekend that the Andalusia gig ended, Hank got drunk. Audrey pitched a fit, Hank threw her clothes into the mud out in front of the trailer, and she called the police and had him put in jail. Don Helms had to get him out. "I was embarrassed," says Helms, "but I went back in there. He was sitting on a bench in his cell watching me. I didn't know what to say, but he was staring at me. He said, 'What d'ya want me to do? Stand on my darn head?' I paid the thirty dollars and got him out. As we were leaving, one of the policemen said, 'Come back 'n' see us, Hank,' and he said, 'All of you can go to hell.' "

By 1945, Hank was back in Montgomery, reestablishing himself as the most popular hillbilly act in town. He sold a self-produced folio of songs called *Original Songs of Hank Williams*, printed by Leon Johnson, a local musician who ran a print shop. Johnson had been printing fly-posters for Hank since the late 1930s, although it was usually Lilly who came to pick up the order and take care of the account. Johnson didn't take much notice of Hank until he got a call for a second printing of the songbook. This time, Hank arrived with a half-gallon jar of nickels, quarters, and dimes to pay the bill. He sold the books for thirty-five cents and he'd tell the audience that the money was for handling. "You send in the money," he'd say, "and I'll handle it."

Only the words were published in the songbook — not the music. Hank told Johnson that if people wanted to learn the tune, they'd have to listen to his radio show, but the truth was that Hank didn't know musical notation and wasn't about to pay somebody to transcribe it for him. The little folio included "I'm Not Coming Home Any More" as well as several songs that were recorded later and several more that never surfaced again. Among the latter was a saber-rattler called "Grandad's Musket," possibly born of Hank's guilt for having done so little toward the war effort:

> The boys up in the mountains have closed down their stills
> They've moved to the city and are making leaded pills
> While me and Grandad's Musket, when we are off to War
> We'll join up with MacArthur and even up the score.

After the gig in Andalusia ended, the band moved to Lilly's boardinghouse in Montgomery, and resumed the prewar routine of schoolhouses during the week and beer joints on weekends. Hank usually paid five dollars a night on top of room and board. Audrey would ride with them, sitting on Hank's lap all the way down to the show and all the way back because Lilly's '37 Chevrolet was packed full. The bass sat on top. Most nights, Lilly came to watch the door.

The lineup of the Drifting Cowboys was never stable for more than a few weeks. Helms quit the group shortly before he went into the service in 1945, but Pruett stayed on a little longer. Shortly after Helms was drafted, Hank hired Doyle and Bernice Turner, a husband-and-wife team living in Panama City, Florida. Helms had recommended them to Hank, and when they came home one night they found that he had called. "Doyle had made me practice and practice barre chords," said Bernice, "and when Hank heard me he had a fit. He had a good sock rhythm playing open chords, but he couldn't play barre chords. We auditioned at the boardinghouse, done two or three songs, and he hired us. He knew we were exactly what he wanted." Bernice remembered them playing throughout Alabama, the Florida panhandle, and parts of Georgia. There was talk of a USO tour, but, according to Turner, Hank would have had to sign papers promising to be sober, and refused to do so. The Turners were furious because Doyle was eligible for the draft, and the USO tour would have earned him a deferment.

Playing with Hank was still no plum job. Even the relatively unsophisticated musicians he hired looked down on his music. "I always thought Hank was too corny," said Sammy Pruett in conversation with radio interviewer Jim Owen, "because whenever he'd end a tune, instead of playing a chord up on the neck of the guitar, he'd do an [open] A or G or D, just as plain as you could get. We used to set around backstage, and he'd play a few tunes with a little pop taste, and he'd say, 'Awright boys, get them pop licks outta ya before we get out onstage 'cause we're gonna keep it vanilla.'" "Vanilla" meant unadorned hillbilly music. Occasionally, he would let his two guitar players cut loose in unison on a western swing tune, but he usually derided western swing as "longhair crap." The only music other than hillbilly and gospel that seemed to reach him was cottonpatch blues. Band members remember him sitting around backstage and at home playing songs like "Matchbox Blues" and "Bottle Up and Go." He would even sit in with blues singers on the sidewalk.

In the summer of 1946, Hank appears to have deviated briefly from his course. He led a band that featured E. B. Fulmer on piano, an instrument he later said had no place in country music, and Lefty Clark on saxophone, an instrument even more at odds with his music. Lum York was on bass, and the group was rounded out with a steel guitarist and a drummer. They played dance music. The sharp double-breasted gabardine suit that Hank wore around this time seems to imply that he was giving some thought to changing direction. As always, he had his ear cocked toward his audience, and he was probably hearing that they wanted the old Hank Williams back.

Hank was off WSFA from February 1945 until January 1946. Starting January 26, 1946, he was on between 6:35 and 7:00 a.m., and that September he was given another sponsored show at 4:00 p.m. By the close of 1946, Hank was so popular that even the radio shows were an event. Fans would turn up to see him at the station, creating a disturbance in the hotel lobby. WSFA still cursed him for his unreliability, but tolerated him as a necessary evil. Hank started using his clout to wrest concessions from the station. One stipulation was that WSFA wouldn't hire a competing hillbilly band. WSFA acceded, although the agreement warped opinion against Hank among the other bands in town. The station's ownership couldn't comprehend his appeal; they simply knew they couldn't afford to lose him. In radio stores, the question from the country folk was often, "Will it pick up Hank Williams?"

"Hank was a big drawing card," said WSFA engineer Sebie Smith, "but the band didn't always dress up too well. They'd come straggling through the Jefferson Davis Hotel. Finally the manager of the hotel asked [WSFA owner] Howard Pill to have Hank's crew come in the back way." At the same time, Hank was attracting a lot of jealousy from the other local acts on WSFA, chief among them Camille Brown, the Oprah of Montgomery. She hosted a show called *Around the Town with Camille Brown,* and griped loud and often to the station's management about the amount of sponsorship Hank got.

Part of the chronic unreliability that dogged Hank can be attributed to the tensions at the boardinghouse. Lilly and Audrey were both strong willed, belligerent, and grasping. In the name of loving Hank and helping his career, they tried to wrest control from each other. The conflict started early, and never really ended. As Audrey told Dorothy Horstman:

> When I first met Hank, he kept saying, "I want to tell you. There's something I want to tell you." Each time, he'd back out. Finally, one day we were at my dad's and we were sitting on the grass, and I said, "Hank, you've got to tell me what it is on your mind." He said, "It's my mother." I was so innocent then, I didn't know if she was dead. He said, "I want to take you home and introduce you to her," then he said, "You know what she's gonna say when she meets you? She's gonna say, 'Where did you meet this whore?' I said, "Hank, your mother couldn't possibly say that. I know she couldn't." You know, we walked in, and that's the first thing she said. I ran back to the car. Hank and [his] mother fought like men would fight. I tell you, *she* was his trouble.

Lilly even hinted at the squabbles in a small booklet she published in 1953. "I must admit I was a little jealous at times," she wrote, adding quickly and unconvincingly, "Not really. I'm joking. Hank's mother was always his first girl, and he never forgot it." She never let him forget it, either. "She would dictate to him," said Don Helms. "She'd say, 'You cain't do this. . . . I ain't puttin' up with that. . . . ' I can't remember the times I heard Hank say, 'Goddamn, don't tell her.'" Lon's absence not only meant that Hank didn't have a male role model, but also meant that he never matured from the dependent mother-child state. He simply transferred his dependency to Audrey, a shift that Lilly felt acutely.

It's doubtful that Hank appreciated the full ramifications of the dangerous curve that Audrey had thrown into his relationship with Lilly. He tended to see it in simpler terms. "No wonder you and Audrey don't get along," Hank told Lilly on one occasion. "Because one of you's afraid the other one's gonna beat you to my pocket when I get drunk." Occasionally when Hank went on a bender, Audrey would take off, perhaps back to Banks. Then it was left to Lilly to organize a search of the local joints and hotels for Hank. Sometimes he would go to WCOV and pick a fight with Dad Crysel, and Crysel's band would take great pleasure in beating him senseless and tossing him out onto the street.

Occasionally, when the three-way strife mounted and he could bear it no longer, Hank would take off for the Florida panhandle. He would hole up in the San Carlos Hotel in Pensacola, and stay drunk for several days, often a week or more. Sometimes Lilly would send Hank to Lon's house when he was on a bender. Watching him sober up one morning, Lon's daughter, Leila, came to know why Hank would refer to himself as her "half a brother." Everyone knew that Hank's drinking was abnormal. His cousin, Walter McNeil Jr. (or "O'Neil McNeil," as Lilly called him), had never — and would never — see anyone who drank with such singlemindedness as Hank. Whether he was a happy drunk or a mean drunk depended on his mood when he started drinking. Lilly couldn't understand it at all. "She'd *demand* that he stop drinking," says McNeil, "but he needed to pitch his drunk and get it out of his system for a few weeks or a few months." Lilly saw Hank's alcoholism in terms of weakness of will. She railed against it, cursed him, but never cast him out, perhaps because he was her only son, and perhaps because she guessed that he would one day amount to something despite himself.

Bernice Turner remembers driving to a gig in southern Alabama.

Hank couldn't drive because his license had been revoked, so he sat between Doyle and Bernice, asking them to stop every few miles so that he could get another beer. Doyle and Bernice decided to let him pass out, hoping that he would sleep it off and sober up in time for the show. "Hank mumbled something about wanting to lay his head in my lap," said Bernice, "and as he said it he was falling anyway. When we got there, I eased out from underneath him, went in and set up." They'd almost played a complete set when Hank came weaving in. He picked up his guitar and started singing "There's a New Moon over My Shoulder." "He was singing in one key and playing in another," said Bernice. "Doyle looked at me and said, 'Blue Steel Blues,' and we started playing to try and drown him out. The place was packed, and Hank looked at us — a dirty look, then he looked at the fiddle player. He was gonna leave and take the musicians with him, but they didn't go." Later, there was a commotion outside when Hank picked a fight with a policeman. He was hauled off to jail, and the Turners went to get him out after the show, but found that the police had decided to keep him. They drove home, gave the takings to Lilly, and went to bed. The next day Lilly and Audrey drove down to get him out.

It seems that Hank was first treated for alcoholism early in 1945 at a sanatorium in Prattville, Alabama, although the treatment probably consisted only of rest and deprivation. As such, it was no more successful than any of the other treatments Hank was forced to take. Going on a spree was his way of dealing with life's problems. It was also a means of relieving the back pain. When the band saw him gobbling aspirins, they knew that a bender was imminent. It probably never occurred to Audrey and Lilly that if Hank had a low tolerance for stress when the load was light, the success they craved might be a mixed blessing. "I'll tell you something," Audrey said many times, "if some woman, equally as strong as I am, had not come along, there would never have been a Hank Williams."

Everyone associated with Hank felt that he could be their passport to better times, and they all fell into a dispiriting cycle with him. For several weeks everything would be fine. Hank would be straight, on time, and in tune for every gig. They'd go fishing down on the Alabama coastline. Hank and Audrey would be holding hands in the car, and the talk would be upbeat. Then something would snap, and Hank would be off on a drunk. The Turners eventually quit because he damned so many promising opportunities with his unreliability, which they — like everyone else — saw in terms of lack of willpower.

Toward the end of 1946, Hank tried to solve part of the problem by moving out of the boardinghouse and into a small rented house at 409 Washington Avenue. From the time that Audrey took up with Hank, Lycrecia had been living with her grandparents in Banks, but now she joined her mother and new stepfather. For the first time since he had lived with the McNeils, Hank was part of a mom-pop-and-the-kid relationship. He tried desperately hard to fill the role for which life had ill prepared him. When Hank was sober, Hank and Audrey's relationship looked like true love. He tried especially hard not to drink around Lycrecia, and with encouragement and not-so-subtle pressure from Audrey, he began to look beyond the limited horizons of south-central Alabama.

At some point in 1945 or 1946, Hank went to Nashville, intending to try out for the *Opry*. He went to see announcer Jud Collins at WSM, the home station of the *Opry*. "They said someone was outside to see me," said Collins, "and there was this guy with blue jeans and a white hat. He said, 'I'm Hank Williams. Charlie Holt from WSFA told me to come up here and see you. He said you'd tell me what I have to do to get on the *Opry*.'" Collins told Hank that there were no shortcuts and that he would have to audition for Jack Stapp like everyone else. "He wouldn't go see Jack," said Collins. "He said, 'You tell Jack Stapp I'm here.' I think he was disappointed that I couldn't take him by the hand and say, 'Hank, you're on the *Opry* tonight at eight.'" Hank heard the same thing that thousands of others had heard. Some might get as far as "Judge" Hay, who had the last word on the *Opry* artist roster. Usually, he would listen politely and then say, "Boys, come back and see me when you're hot 'nuff to draw flies."

Although he returned home empty-handed, word about Hank Williams was slowly seeping out of Montgomery. Ernest Tubb remembered him opening an *Opry* show as a local added attraction around the time the war ended. In exchange for a spot on the show, Hank would promote it on WSFA. "When I got there, Hank had already started the show," remembered Tubb. "He was supposed to do twenty minutes, and he was tearing the house down. He came off and they kept applauding. We like to never got him off the stage." Tubb suggested to his booker, J. L. Frank, that he take on Hank, but Frank knew Hank's reputation firsthand from working with Pee Wee King and told Tubb to stay clear.

There have been persistent claims that Hank sold songs to visiting *Opry* stars, but there is no firm evidence that he ever sold anything other than "(I'm Praying for the Day That) Peace Will Come." One of the prime candidates for purchasing the kind of songs Hank wrote was his idol, Roy Acuff. In common with most of his contemporaries, Acuff bought songs outright when he could. When he became successful, he tried to administer his own music publishing, but then decided to go into partnership with Fred Rose, the man who would secure his future — and Hank's too.

Fred Rose wasn't a hillbilly, although he was born on the Kentucky-Indiana line in Evansville, Indiana, on August 24, 1897. He spent a miserable childhood in St. Louis, then set out for Chicago when he was in his teens. He later told an interviewer that he had been on his own since he was seven. He played piano, sang in the speakeasies, and was part of a twin piano feature on the Paul Whiteman show. Almost inevitably he turned to songwriting. He scored his first hit in 1921 with "Sweet Mama (Papa's Gettin' Mad)." Then in 1924, Sophie Tucker popularized "Red Hot Mamma," and Isham Jones cut the first of many versions of "Honest and Truly." Rose's most enduring song, "Deed I Do," was published in 1926. He married for the first time while in Chicago, and had two sons, Wesley and Lester, whom he would later bring into Acuff-Rose.

Through the Jazz Age, Rose was a featured radio performer on WBBM in Chicago, and he wrote prolifically. He remarried, and began grinding out show tunes, novelties, and topical songs, but the Depression and a bad drinking problem scuppered his career. He was thrown off radio in Chicago, moved to New York, and then, in 1933, he joined WSM in Nashville. This was not the comedown that it might seem. Much of WSM's broadcast day was devoted to pop music despite the fact that it owned the *Grand Ole Opry*. Its orchestra was among the most renowned in the NBC network. Rose had his own show, *Freddie Rose's Song Shop,* and he toured the mid-South with a trio. He also married for the third — and last — time during his first stint in Nashville.

In late 1935 or early 1936, Rose converted to Christian Science. He was back in New York, and his career was in a trough. His newfound faith enabled him to lick his alcoholism and try for a new start in Hollywood. He wrote many songs for Gene Autry, all the while commuting back and forth to Nashville. He also worked a stint at KVOO in Tulsa, where he met Bob Wills, whom he would later produce for Columbia.

Rose's conversion to country music was more gradual and less spectacular than his conversion to Christian Science, and it probably started soon after he arrived in Nashville. "Fred Rose came to Nashville to laugh," Hank told Ralph Gleason in 1952, "and he heard Roy Acuff and said, 'By God he means it.'" In the summer of 1942, Acuff approached Rose, who was back on WSM, with the proposition that they form a joint music publishing venture. Acuff offered to bankroll the company with twenty-five thousand dollars, but Rose apparently never needed to draw on that capital. The partnership, technically between Rose and Acuff's wife Mildred, was launched in October 1942. It would be Nashville's first professional music publishing company.

While Acuff was at the pinnacle of his career, Hank was just a local star in a small market. He wasn't even semi-itinerant like most country musicians. No one was sick of him in Montgomery, but he couldn't use his local success as a springboard to a bigger market because he was already damned as unreliable, and, in a business full of problem drinkers, his reputation was among the worst.

Chapter

4

• •

SONGS FOR HOME FOLKS

• • • • • • • • • • • • • • • • • • • •

*E*VERYONE has a celestial city. For Hank Williams and subsequent generations of wanna-billies it has been Nashville. It wasn't always that way, though. When Hank and Audrey visited one weekend in 1946, country music had a low profile in Nashville, but not low enough for the city elders. The hillbilly music business was anathema to the city's view of itself as the Athens of the South. In 1943, celebrating the fact that his radio show was relayed to 129 stations nationwide, Roy Acuff had thrown a party at the Ryman Auditorium. Governor Prentice Cooper was invited to attend, but declined, saying that he would have no part of a "circus," and that Acuff was bringing disgrace to Tennessee by making Nashville the hillbilly capital of the United States. Acuff responded by running, unsuccessfully, for governor in 1948. Only gradually, over the last fifty years, has the music industry won the city's embrace, and now of course the only reason that Nashville is known at all throughout most of the world is because of its association with country music.

The country music business has not merely grown, but centered itself in Nashville to the point that the two are now synonymous. In 1946, country music was a sidebar to the music business, and often treated with derision. It had no focal point. According to a poll of record company artist and repertoire (A&R) men in 1946, Chicago was reckoned to be the city with the greatest concentration of country musicians. Country recordings were made there and in Dallas, Cincinnati, New

York, and Los Angeles. Almost no recordings were made in Nashville in the year Hank Williams first recorded.

Unlike the equally maligned R&B record business, which was dominated by feisty independent labels, the country record business was dominated by the three major labels, Columbia, RCA Victor, and Decca. The only quasi-majors with sufficient volume to make a blip on industry surveys were Capitol Records (launched in Los Angeles in 1942), Mercury Records (Chicago, 1945), and the long-gone Majestic Records (Elgin, Illinois, 1944).

The majors assigned just one man to look after country music, then known as "hillbilly," "folk," or "western" music. At RCA Victor, it was Steve Sholes. "In sales meetings when it got to Steve's department, a lot of guys would say, 'Hey, I gotta go to the john,'" remembered field rep Brad McCuen. Sholes himself remembered the same thing. "I was never allowed to play more than six or eight revolutions of one of my records," he said. "The gospel records I wasn't permitted to play at all: just announce the titles. There was no attention paid to merchandising — special merchandising or *any* merchandising. There was no promotion or publicity to speak of."

At Columbia, the head of country A&R was Arthur Satherley, an expatriate Englishman who looked and spoke as if he were an Oxford professor of some arcane discipline. Satherley still did what prewar record men had done; he traveled more than seventy thousand miles a year making recordings in the field onto acetate discs. Tape wasn't in common use until around 1950. Decca's country division was in the hands of a gregarious hard-drinking salesman, Paul Cohen, originally from Chicago.

If current country musicians have a homogeneity born of the fact that they've been weaned on an identical diet, that wasn't the case when Hank was starting out. As Art Satherley explained to the *Saturday Evening Post* in 1944, "I would never think of hiring a Mississippi boy to play in a Texas band. Any Texan would know right off it was wrong." In the mid-1940s you could listen to a country record and stand a good chance of guessing where the performer was based. When Fred Rose sent out demos of Hank Williams, A&R men would have known at once that he was from the South or Southeast. No one would have confused his music with East Coast country music, cowboy music, or western swing, and Hank had so little in common with Eddy Arnold's country-pop hybrid that the two barely deserved to be categorized together. Hank's music was called "hillbilly music," and the little respect it had could be attributed almost entirely to Roy Acuff. Most country music in the mid-1940s was smooth, shading ever closer to pop. Only hillbilly music retained the fierce insurgency of mountain music. "Hillbilly" was a pejorative term to those who played the music. When asked, Hank always called his music folk music.

The industry put-downs gnawed at Fred Rose, and, with the zeal of the new convert, he made a spirited defense of hillbilly music in a letter to *Billboard* in August 1946:

> We pride ourselves in being a very intelligent people and good Americans, but are we? We put on our best bib and tucker and make quite an affair of spending an enjoyable evening being entertained with Russian, Italian, French, etc., folklore. . . . We read all kinds of books that will give us an understanding of foreign folklore, but what do we say and do about our own good ol' American folklore? We call it "hillbilly" music and sometimes we're ashamed to call it music.

Hank, too, was fiercely protective of his music and its populist base. "It makes me mad," he told an interviewer in 1951, "to hear these popular orchestras make a jammed-up comedy of a song like 'Wreck on the Highway.' It ain't a funny song. Folk songs express the dreams and prayers and hopes of the working people."

Billboard abandoned its "Folk Tunes" tag in June 1949 in favor of a new coinage, "Country & Western," acknowledging that country music was no longer folk music, but a commercial discipline, and that "folk music" now meant something entirely different. By then, Nashville had become the music's hub. It happened quickly, and the major reason was WSM's *Grand Ole Opry*. Immediately after the war, the *Opry* was just one of hundreds of Saturday night radio jamborees; it wasn't the first and it wasn't the only one broadcast over a maximum-wattage station, but it *was* the only one with network airtime. Starting in October 1939, NBC radio picked up thirty minutes of the *Grand Ole Opry* every Saturday night, and for those thirty minutes, the *Opry* blanketed the nation. Quite suddenly, the *Grand Ole Opry* was the place to be. The other pieces fell into place. Music publishers, bookers, and A&R men all began coming to Nashville. They knew that the big stars would be in town on Friday and Saturday because the *Opry* would dismiss them if they weren't.

Aside from a few prewar field recordings, the first professional recording session held in Nashville is generally reckoned to be Eddy Arnold's debut session on December 4, 1944, at the WSM studios. The following year, three WSM engineers started a recording studio as a separate enterprise within the WSM studio complex, and in 1947 they built a self-contained studio in a remodeled dining room at the Tulane Hotel. Their business was called the Castle Studio because WSM was known as the "Air Castle of the South," and it was there that Hank Williams cut most of his sessions.

Country music began earning industry respect not, as official histories like to say, for its ability to express the hopes and feelings of the common man, but for its ability to generate good revenue with low overhead. *Billboard* offered a snapshot of the music industry's thinking in a review of a Carnegie Hall concert in September 1947 that featured *Opry* acts. "A cornbilly troupe called the *Grand Ole Opry* . . . took over the house and proved to the tune of $12,000 gross that the big city wants country music. The promoters, Sol Gold, Abe Lackman and Oscar Davis, got more than a kick out of it because they garnered about $9,500 with a talent nut of about $5,000."

By the time Hank, nudged as always by Audrey, started thinking seriously about a shot at the songwriting or recording end of the business, Nashville wasn't *the* place to go, but it was the only country music hub within easy reach of Montgomery. Early on Saturday, September 14, 1946, they took the train to Nashville, knowing that Saturday was very much a business day. "I knew about Fred Rose," Audrey said later, "and I knew that he had started a publishing company with Roy Acuff. I knew that Fred had written some pretty good songs, and I felt that he could maybe help Hank. So we called and set up an appointment. It was at WSM radio station, studio B. It was for one o'clock, but I don't remember the day. The nearer the time came, the more Hank backed out. He said, 'I ain't going. I ain't gonna let him hear my songs.' I said, 'You're going if I have to push you every inch of the way.' I just literally made him go." According to one of Hank's band members, R. D. Norred, Audrey had already been to Nashville to make the appointment.

That was not the way that Fred Rose's son, Wesley, remembered it. According to Wesley, he and his father were having a lunchtime game of Ping-Pong in WSM's recreation room on the fifth floor of the National Life and Accident Company building when Hank and Audrey walked in unannounced and asked to audition some songs. After listening to his songs, Fred is supposed to have asked Hank to prove that he hadn't bought the songs by telling him to write one on the spot. Rose suggested a not particularly original theme: a woman leaves the one she truly loves to marry a man with money. Hank is supposed to have taken himself off into a side room and to have emerged with "A Mansion on the Hill." Fred signed him; Wesley nodded in accordance.

The fine details of how Fred Rose came to sign Hank Williams aren't clear, but it's almost certain that Hank wasn't making a cold call, that Wesley wasn't there, and that "A Mansion on the Hill" wasn't written until a year later. Despite what Wesley thought or said, Hank Williams had almost certainly come to Nashville by invitation. Country band-leader Paul Howard remembered working show dates in Alabama during the mid-1940s. Hank, he said, attended some shows and played him some songs. "I told Fred Rose about him," Howard later recalled, "and Fred told me to have him come up and talk to him." Howard, who later became one of Hank's friends, said that Hank came to Nashville and set up an appointment from Howard's hotel room.

Although Paul Howard's scenario is possible, it's even likelier that Hank Williams and Fred Rose came together through Rose's need to find songs for Molly O'Day, an act he was about to produce for Art Satherley. Molly O'Day's early career was a template for what Hank's would have been if he had been more reliable. Born Lois Laverne Williamson in Pike County, Kentucky, she was torn between sacred and secular music, a conflict she eventually resolved by shunning the world. A month older than Hank, Molly O'Day (as she began calling herself in 1942) had been shuttling around the mid-South for six or seven years, playing radio stations and schoolhouses, and slowly building her career. She sang in Roy Acuff's emotional, full-throated mountain style, and neither knew nor cared that she strayed off-key. Her husband and bandleader, Lynn Davis, took care of business. Davis had met Fred Rose when they worked on KVOO in Tulsa, Oklahoma, in the mid-1930s, and Rose had kept abreast of Molly's career. During the war, she was playing a show sponsored by Black Draught laxative over a small network of stations in the South.

One of the stations that picked up the feed was WSFA in Montgomery. "We'd go into the towns that picked up the show, and I'd bring in big acts and we'd play over the network," says Lynn Davis. "One time we were in Montgomery. Hank had announced the show on his program, and he was to be the local added attraction. He sang 'Tramp on the Street' and done four encores on it, and Molly said she had to have that song."

"Tramp on the Street" was first recorded by its writers, Grady and Hazel Cole, for RCA Victor in August 1939. The Coles were based in Rome, Georgia, but worked for a short time in Gadsden, Alabama, and toured throughout Hank's area, so there's no telling where he heard their song. Hank probably didn't know it, but the Coles' song wasn't *that* original. In 1877, Dr. Addison D. Crabtre had written a very similar song, "Only a Tramp!"

> *He's somebody's darling, somebody's son*
> *For once he was fair and once he was young*
> *Somebody has rocked him, a baby to sleep*
> *Now only a tramp found dead on the street*

The Coles' song, based closely on Crabtre's refrain, became especially poignant during the late years of the Depression. The punchline in the song's last verse hit home: what if the tramp knocking on your door were Jesus, and you turned him away? Then God would deny you on the great Judgment Day. For all its emotive power, the Coles' record was almost a dreadful parody of hillbilly music. They treated it as a brisk waltz, but their harmony completely dissolved on the low notes, and it's a testament to the song's strength that it survived their rendition. Hank clearly loved it. He slowed it down, remodeling it almost as a blues. It appeared in one of his WSFA songbooks, where the byline coyly read "Author Unknown."

After Molly O'Day heard Hank perform "Tramp on the Street," she asked for a copy of the lyrics. Hank reached into his guitar case and gave them to her. This must have been no later than 1943 because the song appeared in a folio that Molly published in January 1944. Hank and Molly's paths crossed several times after that. Lynn Davis remembers that Molly was back in Montgomery for a show in 1946 and he was handling the box office. Hank appeared; he was drunk and offered to sell a folder of songs for twenty-five dollars. Davis bought them and asked

Hank to come to the hotel the following morning to complete the paper-work. When Hank appeared the following day, Davis gave Hank his songs back and told him that he was sitting on a gold mine. Hank said he didn't have the twenty-five dollars anymore, and Davis said it didn't matter.

In the summer of 1946, Fred Rose was vacationing in Gatlinburg, Tennessee, and according to Lynn Davis, Art Satherley was with him. They heard Molly sing "Tramp on the Street" on the radio, and Satherley asked Rose if he knew the group. Rose said he did. At Rose's prompting, Satherley signed Molly O'Day and gave Rose the responsibility of scout-ing out some repertoire for the session. Rose asked Lynn Davis where "Tramp on the Street" came from, and Davis told him about Hank Williams and suggested that they contact him. Perhaps Rose had already heard the same suggestion from Paul Howard. Rose even said later that he'd met Hank around 1945 on one of his junkets through the South, so he must have known Hank or known of him before September 1946, but it was almost certainly the need to find songs for Molly O'Day that brought them together. No one else in Rose's little pool of writers was producing the sort of songs that Molly O'Day needed, so, according to Davis, Rose wrote to Hank, and Hank sent back an acetate with a few songs on it. Rose then invited him to Nashville. Perhaps Hank men-tioned that "(I'm Praying for the Day That) Peace Will Come" had already been published by Acuff-Rose, but no one had yet recorded it, and no one was likely to record it until there was another war. In November, Rose issued contracts on several of Hank's songs. On Novem-ber 23 he wrote to Hank, telling him that he'd shown the songs to Molly O'Day, "and I feel sure she will like them, although I have changed the lyrics around in order to make them consistent. These will be minor changes and will not interfere with what you have written."

In 1946 and 1947, Molly O'Day recorded four of Hank's songs: "When God Comes and Gathers His Jewels," "Six More Miles (to the Graveyard)," "I Don't Care (If Tomorrow Never Comes)," and "Singing Waterfall." All of them had appeared in the song folios that Hank had self-published in 1945 and 1946, so if Hank wrote anything especially for her in 1946 it must have been rejected. The only song that he is known to have written specifically for Molly was "On the Evening Train," which was also the only song ever credited to Hank and Audrey. Molly O'Day recorded it in April 1949.

Shortly before Molly's first session, Rose got a call from Al Middleman, the president of Sterling Records in New York. Sterling had started with grandiose plans. It was incorporated in July 1945, bankrolled by three investors, George H. Bell, Pearl Richards, and Eleanor Benedek of New York. It was to have wholly owned distributors in major markets and its own pressing plant in Los Angeles. Art Rupe was brought in as A&R manager, and his label, Juke Box, was made an affiliate of Sterling and was bankrolled by the same three partners. By the summer of 1946, though, Rupe reclaimed his repertoire, using it to start the hugely successful Specialty label. Shortly after Rupe quit, Middleman convinced himself that Sterling needed a hillbilly and black gospel line to complement its jazz, pop, and R&B series. He asked Fred Rose to find some acts for the hillbilly series, record them in Nashville, and ship the masters up to him.

Again, it's unclear exactly how Rose came to think of Hank as a potential Sterling recording artist. According to Hank's bass player, Lum York, he and Hank had already made a trip to Nashville to demo some songs, and during the session, Fred told Hank that he ought to be on a label himself. According to Murray Nash, then an RCA field rep and later Rose's factotum at Acuff-Rose, it was Rose's secretary, Eleanor Shea, who actually remembered Hank and suggested that Rose contact him. According to Wesley, he was the one who remembered Hank. According to Hank, Fred Rose's first thought had been to sign Johnnie and Jack, and he only thought of Hank after Johnnie and Jack told him of a prior commitment. Johnnie and Jack made their recording debut ten weeks after Hank for another New York indie, Apollo Records, so it's possible that they were already under contract when Rose approached them, which might, as Hank said, have prompted Rose to contact him. Whether he did so at his own initiative or that of Wesley or Eleanor Shea is unclear.

Rose also contacted a group called the Willis Brothers, who also went under the name of the Oklahoma Wranglers. Vic, Guy, and Skeeter Willis had grown up in rural Oklahoma, and had been making the rounds of five-hundred-watt stations before they came to Nashville in June 1946. "We were doing guest appearances on Saturday on a show called the *Checkerboard Jamboree* at the old Princess Theater on Church Street," remembered Vic Willis. "Fred Rose approached us on a flat-fee, no-royalty recording deal with a New York company, Sterling Records."

Rose then asked the Willis brothers if they wouldn't mind backing Hank, who was coming up from Montgomery. He forewarned Vic Willis that Hank sang out of meter. Willis said that wouldn't be a problem because they'd backed a duo called Polly and Molly at the Kansas City Brushcreek Follies who were the world's worst at breaking meter.

On Tuesday, December 10, 1946, Hank Williams took the bus from Montgomery to Nashville. "He had on an old beat-up-looking coat and a big dirty cowboy hat," said Vic Willis. "He was a skinny, scrawny guy. He could sit in a chair, cross his legs, and have both feet on the floor. When I saw him I remembered I'd seen him once before. It was at the Princess one afternoon about two months before that. He had been trying to pitch a song to Ernest Tubb."

They rehearsed the day Hank arrived in Nashville, and made plans to record the following day at the WSM studio. "We did ours first and Hank hung around in the control room," remembered Willis. Everyone broke for lunch. Hank and the Willises walked down Seventh Avenue North to the Clarkston Hotel. "Hank was a quiet guy and kinda negative," said Vic Willis. "But he had a hell of a dry sense of humor. Someone asked Hank if he wanted a beer with his meal, and he shook his head. 'You don't know ol' Hank. Hank don't just have *one* beer.'" Vic Willis finished before the others and went back to the studio, where Fred and Wesley were having a game of Ping-Pong. Fred asked Vic if Hank was drinking. Vic said, "No." Fred said, "Good." Vic didn't understand why at the time.

Fred Rose clearly hadn't taken much notice of what Art Satherley had said a couple of years earlier when he told the *Saturday Evening Post* that he wouldn't put a Texas boy with a Mississippi band. The Wranglers played western music: tight harmonies with a little taste of jazz in the rhythm section and in the solos. Hank Williams played hardbitten, unornamented hillbilly music. "My brothers and I weren't used to anyone that *country*," said Vic Willis. One episode stuck in his mind. Hank pronounced "poor" as "purr" on "Wealth Won't Save Your Soul," so the tag line became "[wealth] won't save your *purr* wicked soul." The Willises were supposed to join in on that line, but sang "*poor* wicked soul," expecting Hank to wise up. Finally, in exasperation, Fred Rose said, "Dammit, Wranglers, sing it the way Hank does."

After the session, Rose gave Hank and the Willises a prepared letter to sign in which they agreed to record in exchange for union scale

($82.50 for leaders, $42.50 for sidemen) and waived their rights to future royalties. With his signature, Hank stepped on the bottom rung of the recording ladder. "He wanted to get that check cashed before he got the bus back to Montgomery," remembered Vic Willis. "The Clarkston wouldn't cash it, so we went down to the Tulane Hotel. We knew the girl on the desk and got her to cash Hank's check."

Rose made acetate masters of Hank's four songs and the four by the Oklahoma Wranglers, and shipped them to Sterling Records. In addition to "Wealth Won't Save Your Soul," Hank recorded "Calling You," "Never Again," and "When God Comes and Gathers His Jewels." All four were traditional in form and execution, and only one, "Never Again," was secular. Sterling coupled "Calling You" with "Never Again" for the first record, and released it during the second week of January 1947. WSM's recording quality was poor, and the muddy overall sound was made worse by Sterling's pressing quality. If not for the electric guitar, these could have been field recordings from the 1920s or 1930s. *Billboard* magazine reviewed Hank's debut in glowing terms: "With real spiritual qualities in his pipes, singing with the spirit of a camp . . . meeting, Hank Williams makes his bow an auspicious one." The praise might well have been related to a full-page advertisement that Sterling took out to promote their hillbilly and western releases, but, even if the reviewer was feigning appreciation, he still understood more of what Hank was about than Sterling Records.

Sterling's art department came up with an advertisement that neatly encapsulated everything country music was trying to live down. Two peckerheads without a full set of teeth between them, with patches on their britches and a bottle of hooch beside them, are fiddling and, incongruously, playing a bull fiddle with a classical bow to announce Hank's debut. The advertisement reflected the attitude that Fred Rose had railed against in his letter to *Billboard* a few years earlier, an attitude that was still prevalent in New York. Sterling was no less dismissive in its trade literature. "Hank Williams is the Acuff type of hillbilly," it said. "[He] sings a real country song, the kind folks buy." Then, in describing the Oklahoma Wranglers, it went on to say, "The Wranglers do a higher class song and can sell anywhere."

No one at Sterling could understand it, but Hank's first record sold well. Fred and Wesley Rose probably had a greater role in the success than Sterling. Assiduous promoters of their copyrights, they would send sheet music to every radio station that programmed country music, prompting the station's on-air performers to sing Acuff-Rose songs. The Roses also had a full-time promo man, Mel Foree, out on the road handing out record samples to deejays, and promoting the copyrights at Saturday night radio barn dances. More than anything, the success of Hank's first record showed that the country music market wasn't heading uptown as fast as some people thought. The top-selling country record during the spring of '47 was Merle Travis' "So Round, So Firm, So Fully Packed." In that context, Hank's music was an anachronism. Travis' record had horn *obbligati* and included references to bobby-soxers, Frank Sinatra, and then-current ad slogans like "The Pause That Refreshes." Hank's music was, as he later told session guitarist Harold Bradley, "from a mean bottle."

The second Sterling single coupled "When God Comes and Gathers His Jewels" and "Wealth Won't Save Your Soul." It was released just three weeks after the first. Then, on February 13, 1947, Hank cut his second and last Sterling session. Rose probably recognized his mistake in using the Willis Brothers, and opted instead for a group of WSM staff musicians. By this point, he had trawled through Hank's songbooks and demos and had selected four secular songs. Two of them, "My Love For You (Has Turned to Hate)" and "Honky Tonkin'," were classic Hank Williams.

Hank had published "Honky Tonkin'" in his first song folio, where he called it "Honkey-Tonkey." As originally written, it contained the couplet: "We are going to the city, to the city fair / We'll get a quart of whiskey and get up in the air." At Rose's behest, those lines were changed to the more anodyne "We're going to the city, to the city fair / If you go to the city, baby, you will find me there." Even then, it's hard to know what a skilled musician like Rose thought of a song that stayed in one chord for fifteen and a half of its sixteen bars.

"Pan American" was about the Pan American Clipper, a train that ran daily on the Louisville and Nashville Railroad from Cincinnati to New Orleans via Montgomery. It highballed through Greenville, Georgiana, and other small southern towns that Hank knew very well. Since 1935, the Pan American's whistle had been broadcast every day over WSM in what was then a feat of remote engineering. Country folk would set their watches by it and could tell which engineer was at the throttle. Hank's melody came note-for-note from "Wabash Cannonball," a Carter Family song that Roy Acuff performed regularly on the *Opry*.

The second Sterling session saw the birth of one of Hank's trademarks, the "crack" rhythm: an electric guitar keeping time on the deadened bass strings. Without drums in his lineup, Hank used the electric guitar to emphasize the pulse. It was the sound that Johnny Cash later made into a trademark, adding a little rhythmic flourish to make "boom-chicka-boom."

So, as of March 1947, Hank Williams had two records on the market, four songs in the can, and two of his songs recorded by Molly O'Day, but was still virtually unknown outside WSFA's listening area. He had a more or less permanent band for the first time, though. Steel guitarist Don Helms had returned from the service and worked with Hank again, but soon quit and was replaced by R. D. Norred. Joe Penney, who took the stage name Little Joe Pennington, was on lead guitar. Lum York, who'd met Hank in the shipyards, played bass, and Winston "Red" Todd was on rhythm guitar. Audrey joined them occasionally on bass and drums, bringing along Lycrecia, who'd sleep backstage in Lum's bass fiddle case.

Norred was a fairly sophisticated musician, unhappy to find himself in a hillbilly band. He wanted to play western swing, not three-chord hillbilly music, and lost no opportunity to run down Hank's music in front of him. Little Joe Pennington was from the Tampa Bay area. He replaced a guitarist called Chris Criswell in Hank's band. Criswell was also from Tampa, and Pennington had taken the job that Criswell had held down there before he joined Hank. Criswell then wanted his old job back because his wife wouldn't move to Montgomery. "He phoned me and said, 'Boy, you wanna get this job playing five or six nights a week,'" said Pennington. "He said he'd call Hank for me, and Hank says, 'Chris tells me you're a pretty good guitar man. Do ya want to come up and try it?' I said, 'Well, guess I could. Ain't there no good guitar players up around Montgomery there?' He said, 'None I'd want to hire.' Found out later he'd hired every one of them and run 'em off."

The promise of five or six nights' work a week was hollow. That Hank was now a Sterling recording artist made little difference to his routine. At best, they worked three or four schoolhouse dates a week and the joints on weekends. Norred remembered one night in particular:

We was playing a dance at a juke joint and there was a poppin' sound and someone come up and said there was a fella out there shootin' with a gun. Directly, he come in. He was wearin' overalls — no shirt — and he had a big ol' loaded pistol and one of them bullets hit a heater and richocheted 'round the room. Man, you talk about huntin' a table. Lum run into the girls' toilet — Hank had to go get him out. Another place down near Fort Deposit they had chicken wire out front of the bandstand so if they started throwing bottles they wouldn't hit the band.

Some of the band lived with Hank's mother, although Lum York lived with his own mother. Norred was paid fifty dollars a week regardless of whether they worked because he had a family to support; the others were paid around seven dollars a gig. No one was getting rich, and no one thought that Hank was on the brink of next-big-thingdom. "I couldn't stand Hank's music," says Norred. "I'd tell him so too. I'd make fun of it. He'd get on Audrey for not being able to sing, and I'd say, 'Hank, you ain't so hot y'self. I'm just puttin' up with you.' He wasn't nothin'. If you played with Hank, you was kinda looked down on."

The Drifting Cowboys had to grudgingly admit that Hank knew how to draw a crowd, though. For a few weeks toward the end of 1946 they headlined a Saturday afternoon jamboree with the Henley Harmony Boys featuring Leaborne Eads at the Capitol Stockyards in north Montgomery. The L. C. Henley Monument Company co-owned the yard, and the show was promoted by Marvin Reuben and Charlie Holt from WSFA. Hank and the Harmony Boys performed off the auctioneers' stand, singing to around 250 people in the risers that had been erected for the cattle buyers. The show was starting to do decent business when Reuben and Holt decided that it would do as well without Hank and tore up his contract. They found out how big a draw he was when almost no one turned up the following week.

From the on-air personalities to the engineering staff, no one at WSFA could understand Hank's appeal. The station management despised his unpredictability and occasional fits of arrogance, and would have loved to rid themselves of him, but knew they couldn't. Hank knew it too. "Fans? I got a mob of 'em up here every morning and every afternoon," he told the *Montgomery Advertiser* in 1948:

Some come from fifty miles! A lady from Opelika wrote me just this mornin'. She says, "Say Hank, how much do it cost to come up and hear you sing? If it don't cost too much, we may come up there." If anybody in my business knew as much about their business as the public did, they'd be all right. Just lately, somebody got the idea nobody didn't listen to my kinda music. I told ever'body on the radio, this was my last program. "If anybody's enjoyed it, I'd like to hear from 'em." I got four hundred cards and letters that afternoon and the next mornin'. They decided they wanted to keep my kinda music.

During the early months of 1947, Hank probably sensed he was on the brink of something, and tried to stay straight, but something always triggered a bender. R. D. Norred remembered seeing a crowd gathered in the road and he went over to find his boss lying there with the cars going around him. The police came and hauled him home rather than to the drunk tank. Sterling Records artists were extended that small courtesy.

Hank's success probably surprised Fred Rose, as he watched Roy Acuff's sales slowly tail off, but the sales of the Sterling records made a believer out of him. Getting a true picture of his role in Hank's career is hard because the company's history was later filtered through Wesley Rose, who felt the need to cement himself to every critical moment in the Acuff-Rose saga. Wesley never understood Hank, although he later asserted that they had been best buddies. Rarely have a father and son been as different as Fred and Wesley Rose. Fred was artistic and temperamental. Wesley was sere and guarded. He was the parish priest who knew everything and told nothing. Born in Chicago on February 11, 1918, Wesley stayed with his mother when Fred and his first wife divorced, and hadn't seen his father for twelve years when they met in 1945. By then Wesley was an accountant for Standard Oil in Chicago, and never shed his accountant's skin. It wasn't until he made a trip to see an aunt in St. Louis in April 1945 that he was persuaded to visit Fred. When they met, they didn't recognize each other.

Fred often came to Chicago because Acuff-Rose's first selling agent was there, and he began calling on Wesley. He offered him a job, but Wesley cared nothing for country music, and even less for the prospect of living in Nashville. He held out for the position of general manager with responsibility for all business decisions, and finally joined the family business in November or December 1945. His name quickly appeared on the letterhead just beneath the company slogan: "Songs for Home Folks."

Wesley's skills as an administrator were unquestionable. In hiring him, Fred freed himself to do what he did best: handle the music and the writers. After his father's death, Wesley began assuming credit for all manner of decisions and began to fancy himself a music man. His magnified view of his importance was reflected in sycophantic articles he commissioned, such as "Wesley Rose Chooses Nashville — a Crucial Decision for the World of Music."

It was almost certainly Fred rather than Wesley who realized Hank's dilemma, though. Hank's promise was wasted at Sterling, and Rose began looking elsewhere. He had a good relationship with Art Satherley at Columbia, but Satherley passed on Hank, although he hung onto an acetate of several songs that Rose sent him (an acetate that later surfaced on an Arhoolie Records EP and a Country Music Foundation album). RCA's head of folk and western music, Steve Sholes (who later signed Elvis Presley to the label), passed too. Capitol was generally geared toward West Coast country music, and Mercury had only been in business a year or so and wasn't a much better bet than Sterling. Fred took the Sterling dubs to New York and pitched them to Paul Cohen at Decca. Then he waited.

A good record deal was crucial. Fred Rose knew that Hank couldn't follow the normal pattern: working stations in ever bigger markets, then using the radio work as an entrée to recording. Hank was generally considered to be too much trouble and too hillbilly by half. He needed to reverse the paradigm by getting some hits that would convince a bigger station to take a chance on him, and that in turn would increase his exposure. Records were the key.

Chapter
5

THE YEAR OF THE LION

O NE more opportunity was opening up for Fred Rose as he tried to place Hank Williams with a major record label in the spring of 1947. The giant Loews corporation, which owned MGM Pictures, had just started a record division. The same economic conditions that had prompted the formation of Sterling Records hadn't gone unnoticed further up the corporate pecking order. MGM had seen songs from its fabled musicals go on to sell hundreds of thousands of records for other companies. They had, for instance, stood by helpless as José Iturbi's "Polonaise in A-Flat" from *A Song to Remember* sold more than eight hundred thousand copies for RCA. Loews saw this income slipping through its fingers. Viewed from the outside, the record business seemed like a no-lose proposition in those immediate postwar years. But MGM didn't want its record division to be a lowly independent, so industry veteran Frank B. Walker was hired away from RCA in August 1945. MGM bankrolled him for a couple of years as he prepared to launch a fully functioning quasi-major label.

Born in upstate New York in October 1889, Walker had, as he liked to tell Hank and Fred Rose, been cutting country records since before Hank was born. One of them had been the Coles' "Tramp on the Street." Walker had broken into the music business in 1919 as a concert booker with Central Concerts in Detroit, then joined Columbia Records in 1921. As the label's head of "race" music, he signed Bessie Smith in 1923, and recorded country music on his field trips. He liked to recall how he rode horses back into the woods in search of a singer or musician that someone had told him about. He sold records in the rural areas by renting vacant storefronts, setting up benches, playing the new releases, and taking the cash himself.

In 1933, Walker moved to RCA and launched Bluebird Records as a Depression-era budget label. During the Second World War, he was seconded to the government's V-Disc unit, resuming with RCA before being seduced by MGM. Walker had seen and done it all. He could talk as easily about injection molding in the plant as he could about the innards of music publishing, or the respective merits of two blues singers. He was the sort of generalist that doesn't exist anymore. Short and dapper, with steel-rimmed glasses and a patrician air, he wasn't entirely convincing in his attempt to make Hank feel as though they were both ex–farm boys, but of all the record company CEOs in New York or Los Angeles, he was the only one with much understanding of what Hank Williams was doing.

After Walker came onboard, MGM paid $3.5 million to convert a munitions plant in Bloomfield, New Jersey, into a pressing plant capable of churning out forty million discs a year. Walker then set up distribution through Zenith Radio stores, supplemented by a network of independent distributors. Despite MGM's clout, MGM Records never really became a major player. For one thing, Walker was notoriously cheap. He told his promotion staff to write to radio stations because it was cheaper than phoning, and he didn't like to give away promotional copies. His first signings were in December 1946 for a scheduled launch in March 1947. Waving MGM's checkbook, he culled Jimmy Dorsey, Kate Smith, Ziggy Elman, and Billy Eckstine from the ranks of established artists whose contracts were up. His initial signings in what could loosely be termed country music were Sam Nichols, the Korn Kobblers, and Carson Robison. Of those, Robison was the best known. He'd written topical songs through the Depression and the war (such as "Prosperity Is Just Around Which Corner?" and "Hitler's Last Letter to Hirohito"). To give MGM a little filip at launch time, Walker lowballed the price of his records to sixty cents instead of the usual seventy-five cents, maintaining the lower price until May 1948. By the time he hiked the price, the label had its first hits, one of them by Hank Williams.

Most writing about Hank Williams has taken its cue from Wesley Rose, who said that it was the success of "Honky Tonkin'" on Sterling that encouraged his father to seek a better deal and persuaded Walker to sign Hank. This could not have been the case, though. The MGM contract was dated March 6, 1947, two months before "Honky Tonkin'" was released, and it became effective on April 1, 1947. Hank received an artist royalty for the first time: two cents per record, or roughly 3 percent of MGM's low list price of sixty cents. Three percent was, if anything, on the high side of what an untested act could expect. There is an apocryphal — but probably true — story that Hank didn't understand percentages and opted for a flat fee instead.

According to a deposition that Walker gave in February 1963, he had known Fred Rose since the early 1930s, and seemed to imply that he had met Hank before the Sterling contract. "[Hank] was submitting songs he had written to Mr. Rose for potential publication," Walker said. "Mr. Rose and I looked at them together, and we agreed to the possibilities." Walker also said that he, Fred Rose, and Hank jointly chose all the Hank songs recorded for MGM, although he's probably overstating his involvement. Rose acted as producer, or "A&R Representative." Today, a producer would expect to receive around 3 percent of a record's gross, but Rose, like many A&R men at the time, worked solely for the music publisher's share of the songwriter's royalty. RCA Victor's legendary A&R man, Ralph Peer, reportedly received just one dollar a year from RCA, but secured the publishing on almost everything he recorded (thereby acquiring songs that became standards, like "Walk Right In" and "Wildwood Flower"). Rose agreed to give MGM a bargain rate of 1.25 cents per song when the standard rate was 2 cents per song. This income was split fifty-fifty with the songwriter. When Hank's contract was renegotiated in April 1951, the publishing royalty (or "mechanical," as it was known) was upped to 1.5 cents.

Hank's first MGM session was held on April 21, 1947, with the core of Red Foley's band. Rose knew what was at stake. Hank would get one or two shots on MGM, and if the sales weren't there, he'd be dropped. Nashville had no session men in April 1947, and Foley's band was the sharpest in town. Rose probably figured that he needed a touch of class on the instrumental track to offset Hank's hillbilly edges. Guitarist Zeke Turner would play on several of Hank's sessions, and his brother Zeb would play several more. The backwoods aliases (Zeb and Zeke's real names were Edward and James Cecil Grishaw) disguised two of the more adroit pickers Hank ever used; they were perhaps too fancy for his taste. Brownie Reynolds played bass. Tommy Jackson was on fiddle, and

Smokey Lohman on steel guitar. This was a group capable of delivering exactly what Rose wanted, and more than Hank wanted.

"Move It on Over" was the first song Hank cut for MGM. More than any other song he'd recorded to that point, it betrayed his debt to black music. It rocked. The melody was as old as the blues itself; a variant had done business as "Your Red Wagon" and another variant became "Rock Around the Clock." Hank, like Elvis Presley some years later, never played black music in the tragically white way — oversouling and over-playing. "Move It on Over" was a lazy record even at its brisk tempo. This may have been Tee-Tot's legacy to Hank, and — if it was — it was worth all the nickels and dimes Lilly had scrimped to pay him. Zeke Turner played a lovely little solo, a model of brilliant economy. If the melody of "Move It on Over" had been around the block, the lyrical content was pure Hank Williams. As Hank's future fiddle player, Jerry Rivers, once said, "[Hank's] novelty songs weren't novelty — they were serious, not silly, and that's why they were much better accepted and better selling. 'Move It on Over' hits right home, 'cause half of the people he was singing to were in the doghouse with the ol' lady."

The sound edged closer to Roy Acuff on the session's second song, "I Saw the Light." It remains Hank's best-known hymn, but if gospel composer Albert E. Brumley had been a litigious man, his name would be bracketed alongside Hank's in the composer credit. Not only was the melody very close to Brumley's "He Set Me Free," but even the lyrics bore a passing resemblance. The hugely prolific Brumley, best known for "I'll Fly Away," had published "He Set Me Free" in a 1939 songbook titled *The Gospel Tide,* and it had been cut in March 1941 by the Chuck Wagon Gang. Another white gospel group, the Southern Joy Quartet, recorded it shortly before Hank wrote "I Saw the Light."

By all accounts, "I Saw the Light" was written on the way back from a dance in Fort Deposit. If all the people who later claimed to be in the car with Hank that night had actually been there, he would have needed a twenty-passenger bus. One who claimed to be there was Leaborne Eads, who had flyposted the dance for Lilly. He remembers:

Mizz Williams had given me money to hand out circulars at Fort Deposit. Hank was higher than a kite by the time the show was over. She drove home, and he was in the back seat sleepin' it off. There was a beacon light near Dannelly Field Airport, and

Mizz Williams knew it always took time to get Hank awake when he was drunk like that, so she turned around and told him, "Hank, wake up, we're nearly home. I just saw the light." Between there and home he wrote the song.

"I Saw the Light" wasn't just "He Set Me Free" with new lyrics, though. It was the prayer of the backslider, who lives in hope of redemption. Hank wrote at least two drafts, which was unusual for him. The first was dated Sunday, January 26, 1947, so perhaps, as Eads said, it was written right after the Saturday night dance in Fort Deposit. "Lord" was spelled "Loard." Why? Probably because the words Hank knew best were "Room and Board" posted outside Lilly's boardinghouse. If "board" was "b-o-a-r-d," then "Lord" was "l-o-a-r-d." Hank was the first to record the song, but wasn't the first to release it. His version was held back until September 1948, but Rose pitched the song around. On August 13, 1947, Clyde Grubbs recorded it for RCA, and then on November 18 the song's copublisher and spiritual mentor, Roy Acuff, recorded it. Both versions were released before Hank's.

The other two songs from that first MGM session, "(Last Night) I Heard You Crying in Your Sleep" and "Six More Miles (to the Graveyard)," became flip sides for "Move It on Over" and "I Saw the Light," respectively. An embryonic version of "(Last Night) I Heard You Crying in Your Sleep" exists as a lyric sheet in the Alabama Department of Archives and History. As with the early version of "I Saw the Light," the words are quite dissimilar, suggesting that songwriting wasn't quite the spontaneous act that Hank later made it out to be.

"Move It on Over" was released on June 6, 1947, and, two months later, it became Hank's first *Billboard* hit. On August 21, 1947, he received his first extended write-up in the *Montgomery Examiner*. Calling him the "spur-jangling Sinatra of the western ballad," the writer stated that Hank had already sold more than one hundred thousand copies of "Move It on Over." Then, inviting gales of laughter from those close to Hank, the article went on to say, "Where the inspiration for the song came from [Hank] couldn't say," adding, "it's not his own married life. Mr. and Mrs. Hank Williams lead a model domestic life." The model for the Bickersons, perhaps.

Around the same time, there was another write-up, this one by the Reverend A. S. Turnipseed in the *Montgomery News*. Turnipseed had evidently attended one of Hank's shows. He described the audience as young and "not dressed as to indicate any affluence." It was, he noted, a mostly restrained crowd. "Any preacher who has preached in the rural sections of the white counties of Alabama has observed the same restraint even when highly emotional preaching was going on," he said. Turnipseed went on to say that fully half of Hank's program was devoted to comedy routines and horseplay. There was one religious number, but the only time the crowd was whipped up was when Hank sang "Move It on Over" and "Pan American." Turnipseed concluded by trying to put Hank in a broader context. Changes were taking place in Montgomery as white sandyland farmers like Hank moved into town, challenging the right to rule of the state's old-money families. "As Hank Williams plays," Turnipseed noted apocalyptically, "Rome is burning." There was a half-valid point beneath the bluster. There *was* a migration into town from the rural communities, and even if the new migrants weren't challenging the old money's right to rule, they were certainly bringing their music with them. The former farmers weren't stopping in Montgomery, either. That's why Hank had ready-made audiences when he eventually appeared in places like Cleveland, Washington, and even Oakland. He was a letter from home.

On August 4, just as "Move It on Over" was breaking, Hank was called back to the studio. This time he brought up a band from Montgomery, but they weren't used to recording and Rose quickly became frustrated. Midway through the session, he sent for Red Foley's fiddle player, Tommy Jackson, to replace the man Hank had brought up. Two of the four songs recorded, "Fly Trouble" and "I'm Satisfied with You," were written or cowritten by Fred Rose. As incomprehensible as it seems now, it was common during the 1940s to release a new record just as a hit was peaking, so "Fly Trouble" was released in September 1947, just as "Move It on Over" reached number four. Rose wrote it with the blackface comedy team of Jamup and Honey, modeling it on slick West Coast country novelty songs like "Smoke! Smoke! Smoke! (That Cigarette)." It seemed to signal Rose's intention of easing Hank uptown. From the hokey lyrics to Sammy Pruett's jazzy guitar breaks, the entire production was precisely what Hank's music was *not* about, and it was precisely what white sandyland farmers who had just moved to town did *not* want to hear. Rose issued it with "On the Banks of the Old Pontchartrain," a ballad along traditional lines, in the sense that it related a story. The writer was Ramona Vincent, a crippled woman from Louisiana. She had mailed the song to Hank as a poem, and he put a melody to it. There's correspondence in which Hank asks Fred Rose how to go about buying a song. It remains the least typical song with Hank Williams' name on it. The coupling of "Fly Trouble" and "On the Banks of the Old Pontchartrain" flopped miserably, and in later years Hank would use it as a personal metaphor for a poor-selling record. "Sure am glad it ain't another damn 'Pontchartrain,'" he'd say when people would congratulate him on a hit. More than anything, it proved how much Rose had yet to learn about Hank's music and his audience.

At this point, Hank was no more than a sidebar to Fred Rose's activities and was far from MGM's best-selling artist. In October 1947, Rose was in Chicago producing Bob Wills' last Columbia session for Art Satherley. As Satherley knew, Wills had been seduced away by Frank Walker, an acquisition that seemed to be the coup Walker needed. By the end of October 1947, MGM's country roster consisted of Bob Wills, Hank Williams, Carson Robison, Denver Darling, Jerry Irby (who'd written the beer-joint anthem "Driving Nails in My Coffin"), and another Rose protégé, Rome Johnson. It was Robison who would give the country division its biggest hit in 1948 with "Life Gits Tee-Jus, Don't It." Bob Wills' career was in a slow, inexorable decline, and it would be another year and a half before Hank got his career back on track.

"Move It on Over" gave Hank the first serious money he had ever seen. When he talked to the *Alabama Journal* in 1947, he estimated that his songwriting alone would bring him between $15,000 and $20,000 that year, but he was a little overoptimistic. His MGM royalties came in at $439.55 (equating to roughly twenty-two thousand copies of "Move It on Over"), and his Acuff-Rose royalties totaled $1,709.11. Under pressure from Audrey, Hank put some of that money down on a house — his first — at 10 Stuart Avenue in Montgomery, and some toward a fur coat for Audrey. Citizens Realty (owned by Bill Perdue, who co-owned Radio Recording, where Hank cut his songwriting demos) had to give Hank the commission it made on the sale to help him with the $2,200 deposit.

The delays built into royalty accounting meant that more "Move It on Over" money came through in 1948, and it seems likely that some of it was earmarked for 318 North McDonough Street, a large boarding-house that Lilly purchased that year. Perhaps she had made it unambiguously clear that since she had supported Hank from the first guitar to the first hit, the bill was now due. Lilly was a married woman again. On May 1, 1946, she had divorced J. C. Bozard, and on March 1, 1947, she married one of her boarders, William Wallace "Bill" Stone, from Tuscaloosa, Alabama. Everyone liked Stone, a widower some years younger than Lilly, but he had a fondness for the bottle and remained a shadowy presence in Hank's life. Stone had been a taxi driver and had apprenticed as a carpenter with Crump Craft, but was working at Pelham and Shell Antique Reproduction Furniture when he married Lilly. Later, he brought one of Hank's cousins, Walter McNeil, into the company as an apprentice.

Number 10 Stuart Avenue was small, boxy, and sparsely furnished, and Audrey spent money that should have gone into stocking the icebox on tony metal awnings over the windows. It might have been home, but if Audrey and Lycrecia were out of town, Hank would do anything to avoid being in his little house by himself. "He'd come over to where I lived," said Lum York. "He'd say, 'Come on, go with me.' I'd say, 'Where you goin'?' He said, 'I'm goin' to the house.' I'd say, 'Hank, I don't want to go out there, all you gonna do is git a funny book and sit there and read, and I'll be sittin' there with nobody to talk to.'" Like many entertainers, Hank always needed an audience. Nothing unsettled him more than his own company.

Lycrecia insists that times were good on Stuart Avenue; others, particularly band members, remember the spats. Both Hank and Audrey had low boiling points, and arguments would blow up out of inconsequentialities. Once, Hank called the Radio Hospital to come and repair his wire recorder (the forerunner of the tape recorder) and the bill came to $17.50. Audrey hissed at him for squandering all that money on his recorder, and Hank grabbed Audrey's fur coat and began trashing it. The repairman ran for the door. A couple of days later, Lilly appeared at the store with the $17.50. Peace had returned to Stuart Avenue. On another occasion, Fred and Irella Beach were at the house working up a new song (Fred had worked in one of the earliest incarnations of the Drifting Cowboys). "Audrey was whining and whining," said Irella. "Then Hank said, 'Fred, let's us try another song,' and Audrey went storming off into the bedroom and sent her little girl into the living room. She said, 'My momma says for you all to go home.' When we left, Hank was yelling at Audrey and screamin' at her like nothin' you ever heard. He hit her hard, too."

The Beaches had walked in on one of the problems that plagued Hank and Audrey's relationship. From the time they married, Audrey had been a part of the show. She played bass, even drums on occasion, and she sang. Now she sensed Hank distancing himself from her professionally. She wanted to be more than a happy homemaker, which would be easier to applaud if her singing were better. It's hard to know if Hank was trying to ease her out of the picture because she couldn't sing, or because he thought she should be at home cooking and cleaning. Clearly, it was a source of tension. In a letter to Fred Rose dated August 19, 1947, Hank mentioned that he had mailed a demo of himself and Audrey singing "I Saw the Light." He'd already recorded it for MGM, but it hadn't been released, so perhaps Audrey wanted to redo it as a duet. "We didn't do much on [it]," Hank wrote, as if trying to discourage Rose from doing much on it either. "We never had tried it until we went to make the record." Rose had no problem resisting the notion that Hank and Audrey should record together, but, as Hank became more successful and Audrey more insistent, their pairing on record became inevitable.

If Rose didn't already know it, the demo would have told him that Audrey's singing voice was shrill and tuneless, and, like many people who sing badly, she seemed to have no sense of how bad she was. "Audrey couldn't carry a tune in a bucket," said R. D. Norred, "and the more she practiced, the worse she got." Her duets with Hank were like an extension of their married life as she fought him for dominance on every note. For the present, she would be confined to occasional show dates and morning radio in Montgomery, but she wouldn't be denied much longer.

In late 1947, the music trade papers were consumed with talk of an upcoming recording ban. It soon became clear that the American Federation of Musicians would call a strike effective December 31, 1947, when agreements with all the record companies expired. The problem was a dinosaur named James C. Petrillo, who held the presidency of the AFM as a virtual fiefdom. Petrillo was bitterly opposed to records, the use of records on radio, and the network broadcasting of live and prerecorded music. All of these, he declared, were inimical to his members' best interests. The AFM's agreements with radio were good until 1949, but, with the recording agreements running out at the end of 1947, Petrillo wanted to send a message to the networks via the record companies. It was a more direct hit than it seemed because two of the three major labels, RCA and Columbia, were owned by NBC and CBS, respectively. As a long-term goal, Petrillo wanted to shut down the record business; one of his oft-repeated lines was, "These records are destroying us." In the short term, though, he wanted to test the union's strength against the Taft-Hartley bill, wring a few financial concessions from the record companies, and fire a warning shot over the bows of the radio networks.

Petrillo's first attempt at strangling the record business had come a few years earlier. He'd called a strike in August 1942 that lasted until various points in late 1943 and early 1944. One by one, the companies settled with him, and he won some concessions. In 1947, the companies were ready for Petrillo and began stockpiling masters as year-end approached. The majors viewed the ban as a blessing in disguise; they could work through their backlog of masters, press up catalog, squeeze out the independent labels and, as one unnamed executive said, "There'll be no placating artists with expensive sessions." Petrillo's crusades against records for home use and broadcast as well as the networking of live broadcasts were all doomed. Fewer remotes of live broadcasts were being picked up every year, and more deejays were being hired. And, by 1947, the growth of the home record market was a tide that no one — least of all Petrillo — could stem.

Down in Montgomery, Hank Williams was barely aware of this. He knew he was being called to Nashville for two sessions on November 6 and 7, 1947, and needed to have some songs ready. Rose wanted eight usable sides that could be doled out over the length of the strike. MGM, only in business for nine months, had more reason to feel jittery than the other major labels because its overhead was already high and its back catalog was shallow.

"We had worked up some songs 'cause of the ban coming," says R. D. Norred.

Fred Rose had called Hank and told him to get his songs together, and we had maybe fifteen worked up. I knew you made forty dollars a session, so I went down to Art Freehling's [music store] and got me a real steel guitar and we was ready to go. We had it pretty well complete, then Fred come down to go over things, and he said he couldn't use the band. Hank said, "Why?" and Fred says, "You know how Lum was the last time he was up there. Fidget, fidget, it took all night cutting songs. This time, you ain't gonna get to try it twice." He said, "Them staff musicians up there, you're not gonna have to practice with them boys, you just do your part and they'll do theirs." Hank said, "Well, I'll take Norred with me, anyway," and Fred said, "No, you just can't put Norred with Zeke Turner and expect it to work." Hank didn't like it, but there wasn't too much he could say about it.

Hank arrived in Nashville to find a group drawn from two *Opry* bands. Zeke Turner was back, together with two other members of Red Foley's band, steel guitarist Jerry Byrd and rhythm guitarist Louis Innis. Rose paired them with Bill Monroe's fiddle player, Chubby Wise, and might have played the barely audible piano himself. The first song they cut, "Rootie Tootie," was one of Rose's songs. He'd already pitched it to Pee Wee King and country bandleader Paul Howard, and all three versions were released in January 1948. Rose did very well from King's version because it got a free ride on the flip side of King's original version of "Tennessee Waltz," but the song otherwise did little business.

Hank then cut three of his own songs, "I Can't Get You Off of My Mind," "I'm a Long Gone Daddy," and a remake of "Honky Tonkin'." The following day, he cut three more original songs, "My Sweet Love Ain't Around," "The Blues Come Around," and "I'll Be a Bachelor 'til I Die," and one not-so-original song, "A Mansion on the Hill." The originals were a marked departure from the Sterling songs, recorded just one year earlier. Perhaps the success of "Move It on Over" had shown Hank the way, and given him some encouragement. These recordings sounded like hits, not like 1930s field recordings caught out of time.

"A Mansion on the Hill" was credited to Hank and Fred Rose. The old story that Hank had written it in a side room when he first met Rose wasn't the way Audrey remembered it:

Fred said . . . "To prove to me you *can* write, I'm gonna give you a title, and I want you to take it back to Montgomery and write a song around it." Hank worked with it and worked with it, but he never could do too much good with it, and the reason he couldn't was because it wasn't his idea. One night I had just finished with the dinner dishes, and I started singing "Tonight

down here in the valley . . ." After I got through with it, I took it
in to Hank and said, "Hank, what do you think of this?" He
really liked it, and it was a mixture of my lyrics, Hank's lyrics,
and Fred Rose's lyrics. Hank sent it in, and for a long time I
wouldn't tell anybody that I had anything to do with that
because I wanted it to be all Hank.

The reason Hank had a problem with "A Mansion on the Hill" was
that he couldn't write narrative ballads. All of his best songs froze a
moment, a feeling, or a grudge. The only shred of personal experience he
could draw on for "A Mansion on the Hill" was the unrequited ardor
he'd once had for the daughter of the mayor of Montgomery. Boots Harris remembered driving him around in Lilly's station wagon looking for
her night after night in theater lineups, knowing all the while that she
was unattainable. Perhaps a little of that surfaced in the song.

Hank set "A Mansion on the Hill" to a melody he'd poached from
Bob Wills' 1938 recording of "I Wonder If You Feel the Way I Do."
Released in December 1948, just as the ban was ending, "A Mansion on
the Hill" did little business until March 1949, when it was caught up in
the tidal wave of Hank's career.

The two sessions before the record ban were a template for the years
ahead. Under Rose's guidance, Hank began to realize his strengths and
weaknesses as a writer, and he brought along songs that improved with
every session. The sessionmen might have looked down their noses at
Hank's music, but they were attuned to the challenge of bringing the
Acuff sound into the honky-tonk. Rose's role was to hone Hank's songs
before the session and work with the pickers during the session to keep a
tight commercial focus. He seemed happiest to let Hank follow his
instincts, although he continued to feed him dumb little novelties like
"Rootie Tootie." Perhaps Rose included his own songs to double his
money from MGM, but it's likelier that Hank simply wasn't generating
enough material that Rose considered worth releasing.

At the time the ban came into effect, Hank's band was still composed of R. D. Norred, Lum York, Little Joe Pennington, and Red Todd.
The stability in the lineup was itself an indication of the growing confidence level around Hank. That November, it looked as though Rose
would land them a gig on WLAC in Nashville, which would be a step

toward the *Opry*. Penington recalled the group buying matching outfits in anticipation:

> We'd ordered in western outfits. Pea-green shirts, western-cut khaki pants, and western boots. [Hank's cousin] Marie did appliqué embroidery on the shirts from a pattern that you ironed on. We were a real band when we had suits like that, but those outfits cost thirty dollars each, and thirty dollars was about what we made a week, and we had to pay our board out of that. Hank paid for all the outfits when the order come in. He said, "Boys, any y'all got the money you can pay me off, the rest that don't come on down to the loan company and we'll sign you up." So Lum and Red and me went down and signed up with the Montgomery Loan and Finance Company to pay off these outfits.

The loan agreements were dated November 3, 1947.

Rose's approach to WLAC fell through, and in February 1948, Hank thought about moving to the Washington, D.C., area. A promoter there, Connie B. Gay, had a show, *Town and Country,* that needed a star. On February 23, Hank wired Lilly from Cincinnati, telling her to tell the boys that he was heading for Washington. Lum York says that he'd left tickets for them, but the band had so little faith in Hank's ability to deliver on the promises that they cashed in the tickets and waited for him to return.

It was still a rare day that the band got more than a day's drive out of Montgomery. On one occasion, Hank was booked as a supporting act on a show at the Temple Theater in Birmingham. Pennington discovered that it was a union gig, checked with the union hall, and found out that scale (the minimum that could be paid) was roughly twice what Hank was paying. Norred recalled:

> Hank said, "I want y'all in the back room." We got in there and he said, "Who's the little bright boy been down to the union office?" Joe said, "'I did." Hank said, "Did you find out what you wanted to know down there?" Joe said, "Yeah, union scale is fifteen dollars." So he paid us. Joe said, "I just wanted to

make sure I was gonna get what was coming to me," and Hank said — sarcastic like — "Friend, you'll get what's comin' to you."

It was a pattern Hank would follow throughout his professional life. He would leave a twenty dollar tip on a fifty-cent breakfast, or simply forget where he had stashed the night's takings, but would chisel his band members out of five bucks if he could.

After it became clear that Hank would not be moving to Nashville or Washington, he could do no more than cement his already high standing around Montgomery. As he told the *Montgomery News* that year, "I got the popularest daytime program on this station" (the nighttime programming was drawn from the NBC feed). During the spring of 1948, the group landed a regular gig at the 31 Club, a juke joint in Montgomery with a big dance area. But that spring, Hank slowly unraveled. His disintegration is documented in a series of letters from Fred Rose. Over the course of eighteen months, Rose had taken a profound interest in Hank's well-being. "I'm opening up my heart to you," he wrote in one letter, "because I love you like my own son, and you can call on me anytime when you are in a problem." Going well beyond professional interest or self-interest, Rose dispensed advice on every aspect of life.

In February, Audrey gave up on Hank and took Lycrecia back to Banks, leaving Hank despondent. "The trouble with you kids is that both of you want to be boss," wrote Rose. "Both of you have pride. Pride is one of the most destructive lies on earth. . . . It is something we should all get rid of as quickly as possible so that we can enjoy the happiness of humility. . . . If Audry [*sic*] wants you to wreck your life because of this misunderstanding, fool her, show her you can be a success in spite of her, not because of her."

One month later, on March 19, Rose wrote to Hank, castigating him.

Wesley [Rose] tells me you called this morning for more money after me wiring you four hundred dollars just the day before yesterday. . . . We have gone as far as we can go at this time and cannot send you any more.

Hank I have tried to be a friend of yours but you refuse to let me be one. I feel that you are just using me for a good thing, and this is where I quit. You have been very unfair, calling the house in the middle of the night and I hope you will not let it happen again.

When you get ready to straighten out let me know and maybe we can pick up where we left off, but for the present I am fed up with your foolishness.

One week later, Rose wrote to Lilly. Apparently, Hank was holed up in Pensacola, Florida. Rose had sent him some contracts, and Hank hadn't returned them. "The reason I am asking Hank to sign this particular legal type of contract is for his own protection," Rose wrote, "so that he won't get too full of firewater and sign a bad contract with someone else."

By April 3, Hank had returned to Montgomery, and Rose thought he had come to his senses.

I hear you have been doing a pretty good job of straightening yourself out and nobody is more glad to hear it than me. Hank, anything I've written you or said is for your own good as I know what a fool a man can make of himself with drinking. . . .

You are destined for big things in the recording and songwriting field, and you are the only one who can ruin this opportunity. In the future, forget the firewater and let me take care of your business and you'll be a big name in this business.

Remember that women are revengeful and do all in their power to wreck a man when they separate from him and the only way to win is for the man to become successful.

In fact, Hank hadn't straightened out. That day, he sold his house at 10 Stuart Avenue. He got his $2,200 deposit back, and the new owner assumed the mortgage. Hank went on a spending spree. Five days later, on April 8, a package show came to the Charles Theater. Cowboy Copas and Johnny Bond were the stars, and Hank was to open for them while the group played the 31 Club. Perhaps he was drunk, but he didn't go over well at the Charles. Johnny Bond took it upon himself to tell the people of Montgomery not to take Hank for granted. "You people don't know 'bout this boy here," Bond told the crowd. "He won't be 'round here very long. His records are going like wildfire all over the West Coast."

Hank had promised that he would bring the headliners back to the 31 after their show, so the band was surprised when Bond appeared without Hank. "Johnny come in, sang a song," remembered Pennington, "and we said, 'Is Hank with y'all?' One of them said, 'Well the last we saw him, him and Copas was backstage with a couple of women and a bottle.' R.D. said, 'Well, you needn't look for him for a while.'"

Two or three nights later, Hank showed up. He hadn't shaved since before the Charles show, and was still pitifully hungover. He went up to the bandstand and tried to play a few songs, but he'd known better nights. He tried to smooth things over with the bartender, who was also the owner, but it didn't work, and he staggered off into the night. The band was offered Hank's job and they took it. "Now, who's gonna tell Hank?" said Pennington.

> They decided I was gonna do it, and me and Red went up there — a sanatorium somewhere. Audrey was up there and Hank was propped up in bed. They knew where to take him. Hank said, "How you fellas doing? What's happening down at the club?" I said, "Well the owner's fixin' to get another band." Hank said, "Oh?" I said, "Well, he's offered us the job, and we thought we'd go ahead and take it." He said, "Well, do what you want to," and he got kinda surly.

Hank never held down another regular gig or assembled another band in Montgomery. His life was a series of peaks and troughs. During the downward spirals, Hank would go to the brink, then pull himself back in the nick of time. He did it so many times that he probably made the fatal mistake of thinking he could always do it. The spring of 1948 was one of his deepest troughs, but he slowly came around. On April 12, he finally signed Fred Rose's contracts, and Rose placed him on a fifty-dollar-a-month retainer. The first check came through on April 30. Audrey, though, had decided to file for divorce, and it was too late to change her mind. "Hank Williams my husband is twenty-four years of age," she said in her complaint. "He has a violent and ungovernable temper. He drinks a great deal, and during the last month, he has been drunk most of the time. My nervous system has been upset and I am afraid to live with him any longer." On May 26, after three and a half years of marriage, Hank and Audrey were divorced.

In Audrey's complaint and in Rose's letters we can sense the frustrations involved in dealing with Hank Williams. He was manipulative, selfish, violent, and indiscriminately unfaithful when drunk. Audrey saw Hank's talent and saw him shooting himself in the foot. He seemed to be damning himself to the joints of south-central Alabama, and she railed against it. Like Lilly, she saw the alcoholism in terms of self-control, a view that was reinforced by the fact that there were times when Hank *could* control it.

After the separation, Hank moved back to Lilly's boardinghouse. His old band members would see him there sometimes sitting on the swing, wearing his hat and his suit. He and Audrey reconciled, although the divorce remained in effect. The bridge to Acuff-Rose was mended. Rose inserted a clause into the contract that he subsequently crossed out: "During the three-year period from the date of this contract, the said Hank Williams agrees to conduct himself in a manner not detrimental to Acuff-Rose Publications." The contract also stated that Acuff-Rose could "accept as liquidated damages all future royalties to which . . . Hank Williams may be entitled." Rose's faith in Hank clearly had boundaries.

Everyone but Lilly knew that Hank had to get out of Montgomery. "Aunt Lilly had mixed emotions about Hank leaving Montgomery," said Hank's cousin, Walter McNeil. "She felt that he could stay here and eventually make the *Grand Ole Opry*. But Audrey knew better." Fred Rose shared Audrey's opinion that Hank must move to a bigger market or at least a station with more wattage. Hank, though, was tainted with the twin curses of unreliability and drunkenness. The industry was small, and even though Hank hadn't been far outside south-central Alabama, his reputation had. The *Opry* was out of the question, but Saturday night jamborees were proliferating.

Down in Shreveport, Louisiana, radio station KWKH had started a Saturday night jamboree while Hank was on his springtime bender. It didn't have any big-name acts yet, and it was the best Fred Rose could get. On Thursday, July 29, 1948, Hank signed off WSFA. One way or another, he had to get out of Montgomery, and Shreveport seemed to be the place to take a stand.

I'll tune up my fiddle, rosin up my bow,
I'll make myself welcome wherever I go.

"Rye Whiskey" (unknown)

• •

THE *HAYRIDE*

• •

*S*HORTLY after signing off WSFA, Hank and Audrey loaded Lycrecia and a few possessions into an old Chrysler and set off for Shreveport, Louisiana. They stopped in Houston on July 31 so that Hank could make an appearances at Pappy Daily's Record Ranch and Daily's jukebox distributorship, Southern Amusements. Daily would someday have the thankless task of managing and producing George Jones, but in 1948 he was still a retailer and distributor. His young son, Donald, shot some photos before Hank drove on to Shreveport.

Hank Williams spent just ten months in Shreveport, but during those months he became a star. Country music was localized, and cities like Shreveport were self-contained scenes. Artists would usually work a city until they'd "played it out," and it's a testament to Hank's appeal that he'd worked Montgomery on and off for ten years without coming close to playing it out. Every artist's goal was to join one of the premier radio barn dances, such as WLS's *National Barn Dance* in Chicago, WLW's *Boone County Jamboree* (later known as the *Midwestern Hayride*) in Cincinnati, the *Renfro Valley Barn Dance* (also in Cincinnati), and of course Nashville's *Grand Ole Opry.* Hank had a lot to prove before one of those would touch him.

The *Louisiana Hayride* was a minor-league jamboree when Hank joined, but, between 1948 and 1954, it gave the all-important first break to Webb Pierce, Faron Young, Johnnie and Jack, Kitty Wells, Johnny Horton, Slim Whitman, Jim Reeves, the Browns, Elvis Presley, Johnny Cash,

Tommy Sands, Claude King, Billy Walker . . . and Hank Williams. One by one, they left, together with a crew of backing musicians that included James Burton, Floyd Cramer, and Jerry Kennedy. If only a few had stayed, Shreveport might have taken a run at Nashville's preeminence, which was newly established and vulnerable. As it was, the *Hayride* simply became an *Opry* farm club, or, as it called itself after everyone had left, the Cradle of the Stars.

Just as WSM was the key to Nashville's preeminence, so KWKH could have made Shreveport's hillbilly music business achieve critical mass. The station's long and tangled history began with a local businessman, W. K. Henderson, whose initials it bore. Henderson conducted quixotic crusades against chain stores, and his abuse of clear-channel wattage made him an early target of the Federal Radio Commission (the forerunner of the FCC). Not content to own the station, Henderson went on the air with his trademark greeting, "Hello world, doggone ya!" Jimmie Davis was one of the station's early mainstays. Twice governor of Louisiana and the man who popularized (and claimed to have written) "You Are My Sunshine," Davis made his first recordings for Henderson's short-lived "Doggone" label.

Henderson sold KWKH in September 1932 to a Shreveport consortium that brought the station into the CBS network, and then, in 1935, it was purchased by John D. Ewing, owner of the *Shreveport Times*. In 1939, KWKH became a fifty-thousand-watt clear-channel station. Fifty thousand watts (compared with WSFA's one thousand) was the maximum allowable in the United States, and the clear channel meant that the frequency was assigned to just one station. The only stations with more power were the five-hundred-thousand-watt border stations that operated from Mexico, with a signal so powerful that it obliterated everything within fifty kilocycles of the stations' frequency path. Fifty thousand watts was enough for Hank Williams, though. It would bring him to a larger audience than he'd ever known.

As far back as 1936, KWKH hosted a radio jamboree, the Sunday afternoon *Hillbilly Amateur Show* with Bob and Joe Shelton (the Sunshine Boys). The following year, the Sheltons' show became the *Saturday Night Roundup*, but it was discontinued during the war. Immediately after the war, John Ewing's daughter, Helen, married a naval pilot from Atlanta named Henry Clay, and Clay was handed KWKH as part of Helen's dowry. He'd managed a radio barn dance, the *Dog Patch Jamboree*, in

Florence, Alabama, before the war, and now he decided to start another. The new show's producer would be Horace Logan, who'd been in and around KWKH since 1932. Logan, whose stories usually demand close scrutiny, claimed to have started the *Louisiana Hayride.* "They were toying with the idea of starting another show like the *Saturday Night Roundup* but hadn't reached a decision," he said. "Then after I came back, they decided that they would go with it because I had worked with the prior show." Contemporary reports downplay Logan's role, giving credit for the show's structure to Dean Upson, the station's commercial manager, who'd worked for the *Grand Ole Opry*'s parent station, WSM. "Prior to starting the *Hayride,* we had a lot of talent on daily," Clay once said. "Dean Upson knew a lot of hillbillies, and that helped too."

Louisiana Hayride was a name that carried connotations of the state's infamous governor Huey P. Long; one of the first books about Long was Harnett P. Kane's *Louisiana Hayride: The American Rehearsal for Dictatorship,* published in 1941. There had also been a pop hit in 1932 called "Louisiana Hayride" from the Broadway show *Flying Colors,* so it was a far from original name, but Logan says he decided upon it because "I wanted something that would connote country music — and then localize it." Logan also takes credit for the show's presentation. He went to the *Opry* for what he claims was his first and only visit, and came away with a rival vision:

> With the *Opry,* they'd bring a guy on, and you'd have to suffer through him for a half hour whether you liked him or not. He'd bring on some guests, but essentially you had the same guy, say, Roy Acuff, for a half hour. If you liked him, it was great; if you didn't, it wasn't. My idea was to put the artists in extreme competition with each other. If they were going to be stars, they had to establish themselves and then reestablish themselves every Saturday night. When one of my artists came onstage, he did two numbers. If he encored, he came back later and did another two numbers, and that was all for the evening. It forced the artists to reestablish their eminence; it was a terribly difficult show to work.

The first *Louisiana Hayride* was held on Saturday, April 3, 1948, in Shreveport's Municipal Auditorium. That was the day Hank sold his house in Montgomery, and tried hard to blow the proceeds. The Bailes Brothers headlined the first *Louisiana Hayride*. The Baileses were on Columbia Records and they'd been *Grand Ole Opry* stars before their enforced exile to Shreveport in December 1946. In October 1946, Johnnie Bailes' girlfriend had stabbed herself three times, then jumped to her death from his room in Nashville's Merchants Hotel. The *Opry* immediately canceled the Baileses' contract, and five weeks later they were in Shreveport; that's how quickly the *Opry* blackballed its transgressors. Hank almost certainly knew what happened to Johnnie Bailes and should have paid attention. The Baileses' supporting acts included Johnnie and Jack, together with Johnnie's wife, Kitty Wells, and another Nashville act, Wally Fowler's Oak Ridge Quartet. The other acts were mostly local, but within weeks of launching the *Hayride*, Henry Clay attracted Curley Williams and his Georgia Peach Pickers, still featuring Hank's former sideman, Boots Harris, on steel guitar. It was the beginning of a great lineup.

Hank arrived in Shreveport four months after the *Louisiana Hayride* started, but it's still unclear exactly how he came to be there. Horace Logan's account strains credibility:

When we started the *Hayride*, we publicized it through *Cashbox* and *Billboard* and the like, and we immediately started getting deluged with audition tapes to be on the show. Hank was one of the fellows who phoned in, but [it was] Fred Rose [who] decided to try and get Hank on the *Hayride*. He called KWKH and talked to Henry Clay, and Henry talked to me about it. I'd heard of Hank Williams, heard his records on some little ol' label. I'd also heard that he was a drunk. I suggested that we tell Fred Rose if Hank could stay sober for six months and prove it, we'd put him on the *Hayride*. Hank called me every week, and almost invariably he would have the manager of his radio station with him. "Mr. Logan, Hank has been sober, he's been here every morning, he hasn't missed a single morning. He's sober as a judge," and Hank'd say, "That's right! I'm sober." And at the end of six months, we told him to come on over.

It's just possible that Hank tried to get on KWKH before Rose got into the picture, but what are the chances that the manager of WSFA would smile benignly while his star tried to secure a job elsewhere? And, of course, Hank was anything but sober during the six months before he joined the *Hayride*. The key factor was probably Dean Upson's longstanding relationship with Fred Rose. Upson had sung in a pop quartet, the Vagabonds, who were on WSM when Rose had first come to Nashville in the 1930s. They'd written songs together, and it's likely that Rose prevailed upon Upson to give Hank a chance. To confuse the issue, though, Johnnie Bailes insisted that he had known Hank for several years, and told people that he arrived at KWKH one day to find Hank leaning disconsolately against a parking meter. Hank told him he had been turned down by KWKH, and Bailes says that he went to see Upson to insist that Hank be hired.

It's possible that Hank's reputation was already so bad that it took Bailes, Rose, and Upson to prevail upon Henry Clay. What *is* clear, though, is that KWKH wasn't mortgaging the farm to acquire him. Like the *Opry*, the *Hayride* paid only American Federation of Musicians scale. Financially, Hank was going to be in worse shape than if he had stayed in Montgomery; only KWKH's fifty thousand watts made the move attractive.

Hank and Audrey appear to have made a brief preliminary trip to Shreveport to meet Henry Clay. They also met the KWKH regulars at the Bantam Grill opposite the studio. Hank was wondering how he could supplement his meager income from the station. Homer Bailes went to get Tillman Franks. At one time or another, Franks has been a bass player, booking agent, songwriter, song plugger, producer, and manager. He managed and booked Johnny Horton, Claude King, David Houston, Faron Young, Webb Pierce, and Elvis Presley. Hank's WSFA paycheck had amounted to around $120 a month, but he was so well known around Montgomery that he could fill his datebook. Remebered Tillman,

Hank said Henry Clay had offered him fifty dollars a week. He said he couldn't live on that, but if I booked him into schools, he'd stay. I said I'd do my best, but people didn't really know him. I told him, "If you can get a program on the radio and announce a few times that you're open for bookings I'll take a crack at it." I was starvin', and me and my wife was living with my mom and daddy, and I invited Hank and Audrey out for

Sunday dinner. We had a catfish supper and Hank and Audrey really put it away. After the meal, Hank sat down at this old upright piano and played "When the Roll Is Called Up Yonder" and "Will the Circle Be Unbroken," chording the piano like a guitar, and Audrey was singing with him. After he'd finished playing my daddy got me in a corner and he said, "Son, I hope you ain't thinking of making any money with him, 'cause he just cain't sing."

Hank then launched into one of his set pieces, said Tillman.

He was talking about how he had to leave Montgomery 'cause he owed ever'body in town. He said, "I bought this stove and bed on credit at this furniture store, and ever' month they'd send me a nasty note, and ever' month they was getting nastier. I went down to see the owner of the place, and said, 'I'm Hank Williams. I thought I'd come by and tell y'all how I pay my bills.'" The guy said, "Good," and Hank said, "Ever' month I take ever'one I owe, I write their names on a little bit of paper, put them all in a hat, shake 'em up real good, and I pull out one name and that's the one I pay. You write me one more nasty note and even if I pull your name out, it's going back in the hat."

On August 7, 1948, Hank made his first appearance on the *Louisiana Hayride*. He was the fifth act on the opening 8:00–8:30 p.m. segment. Merle Kilgore was a starstruck teenager hanging around the *Hayride* that night. Later, Kilgore was a performer and composer ("Ring of Fire" and "Wolverton Mountain"); later still, he was an opening act for Hank Jr., and after that, vice president of Hank Williams Jr. Enterprises. "Hank had the same look in his eye that Elvis had," said Kilgore. "That 'I know somethin' you don't know' look. Hank was cocky. That first night, the Baileses were on before him and he said, 'How did they do?' I said, 'Real good. I hate that you have to follow 'em.' He said, 'I'll eat 'em alive.'" In fact, Johnnie and Jack separated Hank and the Bailes Brothers that first night, but clearly Hank wasn't suffering from stage fright. He sang "Move It on Over," then gave way to a commercial for the Asco Loan Company. Johnnie and Jack launched the second half with a gospel song, followed by a comedy sketch. Next, Curley Kinsey's band played an instrumental, "Red Wing," then Hank and Audrey came out to sing an old wartime song, "I Want to Live and Love." Hank was through for the night, and the show was rounded out by the Four Deacons, the Mercer Brothers, and Johnnie and Jack.

Three days earlier, Hank had started his regular fifteen-minute show at 5:15 a.m. He arrived in Shreveport with a band he'd recruited in Montgomery. Lum York dutifully rejoined, and Hank recruited a fiddle player, George Brown, and guitarist Chris Criswell. He tried to get Don Helms to join him, but Helms was earning more money in a band with Boots Harris' brothers. Boots had briefly quit Curley Williams to join his brothers at a skating rink in Andalusia before moving back to California to rejoin Curley. Helms was brought in to replace him. The skating rink gig paid well, so when Hank called, Helms turned him down. "I'm gonna let you off this time," Hank told him, "but one of these days I'm goin' to the *Opry* and I ain't gonna take 'no' for an answer." Helms wouldn't have bet much on the chance, but he told Hank he would go with him when that day came.

Hank rented a garage apartment at 4802 Mansfield Road and the band lived in a trailer, but the arrangement didn't last long. He meant nothing in Shreveport, and couldn't get enough gigs to support the band. Most of them drifted back to Alabama. "He said he'd let me stay out at the house, and he'd feed me and buy me cigarettes," said Lum York, "and as soon as he got started again, we'd start playing, but I went back to Montgomery to work with Uncle Bob Helton."

By late September 1948, Hank was picking up some work in schoolhouses and honky-tonks around Shreveport on weeknights, pulling musicians from the *Hayride* staff band as needed, or booking out with other *Hayride* acts so that he could share their band. Tillman Franks' diary for September shows Hank working doubleheaders with Johnnie and Jack in little towns like Plain Dealing. Tillman booked school auditorium shows, and remembers Hank preferring schoolhouse dates to honky-tonks. "I think he'd got beat up a few times," he says. "In schoolhouses and auditoriums he could really put on a show." Staying away from the joints was probably part of Hank's sobriety program too.

Hank got his stage outfit from Tillman. A year or so earlier, Tillman had worked briefly in Houston with Claude King and Buddy Attaway. A car dealer named Elmer Laird sponsored them on radio, bought them matching uniforms, and helped them write a song called "Poison Love."

Then an angry customer stabbed Laird to death on the steps of the dealership. The trio returned to Shreveport, and their song eventually
became Johnnie and Jack's first hit. Tillman had no use for his stage outfit now that he was booking acts, so he sold it to Hank Williams. Tillman
was short and rotund; Hank was tall and almost anorexically thin, so the
outfit was far from a perfect fit. "Mrs. Maxie Goldberg, who had a tailor-
ing place across from KWKH, tailored it to fit Hank, but the britches
never did fit," says Tillman. "I sold it to him for sixty dollars, but he
never did pay me."

The fact that Tillman Franks was booking acts into schoolhouses in
northern Louisiana and eastern Texas was symptomatic of the problem
that plagued the *Hayride* throughout its existence: the Ewings had no
commitment to the music business. Franks remembers Henry Clay
telling him that the family patriarch, John D. Ewing, viewed KWKH as a
sausage factory; in other words, he didn't care what went in — only
about the profits coming out the other end. At the same time, WSM had
the Artist Service Bureau assembling and booking *Opry* package shows.
"The KWKH management wasn't interested in the future," said Horace
Logan, in rare agreement with Tillman Franks. "They were interested in
this fiscal year. They wouldn't put up the money to let me start an Artist
Service Bureau, which would have been self-supporting very quick."

In fact, the Ewings were socking some money into the *Hayride* roster, bringing in big second-tier artists like Zeke Clements, Red Sovine,
Sheb Wooley, and America's first singing cowgirl, Patsy Montana. Later,
the Ewings made a couple of half-hearted stabs at setting up a booking
agency, first with Jim Bulleit in 1951, then with Tillman Franks in 1957.
When Hank was in Shreveport in 1948 and 1949, he couldn't unravel
the paradox that hundreds of thousands, perhaps millions, heard his
voice every Saturday night, but the following Monday he was driving all
day to play a schoolhouse in eastern Texas for a hundred people. Then
he'd have to drive back in time to do his early morning show. All that for
thirty or forty bucks.

It might have been a marginal existence, but those close to Hank
throughout his career say that the early months in Shreveport were the
happiest. It was a new start. Audrey was several hundred blessed miles
from Lilly, which improved her disposition enormously. Hank was min-
gling on a regular basis with some of the hottest minor-league prospects
in country music, and he and Audrey got along particularly well with

Johnnie Wright and Kitty Wells. Johnnie and Hank would go fishing on Sundays and have a fish fry that night. All the while, Hank was making a determined effort to stay sober, which improved Audrey's disposition still more. An article in the *Shreveport Times* in November 1948, though, seemed to hint that, in some respects, Hank was still his old self. The Ewings cross-promoted the *Hayride* through the *Times,* so criticism was bound to be muted, but the article said, "The trouble with Hank is that you can't keep him in one place long enough. An announcer in Alabama dubbed his gang as the Drifting Cowboys because of Hank's inconsistency. The name was so appropriate it just stuck."

Starting January 10, 1949, Horace Logan found a new sponsor for one of KWKH's late-morning drive-time slots, just before Arthur Godfrey came in on the network feed. The Shreveport Syrup Company had a brand, Johnnie Fair Syrup, and Logan, together with KWKH's time salesman, Red Watkins, persuaded the company to invest five thousand dollars in sponsoring Hank Williams. Hank dubbed himself "The Ol' Syrup Sopper" and performed alone with his guitar. The KWKH schedule for mid-January 1949 has him on the air for fifteen minutes at 5:45 a.m., again at 6:30, and again at 8:15 for Johnnie Fair. No one else on KWKH's roster had more than one sponsorship.

Back in November 1948, the Ewings had sprung for two state-of-the-art RCA acetate cutters, primarily to record CBS network shows for playback later. Hank made good use of these machines, cutting shows to be played on air when he was out of town. A few shows survived on acetate, and around 1955, they ended up in the hands of Leonard Chess, boss of the R&B label Chess Records. Chess turned around and sold them to MGM, then in dire need of some new Hank Williams material.

The Johnnie Fair transcriptions rank alongside Hank's most affecting work. With few hits of his own, he filled the show with his favorite songs. He sang both sides of Jimmy Wakely's current hits, "I Wish I Had a Nickel" and "Someday You'll Call My Name." The songs were trite and affectless in Wakely's hands, but Hank filled them with vengeance and unrequited longing. The Sons of the Pioneers' "Cool Water" became an eerie haunting blues. Bill Carlisle's song about returning servicemen, "Rocking Chair Money," *really* rocked. "I love to rock, yeah rock," Hank sang. He needed no more than his guitar, never appeared to strain, yet never let the tension falter. He once told Tillman Franks that he loved the sound of his own voice, something these shows make clear. Parodists have him singing in a high nasal whine, but he actually had a light baritone; without a band behind him, he explored the natural warm contours of his voice. After every song, he would pitch Johnnie Fair Syrup in two delicious flavors, maple and cane. "Remember, friends," he would say in closing, "meals are easy to prepare when you set your table with Johnnie Fair."

During those early days in Shreveport, Hank and Audrey hung out with Curley Williams and his wife a good deal. They'd introduce each other onstage or on the radio as if they were brothers. Curley flitted in and out of Hank's life from the time he poached Boots Harris in 1942 to the time Hank recorded one of his songs, "Half As Much," a decade later. Born in southern Georgia in June 1914, Curley had been christened Doc Williams because family legend held that the seventh child would be a doctor; instead, he was a fiddle player. He changed his name to avoid confusion with Doc Williams on the Wheeling, West Virginia, *Jamboree*. The Peach Pickers' music was far removed from Hank's; it was light, jazzy, sophisticated western dance music. Curley, who talked so slowly it seemed like a put-on, rarely sang and used a rotating cast of singers to share the spotlight with his daughter, Georgia Ann. Curley's Peach Pickers joined the *Opry*'s parent station, WSM, in December 1942 — shortly after Boots Harris quit Hank. Their *Opry* tenure started the following September, and they landed a Columbia Records contract in November. Curley recorded for Columbia for seven years, and even backed Fred Rose (then recording for Columbia as "The Rambling Rogue") on one session. He lit out for the West Coast to play dance halls late in 1945, returning east to join the *Hayride*. Curley and Hank became good friends, and Hank and Audrey lived with Curley and his wife, Louise, when money was tight.

The 1948 recording ban was in effect for the first five months that Hank was in Shreveport, and MGM worked through its backlog, releasing a new Hank Williams single every two months or so. Just before he arrived in Shreveport, MGM issued the recut of "Honky Tonkin'." *Billboard* lauded its "deft ork beat," and its brief appearance in the country charts in July probably helped secure the *Hayride* spot. To avoid confusion with the Sterling record of "Honky Tonkin'," Fred Rose bought all of the Sterling masters on May 17 for two thousand dollars, then sold them to MGM. One thousand dollars was charged back to Hank. "This was a real break," Wesley Rose wrote to Hank, "as you will now get artist royalties on these as they are released on MGM."

Hank arrived in Shreveport promoting "I'm a Long Gone Daddy." It was in the charts the week he joined, peaking at number six during a three-week stay. Unsure how long the ban would last, Fred Rose paired "Pan American" and "I Don't Care (If Tomorrow Never Comes)" from the Sterling sessions in June 1948, then released two abandoned cuts from Hank's first MGM session, "I Saw the Light" and "Six More Miles," in September. After that, there were only three cuts left before MGM was staring at the bottom of the Hank Williams barrel. MGM scheduled two of the remaining cuts, "A Mansion on the Hill" and "I Can't Get You off of My Mind," for December 1948, but by then the ban was falling apart. Some companies were cutting instrumental tracks overseas, then over-dubbing the vocalists (who were members of a different union) at home; others were simply violating the ban. MGM, RCA, and Columbia played closest to the rules because they had union-staffed affiliate companies and couldn't risk a strike. The ban was ended by an agreement reached on October 27, 1948, which became effective December 14. After all the upset, the union gained a very marginal increase in its pension fund contributions, and a couple of other minor concessions.

Hank usually wrote songs without regard to upcoming sessions, so it's hard to know if his barrenness in Shreveport was the result of the strike or the side effect of a better relationship with Audrey. In late 1948, Fred Rose sent his promotion man, Mel Foree, down to Shreveport to see what was going on. Hank and Foree went on the road together to Jacksonville, Texas. Hank had just bought a new fishing rod, and threw a line into every creek along the way. Foree's presence seemed to spur him and they wrote four songs on the road. As soon as they got back, Hank went into the KWKH studio to cut the songs onto acetates. Foree mailed them to Rose. "When I come back Fred had these acetates on his desk," Foree said. "Each song was written to a melody he [Hank] had already written." Rose found just one usable song in the batch, "'Neath a Cold Gray Tomb of Stone." Bill Monroe's brother, Charlie, recorded it in October 1950. Hank also worked with Curley Williams on some goofy novelty songs like "No, Not Now" and "Honey, Do You Love Me, Huh?" which Curley recorded for Columbia. Hank gave Foree some lyric sheets to take back to Rose, but Foree put them in a suitcase that was stolen before he got home.

Audrey became pregnant just days after arriving in Shreveport, but pregnancy made her sick and irritable; clothes made her skin hurt and she found little joy in bearing a child. The spats continued, but Hank seriously tried to curb his drinking, and Lycrecia was there to bring a little stability. Hank took the rituals of procreation, gestation, and birthing very seriously, and was trying to be a strong family head — a role for which Lon and life in general had done little to prepare him.

Until Audrey outgrew her outfits, she continued to insinuate herself onto Hank's shows. Horace Logan recalled:

Audrey was a pure, unmitigated, hard-boiled, blue-eyed bitch. She wanted to be a singer and she was horrible, unbelievably horrible. She not only tried to sing, she *insisted* on it, and she forced herself out onstage when Hank was out there. I'd never let her out, but Hank would say, "Logan, I've got to let her sing, I've got to live with the woman." I said, "OK, Hank, here's what we do. We put two mics out there. Don't let her sing on your mic. I'll bring down the volume on her mic, and keep yours up." We let her sing some just so Hank would get along better with her.

By the fall of 1948, the move to Shreveport still couldn't be called a success. Hank hadn't recorded for a year because of the recording ban, and although the records from the stockpile were doing decent business, they weren't exploding over the charts. Then, during the late months of the year, he began performing "Lovesick Blues." He'd played it in Montgomery. His former band remembered it clearly because they had to hit minor chords on the bridge, which was *very* unusual for a Hank Williams song. When R. D. Norred heard it on the radio, he turned to his wife and said, "There's that blamed old song." It's likeliest that Hank played it on a whim at some schoolhouse dates, got a good response, then played it on the *Hayride.*

"The first time Hank did 'Lovesick Blues' on the *Hayride,* he didn't have his own band," remembered Tillman Franks.

Dobber Johnson was on fiddle, Buddy Attaway was on guitar, Felton Pruett was on steel guitar, and I was on the bass. We were rehearsing up there and Hank was singing it in F. Then

there was this part where it went from F to B-minor or something, and I said, "Hank, that one chord you got in there, I can't
figure it out." He says, "Don't worry 'bout it, hoss, just stomp
your foot and grin."

When the *Shreveport Times* published a feature about the *Hayride*
stars on November 21, 1948, it said, "Hank's rendition of 'Love Sick [*sic*]
Blues' is one of the most requested songs." Presumably, he'd been
singing it for a while by then, and had figured out that he was onto something. He cut a demo at Curley Williams' house with Boots Harris on
steel guitar, Smokey Paul on electric guitar, and Curley on fiddle. Hank
sent it to Fred Rose, but, according to Boots, Rose wrote back and told
Hank that he wanted nothing to do with it.

With the end of the recording ban in sight, Rose began scheduling
sessions. Hank insisted that he record "Lovesick Blues," and he'd written nothing better. On December 22, 1948, eight days after the ban
ended, Rose scheduled a session in Cincinnati. Around the twentieth,
Hank and Audrey, Johnnie and Jack, and Kitty Wells left Shreveport in a
convoy. They dropped off Lycrecia at her grandparents' house in
Alabama, then drove on to Nashville, where they left Johnnie and Jack
and Kitty, all of whom were from the Nashville area. Then Hank,
Audrey, and Johnnie and Jack's mandolin player, Clyde Baum, drove on
to Cincinnati, where Fred Rose was waiting for them at the E. T. Herzog
studio. Rose had fronted one hundred dollars to cover expenses on the
trip. He'd also enclosed a song of his that he wanted on the flip side of
"Lovesick Blues," although it's hard to know what that song was. "Blue
it up as much as you can," Rose wrote when he sent it to Hank, "and
if you can better the melody, go ahead and do it because I wrote it
quick." Rose also mentioned that Nelson King would get behind the
song. King was one of the first country deejays, and his show, *Hillbilly
Jamboree,* went out every night between 8:05 p.m. and midnight over
fifty-thousand-watt clear-channel WCKY.

It's almost impossible to sort out exactly what happened in Cincinnati. Hank didn't do the song that Rose sent him unless that song was
"There'll Be No Teardrops Tonight." Rose's letter, though, seemed to
indicate that *he'd* written the song, and "There'll Be No Teardrops
Tonight" was credited to Hank with a half-share assigned surreptitiously
to Nelson King. King always insisted that he and Hank had written the

song together one night. He said that Hank stepped out onto the street and bought a guitar from a passer-by who was glad to sell it to him because he was Hank Williams. The problem with King's account is that in late 1948 a passer-by was likely to have said "Hank who?" Also, judging from Rose's correspondence, Hank didn't arrive in Cincinnati until the morning of the session. A more plausible account of how King came to own half of the song came from Tillman Franks, who remembers a conversation with Hank in 1952 when he came to the *Opry* with Webb Pierce. All three of them went fishing on Hickory Lake and started talking shop. By then, Tillman had more or less invented payola in the country record business. "I'd given Nelson King half of [Johnnie and Jack's hit] 'Three Ways of Knowing' to get him to play Webb's record of 'Wondering,'" said Tillman, "and Hank said, 'Franks, you and Pierce have done fucked up business giving these deejays songs.' I said, 'Hank, I didn't start it. Nelson told me you'd given him half of "There'll Be No Teardrops Tonight."' Hank said, 'I didn't mean to, I was drunk.'" Probably not drunk, but grateful for the spins, and hopeful of more.

Hank only had two other original songs to record in Cincinnati; one was a hymn he had written, "Lost on the River," and the other was a hymn Audrey had written, "I Heard My Mother Praying for Me." After the session, Hank and Audrey and Clyde Baum drove back to Nashville, where they ate supper with Johnnie Wright's in-laws and dropped off Clyde Baum. Then they headed to Montgomery for Christmas. Shortly after Hank returned to Shreveport, he met Johnny Bond backstage at the *Hayride.* Bond was the writer of several big hits like "I Wonder Where You Are Tonight," "Bartender's Blues," and "Drink Up and Go Home," and he'd met Hank at the Charles Theater in Montgomery earlier that year. Now he found him almost despondent. "I'm tired of tryin' to get on the *Opry*," Hank told Bond. "It's just too rough. I've recorded one song that's in the can now, a thing called 'Lovesick Blues'; if that don't make it, I'm thinkin' seriously of gittin' out of the business."

· ·

A FEELING CALLED THE BLUES

· ·

*I*T wasn't a blues, it wasn't a country song, and it wasn't even from Hank Williams' pen, but "Lovesick Blues" *was* the spark that ignited his career. It was a phenomenon that no amount of punditry, conventional wisdom, or research could have predicted. It was one of those times when the public saw something that the seasoned professionals missed.

Hank, Audrey, and mandolinist Clyde Baum arrived in Cincinnati on Wednesday, December 22, 1948, and met the core of the band that had backed Hank in Nashville before the ban. Zeke Turner was on electric guitar, Jerry Byrd on steel guitar, Louis Innis reinforced Hank's rhythm, Tommy Jackson played fiddle, and WLW announcer Willie Thawl was on bass. That group, with the exception of Thawl, had worked with Red Foley in Nashville until WLW offered them twice the money to relocate. They dubbed themselves the Pleasant Valley Boys and worked the *Mid-Western Hayride* and other local radio and television shows.

The first two songs on the slate were the duets with Audrey, "Lost on the River" and "I Heard My Mother Praying for Me," both featuring Clyde Baum's mandolin. Hank loved string band music, but rarely brought the mandolin into his lineup; he preferred the electric "take off" guitar that Ernest Tubb had popularized. The sound of the electric guitar could cut through a noisy barroom as no mandolin ever could. By the time they'd finished the duets and recorded "There'll Be No Teardrops Tonight," there was less than half an hour left on the session. Hank pulled

"Lovesick Blues" from his guitar case and ran it down for the band. "It was all out of meter," said Jerry Byrd, "and Fred said, 'That's the worst damn thing I ever heard.' He had eyes that went different ways — he couldn't look at you with both eyes — but he was starin' as hard as he could at Hank."

Clyde Baum remembered that Rose and Hank got into an argument. "I'll tell you one damn thing," Hank said to Rose. "You might not like the song, but when it gets so hot that I walk off the stage and throw my hat back on the stage and the hat encores, that's pretty hot. And you said that 'Pan American' was no good, and that sold pretty good." Rose started to walk out to get a cup of coffee, telling Hank to cut it if he liked, but he was having nothing to do with it. As he got to the door, Rose turned to the musicians (whose fees were deducted from Hank's royalties) and told them that he would give them time and a half if they finished before the three hours of studio time were up. "You're mighty damn free with my money!" yelled Hank, just as the musicians were kicking it off.

With so little time left on the session, the band was under the gun to come up with an arrangement. Byrd and Turner had worked on an Ernest Tubb session shortly before the recording ban when they'd cut Jimmie Rodgers' "Waiting for a Train." They remembered a little unison lick they'd worked up for Tubb's record, and, with no time to prepare anything else, replicated it on "Lovesick Blues." "We made two cuts," said Jerry Byrd. "I said to Hank, 'That's the sorriest thing I ever did hear.'" Faced with criticism from all sides, Hank started to become defensive. "Well," he said, "maybe we'll put it on a flip side or something."

Fred Rose had good reason to be upset. After a year away from the recording studio, the best that Hank could come up with was two mediocre hymns that Audrey made almost unlistenable, one undistinguished secular song, and "Lovesick Blues." It wasn't much to show for a new start and a year's creativity, but if Rose had set aside his musicianship he would have heard something strangely compelling in Hank's treatment of "Lovesick Blues." The brisk tempo and unusual structure, together with the yodels and little flashes of falsetto, made it wholly unlike any other country record.

Hank told Fred Rose that "Lovesick Blues" was an arrangement he'd bought from Rex Griffin, but probably had a suspicion that it dated back beyond Griffin's 1939 recording. He almost certainly didn't know that the song had been kicking around a year longer than he had. Irving Mills, later the gray eminence behind Duke Ellington's music, had written the words, and vaudevillian Cliff Friend, who later wrote "When My Dreamboat Comes Home" and "Time Waits for No One," had written the melody. "Lovesick Blues" was first recorded in March 1922 by a popular contralto named Elsie Clark, but it was Emmett Miller's 1925 and 1928 recordings that Hank had probably heard. Miller was a blackface vaudevillian with a trademark trick yodel; his influence stretched from Jimmie Rodgers to Bob Wills and on to Hank Williams. His few recordings offer a little glimpse into the black hole of the prerecording era. It's impossible to know if Hank heard him on record or in person, but the trailing yodel he later used on "I'd Still Want You" is Emmett Miller note for note. On "Lovesick Blues" and many of his other records, Miller used subtle tempo shifts and minor chords that were never part of Hank's music, but the Miller influence is still there.

The missing link between Emmett Miller and Hank Williams was Aulsie "Rex" Griffin. In September 1939, Griffin cut "Lovesick Blues" for Decca Records with just his guitar, modeling his approach on Emmett Miller, but using the arrangement that Hank would use. When Hank spoke to an interviewer from *National Hillbilly News* at the end of 1949, he mentioned Emmett Miller's record and confirmed that he had been performing the song for years, but gave no clue where he'd first heard it. He didn't mention Rex Griffin at all.

Originally from Gadsden, Alabama, Griffin was a problem drinker and a fine songwriter. Inasmuch as he's remembered at all today it's for "The Last Letter," the suicide note of an older man besotted with a younger woman ("I cannot offer you diamonds and a mansion so fine / I cannot offer you clothes that your young body craves . . ."), but he ought to be remembered for "Everybody's Trying to Be My Baby," a song that Carl Perkins later adapted and the Beatles recorded. Hank Williams and Rex Griffin played shows together, and one of Hank's early sidemen, Pee Wee Moultrie, joined Griffin's band, but it's still unclear what transaction, if any, made Hank think that he'd bought "Lovesick Blues." Griffin later told Lum York that he wanted to sue Hank over what he thought was an infringement of *his* arrangement of a public domain song. Unfortunately, Griffin never gave a full account of his dealings with Hank to anyone, and died of tuberculosis in the charity ward of a New Orleans hospital in 1958.

In Rex Griffin's hands, the melody of "Lovesick Blues" became simplified, and Mills' first verse ("I'm in love, I'm in love with a beautiful gal") became the chorus, while the original chorus ("I've got a feeling called the blues . . .") was used as a verse. Structurally, it was, as Fred Rose wasted no time telling Hank, a mess. When Rose submitted writer and publisher information for "Lovesick Blues" to MGM in January 1949, it read "Composer: Rex Griffin; Arrangements by Hank Williams; Publisher: Acuff-Rose," although the composer credit on the original pressings was ominously blank. When the *Shreveport Times* announced the release on January 9, it said, "Hank Williams' recording of 'Love Sick Blues,' the authorship of which is much disputed and under investigation, will be released next week. . . . Capacity crowds at the *Hayride* nearly tear the house down for encores of 'Love Sick Blues.'" Doubts over ownership are probably what delayed the release until February 11, 1949. Rose coupled it with one of the Sterling cuts, "Never Again," clearly not wanting to waste "There'll Be No Teardrops Tonight" on the flip side of what he considered a dog. Still, he took out advertisements in *Billboard* plugging what he thought was *probably* his song, and published sheet music showing Acuff-Rose as the publisher.

In March 1949, Wesley Rose wrote to Hank saying that he had just returned from New York, and "had a hint" on who owned "Lovesick Blues." He asked Hank to send along the records by Griffin and "Emmett something or other" so that they could try to prove it was a public domain song. A few weeks later, Irving Mills got wise and sued. In a settlement arbitrated by Frank Walker, effective November 1, 1949, Mills and Rose shared the publishing on Hank's recording only, each collecting five-eighths of a cent from MGM in recognition of the promotional work that Acuff-Rose had done on the song's behalf. Mills retained 100 percent of all other rights to the song. By that point, Mills was apparently the song's sole owner. A report in *Billboard* stated that, at the depth of the Depression when Friend had forty cents to his name, he sold his interest in the song to Mills for five hundred dollars, although that seems an exorbitant amount for a song that was, to all intents and purposes, dead.

Rose was not only proved wrong in his judgment of "Lovesick Blues," but proved very wrong very quickly. Even Hank seemed a little surprised at the song's overwhelming success. When he played at the Brackin Theatre in Ozark, Alabama, in September 1950, a local reporter asked him about "Lovesick Blues." "I'd been singing it for years," he said in words that don't seem to be entirely his own. "It was an old minstrel tune. I liked it and my audiences liked it, but I never realized it would be such a hit as it is today."

For all its flaws, "Lovesick Blues" was a riveting record, and all those people who nearly tore the house down at the *Hayride* were already waiting to buy it. By the end of MGM's royalty accounting period just seventeen days after release, "Lovesick Blues" had already sold more than forty-eight thousand copies. On March 5, it showed up on the country charts. Rose was dumbfounded to the point of questioning his commercial instincts, and the Cincinnati session crew was dismayed that, as Jerry Byrd said, "anything as sorry as that could be a hit." A hit it was, though. On May 7, 1949, "Lovesick Blues" dislodged George Morgan's "Candy Kisses" from the number one slot.

"Hank was eating at the Bantam Grill," said Tillman Franks. "I'd bought *Billboard* at the newsstand and 'Lovesick Blues' had just had gotten to number one. I walked in and I showed it to him. It shook him up pretty good. He just sat there silent the longest time. He realized what that was." By the time Hank met his band later in the day, he had already turned it into a typically self-deprecating joke. When one of them said, "You got it made now, boy, you're number one in Nashville," Hank said, "I sure am glad it ain't another damn 'Pontchartrain.'" "Lovesick Blues" stayed at number one for sixteen weeks, and lingered on the charts until the following January. Whenever he was introduced onstage, Hank was "that 'Lovesick Blues' boy," and no hit from his own pen would ever eclipse Rex Griffin's adaptation of that Jazz Age novelty song. As he performed the song late in his career on a Sunday park date in Pennsylvania, he said, "I've sung this song 'til honestly I've woke up at night singin' it. But I don't guess I should complain, it's been feedin' me for about five years. We never did miss no meals, but we postponed a few." Hank knew very well what "Lovesick Blues" meant to his career, and even in 1952, after he'd scored another twenty-five hits, it was still his show closer.

Even before "Lovesick Blues" was released, Hank was becoming very popular in and around Shreveport. He reassembled a band at some point between the song's recording and release. On the way back from the session, he stopped in Montgomery for Christmas, and while he was there he asked his mother to call down to the radio station where Lum York was working. Hank told Lum that he was thinking about putting another band together, and Lum rejoined him. Hank then recruited guitarist Clent Holmes and steel guitarist Felton Pruett from the *Louisiana Hayride* band. Holmes had met Hank in Houston when he was working on KLEE with Hank Locklin, and, after falling out with Locklin, went back to Mobile. He was on his way to join his brother in Abilene when he stopped by the *Hayride.* Hank cornered him and asked him to join his group. Holmes played the "sock" rhythm guitar that took the place of brushes on a snare drum and reinforced Hank's guitar. Steel guitarist Felton Pruett, from Sabine County, Louisiana, was only eighteen years old, and joined the *Hayride* staff band after a stint with Harmie Smith on a KWKH morning show.

Lead guitarist Bob McNett was the only northerner Hank ever hired. Originally from rural upstate Pennsylvania, he had arrived in Shreveport with the singing cowgirl Patsy Montana. Just as she was getting ready to dissolve her band, Hank walked up to McNett backstage at the *Hayride,* and, dispensing with formalities, asked, "Can you make the introduction to 'Lovesick Blues'?" McNett said he could, and was hired. The band was rounded out by Tony Francini (or Franchini) on fiddle. Originally a classical violinist somehow stranded in Shreveport, Francini was already fifty years old when he joined Hank. He learned his parts from listening to the records and copying out the fiddle lines. He hated the traveling, and, according to Pruett, hated country music. One day when they were playing a *Hayride* show in Brownsville or Harlingen, Texas, Hank took his band across the border to Matamoros, Mexico. On the way back, Francini surprised everyone by producing an Italian passport. Canadian country singer Hank Snow was with them that day, and his green card had expired. Hank had to sweet-talk the customs agents into letting Snow back into the United States.

Hank placed the band on a salary of between fifty and sixty dollars a week. On top of that, the band members went out into the crowd during the intermission and sold songbooks and photographs on commission. Admission was fifty cents, roughly double the 1941 price. Often, Hank would come home with his pockets stuffed full of cash. "One night we worked a schoolhouse date, and I was wanting to talk to Hank about something," said Felton Pruett, "and I was standing there while he and the principal was countin' out the money, and they counted out eight hundred dollars. We'd played two shows that night, but eight hundred dollars. Man!"

Ever since Hank had ridden in Curley Kinsey's seven-seater '48 Packard sedan, he had coveted it. The note on the Packard was carried by guitarist Billy Byrd, who had come to Shreveport with Kinsey and the Four Deacons. The Deacons split up, and Byrd joined Curley Williams' Peach Pickers, bringing the Packard with him. Then the Peach Pickers disbanded, leaving Byrd toting the note. Hank paid five hundred dollars to Byrd and assumed the loan. He attached a trailer to the car for the instruments, but could never figure out how to reverse the car and trailer into his driveway, so someone from the band always drove home with him. Immediately after buying the Packard, Hank drove overnight to Montgomery so that he could show it off to WSFA owner Howard Pill and advertising boss Bill Hunt as they sat having coffee at the Jefferson Davis Hotel. Both had probably told him that he'd never amount to anything. Then he went on air to say howdy to all his old fans. Hardrock Gunter, who'd last encountered a very drunk Hank Williams at the Labor Day show in 1943, was in town that day. He heard Hank and went to WSFA to reintroduce himself. Hank quickly proposed that Gunter come back to Shreveport with him to lead his band and act as his manager. Gunter thought about it for a while, then refused. "We'll make a lot of money," said Hank. "I know we will, but I couldn't spend it from prison," said Gunter. Hank said, "Whaddya mean?" and Gunter said, "In time, I'd want to kill you. If I booked you on a show with several hundred dollars at stake and you were drunk someplace, I'm liable to kill you."

Hank's career had turned around in the space of weeks. Now he had a band, a touring sedan, and a hit to pay for both. The gamble on the *Hayride* had paid off. The show's blanket coverage of the central United States offered a launching site that no station in Montgomery could have provided. "When Hank sang 'Lovesick Blues' on the *Hayride*," said Tillman Franks, "he would wobble his knees during the yodel. Ray Atkins, one of the guys who played with Johnnie and Jack, would stand underneath the stage on a platform and turn a flip right at that moment, and the roof would just come in. The auditorium had that natural echo, and, boy, it sounded great."

When Hank finally joined the Shreveport local of the American Federation of Musicians on February 4, 1949, he was living in an apartment across the Red River in Bossier City. Then in March 1949 he signed an agreement to purchase a small house for $9,500 on Charles Street in the Modica subdivision in Bossier. It was a typical postwar subdivision; the houses were small, boxy, and plentiful. Hank still had no inkling of the changes that "Lovesick Blues" would bring; he just knew that he had a wife (or, more precisely, an ex-wife, as they'd been divorced) seven months pregnant and a chance at some decent income for a while.

As the heat and humidity kicked in that spring, Audrey became increasingly irritable. What had once been *their* career was now Hank's career. "God, she was difficult to get along with then," said Horace Logan. "I saw her stand there, pregnant with Hank Jr., and Hank had given her a set of crystal ware and she threw it out, every bit of it, piece at a time into the carport and broke it." One day, returning from a tour, Hank went upstairs with Clent Holmes and tripped over a vase. Probably thinking he was drunk, Audrey picked up some tea glasses and hurled them at him, sending him to the hospital. Even in the relationship's most quiescent period, antagonism simmered just below the surface. Audrey, everyone agrees, acted as though she had a permanent chip on her shoulder, and now an uncomfortable and encumbering pregnancy was thwarting her ambitions. Hank, as always, had a deep-seated need for a strong woman to lean on, especially as the pressures mounted. In his autobiography, Hank Snow recounted an episode from the late months of Audrey's pregnancy. Snow had guested on the *Hayride* and Hank had invited him home. They'd driven downtown to pick up some photographs and a ring for Audrey. She refused to leave her room, so Hank took the ring in to her, then suddenly came back out. Audrey had thrown the ring back at him, saying, "If you can't do any better than that, forget it."

Before long, Hank was back to his old ways: drinking as soon as he left the house. In March 1949, just as "Lovesick Blues" was breaking, he booked some show dates in Lake Charles, Louisiana. He was half-drunk before he left town, and bought another jug for the road. He and Lum York were tussling while Felton Pruett was strumming Hank's guitar. "Lum got sick of it," said Pruett, "and Hank made a swipe at me and I ducked down, and his ol' bony knee came upside my nose. We went on down the road, found a doctor, and got my nose to stop bleeding. The doctor said, 'Was your nose crooked like that before?' and I said, 'No sir,' so he grabbed a hold of it and yanked it back into position." They carried on to Lake Charles. "We poured Hank out," said Pruett.

He always wanted to play the fiddle when he was drunk. He got out and played "Sally Goodin" for five minutes. We kept sayin', "That'll do, Hank, that'll do." He'd say, "Naw, naw, them people jus' eatin' it up." They were, too. We sold ninety-seven dollars' worth of pictures that night at ten cents apiece. We give him the money two or three days later when he'd sobered up and he never did know where it come from. They loved him down there. Drunk or sober, it didn't matter. Funny thing was, his time was right on. If you could get him out there and prop him up, he'd do the show.

Soon after the trip ended, the *Hayride* performers and their families went out for an Easter picnic northwest of Shreveport on Caddo Lake. There was an egg hunt and a wiener roast. There was also a big tub of beer, and Hank partook. While the others were hunting for eggs, Hank was quietly getting plastered. The party moved to Johnnie Bailes' house, and while the Baileses and Johnnie and Jack were working up some quartet pieces, Hank continued drinking. Audrey stormed off home with Lycrecia, and when Hank straggled back later she took an ice pick to the tires of the car. Hank retaliated by breaking some of the furniture and threatening to attack Audrey. She called Johnnie Wright and Kitty Wells, and asked them to come over, but by the time they arrived Hank had passed out on the bed.

The Wrights agreed to stay that night. Johnnie climbed into bed with Hank, and Audrey went looking for her tranquilizers. She found just one or two left, then realized that Hank had gobbled almost the entire bottle. Panicking, she called a doctor, who came and shook Hank, raising him up on the bed. "Hank," he kept saying, "how many of those pills did you take?" Finally, Hank's eyes half-opened. "You know too damn much," he said, then slumped back again.

The following week, Hank went out on tour with 125 businessmen from the Shreveport Chamber of Commerce. The city had hired a train to make a goodwill trip through Louisiana and into Texas. It was a three- or four-day junket, and everywhere Hank went people remarked on his scarred appearance. Audrey had wreaked her vengeance at some point. As they sat on the train, Clent Holmes watched Hank. The muscles in his face were tensing and slacking, and he was grinding his teeth. Finally, he slammed his fist on the table, and said, "Dammit, Clent, don't be lookin' at me. I ain't gonna drink nuthin'. All my life, I got people watchin' me.'" He stormed off up the corridor, and returned with a fifth.

It didn't take much to make Hank reach for the bottle. For a few months, he'd kept his drinking in check, but now the old pattern was returning. He was drinking, and now that he was going farther afield, he needed to beat the torpor that overcame him on the long hauls, so he began using a brand of nasal inhalers fortified with Benzedrine. He'd work his way through a sackful at a time, then tear them open and lick the lining. The band was disgusted.

In endless gestures of appeasement toward Audrey, Hank bought jewelry and things for the home as she performed the sacred task of perpetuating his line. All the while, Audrey was more interested in perpetuating her career. She could truly see no reason why Hank's applause should not be hers. After four years as a singer, she still had little grasp of how she really sounded. The pickers said that she sang "between the frets" (meaning she hit neither one note nor the other). If she screwed up onstage, she'd chew out the musicians. The pregnancy allowed Hank a reprieve from the problem of what to do about Audrey, but he knew it would return. He was trying to run a professional show and get out of Shreveport. If his guitar player screwed up, he'd fire him, but come July, Audrey would demand to be reinstated on the show, and there was nothing Hank could do about it.

Seven months pregnant, Audrey insisted on another "Hank and Audrey" session, and so, on March 1, 1949, she, Hank, and Clyde Baum drove to Nashville for a double session. Fred Rose was there with a new lineup of backing musicians led by Zeke Turner's brother, Zeb, on electric guitar. First, they recorded two duets, "Jesus Remembered Me" and the maudlin "Dear Brother." Just over three weeks later, Johnnie and Jack, again with Clyde Baum, cut "Jesus Remembered Me" and were the first to release it; Hank and Audrey's version was held back until August 1950. "Dear Brother" was coupled with "Lost on the River" from the "Lovesick Blues" session, and shipped in MGM's all-hillbilly *After Planting* release in May, when its chances were thought to be the brightest.

Hank rounded out the first session with "Lost Highway" and "May You Never Be Alone." In recent years, "Lost Highway" has been the title of several books, a stage show, a record label, and a television series. It's seen as one of Hank's defining records, if not a defining moment in country music history, which makes it ironic that it barely dented the charts on release and doubly ironic that it's not even one of Hank's songs. The writer was a blind east Texas honky-tonk singer, Leon Payne, otherwise best known for an altogether different song, "I Love You Because." Payne's original version of "Lost Highway" had been released on the Nashville-based Bullet label in October 1948. Hank changed a few lines ("Just a deck of cards and a jug of gin / Sent me down this road of sin . . ." became "Just a deck of cards and a jug of wine / And a woman's lies make a life like mine . . ."), but the song's combination of perdition and misogyny made it sound like pages torn from his diary.

"May You Never Be Alone" trod the same ground. It was one of Hank's first truly great songs. He was starting to experiment with imagery: "Like a bird that's lost its mate in flight . . ." and "Like a piece of driftwood on the sea . . ." It was a song that had been kicking around a while (it dated back to a 1946 songbook, when it was called "I Loved No One but You"), and the fact that he resuscitated it seemed to underscore the fact that he'd run dry. Clyde Baum took the only mandolin solo ever heard on a Hank Williams record.

After a half-hour break, Hank and the band resumed, working until two o'clock the following morning. They took a second stab at "Honky Tonk Blues," but Hank broke meter, so Rose set it aside. This version had a light, jazzy feel. Zeb Turner took a solo that was probably too intricate for Hank's taste, and there was a bass solo that would have been inaudible on most car radios. The song had to be attempted a fourth time in December 1951 before Rose heard something he wanted to release. Hank also took a first stab at Jewell House's maudlin "My Son Calls Another Man Daddy," but it too was put on hold. House, who died in 1971, ran Jewell's Record Shop and Fun House in Texarkana, Arkansas, and doubled as host of the *Hayloft Jamboree.* The only usable cuts from the double session were "You're Gonna Change (Or I'm Gonna Leave)" and "Mind Your Own Business," both clearly born of the dissent on Charles Street. Hank had bought the genesis of "Mind Your Own Business" from a Montgomery musician, Smokey Metcalfe, but refashioned it and adapted it to the melody of "Move It on Over." His delivery was measured, laconic, and dry. Introducing it in October 1949, he told his radio audience that it was a "little prophecy in song," and indeed it would prove to be.

Right after the session, Hank, Audrey, and Clyde Baum got back in the Packard and headed for Shreveport. It was a bright moonlit night. Hank told Baum to drive fast and not to stop suddenly for dogs because the jolt might make Audrey miscarry. Six months after the session, Zeb Turner recorded one of Hank's least distinguished songs, "Never Been So Lonesome," so Hank might have used the session to pitch songs.

All the songs from the double session were held back. The follow-up to "Lovesick Blues" was of paramount importance and none of the songs just recorded seemed to hold the magic. Seventeen days later, on March 19, 1949, Hank took his first-ever flight, to record a split session the following day with Red Sovine. "It's the only way to travel," he later enthused to the *Shreveport Times,* but was considerably more cautious when he telegrammed Rose just before take-off: "Flight 58 will arrive 5:45. I hope." Hank had two songs by other writers on the slate. "I've Just Told Mama Goodbye" was a dirge by two *Hayride* performers, "Sunshine" Slim Sweet and Curley Kinsey. Sweet's version for Mercury Records had just been released, and Hank wanted to get his own record on the market by Mother's Day. It was as close as he would ever come to the Acuff sound. Don Davis' steel guitar mimicked Acuff's tremulous Dobro. It would be tempting to impute some significance to the fact that in three weeks Hank had recorded two songs that had killed off his mother ("Dear Brother" was the other), but dying mothers were to hillbilly music what fair maidens walking through the dingly dell were to English folk song.

The other side of the record was "Wedding Bells," an apparently undistinguished song that had been passed over by many other artists. To that point, the only version to hit the streets was by Knoxville radio veteran Bill Carlisle, who'd recorded it for King Records in 1947. The name in the composer credit was Claude Boone, a guitarist with Knoxville bluegrass star Carl Story. Boone, though, had bought it from a local drunk, James Arthur Pritchett, who performed locally as "Arthur Q. Smith." According to Carlisle, Smith offered to sell him "Wedding Bells," but Carlisle told him that he should hang on to it. For Arthur Q., hanging on to a song was never an option, and Claude Boone appeared with the all-important twenty-five dollars.

Piecing together Smith's story isn't easy. He left the Army in 1943 and joined Johnnie Wright and Kitty Wells as their business agent, all the while writing and selling songs. He's reckoned to have written the wartime classic "Rainbow at Midnight" (later a number one country hit for Ernest Tubb) as well as "If Teardrops Were Pennies" (a hit for Rosemary Clooney in 1951), "I Wouldn't Change You If I Could" (a hit for Ricky Skaggs), and "I Overlooked an Orchid" (first recorded by Carl Smith, and later an *Urban Cowboy*–era hit for Mickey Gilley). Smith would stand outside the studios at WNOX in Knoxville with a little box of songs, priced between ten and twenty-five dollars. Anyone buying them knew they'd better hightail it to the studio before Arthur Q. sold the same song to someone else.

Hank loved the soap-opera bathos of "Wedding Bells," although he knew nothing of its provenance. "He told me it was the prettiest song he'd ever heard," said Boone. Surprisingly, for someone who rarely lapsed into cheap Victorian sentimentality, Hank seemed to be a sucker for such lines as "a blossom from an orange tree in your hair." Tillman Franks' wife, Virginia, logged the songs played on the *Hayride,* and Hank was singing it as early as February 5, 1949, some six weeks before he recorded it. Around the same time, he worked a show date in Houston and called some local musicians, including Claude King, over to his hotel. He sang "Wedding Bells" for them, and asked what they thought of it.

"Wedding Bells" backed with "I've Just Told Mama Goodbye" was released at the beginning of May 1949. Both were shipped a couple of weeks before "Lovesick Blues" began its stint at number one. "Wedding Bells" broke into the charts on May 14, peaked at number two, and spent the rest of the year on the *Billboard* listings. That alone would have stocked Boone's refrigerator for years, but the song had an even bigger payday when the pop-western duo of Margaret Whiting and Jimmy Wakely placed it on the flip side of their chart-topping pop and country hit "Slippin' Around." By 1951, Boone had made more than forty thousand dollars from his twenty-five-dollar investment, but had the misfortune to live in the same city as Arthur Q. Smith, thus becoming Smith's first port of call for a loan.

In February 1950, MGM made out its royalty statements for the preceding six months. "Lovesick Blues" and "Wedding Bells" were just finishing their run on the charts, and during that period "Lovesick Blues" had sold 148,242 copies and "Wedding Bells" had sold 81,813 copies. Hank and Audrey's "Dear Brother" had sold 739 copies. Altogether,

Hank received a check for a shade over ten thousand dollars, his biggest payday to that point.

The success of "Wedding Bells" coming on top of "Lovesick Blues" compounded Hank's sense of isolation on the schoolhouse circuit in Louisiana and eastern Texas. Before he left Montgomery, he'd met a promoter, Oscar Davis, who booked Roy Acuff, Pee Wee King, and other *Opry* acts. In testimony given at a 1975 court case, Davis said that he'd met Hank as far back as 1940. He managed a show called the Garrett Snuff Varieties in Memphis, and several people at WSFA had told him about Hank. "I set up a meeting with him, but he didn't show," said Davis. "Then he finally showed up and worked for me for some time." Davis didn't clarify his point, but presumably he was talking about the war years. Known as "The Baron," he was originally from Rhode Island, where he was born in 1902. He had drifted into country music promotion in 1936 after a spell in vaudeville and motion picture promotion, and was chiefly famous as the man who had promoted the 1947 Carnegie Hall concerts that brought country music to New York. Davis did his own radio ads, shouting "Don't you dare miss it!" and wasn't afraid to spend money promoting a show. In Nashville, the joke was that Oscar would still be promoting a concert two weeks after it had happened. If you were a performer, you might not make any money on an Oscar Davis show, but you'd get a full house.

Hank called Davis before he recorded "Lovesick Blues." "Now I'm ready for you. Now you'll want me," he told him. Hank went on to talk about the reception he was getting with "Lovesick Blues." Remembered Oscar, "Hank said, 'I do this number, Oscar, so help me God, I get fourteen, fifteen encores.' He played me 'Lovesick Blues,' and in my mind I said, 'This is the most horrible goddamn thing I heard in my life.'" Oscar told Hank to let him know when "Lovesick Blues" was on disc and, like everyone else, was stupefied when it ruled the charts. According to Oscar, Hank promised him 25 percent of his booking fees for life if he could get him on the *Opry*.

Hank was getting too big for the *Hayride*. On the morning of April 12, 1949, Felton Pruett got married. That night, he worked two show dates with Hank at the high school in Many, Louisiana. Pruett remembered turnaway crowds for both shows. A few days later, Oscar Davis signed Hank to a personal management contract and placed him on an *Opry* tour with Ernest Tubb, Red Foley, Cowboy Copas, and two comedians,

Minnie Pearl and Rod Brasfield. This was Hank's first tour as a star, and probably the first to take him more than a day from home. They started in Houston, swung out to Amarillo and Oklahoma City, then headed down to Dallas and on to New Orleans. In six days, the unit grossed forty-one thousand dollars, and although Hank didn't see very much of that and would probably have earned more on the schoolhouse circuit, recognition counts for something. He renewed his acquaintance with Tubb and Minnie Pearl, and got to know the others. His idols, he soon found out, had feet of clay, too. Foley, Tubb, and Brasfield could match anyone drink for drink, although Tubb and Foley had mastered the art of staying drunk for weeks while still making shows, something Hank could never do.

In later interviews, Minnie Pearl could never quite get her places and dates right, but she remembered that tour, contrasting the broke and disheveled Hank Williams she'd met with Pee Wee King back in 1943 with the Hank Williams of early 1949. She recalled:

> I'd never been to the *Louisiana Hayride,* so I'd never seen him perform. They had me closing the show because I was what you call some kind of star. We walked in backstage, and I saw an entirely different Hank Williams. He had a wonderful wardrobe and a clean hat, and shiny boots. He looked great. He went on right before me, and that's the last time he ever went on before me. I told the promoter that night, "'Never again will I follow or try to follow Hank Williams." I knew he was gonna be a star.

In the middle of all the uncertainty, Audrey gave birth to Randall Hank on May 26, 1949. She had been in the hospital several times with false labor pains, and when Hank Jr. was born he weighed ten pounds two ounces, and, as Audrey later said, "practically killed the both of us." Hank and Clent Holmes' wife were at the hospital when Audrey finally gave birth. "It was really a bad scene for Hank," said Audrey. "They couldn't get him away from the door of the delivery room, 'cause he heard me inside screaming."

At 3:51 a.m., Hank excitedly telegrammed Fred and Lorene Rose: "10 lb boy borned this morning at 145. Both doeing fine." The big paychecks were still in the distance, so Hank had to borrow one hundred dollars from Murrell Stancil, owner of the Bantam Grill, to pay the hospital bill. "I can't tell you how happy he was," said Audrey. Frail and gauntly thin all his life, Hank was uncontrollably proud that his son was the biggest in the nursery. Technically, Hank Jr. was born out of wedlock because Audrey had been granted a divorce in Montgomery exactly one year to the day before Hank Jr. was born, but he was legitimized on August 9, 1949, when Hank and Audrey had their first divorce annulled.

With Oscar Davis' promises ringing in his ears, Hank disbanded his group in Shreveport just before he left for Texas to join the *Opry* stars on tour. "He said, 'I'm going to Texas tomorrow,'" remembered Bob McNett. "'If I call you, you have a job. If I don't, you don't.'" He didn't, and the band was offered a job by the *Hayride*'s new hire, Hank Snow. After a few weeks, Snow starved out as Hank had initially done, so Hank's band went its separate ways. Lum York hung around Shreveport for a while, then moved to Baton Rouge. Tony Francini went off to work with Paul Howard. Two years later, Bob McNett ran into him in a hotel in Hot Springs, Arkansas. Francini was destitute, trying to make his way back to New York. Clent Holmes stayed on the *Hayride.* McNett went back to Pennsylvania. Hank later offered Felton Pruett a twenty-five-dollar-a-week raise to seventy-five dollars if he went to the *Opry* with him, but Pruett was ready to quit the business:

> I wasn't really interested in moving up to Nashville. Hank couldn't guarantee the work up there that we were getting, and I thought, "I'm playing with the top man in the nation, and I'm making a whoppin' fifty dollars a week, and I'm gone from home all the time." You git in that doggone car and you drive and drive, gas up, git you a Coke, drink it halfway down, pour a packet of peanuts in it and you was gone again. You'd make it to the next gig, see if they had a dressing room — if they didn't, you'd have to dress outside. We'd play, pack, get back in that durn car, and what sleep you got you got in that ol' car. I knew there had to be a better way of making a living.

The Texas and Pacific Railroad offered Pruett nine dollars for a regular eight-hour day, and he was pleased to accept.

At the time Hank left his band, Fred Rose and Oscar Davis were angling to get Hank on the *Opry.* Clent Holmes says that Rose didn't want the band to accompany him because he wasn't sure that Hank would hold up under the stress, and didn't want the band unemployed far from home. After working the *Opry* tour, Hank went back to Shreveport and played out his remaining commitments with Holmes, picking up a band everywhere they played. As he worked his final *Hayride* dates, Hank told Holmes that he was "fadin' out" of Shreveport, and that is more or less what happened.

The last *Hayride* shows were riotous. Mitchell Torok, who would later write Jim Reeves' breakthrough hit "Mexican Joe," drove up from Nacogdoches just to see him. "Hank was on last," remembered Torok.

> People were hollering for him. Horace Logan introduced him. Horace always wore guns and a cowboy hat, and worked out of a little three-sided booth. Hank came on at 10:30. Skinny as a rail. He had some telegrams. Cocked his hat back. He read out a request from a sergeant and his wife at Barksdale Air Force Base. He'd read a request, then toss it away, then another one and toss it away. I thought, "God, man, is this cool or what?" Then he said, "Let her go, boys." He did nothing but "Lovesick Blues" until sign-off.

> Clent Holmes worked those last shows. "He'd get up and sing that 'Lovesick Blues,'" he said, "and them girls would come from the back of that auditorium, run up there at the stage, and fall down on the floor and pass out and scream. And he'd just take his hat off, and say, 'Ain't this a shame, ain't this a shame.'"

Hank was on the KWKH schedule for June 11, but was almost certainly in Nashville that day for his *Grand Ole Opry* debut. Red Sovine, who'd been on Hank's old station, WSFA in Montgomery, was hired to replace him. Hank's family stayed in Shreveport until Lycrecia finished school and it was clear that there would be enough work to support them in Nashville. With a too vivid memory of the first few months in Shreveport, Hank and Audrey had no desire to move only to struggle as they'd struggled early in Shreveport.

"He was the first real star we had," said Horace Logan. "The last show he encored 'Lovesick Blues' seven times — he could have encored it ten times, and I never let anybody encore more than seven times to keep Hank's record. Hank left saying he was coming back, and there was never any indication that he was not coming back — it was just a question of when." It's hard to know if Hank saw it in those terms, but he would indeed return.

In 1950, I took a little nip
Along with Mister Williams on the way to Mississipp
Stacked eight deep in a Packard limousine
We met Oscar Davis in the town of New Orleans
Oscar told Hank that he liked how he looked
Liked how he sang, liked how he shook
He told us all that we'd soon be rich
And we started believing that fat son of a bitch.

"The Ballad of Hank Williams," to the tune of
"The Battle of New Orleans" (attributed to Don Helms)

"TONIGHT, LIVE FROM NASHVILLE, TENNESSEE . . ."

WITH "Lovesick Blues" and "Wedding Bells" delivering a one-two punch, the *Grand Ole Opry* simply could not afford to ignore Hank Williams much longer. Fred Rose and Oscar Davis were keeping up steady pressure on WSM and the *Opry* management team of Harry Stone, Jack Stapp, and Jim Denny. "I came to Jim Denny," said Oscar Davis, "and Jim said, 'No we won't [have him]. We talked about him with Harry Stone and he's got a bad reputation with drinking and missing shows.' So I plead and plead with him, and finally he agrees to square it away." Stone in particular was vehemently opposed to Hank's joining the show.

Among other things, Oscar Davis guaranteed that Hank would be sober for a year, and reports reaching Nashville from the *Opry* acts who worked with Hank spoke of his newfound sobriety. Stone, Stapp, and Denny had been around enough alcoholics to know that promises of sobriety were as good as a trailing incumbent's election promises, but they also knew that they couldn't afford to ignore Hank Williams if they wanted to remain preeminent. Within a year, the *Louisiana Hayride* had come from nowhere to mount a serious challenge, and there were rumors of a rival jamboree starting in Nashville. Hank Williams was a wild card, but the *Opry* figured that he was now a risk that had to be taken.

To sweeten the pot, it's almost certain that Fred Rose offered the composer credit on a song he'd written, "Chattanoogie Shoe Shine Boy," to Stapp and Stone (he hung on to the music publishing, though). Red Foley recorded it on November 7, 1949, and it became the second-best-charting country song of 1950, and then a big pop hit when Bing Crosby and Frank Sinatra recorded it. WSM executive Irving Waugh remembers Stone and Stapp saying that Rose had given them the song as a token of gratitude for putting him on the air during the 1930s when he was broke, but the timing seems to suggest otherwise, and the fact that Stapp wasn't at the station when Rose was broke in Nashville in the 1930s also makes this claim unlikely.

The *Grand Ole Opry* is the most famous radio barn dance, but it wasn't the first. At some point during the evening of January 4, 1923, WBAP in Fort Worth, Texas, programmed ninety minutes of Captain M. J. Bonner, a Confederate war veteran, sawing away at his fiddle to the accompaniment of a Hawaiian band. No other performer in WBAP's short history elicited as many telegrams and letters, so the station came up with the idea of a radio barn dance. Much the same thing happened in Nashville. On November 28, 1925, Uncle Jimmy Thompson, then age seventy-seven, came to newly launched WSM with his niece and his fiddle. He played a program of fiddle tunes, and the station was deluged with calls, letters, and telegrams. WSM's owner, the National Life Insurance Company, was keen to reach rural areas and immediately okayed a radio barn dance. Dubbed the WSM *Barn Dance,* it was juggled around various time slots until 1927, when it became a fixture on Saturday night. Uncle Jimmy was a bit of a problem. He turned up drunk every now and again, and soon found what other performers on the show would find: he could make much more money just about anywhere else on Saturday night.

WSM wasn't a country station. Affiliated with NBC from 1927, its broadcast day was a mosaic of society doings, drama, news, and music. Some of the music came from network feeds, and some was generated locally. One night, WSM manager George D. Hay was segueing from an opera on the network feed to the WSM *Barn Dance,* and told the listeners to get ready for some "grand old op'ra." The name stuck, but just as

WSM was not an all-country station, so the *Opry* was not an all-country show. There were comedians (some of them in blackface), pop and sacred quartets, dancers, and a black harmonica player named DeFord Bailey. It was a fast-paced vaudeville revue, and its success spurred WSM to begin programming country musicians "live" on air during the early morning hours.

By the mid-1940s, there were countless radio jamborees on stations great and small, but the *Opry* slowly achieved preeminence. It began reaching a much wider audience when WSM was boosted to fifty thousand watts in 1932, then edged ahead of the pack after the 8:30–9:00 p.m. portion of the show was picked up by the NBC radio network in October 1939. The networked portion was sponsored by R. J. Reynolds' Prince Albert Tobacco, and by July 1940, the Prince Albert *Opry* (as it was called) was heard coast to coast on more than 150 stations, and attracted around ten million listeners. The entire show, which ran from 7:30 p.m. until midnight, had an almost biblical importance when Hank joined. Up in the hills and down in the hollers, neighbors would gather on Saturday night. Someone would hook the car battery to the radio, light the coal-oil lamps, and tune in WSM at 650 on the AM dial. Up north, exiled southerners would listen and dream of home. During the late 1940s, photographer Ed Clark came to the *Opry* and realized that the real story was the crowd. He photographed farm trucks, many with out-of-state plates, lined up outside the auditorium. Grandma and grandpa climbed from the tailgate, where chickens had been the day before. Clark photographed a mother breastfeeding her child up in the highest seats, and kids hanging over the balcony. The *Grand Ole Opry* was an institution that not only defined country music, but just about defined the South.

Since 1943, the *Opry* had been held in the Ryman Auditorium. The story goes that the Ryman was built in 1891 by a riverboat tycoon, Tom Ryman, who had come onshore to heckle an evangelist, Sam Jones, holding a tent meeting. But the Reverend Jones chose "mother" as his subject that night — the one subject capable of reducing Captain Ryman to tears. Ryman apparently rushed back to his riverboats, tore out the gambling fixtures, dumped them overboard, and declared that a great preacher like the Reverend Jones should not have to preach in a tent, so he built the Ryman Auditorium for him. Seating was still on wooden pews when the Ryman became home to the *Grand Ole Opry*.

By 1949, when Hank moved to Nashville, the *Opry* had become WSM's principal money-spinner, accounting for two-thirds of the station's advertising revenue. The eighty cents scooped up at the door from the three thousand admissions more than covered the hall rental, talent, and backstage staff. Sponsors were lined up five deep, and WSM would soon start a Friday night jamboree (the *Friday Night Frolics*) and pre-*Opry* shows in WSM's auditorium to increase the sponsorship opportunities. The hokiness, in which the *Opry* took a great deal of inverted pride, disguised ruthlessly aggressive management and shrewd organization. Harry Stone had taken over from Judge Hay in 1930, leaving Hay as the *Opry*'s chief announcer. Stone hired an out-of-work concert violinist, Vito Pelletieri, to work on scheduling, and they divided the show into sponsored time slots, giving each time slot its own star. The structure ensured that no artist would become more popular than the show. The *Prince Albert Opry* made its host, Roy Acuff, into a star, but the entire show could be picked up over a huge listening area, and made stars of Bill Monroe (who joined in 1938), Eddy Arnold (1942), and Ernest Tubb (1943). When Acuff tested his commercial clout by quitting the Prince Albert *Opry* in 1946, the *Opry* replaced him with Red Foley, who had already headlined shows on WLS in Chicago and WLW in Cincinnati. In hiring Foley, Harry Stone and Jack Stapp served notice that they would keep the *Opry* preeminent, but wouldn't let any star eclipse the show.

Hank was eased onto the *Opry* through a guest shot on the non-networked portion. It was the back door, but a door nonetheless. His first appearance was on June 11, 1949, during the 9:00–9:30 Warren Paint segment hosted by Ernest Tubb. Hank sang "Lovesick Blues" and made another appearance on the 11:00–11:15 Allen Manufacturing segment when he sang "Mind Your Own Business." His reception that night guaranteed that he would be offered a spot on the Prince Albert section the following week. He probably remained in Nashville all that week. On June 15, he signed a two-year contract extension with MGM Records. MGM paid him a nonrecoupable bonus of one thousand dollars.

The structure of the thirty-minute Prince Albert *Opry* was much tighter than the non-networked portion. The cast held a rehearsal on Saturday morning to do a complete dry run, with commercials, jokes, and music timed out to the second. Every word, every wordless gooberism was scripted. For his debut, Hank worked with the house band that included Grady Martin on fiddle or guitar, Zeb Turner and Jimmy Selph on guitars, Billy Robinson on steel guitar, and bassist Ernie Newton. The Prince Albert host, Red Foley, introduced him.

"Well, sir, tonight's big-name guest is making his first appearance on Prince Albert *Grand Ole Opry*. He's a Montgomery, Alabama, boy, been pickin' and singin' about twelve years, but it's been about the last year he's really come into his own . . . and we're proud to give a rousing Prince Albert welcome to the 'Lovesick Blues' boy, Hank Williams."

Hank walked out to fairly muted applause. Foley stepped back up to the microphone.

"Well, sir, we hope you'll be here for a good long time, buddy."

"Well, Red," said Hank, coming in right on cue, "it looks like I'll be doing just that, and I'll be looking forward to it."

The band kicked off "Lovesick Blues," and the audience buzz rose noticeably during the song; the crowd may not have known the name, but it certainly knew the song. Contrary to myth, there were no encores, but as Hank indicated to Foley, he had now been accepted for membership in the most exclusive club in country music. When they played acetates of the show at the usual postmortem in Jack Stapp's office on Monday morning, everyone was well pleased. Hank's quick acceptance was such that less than a year later, Easter 1950, when Foley was off for what was called some "much-needed rest," Hank emceed the *Opry*'s flagship Prince Albert show.

After the June 18 show, Hank prepared to go back to Shreveport to mop up some engagements and see his family. He was staying at Nashville's toniest hotel, the Hermitage, when Bob McKinnon, a deejay from Hank's part of the world, came to see him. McKinnon offered a drink while Hank got dressed. "No, I quit," said Hank. "I can't handle it. I don't ever expect to take another drop." And he truly, truly meant it. With the world falling into his lap and a healthy boy child less than three weeks old, he must have thought that he would never again feel the need to take to the bottle.

Soon after he became a fixture on the *Opry*, Hank set about assembling another band. He called Bob McNett in Pennsylvania and asked him to rejoin. Then he tried to find Don Helms. When Helms had turned down Hank's *Hayride* offer, he had been making good money playing at a skating rink that he and Boots Harris' brothers leased in Andalusia. Then one night someone was shot and a local preacher got up a petition to close the rink. This left Helms and the Harrises with two thousand pairs of skates and nowhere to play. The Harrises went off to Mississippi, and Helms went up to Richmond, Virginia, where his wife's sister lived. He'd heard that Buddy Wheeler, the steel guitarist on the WRVA's *Old Dominion Barn Dance* was moving to Phoenix, and Helms hoped to take his place, but by the time he got there, Wheeler had decided to stay. Four or five days later, Helms' wife called and told him that Hank Williams was trying to reach him. Helms called Hank. "You remember when I was going to Shreveport, you told me that if I ever got to the *Grand Ole Opry* you'd go with me," said Hank. "Well, have your ass here next Friday night." Helms said, "You got it, chief."

Helms had probably figured out that the steel guitar was the crucial instrument for Hank; its notes were the wordless cry that completed his vocal lines. The steel guitar sustained the mood and took most of the solos. Nearly all of the great country singers had a steel guitarist who functioned as their musical alter ego. Technically, Jerry Byrd might have been a better player than Don Helms, but Byrd's tone was rooted in the cloying sweetness of Hawaiian music and his melodic invention was sometimes a little too intricate for Hank's liking. Helms had precision, economy, and a bluesy tone that echoed his master's voice. He liked to use the high E6 tuning on one neck of his lap steel, and the notes he found there and juggled into Hank's rudimentary chord changes were simple, direct phrases that precisely complemented Hank's songs.

Fiddle player Jerry Rivers was born in Miami in 1928, the son of a dentist, but grew up in Nashville and started playing semiprofessionally in 1945. Three years later, he quit his job as an electronic parts salesman to become a road musician with the Short Brothers, a breakaway unit from Ernest Tubb's Texas Troubadours. When the Shorts decided to stay in Houston, Rivers returned to Nashville to work with Big Jeff Bess. Big Jeff was a Nashville legend, and his band became known as Big Jeff's Finishing School for the number of top-flight musicians that started there. These days, though, Jeff is chiefly famous for marrying Tootsie, founder of Tootsie's Orchid Lounge, the legendary drinking hole near the *Opry*. Rivers says that Hank had phoned from Shreveport offering him a job at the time the Shreveport band was being put together, but he'd turned him down. Hank was offering fifty dollars a week then, and Rivers was making that much closer to home.

Rivers was still kicking himself for not going with Hank when he heard through Jack Boles, who worked with Little Jimmy Dickens, that Hank was looking for a fiddle player. Rivers headed straight for WSM, looked around, and found Hank at the shoe-shine stand. Hank listened in silence while Rivers made his pitch, then beckoned him into unoccupied Studio C. Rivers opened his fiddle case and was surprised when Hank reached in, grabbed the fiddle and started sawing away at "Sally Goodin." When he finished, he said, "Kin you play 'Sally Goodin,' boy?" Rivers lit into it, and Hank picked up his guitar. "He was stompin' that foot, flailin' on the guitar," says Rivers. "We must have played it for five minutes, then he set down his guitar and I set down the fiddle, and he said, 'Well, anyone can play "Sally Goodin" better 'n me is a darn good fiddle player. You're hired.' " Or, as Hank said, "harr'd."

Rivers found out that Hank still needed a bass player, so he called his friend Hillous Butrum. From rural Tennessee, Butrum had also been raised in Nashville, and he had played with Rivers when they were growing up. He graduated from tent shows with the blackface duo Jamup and Honey to the *Opry* staff band, and by 1949 he was working with Benny Martin and Big Jeff Bess on WLAC. Just after Hank arrived in town, Butrum headed out to North Carolina to work on a tent show, but he starved out a few weeks later and came back to Nashville. When Rivers called asking if he'd like a job with Hank, Butrum told him he'd like a job with *anyone.* Butrum met Don Helms and Hank Williams at eleven o'clock one morning at WSM. They ran through a few tunes, and Butrum was hired. He went straightaway to see Big Jeff and bought a western suit for twenty bucks to look the part of a Drifting Cowboy.

Hank rehearsed the band in an empty WSM studio, then brought in Jim Denny, who was in the position to let them play on the *Opry* or insist that Hank use staff musicians. Denny said, "They sound good to me," and Hank settled their wages at fifteen dollars a show, five dollars over union scale. They could make much more selling songbooks and photos during the intermission. Hank was grossing around $250 a show (from which the *Opry* deducted its 15 percent commission), but his asking price soon increased.

The *Grand Ole Opry* formally hired Hank on Monday, July 11, 1949, and Jerry Rivers reckons that the new Drifting Cowboys first worked together the following Thursday. They played the *Opry* the following

Saturday, then rolled out of town in Hank's Packard en route for Cincinnati. "In those few moments on the stage of the *Opry* watching Hank perform, and watching the audience respond," Rivers wrote later, "I regained a humility I had lost somewhere along the line." The really great musicians evince that kind of respect. "God is in the house," a jazz musician once said when Art Tatum stepped up to the piano stool. Hank had his fellow performers watching from the wings. He was good and he knew it. With the applause of the *Opry* crowd still echoing in his ears, Rivers knew he had met the man who would change his life. Helms and McNett were less in awe of Hank because they had known him earlier, but Helms was overwhelmed at finally playing the *Opry* and meeting all the artists he had heard about all those years.

Hank had never been happier. The atmosphere in the Packard was warm and convivial. Very soon, Hank had given everyone in the band a nickname. Don Helms was "Shag" because, as Rivers said, "before the days of much hair, Don had much." Rivers had a G.I. crewcut so Hank called him "Burrhead." "When I'd tip my hat, he'd say, 'Look at that, looks like a stump full of dead grandaddies,'" said Rivers. Hank called Hillous Butrum "Bew" because he was intrigued by his middle name, Buell, and Bob McNett was dubbed "Rapid Robert" because he played a song called "Fingers on Fire." Occasionally, Hank would call McNett "The Mayor of Roaring Branch, Pennsylvania," and tell the audience that he had to roll peanuts off the mountain to get him to come join the band. That was the sort of homespun humor the crowds liked. The Cowboys called Hank "Bones" or "Gimly" (short for "Gimly-Ass") because he was so skinny he had no ass to speak of.

Hank's early *Opry* tours were organized by Oscar Davis in conjunction with the *Opry*'s Artist Service Bureau manager, Jim Denny. Second only to his relationship with Fred Rose, Hank's relationship with Denny was critical to his professional career, and it was a relationship founded on a mixture of mutual respect and antagonism. With a steely sense of purpose, Denny had worked his way up from the mailroom at WSM's parent company, National Life and Accident, and had persuaded National Life to give him the concession stand at the *Opry* as a side venture. He sold souvenirs, food, and fans, and it became the first of many operations that blurred the line between his interest and that of his employer. One of his moonlight ventures was a short-lived recording studio.

Denny found his niche when he was made Artist Service Bureau manager in November 1946. Originally set up in 1934 to arrange charity appearances, the Bureau controlled how the *Opry* name was used on touring packages, and acted as a coordination point for the various tours and shows that *Opry* stars were on. Denny parlayed his position into one of the most powerful jobs in country music. He could have written the book on winning through intimidation. Although only five feet nine inches tall, he was built like a bear, and had been a bouncer at the *Opry* stage door during the 1930s. He had a habit of staring at people and saying nothing, which spooked the naturally garrulous country performers.

Denny divided the country into regions and assigned them to different promoters who would have the right to book *Opry* shows into those regions. He would then work with the artists' managers or directly with the artists to assemble package shows that he offered to these franchisees. For this service and the right to use the *Grand Ole Opry* name on shows, the Artist Service Bureau took 15 percent of the artist's fee; in fact, the fee was required whenever the *Opry* trademark was used, regardless of whether the Service Bureau had booked the show. That explained how it was possible that Hank Williams was one of the *Opry*'s biggest stars but often owed the show more than he was paid.

If Hank didn't have much leverage at the *Opry,* he had newfound clout at MGM. The first session under his new contract was held in Cincinnati on August 30, 1949. Records were the key to everything now. Hank had to answer the question of whether he was a flash in the pan who'd gotten lucky with a pair of someone else's tunes or an artist with staying power. Increasingly, he decided to stand or fall with his own songs, and on the evidence of this session and every other session until his last, he had quite suddenly become the most accomplished writer in country music.

Country song craft was in transition. From the dawn of recorded country music in 1923, country songs had been a mixture of traditional ballads, dance tunes, Victorian parlor songs, hymns, blues, and vaudeville numbers. Deep introspection was rare. If there was sin, there would be retribution by the final verse. Then honky-tonk singers like Ernest Tubb and Floyd Tillman began writing almost embarrassingly intimate songs, clearly rooted in personal experience. In old parlor ballads, such as "After the Ball," a man lives alone his entire life because he thinks he has seen his fiancée with another man. Tillman's "It Makes No Difference Now" was almost diametrically opposite. Its message was quite blunt: "So you're leaving? Screw you!" Tillman went on to write "Slippin' Around," the first cheating song that neither moralized nor condemned. His vocals were just as revolutionary. He sang as if his world were viewed through the bottom of a shot glass. He slurred words, broke meter, and bent notes. Ernest Tubb wrote sour valentines to his wife, and achingly confessional songs that spoke of weakness, drunkenness, and acute loneliness. Hank's songs began taking their cue from Tillman and Tubb, but he didn't sing with their detached irony; instead, he clung to Acuff's emotionalism. On tour with Tubb in 1949, Hank had told him that he had "found me a place right between you and ol' Roy Acuff."

As far back as a 1947 *Montgomery Advertiser* feature, Hank was dubbed "the hillbilly Shakespeare," though in truth there was more Shakespeare in songs the bog Irish sang on the way back from the pub, or in half-forgotten Tin Pan Alley tunes. Hank's achievement lay elsewhere. He cast the highs and lows of everyday life in terms that were simple enough to register quickly over a car radio or jukebox yet profound enough to bear repeated listening. His songs were the true-to-life blues. Any art form at its best has the one-on-oneness of physical intimacy, and that's what Hank brought to country music. Like most truly great songwriters, he flirted with banality, but nearly always managed to sidestep it. After he'd been writing for a few years, he stopped rejuggling clichés and gave his songs the little flashes of detail that led people to think he was writing about them. He never lost his audience with wordiness or poeticism. From Fred Rose, he also learned the importance of starting with a commanding image, as in "Mind Your Own Business."

One of the enduring myths about Hank Williams is that he purchased finished or half-finished songs. It's true that he bought a few songs, stole a few melodies, and occasionally even wrote new songs to titles he had found on MGM release schedules ("I'm So Lonesome I Could Cry" was one), but many, probably most, Hank Williams songs were the pure product of Hank himself. With few exceptions, the songs that bear his name have the imprimatur of sole authorship. The Acuff-Rose archives are full of lyrics that Hank brought in. He wrote screeds, compulsively diarizing his life. He did most of his writing on the road. There wasn't even room to break out a guitar in the sedan, so he'd beat out a rhythm on the dashboard and someone would get something like a cardboard stiffener from a pressed shirt and take the words down. "We were coming back from a Minneapolis–St. Paul show," said promoter A. V. Bamford. "Hank pulled out a notebook, opened the glove compartment, and leaned into its light. He had a little pencil. A small, stubby, stubby pencil. And he had a notebook. He wrote something and we'd be driving, then he'd write some more. I'd say he wrote, altogether, an hour or so. Next day, he went to Fred Rose's home studio." Hank would come back off the road with a billfold full of scraps of paper on which he had verses, half-completed songs, and abandoned ideas. The band would kid him because his billfold was so thick. They'd say, "Hoss, be careful, you'll fall off that billfold, break an arm and we'll have to get us a new lead singer." All the melodies were in Hank's head.

The other enduring myth is that Fred Rose wrote the songs. Starting with the August '49 Cincinnati session, Hank came closer to hitting a home run every time at bat than anyone in popular music before or since, and some say that Fred Rose was more responsible than Hank himself. It's true that you'd be hard-pressed to see promise in the songs that Hank wrote before his Acuff-Rose contract (although Rose must have seen something), and the dramatic improvement led many to the conclusion that Rose was responsible. The fact remains, though, that Rose wrote hundreds, perhaps thousands, of songs, and few sounded anything like Hank Williams' songs. Rose himself emphasized that point when he spoke after Hank's death: "Don't get the idea that I made the guy or wrote his songs for him," said Rose. "He made himself, don't forget that!" Rose deliberately excluded everyone from his writing sessions with Hank, so we'll never know who did what. In all likelihood, Rose brought no more than a commercial gloss and organizational skills to Hank's work. He encouraged him to write bridges rather than simply string verses together, and provided a much-needed element of quality control. He also probably told Hank to dispense with archaic folk forms like "ne'er" and "o'er," and assert the primacy of everyday speech.

Whenever Hank was asked about his songwriting, he was always careful to downplay the element of song craft, something he perhaps thought unbecoming a "folk" musician. "People don't write music," he told *Pathfinder* magazine in 1952, "it's given to you; you sit there and wait and it comes to you. If [a song] takes longer than thirty minutes or an hour, I usually throw it away." It was up to Fred Rose to separate the gold from the dross and work with Hank to transform the best ideas into integrated, complete statements, taut with commercial logic. If Rose contributed substantially, as he did on "A Mansion on the Hill" and later "Kaw-Liga," he took half-credit; if he simply doctored Hank's songs, he didn't take a share. Rose knew that he would get the publisher's half of the royalty, and there is consensus that he was not a greedy man.

The only person to walk in on Hank and Fred Rose working together was Roy Acuff, and his description was studiedly trite. "They worked as a good team of mules," Acuff said on an MGM Records documentary. "They pulled right together. Hank would come up with the ideas, and Fred would say, 'Well, write it down and let me look at it.' Hank'd bring it to Fred, and Fred would sit at the piano and complement Hank and say, 'Well maybe you ought to express this a little differently, let's change it a little bit,' but Fred never changed Hank's thinking." For his part, Hank took Rose's lessons to heart, worked hard at his craft, and received the best positive reinforcement there was — hits.

Hank's ultimate triumph as a songwriter was that he learned to tell an audience of thousands what he couldn't tell someone sitting one-on-one across the room. "If he'd had the personality offstage that he had onstage, he'd have been all right," said Lum York, so often the victim of Hank's interminable, impenetrable silences. Hank felt the need to mask his tenderheartedness with callousness and shitkicker bravado, but in his songs he let his weakness show, increasingly so once he discovered that everyone else was weak too.

By late 1949, Hank had shaken off the dry spell that had afflicted him in Shreveport, and was in the process of becoming the most accomplished songwriter in country music history. The session held between 2:00 and 5:30 p.m. on August 30, 1949, at the Herzog Studio in Cincinnati was the first convincing proof that Hank had arrived.

Fred Rose still insisted that Hank record with the Pleasant Valley Boys — Zeke Turner, Jerry Byrd, and Louis Innis — and was prepared to go to Cincinnati if necessary. Hank drove down from Milwaukee to meet them. He had been working a weeklong stint at the Palace Theater with Ernest Tubb, Cowboy Copas, and Minnie Pearl. His road band stood in the studio and watched, but didn't play. The first song they cut was "I'm So Lonesome I Could Cry." Its poetic form comes from the fact that it was originally intended to be spoken — not sung. Acuff-Rose staff writer Vic McAlpin said that Hank had written it for his first session of recitations slated for January 1950, but changed his mind. "I think ol' Hank needs to record this," he told McAlpin. Hank was concerned that some of the lines might sound artsy and alienate his audience, so he tried them out on friends, fellow performers, and Fred Rose, and let them convince him that he had excelled. Zeke Turner underpinned "I'm So Lonesome I Could Cry" with recurring figures on the bass strings of the electric guitar. A few weeks earlier, Turner had led the backing on the Delmore Brothers' recording of "Blues Stay Away from Me" using very similar licks, so perhaps they were still echoing in his mind. Jerry Byrd played a solo of unusual simplicity, paraphrasing the melody to haunting effect, subtly adjusting tone and volume. Hank sang with unshakable conviction. It was, as he surely knew, a masterpiece.

"I'm So Lonesome I Could Cry" was the song Hank would cite as his personal favorite, but when it was released on November 8, 1949, it was on the flip side of "My Bucket's Got a Hole in It," another song that Fred Rose didn't want to touch. We'll never know what prompted Hank to record it, but it's his only commercial recording with direct antecedents in black music, and the only one on which he takes a guitar solo. Some have advanced the theory that Tee-Tot taught him the song, but Pappy Neal McCormick also took credit. Perhaps Hank was scouring his mind for ancient, up-tempo songs because "Lovesick Blues" had been so successful, and his own songs less so. The song began in the brothels of New Orleans during the early part of the twentieth century, and it's the kissing cousin of a very similar song, "Keep a'Knockin,'" later recorded by Louis Jordan and Little Richard. The riff that underpins both songs probably came from the church. The first recorded version of "My Bucket's Got a Hole in It" (then called "*The* Bucket's Got a Hole in It") was by Tom Gates on Gennett Records in 1927. Then, in 1933, it was copyrighted by Clarence Williams, one of the first African Americans to cross the line between the music and the business. Williams produced and accompanied Bessie Smith, among others, and worked with Frank Walker for years. His own recordings were part jazz, part hokum, and part blues: in other words, much the same mix that Hank heard from Tee-Tot. Clarence Williams' version of "My Bucket's Got a Hole in It" is very different from Hank's. Among the song's eight couplets, one berates a frigid woman:

Wintertime is cold, dear, summertime is too
You know a doggone iceberg'll turn black to blue.

Five years after Clarence Williams copyrighted the song, blues singer Washboard Sam recorded yet another version that he credited to himself. This one was about pimping, prostitution, and dope dealing.

When you walkin' down Thirty-first Street, boy you better look
   round
The vice squad is on the beat and you'll be jailhouse bound

Standing on the corner, everything is so slow,
Can't make no money, tricks ain't walkin' no more

Gonna start a new racket, gonna start it out right
Sell moonshine at day, peddle dope at night.

Like "Frankie and Johnny," "My Bucket's Got a Hole in It" lent itself to endless additions and permutations, and as the Dixieland jazz revival took shape in the mid- to late 1940s, the song rose to the surface once more. New Orleans old-timers George Lewis and Kid Ory recorded it in 1944 and 1946 respectively. When Hank demo'd the song for the band in the studio, he included a couplet that didn't make it to record:

Me and my baby, we got a Ford,
Now we change the gears from the running board

Fred Rose's opposition to the song had a lot to do with the fact that it mentioned beer, and probably had something to do with the fact that Acuff-Rose didn't publish it. If Hank was to record it, though, the couplet about the Ford definitely had to go. If Hank endorsed Ford, then deejays sponsored by GM, Chrysler, and Studebaker wouldn't spin his record. Hank came to the studio with a guitar solo already worked out. He played it twice as he demo'd it for the band, then reprised it on the record, and while it didn't break new ground, it was loose and swinging, and wonderfully bluesy. The entire record had a mellow compelling swing that showed just how deeply Hank was immersed in black music.

Hank Williams made "My Bucket's Got a Hole in It" into a minor standard. Right away, there were cover versions: Murv Shiner recorded it for Decca, Dave Denny for RCA, and T. Texas Tyler for 4-Star. Fat Man Robinson's R&B cover version for Decca was interesting in that it included the verse about the Ford that Hank dropped, suggesting that either Hank and Robinson were copying another record or that Robinson had somehow acquired Hank's demo. Just as Hank's record was descending the charts, Louis Armstrong recorded it, thereby bringing it back to New Orleans. In 1956, Sonny Burgess recorded a rockabilly version for Sun Records, and Ricky Nelson covered it. With Ozzie Nelson behind the control board, the reference to beer disappeared. The refrain now went, "My bucket's got a hole in it, won't work no more." Completely deracinated, the song finally scaled the pop charts. In fifty years, it had made its way across the breadth of American culture from the whorehouses of Storyville to *The Adventures of Ozzie and Harriet*.

The other two songs Hank cut that day in Cincinnati were somber reflections on what his life had quickly become. "A House without Love" resonates with emptiness and unfulfillment. "We slaved to gain a worthless treasure" and "the simple things have gone forever" were a bleak commentary on what success was doing to the Williamses' ever less-than-stable relationship. "I Just Don't Like This Kind of Living" was a tad faster and had flashes of Hank's dark humor ("You ain't never bin known to be wrong, and I ain't never bin right"). Audrey's thoughts can only be guessed at as she heard the substance of their domestic disputes on the radio, particularly as only one side ever got aired. Perhaps, like a game show contestant, she was willing to live with any amount of humiliation for the prize money.

Audrey was, in fact, spending the prize money, and more that Hank had yet to make. She and Hank bought a house at 4916 Franklin Road from Mr. W. Raymond Denney, and the deal closed on September 3, 1949, the Saturday after the session. Hank was back in town for the *Opry* that day. The Williamses paid $21,000 for a three-bedroom, ranch-style house set back from the road on three acres of land. It was more or less in the country, but still conveniently close to the new Acuff-Rose building at 2510 Franklin that Hank had also partly paid for. Audrey had big plans for the house, which, like Graceland, became a monument to what good money and bad taste can accomplish. A new bedroom, den, breezeway, and two-car garage were added almost immediately, and Audrey went out and bought the most expensive furnishings she could find. The prevailing motif was Oriental: shiny black lacquer and dragons — lots of dragons. To Audrey, kitsch was a step up. The furnishings looked and felt so unusual and cost so much that Hank told his band he was afraid to sit on them. He preferred to lounge on the floor instead. The simple things really had gone forever.

Just days after the house purchase, Hank joined an *Opry* troupe led by Ernest Tubb on a tour of the Northwest, and on September 13, he made his first appearance in Canada when the troupe played in Vancouver, British Columbia. Later that month, Hank was back on the West Coast with the same troupe, this time in California. On one of those trips, he outfitted himself at Nudie's Rodeo Tailors in Los Angeles. When he had arrived in Nashville, his principal stage outfit was still the poorly fitting western suit that Tillman Franks had sold him, but now he had something more flamboyant in mind. Nudka Cohn, better known as Nudie Cohen, was born in Russia in 1902, and came to the United States in 1913. He was a boxer and a bit-part actor before finding his calling in western apparel. There were several other western outfitters in Los Angeles, but Nudie became the most lurid of them all. Tex Williams, chiefly remembered these days for "Smoke! Smoke! Smoke! (That Cigarette)," was Nudie's first country music client, and Hank was one of his first Nashville clients. Hank and Nudie became close friends, and Nudie later told friends that Hank would be sent to his house to dry out. In 1957, Nudie tailored Elvis' gold lamé outfit and designed Webb Pierce's silver-dollar-encrusted Pontiac. Staying abreast of the times, he tailored the infamous rhinestones-inlaid-as-marijuana suit for Gram Parsons of the Flying Burrito Brothers.

Audrey bought outfits for herself, clearly signaling that Hank *and* Audrey were back in business. She hired a nurse / housekeeper, Audrey Ragland, in September 1949, telling her that she would be on the road with Hank. Evidence of what a Hank and Audrey radio show was like comes from Hank's first syndicated radio series, the *Health and Happiness* show, in October 1949. It was an ironic title, as Hank never had much of either. Eight fifteen-minute shows were recorded on two successive Sundays that October. They were the brainchild of Mack Hedrick, advertising manager at WSM. Hedrick pitched Louisiana state senator Dudley J. LeBlanc, inventor of a foul-tasting patent medicine called Hadacol, on the notion of sponsoring Hank. LeBlanc had seen Hank in Lafayette, and was reaping the benefit of having Bill Nettles' "Hadacol Boogie" in the charts, so he leaped at the idea.

LeBlanc had little direct involvement with the *Health and Happiness* shows except to underwrite them, and for once in his life, he was outscammed. Hedrick made sure that Hank never mentioned Hadacol; in that way, he had a set of generic shows he could resell to other sponsors. His philosophy was that you had some pickin' and singin' and then, as he put it, a commercial right after the "Come to Jesus" number. The transcriptions were duplicated onto banded sixteen-inch discs that played at 33 rpm. After almost every song, Hank made an all-purpose pitch, like "Here's someone with some news that'll make you mighty glad you tuned in." At that point, the engineers on the local stations would stop the disc, a local announcer would read the pitch, then the discs would be restarted.

Hank was the new boy in town with something to prove. The frightening conviction of his singing was strangely offset by his molassified between-song patter. Audrey was on the first four shows, joining Hank on the closing hymn and taking her own solo spots. She followed "I'm a Long Gone Daddy" with "I'm Telling You," a song that appears to be a self-composed riposte, but, as always, she shot herself in the foot by singing off-key and breaking meter. It was probably at LeBlanc's request that she was dropped when the last four shows were recorded. Hank was, if anything, in even better form on the four shows without her. He out-Acuffed Acuff on "The Prodigal Son," then invested "Mind Your Own Business" with even more damning sarcasm than the record, throwing in a fresh couplet after the break: "If I get my head beat black and blue / Brother that's my wife and my stove wood too." The shows also included Hank's only surviving recording of "Tramp on the Street," the song that had earned him his break.

The *Health and Happiness* shows were the first recorded evidence of Hank's new Drifting Cowboys. In the three months they'd worked together they had clearly been schooled in what he wanted. Hank hated pickers who were too busy. When he was singing, he didn't want the impact undermined by cute fills, and he wanted the solos as simple and direct as his vocals. He would spin around and glare at any musician who got too close to jazz. "I know a lot of good guitar players," he once said, "who've educated themselves right out of a job." Later, when Hank Garland came to town and proved himself the most technically adroit picker in country music, Hank was dismissive. "Aw," he said, "he's still searchin' for it. I've found it." Hillous Butrum occasionally got too fancy for Hank. "Mostly I'd play two-four time," said Hillous. "Hank come to me one night and he said, 'Hillous, you play as good a bass as anyone I ever heard. At times. Then all of a sudden you'll take off on that thing and I don't know where you're going.' When we'd do 'Move It on Over' I'd switch to four-four on the break and Hank never understood what I was doing. You wasn't supposed to hear a bass note except ever' other one."

Plain and simple — that was Hank's philosophy. It had taken him to the *Grand Ole Opry*, and he wasn't about to try for sophistication now. He'd fought the Willis Brothers on his pronunciation during his first session, and he wasn't about to change now. If he sang "perhaps," it would be "pre-haps." "Picture" was "pitcher." When he sang "Armageddon" in "The Battle of Armageddon," he pronounced it "Am-be-gotten." If he contributed to the social transmission of illiteracy, he didn't care, and Fred Rose learned not to care, either. "Vanilla, boys," Hank had told his band back in the mid-'40s, and that was still his credo.

Right after the *Health and Happiness* shows, Hank and his band hit the road on a tour that took them up into Ontario, Canada, in late October 1949. On November 11, he returned in triumph to Montgomery for a show with Bill Monroe, and then on November 13, he flew to Europe as part of the Prince Albert *Opry* revue. The *Opry* troupe was to play U.S. Air Force bases on a two-week tour sponsored by R. J. Reynolds. In Air Force–speak, it was deemed a "non revenue mission," and according to the protocol of the day, the Russians were informed. Hillbilly music was immensely popular among servicemen overseas. *Hillbilly Gasthaus* was the highest-rated show on Armed Forces Radio (AFRS), and the *Opry* came over at the request of the enlisted men. Hank was issued with a sheet of instructions in Russian in case he mistakenly wandered into the Russian zone. He looked at the Cyrillic script and said, "Aw, they ain't gonna win the next war. They cain't even spell."

Red Foley led the troupe, backed by Roy Acuff, Jimmy Dickens, Minnie Pearl, and Rod Brasfield. Another *Opry* act, Radio Dot and Smokey, were cleared by the Department of the Air Force, but don't appear in any photos from the tour. Harry Stone, Jim Denny, and announcer Grant Turner joined the show, and Acuff took his daughter, Thelma, who did a tap-dance routine. They were all allowed to bring their spouses because they would be away for Thanksgiving. Acuff and Foley brought their own bands, but Hank was to work with Foley's band.

The troupe left Nashville on what had been General Eisenhower's private plane. They went to Washington, flew on to Newfoundland to refuel, then hunkered down for the night flight across the Atlantic. Hank snuggled next to Audrey and put his coat over them. The next morning, they arrived in Paris, France, to refuel, then went on to Wiesbaden, Germany. A German oompah band played "Dixie" to welcome them. They visited all the base hospitals, playing a few numbers for the patients, and put on shows in Berlin, Frankfurt, Munich, and Vienna. The Berlin and Frankfurt shows were recorded for transmission back home on the Prince Albert portion of the *Opry*. Hank and Red Foley had two of the most popular records of the day, "Lovesick Blues" and "Chattanoogie Shoe Shine Boy," and they were called back for encore after encore at every hall they played.

Hank was straight as an arrow and so careful to avoid alcohol that he sniffed his glass at mealtimes to make sure that it contained water — not wine — but that didn't stop him from yelling, "Hey, Herman, bring me the ketchup" any time he was faced with a dish he didn't recognize. Aside from brief forays into Canada and Mexico, this was Hank's first and last experience of foreign lands.

On the way back across the Atlantic, the plane hit an air pocket, and dropped precipitously. The performers clung to their seats, and some flew up to the roof of the plane. Nearly everyone had bought cuckoo clocks in the Black Forest, and the clocks fell from the overhead racks, going "cuckoo, cuckoo" as they hit the floor. The plane touched down to refuel in Bermuda and the troupe boarded a bus to a hotel. The roads were narrow and windy, and, because it was a British colony, oncoming vehicles would suddenly appear on what Hank and the others regarded as the wrong side of the road. On arrival back in Nashville, Hank bent over gingerly and kissed the tarmac.

Oscar Davis had dropped all his other clients to handle Hank exclusively, and now Hank was beginning to understand what real pressure was like. He came home to a full date book and a punishing itinerary. In Montgomery or Shreveport, he'd played within driving distance of home, and if he missed a show date or two, he would do a "make-good" later if he felt like it. Now he was working with structured itineraries that took him away from home all week. Too often, he would arrive home on Friday night and leave again on Saturday night or Sunday morning.

Hank arrived back from Europe to see "My Bucket's Got a Hole in It" climbing the charts. It had reached number two by the end of December. Among the records that kept it from the top spot were the Delmore

Brothers' "Blues Stay Away from Me" and Red Foley's "Chattanoogie Shoe Shine Boy."

After successful tours out west, through the Southwest, and up the Ohio valley into Canada, Oscar Davis had decided to promote Hank on the eastern seaboard during the period leading up to Christmas. On December 8, Hank was to star for a week at the Hippodrome Theater in Baltimore, and was scheduled to follow it with a Potomac River Cruise show and a headline appearance at the Roosevelt Hotel in Washington. He started drinking in Dayton, Ohio, after losing some money in a craps game, and by the time he got to Baltimore he was drunk. It was the first time the new Drifting Cowboys had seen Hank on a bender. They checked into the hotel behind the Hippodrome with everyone on edge because Hank, although drunk, still thought himself able to perform. The band was watching him closely, but when he needed a drink Hank was more resourceful than anyone gave him credit for. He bribed a bell-hop to bring up whiskey miniatures hidden inside a pitcher of ice and arranged for one of the girls in the square dance troupe to hide minatures in her skirts for him.

The rule of thumb that people came to use with Hank was that it would take about three days for him to get good and drunk and then three days to get over it. At first, he would make the shows, swaying precariously but always somehow managing to remain upright. "Here I am in Baltimore," he told the audience. "I ain't never been in Baltimore. If I come back, it'll be twice I been here." He said that every show, four shows a day. Oscar Davis eventually took him off the bill and brought in old-time yodeler Elton Britt as the headliner. Audrey was flown up from Nashville for her expertise, and Helms and McNett went to pick her up at the airport. Later, as she sat disconsolately in the hotel lobby, Audrey turned to McNett and said, "I'm so upset and discouraged, I think I've lost the love I had for Hank." But, since she was there, she decided she would do some shows with him after he'd straightened out.

By December 16, Hank was back on track. He and Cowboy Copas set an attendance record at the Victory Room in the Hotel Roosevelt in Washington. Nine hundred were admitted and five hundred turned away, but Audrey's insistence upon performing led to another rift. Finally, Hank refused to let her sing, so she stormed back home. Hank came into the room that McNett and Butrum were sharing, put his foot up on the window ledge and said, "Boys, it's heck to have a wife in the business that wants to sing, but it's worse'n that to have one that wants to sing and cain't."

A few days later, Hank was home for Christmas. It was his first in Nashville, and his first with Hank Jr. When Hank went downtown to buy a copy of *Billboard,* he saw in the year-end tallies that he had shot from nowhere to become the second-best-selling country singer of the year. Only Eddy Arnold was ahead of him. Hank had placed eight songs in the country charts in 1949, but Arnold had placed thirteen and was still the man to beat.

It wasn't until December that Hank and Audrey finally sold their house in Shreveport, getting back the $9,500 they paid for it and thus drawing a line under that phase of Hank's career.

What was Hank thinking as he wriggled uncomfortably in his Oriental furniture that Christmas? Did he wonder what would have happened without "Lovesick Blues," that "nothing song" that Fred Rose had disparaged? Without its catalytic effect, Rose might have lost interest in the undistinguished songs that Hank was sending up from Louisiana. MGM might have dropped him when his contract was up that year. Hank might even have become so discouraged that he would have gotten out of the business, as he had told Johnny Bond he would do just one year earlier. What if Fred Rose had stuck to his guns and refused to let Hank record "Lovesick Blues"? Instead of soaring in 1949, Hank Williams' recording career might simply have petered out.

More tears are shed over answered
prayers than unanswered prayers.

St. Teresa of Avila

● ●

Chapter 9

"HURRIED SOUTHERN TRIPS . . ."

● ● ● ● ● ● ● ● ● ● ● ● ● ● ● ● ● ● ●

*T*HE new decade dawned with Hank preparing for two recording sessions, scheduled for Monday, January 9, and Tuesday, January 10. Frank Walker came to Nashville to work with Fred Rose on the ninth, the only time Hank worked with anyone other than Rose behind the glass. Hank was using his road band for the first time since the disastrous "Fly Trouble" session in August 1947, and was recording all his own songs for the first time since April 1947. That alone said much for his growing confidence. Just one thing was required from these sessions: another blockbuster hit. "Mind Your Own Business," "You're Gonna Change," and "My Bucket's Got a Hole in It" had all sold well enough, but none of them had come close to eclipsing "Lovesick Blues" or "Wedding Bells." The midsize hits were fine, they kept the pot boiling, but Hank needed a song that would rule the airwaves for months. Like a successful sports franchise, he needed to deliver the big prize every now and again to keep the attendance up.

Hank and Fred Rose decided to take their best shot with "Long Gone Lonesome Blues," a song that had — in almost every sense — been sired by "Lovesick Blues." Rose, of course, couldn't risk another lawsuit from Mills Music, so the melody wasn't litigiously close, but Hank had clearly crafted a deliberate follow-up. It had "blues" in the title and windows for the yodels and flashes of falsetto that had proved so effective on "Lovesick Blues." The tempo was almost identical, and the lyrics were just as inconsequential. The song's architecture and arrangement were kissing cousins, right down to the unison yodeling figure from the lead guitar and the steel guitar at the intro. Hank liked to tell interviewers that he just closed off his mind and let God write his songs, but "Long Gone Lonesome Blues" was squeezed out line by line from a title that Hank had been nursing for a while. The pieces came together on a fishing trip with songwriter Vic McAlpin. They left early to drive out to the Tennessee River where it broadens into Kentucky Lake, but Hank had been unable to sleep on the trip, and was noodling around with the title all the way. As McAlpin told journalist Roger Williams, he and Hank were already out on the lake when McAlpin became frustrated with Hank's preoccupation. "You come here to fish or watch the fish swim by?" he said, and suddenly Hank had the key that unlocked the song for him. "Hey!" he said. "That's the first line!" Then it fell into place. All the old blues clichés he had ever heard about going to the river, jumping in three times and only coming up twice came flooding back. McAlpin contributed a few lines, but Hank later bought him out.

In case "Long Gone Lonesome Blues" didn't make it, Hank had written himself an insurance policy, "Why Don't You Love Me (Like You Used to Do)." It showed that he could still afford to be lighthearted about the persistent troubles with Audrey. "I'm the same old trouble you've always been through," he told her, and that would become truer than either of them dared believe. "Why Should We Try Anymore?" was a wintry variation on the same theme. Based loosely on "I'm Not Coming Home Any More," its four verses limned a bleak picture of a marriage gone sour.

The session was rounded out with another stab at "My Son Calls Another Man Daddy," in which a jailed man loses his son. There were hundreds of similar songs dating back to the dawn of country music. "I'll ne'er know his name or his face," sang Hank, once again resorting to an archaic form as he often would when trying something with a traditional flavor.

After admitting that he was wrong to steer Hank uptown with novelties like "Fly Trouble" and "Rootie Tootie," Rose had realized that Hank was plugged in to a segment of the market that neither craved nor aspired to sophistication. He had come to share Hank's "vanilla" philosophy. Bob McNett remembered that during rehearsals he hit some licks and then looked up at the control room. "Is that too country?" he asked. "You can never get too country," Rose told him. Not on a Hank Williams session.

As they began working together, Rose helped the band define what is still known as the Hank Williams sound. He gave Don Helms the golden rule for accompanying Hank. "Fred said it was useless for me and Hank to be in the same register," said Helms. "He said, 'When Hank is singing something low why don't you play high, and if he's singing high, you play something low,' so the steel was always in a different register." Once, when Helms wasn't playing high enough for Rose's liking, he came out of the control and moved the steel guitar several inches, gesturing with his hands up past the nut to show how much higher he wanted it.

Rose also told Jerry Rivers to play in the traditional double-stop fiddle style in which the melody and the harmony are carried on two strings. Hank always called it the "garden seed" fiddle. There would be no more jazzy single-string western swing fiddle on Hank Williams records.

When Zeb and Zeke Turner had worked Hank's sessions, they had taken solos, but from this point the electric guitar was limited to keeping time with a steady tic-toc on the bass strings. Hank played the acoustic rhythm guitar, although Rose tried to persuade him to drop it and concentrate on singing. Hank probably knew that the guitar helped him keep time, so he hung on to it. Rose wouldn't put a microphone on Hank's guitar, though; instead, he brought along rhythm guitarist Jack Shook to reinforce the rhythm. Shook could play percussive barre chords, which took the place of brushes on the snare drum.

Rose had very precise ideas about the pace of every song. If it was going too fast or dragging, he would come down from the control room, sit at the piano, and pound it out at the tempo he thought best suited the piece. At first, the band was surprised at the way Hank and Fred Rose seemed to be at each other's throats, but the bickering was, they found out, just the way they worked. Hank took note of Rose's suggestions most of the time, and, for his part, Rose gave Hank a lot of latitude. "Hank needed Fred to say, 'That's a good un,'" said Don Helms, "but if Fred said, 'Naw, naw, it needs . . . such and such,' Hank would say, 'I don't see it,' and Fred would say, 'It does. Let me show you why,' and then Hank would usually say, 'Awright, okay.'"

Rose's true feelings about the second day's sessions are hard to guess. After lunch on January 10, Hank cut his first set of recitations and talking blues as Luke the Drifter. The recitation was a little homily, usually with a strong moral undertow, narrated to musical accompaniment. It was a tradition embedded deep in country music, and one that was still kicking as it went down. T. Texas Tyler's narration "Deck of Cards" had been one of the best-selling records of 1948. Hank would have heard Cowboy Slim Rinehart broadcast complete programs of narrations over the powerful unregulated Mexican border stations, and he performed them often on his own radio shows. Bernice Turner, who worked with Hank toward the end of the war, remembered that he'd include a narration on almost every radio show, then he'd walk the short distance from the radio station to Lilly's boardinghouse and the boarders would be gathered around the radio, some of them still crying. "Some," added Turner, "would be drinking and crying, but they'd still be crying." The "talking blues" was part of vaudeville's legacy to country music. Robert Lunn, "the Talking Blues Boy," was still a fixture on the *Opry* when Hank joined. Hank's talking blues were more sardonic than his narrations, and more personal. Over time, Luke the Drifter became Hank's alter ego, a wise and thoughtful soul, dispensing advice that the willful Hank Williams ignored.

Don Helms says that Hank pestered Rose long and hard to cut narrations and talking blues, so they were clearly something close to his heart; in fact, Helms believes that Hank was more deeply committed to the recitations than to his regular songs. Rose's objection was rooted in commercial logic: jukebox operators had huge standing orders for Hank Williams records and, if the recitations were issued under Hank's name, the operators would complain. Virtually all of the operators serviced bars, and the last thing they needed was for someone to punch up a Hank Williams record and get a sermon. Credibility in the marketplace is hard to win and easy to lose, and Hank didn't have enough of a track record to take too many risks.

Rose decided to solve the problem by issuing the narrations under a pseudonym, but from the beginning there was no attempt to disguise the identity of Luke the Drifter. An entry in *Billboard*'s "Folk Talent and Tunes" section made it obvious to the trade. In interviews, Hank never denied that he was Luke the Drifter, and told interviewers that the records were primarily designed for what he called the "take home" trade. Introducing a Luke the Drifter talking blues on one of his radio shows, he would say, "And here's a little number by one of my closest relatives, Luke the Drifter," or he'd say, "Here's one by my half brother."

Rose's concerns were validated by the numbers. The jukebox operators were a hugely powerful force in the industry. In 1950, there were
four hundred thousand jukeboxes on location serviced by fifty-five hundred jukebox operators. Even though the number of operators was
dwarfed by the number of home phonograph owners (then estimated at
between sixteen and seventeen million), the operators bought an average
of 150 records a week, whereas the average record buyer bought fewer
than 10 a year. Wesley Rose estimated that if one of Hank's records sold
250,000 copies, the jukebox operators accounted for 150,000 of those.
The ops, as they were known, were accommodated to the point that
Hank, like most other songwriters, kept his song titles to fewer than five
words so that they would fit onto the jukebox cards, and made sure his
records timed out at under three minutes and twelve seconds, the time
at which a record would automatically eject from a jukebox turntable.

Every year, the operators' organization, the Music Operators of
America, held a convention that was celebrated with special issues of
Billboard and *Cashbox*. Everyone in the industry took out advertisements to greet the ops, thanking them for buying their product. The
record labels laid on entertainment; in fact, Hank was sent to the March
1950 convention in Chicago. Rose didn't want to alienate the ops, but if
he refused to let Hank cut narrations, he would alienate his prize asset.
"Luke the Drifter" was the best compromise he could hope for.

Hank was particularly keen to cut two narrations, "The Funeral"
and "Beyond the Sunset." Just a few weeks before the Luke the Drifter
session, Elton Britt had cut "Beyond the Sunset," and T. Texas Tyler had
just cut both "Beyond the Sunset" and "The Funeral" (which he titled
"Colored Child's Funeral"). Then, a few days after the Luke the Drifter
session, East Coast deejay Buddy Starcher cut both. From this distance,
it's hard to account for this little flurry of activity. As poems, both songs
had been kicking around in one form or another for decades.

By today's standards, "The Funeral" was an uncomfortably patronizing account of a black child's funeral service. Originally a poem by
Will Carleton, it was first published in 1909 and designed for recitation
in caricatured black patois. Unlike Starcher and Tyler, though, Hank
delivered "The Funeral" in his regular voice, and was clearly extending
every ounce of compassion within him. His sincerity, though, was undermined by the words: "I pictured him while livin', curly hair, protrudin'
lips," he said, "I'd seen perhaps a thousand in my hurried southern trips."

Then the preacher arises "with a manner sorta awkward and countenance grotest [*sic*]. The simplicity and shrewdness in his Ethiopian face, showed the ignorance and wisdom of a crushed, undying race."

In the background, an organ (manned by Fred Rose or Owen Bradley) played the reedy chords of Rose's "A House Built on a Rock" with accenting from Don Helms' steel guitar. When Rose submitted artist and publisher information to MGM, he noted that there was to be no songwriter or publisher credit on the record label, but that he was to receive half the composer royalty for "A House Built on a Rock." Later, the Williams estate claimed "The Funeral" as one of Hank's compositions, and in a 1993 edition of his lyrics it appeared in a new, politically correct version (the "protruding lips," for instance, were now "smiling lips").

Bob McNett didn't play on "The Funeral" but he was there. He remembers that when Hank and Helms finished, they both had tears running down their cheeks. "I've formed an opinion of Hank over late years that I had never thought of when I was working with him," he said. "Hank had a deep personal feeling for his fellow man. This didn't show on the outside. You had to get to know him, and then he'd give himself away every now and again about his deep concern for people who were less fortunate. 'The Funeral' touched him. When he did it, he lost himself in it." On his narrations, Hank rarely gave in to mawkishness. He was simply, almost painfully, direct, letting tenderness edge out the knuckleheadedness with which he often greeted the world.

"Beyond the Sunset" was pure Victoriana caught out of time. The words came from "Should You Go First," a poem by Albert "Rosey" Rowswell, the voice of the Pittsburgh Pirates for more than twenty years. The poem first appeared in a book called *Rosey Reflections,* but Hank probably found it in a popular anthology called *Poems That Touch the Heart.* Tillman Franks claimed to have given Hank his copy of the book, but it was on almost as many shelves as the Bible in the late 1940s, and often tucked next to it. Even Elvis Presley, en route to Germany, said at a news conference that he had been reading *Poems That Touch the Heart* on the train and had been especially moved by "Should You Go First." The 1936 hymn "Beyond the Sunset" was first married to "Should You Go First" by Chickie Williams, a performer on WWVA in Wheeling, West Virginia. Elton Britt's version briefly cracked the charts in February 1950, three weeks before Hank's was released, but it didn't linger.

Two other narrations were cut that day. The first was "Too Many Parties and Too Many Pals," a morality play in one mercifully short act by Tin Pan Alley veteran Billy Rose (no relation to Fred) and two other New Yorkers. It was first published in 1925 when Rose, the writer of songs like "I Found a Million Dollar Baby (in a Five and Ten Cent Store)," "Clap Hands, Here Comes Charley," and "I Got a Code id By Dose," was new to the business. One of the first singing cowboys, Carl T. Sprague, recorded it as "The Wayward Daughter," and by the time Hank turned to it, it was a minor hillbilly standard. One of the versions immediately preceding Hank's was by Bill Haley, then leading a group called the Saddlemen. Hank's version was released in June 1950 with his own gently mocking "Everything's Okay," a "What, Me Worry?" talking blues that he'd first sent to Fred Rose back in August 1947.

"Long Gone Lonesome Blues" did exactly what Hank calculated it would, and Rose hoped it would. On March 25, 1950, it shot straight into the charts at number two, staying there until April 29, when it dislodged "Chattanoogie Shoe Shine Boy" from the number one spot. It was the knockout punch Hank needed, and it ended up spending twenty-one weeks on the charts, eight of them at the top. None of the Luke the Drifter releases sold sufficiently well to chart. By August 1950, "Too Many Parties" had sold 20,000 copies and "The Funeral" had sold just 6,600 copies, while "Long Gone Lonesome Blues" had sold 150,000. Hank's credibility was born anew, and "Long Gone Lonesome Blues" set the table for the unprecedented success he would enjoy until his death, success that would create its own ceaseless pressure to keep delivering. For the present, Hank was desperately eager to rise to the challenge.

Nothing else was recorded until June 14, when, at a half-session, Hank cut another Leon Payne song, "They'll Never Take Her Love from Me," and a third version of "Honky Tonk Blues" that, like the other two, was abandoned. After "Long Gone Lonesome Blues" had spent eight weeks at number one, only to be replaced by "Why Don't You Love Me?" Hank was probably disappointed to see "They'll Never Take Her Love from Me" top out at number five. The message was fairly clear: the public wanted brisk, up-tempo juke joint songs. History might decide that Hank Williams was the finest writer and singer of "heart" songs in all country music, but that wasn't what the radio and jukebox audiences wanted in 1950.

Since joining the *Opry*, Hank had worked shows with Bill Monroe, the irascible father of bluegrass music. Hank's feelings toward Monroe's music are unknown, but he probably loved it because it contained much that he held dear. Monroe refused to have electric instruments in his lineup, and voiced some criticism of Hank's singing style ("He drug it to death," he once said, referring not to drugs but to Hank's tendency to hold on to notes), but he was a good judge of songs, and knew that Hank was writing some great ones. Somewhere on tour in Texas, Hank played Monroe a new song, "I'm Blue, I'm Lonesome," and Monroe somehow acquired it. There were rumors that the song's notional writer, "James B. Smith," was a pseudonym for Hank and Bill Monroe, but it appears as though the royalties went solely to Monroe until Acuff-Rose challenged for a share in the 1990s. Monroe later asserted that he wrote some of the song, but his sideman, Jimmy Martin, who was with Hank and Monroe at the time, insists that Hank wrote it all.

Monroe recorded "I'm Blue, I'm Lonesome" on February 3, 1950, during his first sessions for Decca, and it became a bluegrass classic. At the same time, Monroe cut "Alabama Waltz," a song that Hank had written to stoke the ongoing craze for "state" waltzes that had started with Monroe's "Kentucky Waltz" and Pee Wee King's "Tennessee Waltz." Monroe couldn't recall if Hank was at the session, but if he was in town he usually liked to sit on the sidelines when his songs were being cut.

Braxton Schuffert says that Hank was at his recording session five days later, on February 8, although existing itineraries place Hank in Kansas City with Cowboy Copas and Jamup and Honey for that entire week (February 5 through 9). It's hard to know if Hank felt as though he owed a debt to Braxton, or if he truly thought Braxton stood a chance of making it. Since the war, Braxton had been working six days a week for Hormel Meats in Montgomery, all the while performing as a Hormel-sponsored solo act on WCOV and WSFA. Whenever Hank went back to Montgomery, he tried to persuade Braxton to take another stab at the music business, and in January 1950 he took matters into his own hands. He called Brack's wife and told her that he had train tickets ready, a backstage pass to the *Opry*, and reservations at the Hermitage Hotel. Braxton begged off work and took the Saturday morning train to Nashville. He joined the melee backstage at the *Opry*, and the next morning Hank picked him up at the hotel and drove him out to his house.

Hank opened and closed his garage door a few times with the remote control. Braxton had never seen anything like it. Hank then phoned Fred Rose, asked him to come over, and ordered Braxton to sing Rose some songs. Rose had more or less been given carte blanche by Frank Walker to sign country acts to MGM, and he either heard something he liked in Braxton's slightly antiquated style or realized that this was a concession, like the Luke the Drifter session, that he needed to make to keep Hank sweet.

"Fred said, 'What have you got for him to sing?'" said Braxton, "and Hank said he had a couple of songs, and Fred said he had a song by one of the Anglins called 'If Tears Would Bring You Back.'" Among the songs Hank pitched to Braxton was "Teardrop on a Rose," a sentimental parlor piece that Hank had toyed with for years. He asked Braxton what he thought of it. Braxton said:

> I told him it was one of the most beautiful songs I ever heard, and Hank said I could have it if I wanted. Then we needed one more. I was wanting to sing "I'll Still Write Your Name in the Sand," but Fred said, "No-o-o, we don't give other folks royalties. I'm going over to the house for a few minutes. You and Hank write something." So Hank and me wrote "Rockin' Chair Daddy" sittin' on the settee at his house. He'd write a line and I'd write a line. When Fred come back, I sang him "Rockin' Chair Daddy," and he signed me up that evening.

"Rockin' Chair Daddy" was the closest to a Jimmie Rodgers–style song Hank would ever have a hand in writing.

The session was logged at the Castle studio on February 8, 1950, but that was a Wednesday, when Braxton should have been at work, and Hank, as noted, should have been in Kansas City. Braxton says he played Hank's guitar, but insists that Hank didn't participate except, as Braxton says, to "pop that heel — he wouldn't pat, he'd pop that thing." All four songs were released under the name "Braxton Shooford." Like every record that Rose produced for MGM that wasn't by Hank Williams, Braxton's failed to do much business. MGM's initial sell-in on "Rockin' Chair Daddy" accounted for just under thirty-five hundred copies.

At the end of March, Hank was back in the studio. This time he was sitting in on Audrey's first session for Decca. Having just missed the opportunity of signing Hank, Decca's country A&R chief, Paul Cohen, now had the worst-case consolation prize: Hank and the Drifting Cowboys were at a Decca session, but Audrey was singing.

Audrey cut seven songs, and six of them were released. First out of the tape box was a cover version of "Honky Tonkin'." Rose Maddox had revived the song in July 1949, and it had been picked up by Polly Bergen and Teresa Brewer for the pop market — the first pop cover version of a Hank Williams song, and the unlikeliest. Brewer was coming off her first big hit, "Music! Music! Music!" but "Honky Tonkin'" simply wasn't a pop song. Even so, Brewer's version was attracting a little airplay, and Audrey decided to corner some of the action. Her version was released back-to-back with a Hadacol song, "What Put the Pep in Grandma?" (the band yelled "Haddy-cole, Haddy-cole, Haddy-cole"). It was the kind of free advertising only Hadacol's competitors would have wished on it.

When *Billboard* reviewed Audrey's second Decca single in October 1950, its review staff concluded that "Orking [is] much superior to thrush's singing," and gave it one of the lowest ratings of the week. Audrey now had an official recommendation, almost a request, that she stop singing, but she continued to insinuate herself onto Hank's radio shows and occasionally onto his live shows. If they were getting along, Hank would call her onstage at the *Opry* for a duet; if they were on the outs, she would stand backstage and pout while Hank did his portion alone.

Audrey felt excluded from a career she thought, with justification, she had done much to get off the ground. Having Hank's money to spend was not enough of a consolation prize, so peace never broke out for long at the Williams household. Two weeks after the Decca session, the troubles resurfaced. Hank returned from a tour, and Audrey had heard that he was drinking and locked him out. Hank checked into the Tulane Hotel and was later arrested after he fell asleep drunk with a lit cigarette in his hand and set fire to his room.

Audrey always maintained that she had been signed to MGM with Hank, but Rose evidently refused to produce her as a solo act, leading to the Decca deal. Rose did, however, schedule the two unissued Hank and Audrey duets, "Jesus Remembered Me" and "I Heard My Mother Praying for Me," for September 1950. The fall time slot was dubbed the "After Harvest" release, when the market for religious songs was supposed to be especially good. Even then, with Hank's credibility near its zenith, the record fell stillborn from the presses.

Hank's 1949 royalties were reported by *Variety* magazine at $65,000, but the actual figures were substantially lower. The MGM royalties for 1949 were $15,400 and the Acuff-Rose royalties were $8,219, totaling $23,619. Still good money. In 1950 the MGM royalties jumped to $22,574, in part because some "Lovesick Blues" sales from 1949 were accounted for in 1950. Hank's Acuff-Rose royalties for 1950 increased substantially to $18,040 because he was now writing his own songs.

The same *Variety* report stated that MGM's top seller, black crooner Billy Eckstine, grossed more than $100,000 in royalties in 1949. Even if true, there was no disguising the fact that MGM was in trouble almost from the first day. Eckstine, Hank Williams, and MGM's other quasi-major names like orchestra leaders Blue Barron and Art Mooney weren't generating enough sales to cover the giant overhead. When the parent corporation, Loews, was ordered to divide its business into independently operating studio and theater divisions, MGM Records devolved to the theater division. There were rumors in the trade that the theater division would shut down MGM Records when Frank Walker's initial five-year term was up in August 1950, but it was decided to keep MGM Records afloat, and Walker was re-signed.

One expense that MGM hadn't counted upon when it broke ground at its plant in New Jersey was the need to retool the presses to accommodate 45 rpm records and LPs. RCA had introduced the 45 rpm in March 1949 in response to Columbia's introduction of the LP in June the previous year. Trying to sidestep the cost, MGM began pressing its 78s on a supposedly unbreakable compound in October 1949, but Walker soon had to face up to the inevitable and began pressing 45s in May 1950. For all companies, the LP and 45 "micro-platters" as they were called, represented additional overhead for a minimal return. The only benefits were their lighter shipping weight and unbreakability (all record labels made a "breakage allowance" on shipments of 78s). It wasn't until October 1950 that Seeburg introduced the first 45 rpm jukebox, and even though 45s gained acceptance in the pop market, 78s would outsell 45s for years in the country and gospel markets. Jerry Rivers remembers seeing 45s for the first time in Cincinnati when Hank and the band went to Nelson King's house on one of their earliest tours. Hank's first record to be released simultaneously as a 45 and a 78 was "They'll Never Take Her Love from Me" / "Why Should We Try Anymore?" in August 1950.*

For Hank, records and music publishing were icing on the cake. His personal appearance fees made up the greater part of his income, which was estimated at ninety-two thousand dollars for 1950. A record that sold 150,000 copies, as both "Long Gone Lonesome Blues" and "Why Don't You Love Me?" had done, netted Hank just three thousand dollars from MGM. If he wrote both sides of the record, he would receive an additional forty-five hundred dollars from Acuff-Rose. Airplay royalties would filter back from the performing rights society, BMI. But the true value of a big hit lay in the fact that Hank could hike his personal appearance fee or antici-pate a higher turnout, which would increase his share of the gate.

Hank's personal appearance fee fluctuated wildly. The rule of thumb was that you worked for what you could get, and you got it in cash. If Hank was playing a date as a headliner in a major center, he often settled for 50 or 60 percent of the gross after tax; if he filled a four-thousand-seat auditorium at ticket prices that ranged from a dollar for adults to fifty cents for children, he might expect to stuff two thousand dollars into his valise for the night's work. He never took checks after being burned a few times. But then, if he had a free night and was expecting to pass through a small town where he knew a deejay or someone who pro-moted hillbilly shows, he might play a club for a few hundred dollars.

Grand Ole Opry appearances were a loss leader. Like the *Hayride,* the *Opry* paid American Federation of Musicians scale. For backing men, this was seven dollars a spot on the non-networked portion and twenty dollars on the Prince Albert portion. Hank's rate was roughly fifty dollars a show. Soon after arriving at the *Opry,* he was given some fifteen-minute early morning shows on WSM. His sponsors included Duckhead Overalls, Pops-Rite Popcorn, and Mother's Best flour. The net result was that after Jim Denny's Artist Service Bureau deducted the money that Hank owed WSM for using the *Opry* name on shows, he was usually in the hole to the station.

Hank supplemented his income in various ways. Sheet music and song folio sales were a big deal in 1950. At the top end of the scale, Pee

*Of the 188 million records sold in 1950, 177.3 million were still on 78 rpm, 7.3 million were on 45 rpm, and 3.4 million were on LP.

Wee King's "Tennessee Waltz" sold 1.1 million pieces of sheet music in 1951. Hank's sheet music sales were substantially less (between January and June 1950, for instance, "Honky Tonkin'" sold 4,769 copies), but still combined to provide a healthy adjunct to his income. Songbooks were an even better business. Acuff-Rose reported sales of 7,300 copies of *The Hank Williams Country Folio* during the first six months of 1950, and Hank doubled his money by selling many of those himself. The band typically went out into the crowd and sold song folios and photographs on commission during the intermission. The usual asking price for photos was fifty cents, and Hank would sign them for that price. When he returned to Shreveport for a concert on May 31, 1950, he was open for business. "Some guy near Hank's dressing room was selling pictures of Hank," said Tillman Franks, who'd booked Hank in leaner times. "I bought one, and Hank saw me buy it and didn't offer to give it to me. Then I asked him to autograph it, and he spelled my name wrong."

Hank grabbed wildly at every source of income because he had no inkling that his success would last. He saw the opportunities suddenly opening up, and lunged at them. It was a natural reaction for someone who had been trying for success as long as he had. It's true that Audrey was spending the money faster than he made it, but the reason he made it was because it was there to be made.

By paying his band slightly more than scale, he was able to keep the steadiest lineup he'd ever had. The only change during the first year in Nashville came when Bob McNett quit in May 1950. He'd messed up on the networked portion of the Opry, kicking off a song with the wrong intro. No amount of faking could cover it up that night; they had to stop and restart the song. Hank didn't dismiss him, but McNett came to believe that he wasn't cut out for the big time, and as he says, "I wanted to do something on my own. I had the feeling I was traveling all over the country lookin' at someone else's back, and that's as far as I could see." He and his brother planned to open a country music park back in his native Pennsylvania, so he quit the Drifting Cowboys. Rather than recruit a guitarist from the growing pool of Nashville sessionmen, Hank replaced McNett with Sammy Pruett, who had played with him in leaner times. Pruett was a fine guitarist, generally reckoned to know more chords and chord inversions than anyone then working in country music, but Hank's decision to hire him was more indicative of his profound mistrust of Nashville success. He needed to surround himself with familiar faces, and Pruett had stuck with him when they were lucky to walk away from a gig with five bucks apiece and no open wounds. Pruett was working with Happy Wilson's Golden River Boys on WAPI in Birmingham when he got a call from Hank in Sioux City, Iowa. "I got to Nashville about nine o'clock one Saturday morning," he remembered. "Hank picked me up in front of the *Grand Ole Opry* and we left for somewhere out west and we were gone for three weeks." Like McNett, Pruett was confined to playing the tic-toc rhythm that was now one of the trademarks of the Hank Williams sound. Hank called it the "cheap banjo sound" when interviewed, and Pruett soon grew bored playing it.

In June 1950 Hank and Oscar Davis came to a parting of the ways for reasons that Davis never specified. Hank tried to increase his share of the personal appearance pie by managing himself, but things fell apart. On July 4 he was supposed to headline at the Watermelon Festival at DeLeon, Texas, a hundred miles southwest of Fort Worth. The town was small, but the festival drew some of the biggest names in country music in the late 1940s and early '50s because it was a magnet for farming families for hundreds of miles around. The promoter, W. B. Nowlin, was also the mayor of DeLeon, and paid Hank a three-thousand-dollar guarantee for the July 4 date. Hank committed to be there by 10:00 a.m. By 2:00 p.m., there was no sign of him, and Nowlin had eleven thousand farmers baking in the Texas sun, getting madder by the hour. Then, just after two o'clock, Hank's limo came racing into the field where the festival was being staged, and someone calling himself Hank's road manager got out and told Nowlin that Hank was "too sick" to perform. What had seemed like Nowlin's biggest coup earlier that day was now a disaster. Nowlin insisted that Hank at least get out of the limo and appear onstage, but the road manager refused, so Nowlin ordered the chief of police to handcuff the road manager to the steering wheel while two men dragged Hank up onstage. Nowlin got on the microphone and said, "Hank Williams' manager says Hank Williams is too sick to perform, but if you were standing as close to him as I am you would know what he's sick from." Then the two men holding Hank let go for a moment and Hank fell almost to his knees before he regained his balance and staggered back to the limo.

Word got back to Nashville that Hank was on a drunk, so Jim Denny flew Hank Snow to Dallas to do the evening show at the Northside

Coliseum. Still in bad shape on July 5, Hank signed a curious document naming Jerry Rivers as his general manager while in Texas, then checked into the Adolphus Hotel as Herman P. Willis, the band's pet name for anyone who couldn't win for losing. Later that day, Rivers saw Herman P. Willis walking around the hotel wearing dark glasses with a hat pulled low over his eyes. The reason, according to Rivers, was that he was trying to avoid a local booker, Jack Ruby (*the* Jack Ruby). If rumors of Ruby's mob connections are true, Hank probably had valid reasons for keeping a low profile. Rivers said that Hank was hiding from Ruby because he didn't show at a party.

As he was bundled on a plane back to Nashville, even Hank must have drawn the conclusion that he was stretching himself too thin trying to handle his own business. Not long after, his bookings were taken over by A. V. Bamford, the self-styled "Cuban Jew." Right away, Bamford placed him on a package tour with Ernest Tubb and Minnie Pearl. Bamford had arrived in Nashville in 1949 from the West Coast. He had been booking big bands into the Venice Pier when the orchestra business went sour. Then he'd taken a chance on Bob Wills at the pier, saw the huge turnout, and experienced a conversion to country music that eventually brought him to Nashville. Bamford was a packager. He would figure out an itinerary, assemble a troupe of artists, book the halls, print up posters, arrange the advertising, then ride with the artists.

Hank's first Bamford tour took him out to Phoenix on July 17, then on to Albuquerque, El Paso, Odessa, and Lubbock on consecutive nights before heading back to Nashville. After a couple of weeks at home, he took off on another Bamford tour with Lonzo and Oscar and Rod Brasfield that started in Ohio, and swung across to Richmond, Virginia. Hank then returned to Nashville to rest up and prepare for another recording session slated for August 31.

Hank now believed that "blues" was the password to the top of the charts, and he was finishing up a song called "Moanin' the Blues" that he hoped would keep his hit streak alive. Once again, he left plenty of windows for yodels and flashes of trailing falsetto. The end result was greater than the sum of its parts. It rocked and rolled. The bridge was particularly compelling; Hank yodeled over the stops, setting up the smooth segue back to the verses. The rhythm, carried by Jack Shook's prominently mic'd acoustic guitar played up on the neck, was reinforced by big band drummer Farris Coursey playing brushes on the snare. It was one of only two times that Hank worked with drums.

The second song on the slate, "Nobody's Lonesome for Me," was clearly a B side. It had no bridge, and lacked the radio-friendliness of "Moanin' the Blues." Then, for the last half of the session, Hank once again became Luke the Drifter. First, he recorded a trite little homily, "Help Me Understand," a parable for the nag and the philanderer. A little more detail would have elevated it above the mundane. "One word led to another, and the last word led to divorce," said Hank tearfully, clearly cognizant of the threat of divorce hanging over his own head. Audrey had been the first to record the song back in March, and it was one that she and Hank often performed together as a two-part piece; Hank would narrate it and Audrey would sing the little girl's part, a rare occasion when her tuneless singing actually worked.

The last song was Fred Rose's "No, No Joe." The Cold War was heating up, the Korean War had started in June 1950, and the main enemy was Joseph Stalin. Roy Acuff had already recorded "Advice to Joe" ("When Moscow lies in ashes, God have mercy on your soul"); Jimmy Osborne chimed in with the slightly premature "Thank God for Victory in Korea;" and Elton Britt recorded "The Red We Want Is the Red We've Got in the Old Red, White and Blue." Red-baiting briefly became an issue in the music business, but the only casualties were black folk singer Josh White, who was forced to publicly confess that he had once held communist sympathies, and the Weavers, who saw their bookings dry up and were forced to disband.

In the context of McCarthyism, "No, No Joe" was understated and witty. *Billboard* noted as much in its review: "Tune and material are carefully wedded, not forced like so many of the recent patriotic tunes." It wouldn't have been stretching a point to issue "No, No Joe" under Hank's name, but Rose held fast to his original intention and issued it under Luke the Drifter. MGM took out full-page advertisements in trade magazines, but it failed to crack the charts. After Hank died and MGM was looking under every rock for Hank Williams recordings, they never once resorted to reissuing "No, No Joe." Its first domestic LP appearance was on a Time-Life set in 1981.

As the year ended, "Moanin' the Blues" was atop the charts, but the competition was stronger than ever. Two major new players had arrived:

Hank Snow (who stole Hank's bass player, Hillous Butrum, soon after the debacle in Texas) and Lefty Frizzell. Snow's first big American hit, "I'm Moving On," had spent twenty-one weeks at number one (longer than any other country record ever had or ever would), and Hank's "Moanin' the Blues" had to share the top spot with Frizzell's "If You've Got the Money, I've Got the Time." In the year-end tallies Hank was rated the third-best-selling artist of the year. Red Foley and Eddy Arnold were still ahead of him, and Hank Snow and Lefty Frizzell were snapping at his heels.

Chapter

10

A GOOD YEAR FOR THE ROSES

*H*ERE'S a little number me an' the boys been eatin' off of fer a while," Hank would often say in his introductions, and he had been depending on his music for so long that he probably saw it at least partly in those terms. If so, he had written and recorded his meal ticket for 1951 before he went out to play his New Year's show. It was another little cameo of life with Audrey, and if, as some said, the warmest she ever got was thawing, then "Cold, Cold Heart" was one of the most awfully true songs ever written.

Stories of the song's origin vary. The way that Pappy Neil McCormick remembered it, Audrey was in the hospital, probably recovering from an infection that had set in after she'd had an abortion in September 1950. The abortion had apparently been carried out at home without Hank's knowledge, and Audrey would have kept him in the dark if she hadn't developed an infection ("I was in the hospital over some little minor something," she coyly told journalist Dorothy Horstman). The reasons for the abortion are unclear. Audrey probably didn't want the physical pain of another pregnancy, much less the encumbrance of another child. According to McCormick, Hank went to the hospital and bent down to kiss Audrey, but she wouldn't let him. "You sorry son of a bitch," she is supposed to have said, "it was you that caused me to suffer this." Hank went home and told the children's governess, Miss Ragland, that Audrey had a "cold, cold heart," and then, as so often in the past, realized that the bitterness in his heart held commercial promise.

Years later, Audrey told one of her lovers a different story about the song's origin: she'd found out about one of Hank's affairs while she was in the hospital, and that when he brought her some jewelry in atonement, she'd flung it back at him. Other stories surround the song, all of them reflecting the increasingly unhappy times on Franklin Road. Audrey, like most musicians' wives, probably accepted the fact that Hank had dalliances out on the road. It was generally regarded as one of the few perks of the job. What irked her, though, was that Hank would often come back on Friday night or Saturday morning physically depleted, and would be gone again on Saturday night or Sunday morning. She had more stamina than he did, and could have coped with the rigors of the road, but she was left at home. So she began taking lovers to fill the lonely hours, and quite possibly suspected that the child she had conceived was not Hank's.

Talking to the *Wall Street Journal* in October 1951, Hank was economical with the truth. "Cold, Cold Heart," he told the interviewer, had taken about an hour to write; he just sat and waited, and pretty soon, God had written it for him. If so, the most that God gave him was the words; the melody was adapted from T. Texas Tyler's 1945 recording of "You'll Still Be in My Heart." Lyrically, the songs bore some similarities, but melodically there was very little difference at all. "You'll Still Be in My Heart" was originally copyrighted by Ted West in May 1943, then rewritten by Buddy Starcher and acquired in July 1943 by one of Starcher's affiliates, Clark Van Ness. Earlier, Van Ness' adaptation of an old Spanish-American War song of interracial passion, "Ma Filipino Baby," had become a big hit as servicemen returned from the Far East. Van Ness traded as Dixie Music, and, as was common, waited until "Cold, Cold Heart" had racked up some sales before filing suit on December 3, 1951.

Hank's draft of "Cold, Cold Heart" (titled "Your Cold Cold Heart") was dated November 23, 1950. If that was indeed the day he wrote it, it was some two months after Audrey's abortion, so perhaps his upset festered longer than supposed. It was recorded during an evening session on December 21. Hank sang with palpable hurt, never once sinking to mawkishness. His restraint only heightened the record's impact, and left the listener in no doubt that he was living every word. It was the first song recorded that night, but from the outset Fred Rose saw it as a B side because it now seemed to be an immutable law that the faster numbers sold best. The A side — the fast side — would be "Dear John," a song that Acuff-Rose didn't even publish. It was unthinkable that Rose would have wasted another company's song on a B side. B sides were known in the business as "free rides" because the record company paid the publisher of the B side as much as they paid the publisher of the A side. From the paperwork submitted to MGM, it seemed clear that Rose intended "Cold, Cold Heart" to get a free ride on the back of "Dear John."

"Dear John" was written by a hard-luck Texas honky-tonk singer, Aubrey Gass. It was the only hit he ever wrote. The first version was by Jim Boyd, younger brother of Dallas-based western swing artist Bill Boyd. Gass apparently knew Jim Boyd and offered him "Dear John," and Boyd recorded it on March 11, 1949. Soon after, Tex Ritter got his finger in the pie. Ritter probably promised to get the song cut by a big name (himself perhaps), or get Gass a contract with his label, Capitol, if he got a piece of the song. The fact that Gass recorded "Dear John" for Capitol some six months after Boyd suggests that Ritter lived up to his half of the bargain. When MGM filed for a license for Hank's version in January 1951, the application went to Tex Ritter Music in New York.

For all his tales of life in the bunkhouse, Tex (or Maurice Woodward Ritter, to give him his full name) had spent longer at law school than on the trail, and knew the angles when it came to the business end of the music business. If Tex hadn't beaten him to it, Hank could have bought the song from Aubrey Gass and no one would have known that "Dear John" wasn't a Hank Williams song. Clent Holmes, who'd worked with Hank in Shreveport, remembers him singing it there, so Hank had probably acquired Jim Boyd's record and carried the song around in the back of his mind for a year and a half. Needing a fast song for the jukeboxes, he remembered "Dear John." When Hank and the band hollered the tag line, "Dear John, I've sent your saddle home," it invited everyone in the bar, the auditorium, or even the car to holler right along. Once again, the upfront rhythm guitar carried the recording. Hank cruised at the brisk tempo, never once straining.

The last two sides recorded at the "Cold, Cold Heart" session were for another Luke the Drifter single, the fourth that year. "Just Waitin'" was a lusterless talking blues that Hank had adapted from an idea by a Texas songwriter, Bob Gazzaway, but it did little credit to either of them. Gazzaway wrote a few more songs that got recorded, including several by Little Jimmy Dickens, but never wrote a hit. "Just Waitin'" promised more than it delivered. Everyone is "just waitin'" for something. It was a good premise, but a bad song. The other side of the record, "Men with Broken Hearts," was Hank at his absolute bleakest. Later, Montgomery journalist Allen Rankin recalled Hank playing him the song. "Ain't that the awfulest, morbidest song you ever heard in your life?" Rankin remembered Hank saying. The lines about "eyes staring in defeat," "hearts pray[ing] for death," and "know[ing] pain with every breath" were from the darker side of life that drew the poetry out of Hank. "Don't know why I happen to of wrote that thing," he told Rankin, "except somebody that fell, he's the same man as before he fell, ain't he? Got the same blood in his veins. How can he be such a nice guy when he's got it and such a bad guy when he ain't got nothin'? Can you tell me?" It was a theme that Hank harped upon often in his conversation, as he sensed that those claiming to be his new best friends would one day disown him. If those were indeed his thoughts, they were a chillingly accurate premonition.

The year 1951 began with no hint of the changes in store. Hank closed out a hugely successful New Year's weekend bash in Indianapolis when more than sixteen thousand people had paid to see him, and as he looked into the new year, he probably saw the road stretching forever. There was a swing out west, followed by a short tour through the Southeast, both for A. V. Bamford.

During rare days off in Nashville, Hank prerecorded seventy fifteen-minute radio shows for Mother's Best flour, hosting the show with WSM announcer Louie Buck. The format was almost invariably the same. Hank would kick off with "Lovesick Blues" (he was still "that 'Lovesick Blues' boy"), and Cousin Louie would come in over the instrumental backing with a pitch for Mother's Best. There was a secular song, a "Come to Jesus" number, an instrumental, and finally a long closing pitch for Mother's Best. Sometimes a guest would drop in and do a number in place of the instrumental. Most if not all of the Mother's Best shows survived, and they include more than forty songs that Hank never otherwise recorded. He's very unguarded, believing that no one aside from early morning listeners in and around Nashville and mid-Alabama would ever hear him. He laughs a lot, sometimes almost giggles, reminding us that he was only twenty-seven. The jokes are usually self-deprecating and the hymns are riveting.

Some of the hymns were extraordinarily long, but Hank sings them entirely from memory. Most had a dark undercurrent. "The Great Judgment Morning" was possibly the best. It talks of the day when everyone will be equal. Money won't matter; neither will debt. The widow and the orphan will be on an equal footing with the famous as they gather before the "great throne." Roy Acuff had recorded it, but he hadn't included one verse that Hank found especially compelling:

> The gambler was there and the drunkard
> And they who had sold him the drink
> The people who gave them the license
> Together in Hell they did sink
>
> And oh the weeping, the wailing
> As the lost were told of their fate
> They cried for the rocks and the mountains
> They prayed, but their prayers were too late

There were a few surprises, too. The Weavers were in the pop charts with an old folk song, "On Top of Old Smoky," and Hank was clearly amazed that a song his grandmother used to sing was in the charts, so he decided on the spur of the moment to sing it as his grandmother had sung it. The Weavers' record is insufferably jolly, but Hank's rendition is very melancholy. The Drifting Cowboys join him on the chorus to haunting effect. It could have been a hit.

Hank featured both "Cold, Cold Heart" and "Dear John" on his Mother's Best shows, promoting what was then his latest release. The single was shipped on February 2, 1951, and "Dear John" showed up in the charts one month later. Within two weeks, though, "Cold, Cold Heart" overtook it. This left Rose gnashing his teeth because "Dear John" was now getting a free ride on the back of "Cold, Cold Heart." Still, it was good to know that a slow song would sell. "Cold, Cold Heart" eventually peaked at number one for a week in May, then hung around on the charts for the rest of the year. "Dear John" was off the charts in four weeks.

"Cold, Cold Heart" lingered because it acquired a new, and unexpected, lease on life. It's part of Acuff-Rose mythology that, against all odds and against the deeply ingrained resistance of the pop music establishment, Wesley Rose went to New York and persuaded Mitch Miller to record "Cold, Cold Heart" with Tony Bennett. Wesley loved to tell of how he beat on every record company door in New York with the song. "That's a hillbilly song," he was told everywhere, "and there's no use kidding yourself otherwise." Finally, he persuaded Miller, the goateed head of pop music A&R at Columbia Records, to take a listen. The rest, Wesley was fond of saying, is history.

In truth, Wesley took "Cold, Cold Heart" to New York at a time when the market for country songs had never been better. Every pop A&R man in town should have been beating a path to his hotel room. The idea of covering country records for the pop charts gathered steam after Jimmie Davis' "You Are My Sunshine" and Al Dexter's "Pistol Packin' Mama" became huge wartime hits for Bing Crosby. Acuff-Rose's first taste of pop action came several years later with "Jealous Heart." Written by Red Foley's sister-in-law, Jenny Lou Carson, it was a hit for Tex Ritter in 1945, then languished for four years before a Chicago pianist and singer, Al "Mr. Flying Fingers" Morgan, recorded it for a small local label. Morgan's record was picked up by London Records, and it became a top five pop record in 1949. Acuff-Rose had nothing to do with Morgan's picking up the song, but if the Roses ever needed a reminder that pop sales comfortably exceeded country sales, Al "Mr. Flying Fingers" Morgan was it. Later in 1949, Acuff-Rose had another pop hit when Frank Sinatra and others covered Red Foley's "Chattanoogie Shoe Shine Boy."

Pee Wee King's "Tennessee Waltz" provided another vast, unanticipated windfall for Acuff-Rose. Again, no one there had any role in its success, which probably increased Wesley's need to cement himself to the success of "Cold, Cold Heart." His training as an accountant led him to downplay dumb luck, which has always counted for so much in the music business. King had written and recorded "Tennessee Waltz" in 1947 and released it in January 1948 back-to-back with his version of Fred Rose's "Rootie Tootie." It became a fair-sized country hit. King and Cowboy Copas sold roughly 380,000 copies combined, but the song was dead in the water by the time jazz band leader Erskine Hawkins recorded it in September 1950. Jerry Wexler, then a *Billboard* columnist, heard Hawkins' record and suggested to Patti Page's manager that she put it on the flip side of her 1950 Christmas single. By early 1951, it had become one of those inexplicable, uncontainable smashes. By May, Page's record had sold 4.8 million copies and cover versions had probably sold half as many again. Sheet music sales had topped 1.1 million, and it was the highest-grossing song that BMI had ever represented. So, when Wesley Rose went to New York in early 1951 with "Cold, Cold Heart" in his briefcase, he shouldn't have had to twist anybody's arm into recording it.

Mitch Miller downplays Wesley's role in getting "Cold, Cold Heart" to him. He says it was Jerry Wexler who alerted him to "Cold, Cold Heart," but confirms that Tony Bennett had to be coerced into recording it. "When I heard the song, I thought it was made to order for Tony," says Miller. "I thought the last four lines were particularly poetic, and so I played Hank Williams' record for Tony, with the scratchy fiddle and everything, and Tony said, 'Don't make me do cowboy songs!' I said, 'Tony, listen to the words. It's only a record. If it doesn't work out, I won't put it out. I'm not here to hurt you.'"

Bennett had yet to see a chart entry when he recorded "Cold, Cold Heart" on May 31, 1951, so he wasn't the prize catch that Wesley might have been hoping for, but three weeks after the session, his version of "Because of You" shot straight to number one. This gave "Cold, Cold Heart" a head start, and proved again how important dumb luck could be. If "Because of You" had flopped, would "Cold, Cold Heart" have done as well? Would it even have shown up at all? As it was, "Cold, Cold Heart" jumped to the top of the pop charts, and every record label had to have at least one cover version. The Fontane Sisters and Perry Como did it for RCA, Louis Armstrong and Eileen Wilson for Decca, Tony Fontane and Dinah Washington for Mercury, and so on. It wasn't half the phenomenon that "Tennessee Waltz" had been, but "Cold, Cold Heart" served notice that Hank Williams' songs now had a potential that was unthinkable when he sent up his acetate of God, Mother, and Death songs for Molly O'Day just five years earlier. Mitch Miller, always the unabashed populist, came to appreciate Hank's artistry. "He had a way of reaching your guts and your head at the same time," he said later. "The language hit home. Nobody I know could use basic English so effectively." Tony Bennett never really understood what Hank was doing, but in January 1956, he sang "Cold, Cold Heart" on an ABC-TV *Opry* broadcast, while Ernest Tubb stared at him with stunned, icy disbelief.

Hank was tickled. He had always made a policy of spinning his own records on the jukebox in any restaurant he ate in; now he spun Tony

Bennett's record as well. The first couple of times, he would slap the table, grin his shiteating grin and say "Hot damn!" Now when he looked in *Billboard* every week he had a reason to check out the pop listings instead of heading straight for the "Folk Talent and Tunes" section. Miller's success with "Cold, Cold Heart" earned him a promise from Acuff-Rose that he would get prerelease demos of any songs that Wesley or Fred considered to have pop potential. "That way," says Miller, "I wouldn't have to scramble, but I agreed with Fred and Wesley that I wouldn't release my record until the original had got going on the country chart." It was an arrangement that would be mutually profitable for Acuff-Rose and Columbia over the next few years. When Rose spoke to the *Wall Street Journal* in late 1951, he stated that Acuff-Rose's gross for that year would be 40 or 50 percent up on 1950, which had in turn been 150 percent better than 1949. Mitch Miller made a substantial contribution to that.

Looked at in a broader context, the success of hillbilly songs refashioned for the pop market and the success of R&B reconfigured as pop a couple of years later meant that the music of the black and white underclasses was entering the pop mainstream through the back door. That in turn meant that the pop market was being prepped for rock 'n' roll. The "folk tunes boom," as it was termed at the time, caught the attention not only of the *Wall Street Journal* but of virtually every other periodical. The *Collier's* approach was typical in its mixture of surprise and condescension; "There's Gold in Them Thar Hillbilly Tunes" was the headline. Hank was often singled out in the press' musings. Much of the comment focused upon his ability to write hits in half an hour, and Hank played the role of the intuitive folk artist to the hilt, never once mentioning the rigid application of commercial logic that took place in Rose's home studio before every session.

Not only were cover versions of hillbilly tunes selling well, but the original versions were doing unprecedentedly good business as well. Decca Records had tried without success to sign Hank Williams, but had Red Foley, Ernest Tubb, and Kitty Wells under contract. Decca estimated that 50 percent of its sales derived from country music. Even Columbia Records estimated that 40 percent of its gross came from country. The bottom line looked even rosier. A typical pop session of the day used as many as thirty or forty instrumentalists at $41.25 for three hours. Before the session, an army of copyists was required to write out the arrangements, and a contractor had to be engaged to call everyone in. Then, typically, only one or two songs would be recorded during a session. In Nashville, most sessions used no more than six or seven instrumentalists, arrangements were cooked up on the spot, no contractor was needed, and three or four songs were cut in three hours.

Hank was happy to cash the checks as the palm court orchestras played his songs, but on a far deeper level he was suspicious of the trend, seeing it as a dilution of his music. "These pop bands," he told an interviewer in Charleston, South Carolina, "will play our hillbilly songs when they cain't eat any other way." If he saw the trade advertisement for Bennett's "Cold, Cold Heart," it must have confirmed his darkest suspicions. The headline was "Popcorn! A Top Corn Tune Gone Pop." Tony Bennett was caricatured in a policeman's uniform holding up traffic while a witless hillbilly leads a pig and a mule across a busy city street. In terms of denigrating hillbilly music, this was no better than the Sterling ads four years earlier.

For all its success, "Cold, Cold Heart" did little to change Hank's routine. After the *Opry* on Saturday night, he headed out of town on a four- or five-day junket. The crowds were getting bigger as his reputation grew, but otherwise it was all much as before. There was the backstage meet 'n' greet, and no one was more concerned than Hank to sign every autograph. There were deejays to be stroked — the phrases now tripped like a litany off Hank's tongue. If there was time and if he had the energy, there might be a quick dive into a motel with a woman. Sometimes, the band would sit out in the car with the motor running while Hank took care of business. Then there was more wriggling inside that damned old car trying to find a position in which his back didn't hurt so bad, and more grief when he got home. It was a routine that was beginning to pall, but for the present it beat anything Hank had ever known, and he was still happy to be out there.

Hank had been without a manager since he and Oscar Davis parted company, and he tried to bring some order to his business affairs by hiring William R. "Bill" England. Rather than look around Nashville, Hank once again pulled someone from Montgomery. England had been a time salesman on WSFA before coming to Nashville. He moved up in January 1951 and worked from his home at 1950 Richard Jones Road. England's first priority was to assemble a catalog of promotional items that could be sent out in advance of a show. The promoter could pick and choose from an array of predesigned one- or two-column advertisements for "The Sensational Radio-Recording Star Mr. Lovesick Blues Hank Williams with his Entire Grand Ole Opry Show." If Hank was paying to use the *Grand Ole Opry* trademark, he might as well get all the mileage he could out of it. England also wrote some prepackaged stories that could run in newspapers just before the show, and printed up huge stocks of 8 × 10 inch photos for store windows, giveaways, and intermission sales. It wasn't long, though, before England found that Hank really wanted a gofer, not a manager.

At roughly the same time, a power play was unfolding at the *Opry*. In August 1950, Harry Stone quit as WSM manager to become a consultant, eventually working for KPHO in Phoenix, Arizona, where he discovered Marty Robbins. He was replaced by Jack DeWitt Jr., who was already president of WSM. DeWitt's background was in the technical end of radio. He had designed equipment that could bounce radar signals off the moon, and had spent the Second World War working on radar technology, but had little or no feel for hillbilly music. DeWitt had the sense to place Jim Denny in the newly created post of manager of the *Grand Ole Opry*, despite the fact that he and Denny rarely got along. This left Denny the uneasy victor in a protracted campaign against Stone, a campaign waged on the personal and professional front. Although both men were married, they had competed for the affections of Dollie Dearman, a dancer in the *Opry* troupe, and that too was a battle that Denny won. The bitter pill for Denny was that he had to surrender the lucrative concession businesses he had built up.

Jim Denny liked Hank, and had a grudging respect for him. Hank, though, had a deep-seated suspicion of everybody. He would never invest enough trust in either Denny or Bill England for them to act on his behalf. Hank's idea of calculating his net worth was to empty his pockets, and England soon grew frustrated. "We never had a contract because to me a contract represents a lack of trust," he said, "but managing Hank was like a company asking a management consultant to come in and look at their business, make recommendations and so forth, then ignoring everything the management consultant says and going right back to operating the way they did before. I had the title of manager, but did not manage." England maintains that he was paid low and slow, and says that Hank, even at the height of his fame, couldn't cover a ten-dollar check.

Part of the problem was that Audrey was still buying everything that caught her eye, although England asserts that she and Hank were equally bad. "That went back to the early thirties," he says. "They'd never had anything, then the money came rolling in, and anything they saw, they wanted." Automobiles, of course. His-and-hers Cadillacs. Audrey bought a four-thousand-dollar convertible against Hank's wishes — he thought a married woman had no business riding around in one. He bought a Cadillac Coupe for himself, and a six-thousand-dollar seven-passenger Cadillac touring sedan. Audrey shopped at the most expensive couturiers, bought overpriced furniture, and treated herself to jewelry. As Hank sang "Dear John," the words must have rung truer than any from his own pen:

> I went down to the bank this morning, the cashier said with
>   a grin,
> I feel so sorry for you, Hank, but your wife has done been in.

Hank later claimed that Audrey spent fifty thousand dollars during 1951 alone, much of it remodeling and refurbishing the Franklin Road house in what would become the Graceland school of interior decor. Soon after Hank came to the *Opry*, he boasted to a band member that he was now making money faster than even Audrey could spend it, but she somehow caught up. If Audrey were to defend herself, she would probably say that Hank matched her dollar for dollar. Hank had simple tastes, but indulged them to excess. He had partied away the fifteen dollars he had won at the Empire Theater in 1937, and now he was buying guns, riding tackle, or anything else that caught his eye. He left huge tips on a whim, and would sometimes simply lose money, or send it to people who mailed him a hard-luck story. After he came to Nashville, he started banking with John Clay, the brother of KWKH manager Henry Clay, at the Third National Bank. He would often return from a trip with a suitcase full of money that he would simply dump on a cashier's desk. When asked how much was there, he would say that it was his business to make it and theirs to count it.

Hank's fascination with guns was particularly costly. Jerry Rivers remembered that Hank, like Elvis, would befriend members of the police so that they would help him locate guns and even girls. One night, a member of the vice squad in El Paso took Hank and the Drifting

Cowboys on a late-night excursion into Juarez in search of exotic firearms. Members of the troupe that accompanied Hank to Oklahoma City in 1951 remember him buying a gross of expensive cufflinks with pistol motifs. He bought a Tennessee walking horse, figuring that its smooth gait would enhance his cowboy image with minimal damage to his back. And then, on September 1, 1951, he bought 507 acres of land with a derelict antebellum farmhouse south of Nashville in Williamson County. The purchase price was sixty thousand dollars, but Hank put up just fifteen thousand, and then proceeded to dig a deeper hole for himself by stocking the farm with whiteface cattle. So if Audrey was the thrusting arriviste, using Hank's money to buy social credibility, Hank was spending like a lottery winner with a month to live.

Some of Hank's income went into a forlorn retail venture, Hank and Audrey's Corral. Back in 1947, Ernest Tubb had opened his famous Record Shop close to the *Opry*. He mailed records across the nation, and bought up WSM's airtime after the *Opry* went off the air on Saturday night to host his *Midnight Jamboree* from the store. Hank tried to replicate Tubb's formula by opening Hank and Audrey's Corral at 724 Commerce Street, next door to Tubb. The Corral opened in June 1951, and Hank took out a five-year lease on the property at $160 a month, then stocked it with seven thousand dollars' worth of inventory, with furnishings like the western-wear stores he'd seen out west. The walls were covered with barn board, wagon wheels, and hurricane lamps. In addition to the western gear, there were Hank and Audrey dolls, fans, and knicknacks for the Saturday night crowd. The gala opening was broadcast over WSM between 5:00 and 5:30 p.m. on June 16, 1951, and Hank planned to broadcast every week in that time slot, much as Ernest Tubb did after midnight, but the Corral show had to be relocated to the WSM studios after three months because crowds blocked the sidewalk. Hank placed the store in the hands of Mac McGee, but it was too often a refuge for out-of-work musicians waiting for Hank to drop in and buy everyone Krystal burgers. He usually showed up on Saturday morning to sign the paychecks, and Audrey would come by most days to scoop the cash register.

As Hank's success reached its zenith in 1951, the situation deteriorated at home. "Cold, Cold Heart" turned into what he liked to call "a little prophecy in song." Audrey, now shut out from everything to do with Hank's career except the cash flow, closed off her heart. The Hank

Williams she got was either dog tired or shipped home early from a tour because he was drinking. The good times hadn't all passed and gone, but they were fewer now. Two years of almost constant touring had taken their toll on Hank's health, while the career pressures in the wake of "Cold, Cold Heart" were placing an additional strain on his ever less stable psyche.

Through it all, Hank never messed up in the recording studio. At 1:30 on the afternoon of Friday, March 16, 1951, just as "Cold, Cold Heart" and "Dear John" were breaking, he went back into the studio with four songs, four remarkably strong songs even by the standards he had set for himself. They were "I Can't Help It (If I'm Still in Love with You)," "Howlin' at the Moon," "Hey, Good Lookin'," and "My Heart Would Know." It took half an hour of studio overtime on top of the three-hour session to get all four down, but Rose's glee must have been uncontained as he made his myopic way back home that afternoon.

Don Helms' opening notes on "I Can't Help It" held fast to Rose's credo that he must play high if Hank was to sing low. If Helms had played any higher, only dogs would have heard him. Jerry Rivers always said that Hank wrote the song in the touring sedan. He came up with the first line, "Today I passed you on the street," and then asked for suggestions. "What's a good line?" he said. Don Helms answered, "And I smelled your rotten feet." Everyone in the car broke up laughing, but Hank soldiered on. The hand of Fred Rose is clearly at work in some of the lines; the grammatical forms and scansion are unlike pure Hank, but the content and the prevailing mood are identifiably Hank Williams.

In complete contrast, "Howlin' at the Moon" captures the giddiness of new love. Much of its humor was rooted in Hank's passion for hunting. The performance tears along, punctuated by Jerry Rivers' hound dog yodels. It was but a short step from there to rockabilly. Hank had already written another set of words to the same melody, and called it "Countryfied." He pitched "Countryfied" to his opening act, Big Bill Lister, a month later.

"Hey, Good Lookin'" seemed to demand the same breezy treatment as "Howlin' at the Moon." On one level, it seemed to point toward rock 'n' roll (hot rods, dancing sprees, goin' steady, and soda pop), but the rhythm plodded along with a steppity-step piano, and Hank sounded almost dour. If Audrey felt a twinge of guilt over her affairs, she must have wondered if she or another had inspired "Hey, Good Lookin'" and

"Howlin' at the Moon." Hank's *Opry* costar, Little Jimmy Dickens, says that Hank wrote both songs on a plane taking them to a date in Wichita Falls, Texas. Dickens also insists that Hank promised him "Hey, Good Lookin'." "He said he wanted me to record it," said Dickens, "and I was delighted, I thought it would be a good song for me. Then I met him in the hall of WSM, and he said, 'Tater [Hank called Dickens "Tater" after his first hit, "Take an Old Cold Tater (and Wait)"], I cut your song today. It's too good a song for you, anyway.'" Dickens says he laughed it off, but it wasn't the first time Hank had pulled a stunt like that, and it wouldn't be the last.

Typically, Hank would offer a song around, and if enough artists seemed interested, he would record it himself. "Listen here what I wrote," he would say, "ain't that a good un?" Chet Atkins remembers that Hank would "get right up close to you in your face and he'd sing. If you raved over it, he'd love that. He was pitching songs to the hot acts of that time, and they'd say, 'That's a great song, Hank. I want to do that on my next session.' If he got enough people to say that, he'd say, 'No, it's too damn good for you, I'm gonna do it myself.'" The humility that all country performers were, and are, supposed to wear like a crown of thorns often drops in private, but Hank's hubris alienated many of his peers. He placed a surprising number of songs with other artists, but none of them ever amounted to anything. Many, like "There's Nothing As Sweet As My Baby," given to young and struggling Carl Smith, were inconsequential songs, and Hank probably knew he was doing no one a favor in bestowing them. All evidence points to the fact that he knew exactly which ones to keep for himself.

The four songs recorded on March 16, 1951, were released in two couplings. "I Can't Help It" and "Howlin' at the Moon" were released on April 27, and "Hey, Good Lookin'" and "My Heart Would Know" were released on June 22. Together, those two singles kept "Cold, Cold Heart" company in the charts for the rest of the year. "Hey, Good Lookin'" spent most of August and September at number one. Adhering to their agreement with Mitch Miller, the Roses offered him these new songs, and Miller scored pop hits with Guy Mitchell's version of "I Can't Help It" and Frankie Laine's duet on "Hey, Good Lookin'" with Jo Stafford. Laine and Stafford's record had much of the zest that Hank's lacked, thanks to six guitars comping in unison underpinned by a jazz bassist and drummer, all punctuated by Speedy West's steel guitar. The record peaked at number nine on the pop charts at the tail end of 1951.

Hank was back in the studio for another session on March 23, a week after he'd recorded "Hey, Good Lookin.'" Decca Records had jettisoned Miss Audrey, and Hank had persuaded Fred Rose to record her for MGM as a solo act and to cut some more religious duets. The sacred songs they chose were "The Pale Horse and His Rider" and "A Home in Heaven." Hank had probably learned "The Pale Horse and His Rider" from its cowriter, Johnny Bailes, when he worked with the Bailes Brothers in Shreveport, but the song dated back to 1939, when Bailes was working with Molly O'Day and the song's other writer, Ervin Staggs, at WCHS in Charleston, West Virginia. Full of images as spectral and haunting as any Hank ever wrote, it is nonetheless undermined by Audrey, who is strident and often woefully off-key.

"A Home in Heaven" was a song that Hank had kicked around in one guise or another for five years. A version was included on a set of demos sent to Columbia's Art Satherley in 1946, and it would later resurface as "Are You Building a Temple in Heaven?" Once again, Hank and Audrey's domestic disharmony seemed to find its extension on disc as she tried for supremacy on every note. Rose refused to okay the recordings for release, and it would be almost four years after Hank's death, when MGM believed it was staring at the bottom of the barrel, before "Home in Heaven" and "The Pale Horse and His Rider" were shipped.

Part of the appeal of Hank's records was that they gave an inkling of the gulf that existed between the public mask and the inner disquiet. He was now one of the most successful artists in country music. Eddy Arnold might be selling more records, but he couldn't equal Hank's overall achievement as a writer and performer. Most of those who punched up a Hank Williams record on the jukebox probably felt that the mood swing on every record between the bouncy up-tempo song and the slower "heart" song was more than a commercial formula; it was an echo of his life, and many other people's lives. He could josh around with the guys in the limo, bathe in the applause onstage, find a girl and head off to a motel, see his records plastered all over the charts, perform a gratuitous act of charity for someone who was as poor as he had once been . . . but still he seemed to find no peace or real contentment in it.

Everyone who says they were close to Hank usually has to admit that — on some level — they really didn't know him at all. "I never knew anybody I liked better than Hank," Jim Denny said after Hank's death, "but I don't think I ever really got close to him. I don't know if anyone really could. He was so bitter. . . . He thought everybody had some sort of angle on him." The mistrust and secretiveness weren't traits that developed in the wake of success. "This guy was afraid for anyone to get close to him, even to the point of being cold," said Doyle Turner, who had worked with Hank in 1945. "He was never the type of person to be close. Bernice and I were closer to him than any of the group, and it was as though we were a hundred miles away from him." Working the street corners with Tee-Tot, Hank had acquired a cheery mask that led people to believe they were his confidantes, and led many to claim that Hank had befriended them and poured his heart out to them. In fact, they'd heard one of his set pieces, every bit as well rehearsed and sincere as his songs. Audrey's betrayals probably hurt him all the more because she was one of the few to whom he had truly opened up.

Hank craved success until he found it, then wanted less tangible things, like a centered home life. Success alone didn't widen the gap between Hank and Audrey, but it financed their aspirations, which in turn made it clear how different those aspirations were. Audrey wanted to integrate herself into the old-money Belle Meade country club set, while Hank's idea of recreation was to go fishing on Kentucky Lake. He is generally reckoned to have been happiest out on the lake with a cane pole. He didn't even want to go hunting and fishing with the old-money crowd, who took their blinds, their servants, and all manner of expensive tackle and hardware. Several times, Hank apparently embarrassed Audrey at her dinner parties, and even if the stories are exaggerated, they nonetheless show how divergent their paths had become.

Much as Hank blamed Audrey for his poor family life, he knew his own conduct, particularly his drinking bouts, drove a wedge between them. Guilt over his drinking, his inability to spend more time with his wife and son, and his little flings almost certainly gnawed at him. Chiefly, it was the binges, now coming more frequently, that frustrated those who dealt with him. Everyone tried to make him feel guilty about the boozing — and he probably felt the guilt even as he covered it up with truculence. "I tried to shame him," said Oscar Davis. "I said, 'Look, you got your son and your wife,' [but] you can't shake an alcoholic." Bob

McNett says, "Some of the lonesomeness you found in Hank was guilt because he knew in his heart he wasn't living up to what he knew was morally right." The caricature of Hank Williams, with the Bible in one hand and *Billboard* in the other, has its grain of truth. He knew right from wrong, and knew he had been weighed in the balance and found wanting.

The year 1951 would be the last good one, the last of only three. Hank spent the greater part of it on the road. Once in a while, one of his fellow performers told him his pace was killing him. He would shrug to hide the fact that he probably knew it, and say he had to strike while the iron was hot.

*We need applause. That's how we live.
When you don't have a lot of noise
around you, the noise inside you
becomes overwhelming.*
Judy Garland

● ●

FOLK AND WESTERN MUSIC TO SELL

● ●

*T*HE year 1951 was Hank Williams' career
year. Bigger crowds; city reporters taking an
interest in ol' Hank and his songs; the admiration — sometimes grudging, sometimes not — of his peers. "Everywhere we were fixin' to go was
a higher level," said Don Helms. Hank appeared to be cocky, but on
another level the success made him deeply uneasy. Just a few years earlier, he had been refused jobs and turned away from radio stations as a
damn drunk. He knew in his heart he was still the same person, and
deeply mistrusted the embrace of the business. At some moments, the
mistrust generalized to everybody, because everyone seemed to want a
piece of him; everyone that is, except the person to whom he wanted to
give a piece of himself.

After eighteen months on the *Opry*, Hank had sufficient drawing
power to tour as a single attraction. He no longer needed to be part of a
package show. This gave him the opportunity to assemble his own show,
and in February 1951 he hired Big Bill Lister as a warm-up act and
rhythm guitarist. Lister stood out in just about any crowd except basket-
ball players. He was gauntly thin, six feet seven inches tall, and billed
himself as the World's Tallest Singing Cowboy. He loved hunting and
fishing, so he fit right in with the Drifting Cowboys, and his bluntness
and directness endeared him to Hank.

Born Weldon E. Lister in Karnes County, south of San Antonio, on
January 5, 1923, Big Bill grew up in the hill country around Brady and
had been performing since 1938. By the late 1940s, he had been a staple

of San Antonio–area radio for almost a decade. Like Roger Miller's "Kansas City Star," he was well known in and around his hometown. He got stopped in parking lots and his barber told him jokes. He'd even made a few records for small labels, but knew that the future held nothing for him unless he got out of town. Shortly after Christmas 1950, he and his wife, Lila, locked up the house, packed his Nudie suits and his Gibson into their car, and headed for Nashville.

During Lister's first week in Nashville he met Joe Allison, who'd been a deejay in San Antonio before moving to Nashville's WMAK. Allison brought Lister backstage at the *Opry* to meet Hank and Jim Denny. Hank was sitting quietly by himself on one of the pews reserved for performers. He and Lister chitchatted and went out to the alley to smoke a cigarette. Hank clearly didn't tell Lister much about Jim Denny before the two met. Lister recalled:

> Show how naive I was, I didn't know who Denny was. He asked what I was doing, and I told him I'd come to Nashville to get on the *Opry*. I said, "I hear there are auditions over at WSM and some joker's supposed to listen to me over there." He kinda chuckled and said, "I wish you good luck." Joe had set up an audition for me the following week in Studio B at WSM, and I was sitting there with my guitar, and Jim come waltzing in. I said, "Jim, what're you doing here?" He said, "I'm the joker you gotta audition for."

Lister was caught in the hillbilly catch-22. The *Opry* wasn't interested because he didn't have a record contract, and record companies weren't interested because he wasn't on the *Opry*. Tex Ritter, who'd worked shows with Lister in San Antonio, took care of the record contract. "Tex came to town," says Lister, "and he asked if I'd talked to Dee Kilpatrick [at Capitol], and I said he'd turned me down. Tex said, 'Meet me at the office in thirty minutes,' and he told Dee, 'Sign this guy.' As soon as I got that contract I went back to WSM and showed it to Jim Denny. I said, 'I come to find out if you're a man of your word. I've got a Capitol contract, now what you gonna do?'"

Denny placed Lister on a Hank Williams tour, and persuaded Hank to let him guest a few times on his *Mother's Best* early morning show. Lister didn't have any inkling of it at the time, but he came to believe that Denny was helping Hank ease Audrey out of his radio schedule by giving him a supporting act that needed to be featured. It was rare now for Audrey to join the group on a tour. Occasionally she would fly to do a show, then drive with the group for a few days before flying home, but as 1951 wore on, her appearances grew fewer and fewer. As much as this improved the shows, it did nothing for those moments when Hank would try to hold Audrey close.

This was Lister's big chance. He soon found that life wasn't easy for a six-foot-seven-inch singing cowboy in the back of a touring sedan, but the memory of the discomfort later faded, leaving much fonder memories of the camaraderie, the hijinks, and the impromptu baseball games in the middle of nowhere. Travel was usually at night because it was cooler and there was less traffic, but there were often long distances between shows which would involve driving through the day, right up to show time. Before interstates and orbital freeways, the highways went straight through the center of town. "We'd stop to get gas," says Lister, "and at the same time, we'd get a gallon of milk and a dozen doughnuts or cupcakes. We didn't even have time to order hamburgers a lot of time. There were many weeks that we'd maybe check into a hotel twice. The rest of the time you're driving."

When Lister joined, Hank bought a second touring sedan. The biggest item of baggage was the string bass, which sat on top when it wasn't raining. The trunk was usually full of clothes, photos, and songbooks. The one amplifier was shared by Don Helms and Sammy Pruett. Summer months were hell, especially in heavy traffic. For a while, Hank had an air cooler fitted to his limo. The technology wasn't very complicated; a water tank was attached to the roof and a bat of gauze was fitted into the open window. Water was released from the tank by means of a cord, and leached into the gauze. The breeze then blew through the water-filled gauze and supposedly cooled the interior. It seemed to work for a while, but Audrey was pressuring Hank to wear a toupee, which made him hotter still. He shaved off what hair he had on the crown of his head and the toupee was fixed in place with spirit gum. Somewhere in Louisiana, with the temperature inside the car around a hundred degrees, Hank pulled the cord to flush more water into the cooler and the entire contents of the tank disgorged onto his head. He pulled off the toupee, threw it out the window, and told everyone it was the last time he was going to wear the damn thing. Then he junked the air cooler.

Hank's show would usually start at 8:00 p.m. Lister and the Drifting Cowboys warmed up the crowd. Bass player Howard Watts, who had replaced Hillous Butrum, did a little baggy-pants comedy as "Cedric Rainwater," then the band played a few tunes before Hank did the first half of his show. There'd be a short intermission when the Drifting Cowboys would work the crowd, selling photos and songbooks, and then Hank would play again until around 10:00 p.m. Hank would sometimes work three or four days in major centers with other *Opry* acts, but his drawing power was so strong that he didn't need costars to fill a hall. Eddy Arnold might have sold more records nationwide, but Hank was king in the South and Southwest. His only serious challenge came from Lefty Frizzell, so it was a surprise when A. V. Bamford placed the two on tour together in April 1951. Either of them could have filled the halls, so this would be, as writer Dan Cooper put it, "honky tonk's apex, the instant that symbolized the genre's zenith."

The rivalry between Hank and Lefty had simmered for a few months after Lefty broke through at the end of 1950. Hank could see little good in Lefty's style. Once, when he was holed up on a drinking spree with Johnnie Wright and Jack and Jim Anglin, Hank's guard slipped and he took aim at Lefty's singing. It was whiny and no good, he said, ranting on until the others grew sick of it and told him to shut up. Lefty wouldn't sustain a note or let it trail bluesily like Hank. He worried words and vowels, glissing up or down on a syllable. It was a style that shaped latter-day country singing. It was also a style that required a microphone, whereas Hank's full-throated delivery had been forged out of necessity when he sang without amplification.

Hank and Lefty met for the first time in Nashville shortly after Hank had done a radio interview with deejay Hugh Cherry. Hank and Cherry were sitting in Eddie DuBois' Key Club in Printer's Alley. As Cherry recalled to researcher Charles Wolfe:

Lefty came in by himself a little greased and sat down with us. Hank decided to feign displeasure and he started out by saying, "Here, boy, why don't you just stay down in Texas, this is my territory up here." Lefty got that great big smile on his face, and said, "Hank, the whole damn country is the back yard of both of us, can't you realize there's enough room for all of us?" Hank kinda smiled and said, "Well, I was just kidding. It's good to have a little competition. Makes me realize I gotta work harder than ever, and boy you're the best competition I ever had."

The Hank and Lefty road show started in Little Rock on April 1, 1951, and headed south through Monroe, Lousiana; Baton Rouge, Louisiana; and Corpus Christi, Texas; finishing in New Orleans. It came just as Lefty was considering an offer from the *Opry*. Talking about the tour in 1974, he said:

[Hank] had a way of influencing you. He could talk you into anything. We was on the road. I had "Always Late" and "Mom and Dad's Waltz" and "I Want to Be With You Always" on the charts. Hank said, "Lefty, what you need is the *Grand Ole Opry*." I said, "Hell, I just got a telegram from [music publisher] Hill & Range on having number one and number two, and I got maybe two more in there, and you say I need the *Grand Ole Opry*?" He said, "You got a hell of an argument."

Lefty briefly joined the *Opry* that July, but didn't stay.

Lefty said in an MGM Records documentary that Hank was stone cold sober throughout the tour:

I come in to Corpus Christi [April 5, 1951], and I brought in a bottle of bourbon and set it down in there. Hank and me was settin' around getting ready to do the show. I said, "Hey, I'm gonna have a shot. How about you?" He said, "If I was to have what you're fixin' to drink, I'd want another and first thing you know I'd be gone." I thought he was kidding, teasin' me. Found out later that he would have. When I saw that movie [*Your Cheatin' Heart*] it really made me feel bad, 'cause he was always late and always drunk, and I worked two weeks with him and he never sounded better. He was in good shape. But he didn't take a drink — and he put on a show. We flipped coins to see who would go on first. Dad [Naamon Frizzell] was still driving for us, and there's enough stories to fill a book there.

But he never told them.

"All Hank thought about," Lefty said later, "was writing. He recorded a number he wrote because I was having trouble with my better half called 'I'm Sorry For You, My Friend.' We'd swap songs we'd written." It seems very likely that the song Hank acquired from Lefty was "I Ain't Got Nothing but Time." Lefty listed a song of that title on a Hill & Range contract a few days before the tour began, and Hank logged it with Acuff-Rose on June 6, 1951. It's unclear what, if anything, Hank gave to Lefty. Between the show in Baton Rouge on April 3 and another show with Lefty in Corpus Christi two days later, Hank shot north by himself to revisit the scene of his first triumph, the Municipal Auditorium in Shreveport. Bluegrass star Mac Wiseman, then a *Hayride* regular, supported him. The atmosphere throughout the short tour was convivial. Hank, Lefty, and Big Bill Lister would get together in hotel rooms to play Jimmie Rodgers songs. Hank would stand in the wings while Lefty performed, and vice versa. It was the ultimate mark of respect.

After a short break, Hank went north on a tour of Canada. They played Ottawa on May 8, but a day or two later the wheels started to come off. Hank started drinking somewhere in Ontario, and reportedly fell offstage, aggravating the already serious problem with his back. Jim Denny rushed Carl Smith up to complete the tour, and Bill Lister was given the unenviable task of hauling Hank and a suitcase full of money back to Nashville. It was the first time he'd seen his boss disabled in that way. Says Lister,

> Coming back, we stopped one morning just after daylight, and I said, "Hank, you gotta have something to eat, son." He said, "Big un, I just cain't do this." I could understand. His eyes looked like watery fried eggs when he was in that shape, but I knew better than to let him wait in the car, so I just jumped up and paid the bill, and by the time I was outside, he was nowhere to be seen. In the middle of the next block, a big sign said "Cocktails" and I just broke into a dead run, and by the time I got there, he'd already had him one. I paid his bill and drug him back to the car. It just broke your heart, but I knew I had to get him home.

Lister carried on driving and got to the outskirts of Nashville around five in the morning. He stopped to call Audrey, to tell her to expect them shortly.

I said, "I'm at the edge of town, and I got Hank with me and he's in pretty bad shape. I just wanted you to be expecting us." She said, "I don't care what you do with the son of a bitch, just don't bring him out here," so I called Jim Denny, and Jim told me where to take him — the hospital out in Madison. Then I went by the studio and put the money in the safe, then around nine o'clock Audrey called me and wanted to know where her money was at. I said, "Lady, as far as I know you ain't got no damn money. I gave *Hank's* money to Jim."

From Madison, Hank probably went home but continued to mess up and was quickly transferred to the North Louisiana Sanatorium in Shreveport on May 21, 1951. When he was admitted he was complaining of acute back pain and mental worries, and had apparently been drinking for several days. Complete physical examinations under the direction of Dr. G. H. Cassity revealed the extent and nature of the degeneration of his spine, and arrangements were made to fit a lumbrosacral brace. Hank was discharged three days later, sober but still in pain, a pain that would — from this point on — scarcely ever leave him. The brace was uncomfortable. It was made of stainless steel and leather, and it made road travel unbearable, so increasingly and whenever feasible, Hank would fly to the starting point of a tour in a private plane, often a Beechcraft Bonanza piloted by Minnie Pearl's husband, Henry Cannon.

After his discharge from Shreveport, Hank appears to have rested up in Nashville for a few days before preparing for a Luke the Drifter session on the evening of Friday, June 1. The lead-off cut, "Ramblin' Man," was one of Hank's few minor-key compositions. A taut, edgy performance, it was sung rather than spoken, which made it more like a Hank Williams record (a judgment MGM came to share immediately after Hank's death when they reissued it under his name). Hank's keening falsetto was used to particularly good effect, and Harold Bradley's prominently mic'd acoustic guitar punctuated by Don Helms' steel guitar gave the record a folky flavor that wasn't entirely accidental. The Weavers' hit version of Leadbelly's "Goodnight Irene" had sparked a short-lived folk music craze, and it's possible that Hank saw the folk craze as an opportunity for Luke the Drifter.

The second Luke the Drifter cut, "Pictures from Life's Other Side," was a Victorian morality fable. The arrangement was credited to Hank, but it was a much earlier song. Some researchers date it to around 1880, and credit it to John B. Vaughan, a composer and singing-school teacher from Athens, Georgia; others credit it to a gospel songwriter named Charles E. Baer. It was first recorded as a country song in 1926, and it's hard to know which of the twenty or so earlier versions was the one Hank heard. His recitation showed that constant travel had done nothing to change his pronunciation. "Poor" was still "purr," just as it had been on his first session, and "picture" was still "pitcher."

"I've Been Down That Road Before" was another dose of the sage advice that Luke the Drifter seemed endlessly capable of dispensing — and Hank Williams seemed just as capable of ignoring. It was perhaps the most directly biographical song Hank ever wrote, and leaves us guessing at the incidents that inspired it.

The last cut, "I Dreamed about Mama Last Night," was a recitation that Fred Rose credited to himself, although it was actually a poem, "The Mother Watch," by British-born poet Edgar Guest, who worked for years at the *Detroit Free Press*. It came from Guest's 1925 anthology, *Mother,* and it was especially ironic that Rose chose it because it was rooted in an idyllic childhood that was nowhere close to his own experience.

After the session, Hank eased himself back into his public appearance schedule. His July 4 date for 1951 was at a park in Huntingdon, West Virginia. Then, on Sunday, July 15, he was the star of the Hank Williams Homecoming in Montgomery, sponsored by the Jaycees. There was an early afternoon show at the Veterans Hospital, a parade, then a 3:00 p.m. show at the Montgomery Agricultural Coliseum, known as the Cow Coliseum. It was the first music event staged there, so there were inevitable problems with the public address system. Hank headed a cast that included Hank Snow, Chet Atkins (billed that day as a "Teenage Tantalizer"), the Carter Family, and Braxton Schuffert.

For some reason, Hank didn't have a guitar, so just before the first show his cousin Walter McNeil drove him to French's Music store to borrow one for the afternoon. He came back out to the car, sat in the front seat quietly for a while, then said, "You know, I tried to buy a guitar on credit there once when I was comin' up and they wouldn't have nothin' to do with me. Now they want to give me one." It could have been a moment to savor, but Hank always saw the darker side. The city, which had once treated him as a worthless drunk, was now extending its embrace, but Hank knew well that it could be as quickly withdrawn.

Before the show, Hank took the band to eat at his favorite barbecue stand, run by a black couple, and treated everyone to barbecue sandwiches. Bill Lister remembered:

> Just as we were leaving, Hank was fixing to get back in the car, the lady come out and said, "Oh, Mr. Williams, Mr. Williams, you dropped this." He said, "Oh my goodness." It was his bill clip. He told her, "Well, I appreciate that," and he took the money clip off, put it in his hand, put that money back in that lady's hand and said, "Thank you," and left. Hank didn't drop it accidentally. That was his way to give them old people a little bit of what he had. Hank helped a lot of people like that and gets very little credit for it. He was just thinking back to when he'd be hard up for a fifteen-cent sandwich.

At Hank's insistence, Lilly was presented with a gold watch by the Jaycees. Her smile, as she posed for the cameras, was exactly like Hank's. It was a chance for him to acknowledge in front of nine thousand paying attendees the role she had played in getting his career started. Hank could also celebrate a partial family truce held in his honor. Audrey didn't squabble with Lilly, and Lilly didn't squabble with Lon, who'd come from McWilliams for the occasion, but when Lon tried to hold his grandson, Audrey snatched him back.

Braxton remembered sitting backstage at the Coliseum when a kid with a guitar strode up to Hank and asked if he could sing a couple of numbers to the crowd. At first Hank declined, but then, recognizing shades of himself fifteen years earlier, agreed. "This guy said, 'All I do is sing your songs, just let me sing one of your songs,'" said Braxton. "Hank said, 'Well, what d'you want to do?' This guy said, 'I want to do "Hey, Good Lookin'."' Hank said, 'Well, that's my current song.' This guy said, 'Aw, Hank, let me sing it.' Hank said, 'Go 'head, I'll sing something else.'"

Hank's manager, Bill England, negotiated the show with the Jaycees, and he remembered it as a fiasco because of the poor PA, although his attitude could have stemmed from the fact that he and Hank were heading for a parting of the ways. The Homecoming was one of his last acts on Hank's behalf, and they eventually parted backstage at the Ryman. They'd both seen it coming. WSM made England an offer to return to his old job, selling airtime, and he gratefully accepted.

Hank stayed overnight in Montgomery after the Homecoming. Back at the boardinghouse, he took off his shirt to show everyone his new brace. Swarms of people were around him pitching songs or trying to sell him something. The next day, he headed down the oh so familiar Highway 31 toward the Gulf for a string of personal appearances that started in Biloxi, and he continued on through his old haunts in southern Louisiana and eastern Texas. He then returned to Nashville for the *Opry* and to prepare for another recording session, the first under a contract renewal dated July 5 that extended his MGM term for another two years and upped his royalty from two to three cents a single.

The July 25, 1951, session was held between 7:15 and 10:35 p.m., and the studio was stiflingly hot. Air conditioners and fans created too much noise, so there was no alternative but to sweat it out. Another Acuff-Rose songwriter, Helen Hudgins, was there that night. "Hank had his shirt unbuttoned all the way," she told researcher John Rumble, "and he was absolutely soaking wet. It seemed that all he was . . . was voice. It came up from I don't know where." Only three songs from the July 25 session were deemed issuable by Fred Rose. The most unusual was "Lonesome Whistle," a title truncated in the interests of jukebox cards from "(I Heard That) Lonesome Whistle." Credited to Hank and Jimmie Davis, it was one of a long line of prison songs.

Davis was something of an elder statesman in Hank's eyes. After cutting his first record for KWKH's "Doggone" label, he'd become a Jimmie Rodgers disciple. He'd made some wonderfully libidinous blues for RCA Victor, like "Tom Cat and Pussy Blues" and "Red Nightgown Blues," but by the time he signed with Decca in 1934, he was cleaning up his act and his image. His biggest hit on Decca, "You Are My Sunshine," was one he claimed to have written, all evidence to the contrary. He certainly popularized it, though. After a political career in Shreveport, Davis ran for governor in 1944, and won in the face of a viciously negative advertising campaign that tried to make capital out of his old smutty records. His opponent also maintained that Davis couldn't be in favor of segregation, as he claimed, because he owned a "colored honky tonk" in California. After Davis' first term as governor (he stood again and was reelected in 1960), he returned to Shreveport, and it was probably there that Hank met him. There's a grainy photo of them; Hank has the grin that he usually reserved for the times he was getting plastered, and Davis looks none too sober. Three songs are jointly credited to Hank

Williams and Jimmie Davis, but it's unclear how or when they wrote them. On one of the *Mother's Best* shows, recorded between January and March 1951, Hank tells his audience that he's going fishing with Jimmie Davis next week. Perhaps they'd written the songs then or during Hank's brief return to Shreveport in April.

"Lonesome Whistle," like "Ramblin' Man," had folk overtones, and gained what impact it had from the way Hank grafted the sound of a train whistle onto the word "lonesome." It was shipped on September 24, coupled with another song from the July 25 session, "Crazy Heart." The latter was a song that Fred Rose had written with one of his Tin Pan Alley buddies, Maurice Murray Fisher. The single reportedly sold one hundred thousand in its first week, but "Crazy Heart" pegged out at number four and "Lonesome Whistle" reached number eight, spending just two weeks on the charts. Both songs were covered for the pop market, and Guy Lombardo dented the top twenty with "Crazy Heart," underscoring the fact that it was better suited to a palm court orchestra than Hank Williams.

Two other songs were recorded at the July 25 session. "I'd Still Want You" was another bleak commentary on Hank's continuing need for Audrey as she closed off her heart to him, while "Baby, We're Really in Love" was tried and abandoned. Rose wanted to get some more songs in the can before Hank went off on the ten-week Hadacol Caravan, so he scheduled another Friday night session for August 10. Only two cuts from that session were released; the first was the rerecording of "Baby, We're Really in Love," and the other was "Half As Much." Rose played the piano to flesh out the rhythm section, and — for the first and only time on a Hank Williams record — there was a flash of solo barroom piano at the very end of "Half As Much."

The "Williams" in the composer credit of "Half As Much" was not Hank but his buddy from Shreveport, Curley Williams. On September 13, 1951, some two months after Hank's session, Curley recorded it for Columbia. Hank wasn't too interested in touching the song, but Rose insisted that he cut it. Like "Crazy Heart," it boiled down to nothing. Rose wanted to give Curley a head start, so Curley's version was released first, on November 2. When Hank's version was finally released on March 28, 1952, it became a number two hit. That success ensured that the pop cover versions soon appeared, and the pop charts were where the song belonged. Rosemary Clooney took it to number seven. "Later," remembered Curley's steel guitarist, Boots Harris, "Mitch Miller said to Wesley, 'Ol' Hank's done it again, hasn't he?' and Wesley said, 'That was *Curley* Williams who wrote "Half As Much,"' and Mitch Miller said, 'Who's Curley Williams?' and Wesley said, 'A guy that's been on your label about seven years.'"

"Baby, We're Really in Love" was released on November 23, 1951. It was as good as any other bouncy mid- to fast-tempo number that Hank had released, but it stalled at number four. Perhaps the competition was stronger; perhaps repetition was setting in. Hank's 1951 MGM royalties were down from $22,574 in 1950 to $20,224, despite the success of "Cold, Cold Heart" earlier in the year. The declining numbers might have been the reason Hank was trying other people's songs. He was still writing as prolifically as ever, pitching songs to almost every artist he met — all of which flopped. "I Can't Escape from You" went to Rusty Gabbard and Ray Price. "Countryfied" and "The Little House We Built Just o'er the Hill" went to Big Bill Lister, and "Me and My Broken Heart" and "There's Nothing As Sweet As My Baby" went to newcomer Carl Smith. Hank and George Morgan's brother wrote "A Stranger in the Night" for Morgan, and Little Jimmy Dickens tackled the bruisingly sarcastic "I Wish You Didn't Love Me So Much." Jimmie Davis recorded the other two songs he'd written with Hank, "Bayou Pon-Pon" and "Forever Is a Long, Long Time."

Fred Rose, meanwhile, was producing acts so prolifically for MGM that it's hard to see how he found time to work with Hank and run a pubishing company. Between March and June 1951, MGM released roughly one hundred records, and Rose produced nineteen of those. But, just as Hank couldn't write a hit for anyone else, so Fred Rose couldn't produce one for anyone else. The records he cut with the Louvin Brothers have lasted well, but they flopped on release, as did the records he produced on Al Rogers, Carl "Mr. Sunshine" Swanson, Hal White, Gene McGhee, and all the others.

Another of Hank's attempts to make a little money on the side was his booklet *Hank Williams Tells How to Write Folk and Western Music to Sell*. It was published in September 1951 and would have been very interesting if Hank had written a word of it. His major contributions were to put his name and face on the front, and narrate the radio spots. "I set down and started to writing," he said with his salesman's oily charm, "but pretty soon I decided I needed some he'p." That help extended to letting his cowriter, Jimmy Rule, author the entire booklet. Rule was a fifty-year-old math teacher at a local private school who wrote songs on the side, but he had yet to write any folk or western music that had sold. He'd had a hand in a number of pop songs, like Perry Como's first record, "Goodbye Sue," and a wartime saber-rattler, "Let's Sing a Hymn to G.I. Jim," but he had not given up his day job. *Hank Williams Tells How to Write Folk and Western Music to Sell* is full of solid advice for the budding songwriter but it holds little or no insight into Hank Williams.

Toward the end, the booklet lists the titles and publishers of two rhyming dictionaries, but no one remembers Hank sitting at home or in the touring sedan with the *New Rhyming Dictionary and Poet's Handbook* on his lap. Hank's lengthy radio spots were more interesting than the book. As always when he was selling something, he put a little humor into his pitch. WSM announcer Grant Turner was the straight man, and mentioned that Hank's photo was on the front of the book. "Yes, Grant," said Hank. "If any of the folks are bothered by crows gittin' in their corn, it might come in handy to scar' them critters away." The twenty-page booklet sold for one dollar and was marketed through the border station XEDM, in Nogales, Mexico. "It'll be a blessin' to you," said Hank in conclusion. Rule continued writing folk and western music that didn't sell, and died in January 2003 at age 101.

In October 1951, Hank pitched a third song to Big Bill Lister. The chart books have no entry for Lister, but his record of "Beer Drinking Blues" had sold well. "We didn't get no radio play on beer drinking songs," says Lister, "but they was killers on the jukebox, so every session I had to do at least one beer drinking song." Capitol's West Coast–based chief of country A&R, Ken Nelson, scheduled a session for Lister on Friday, October 26. "I told Hank I needed a beer drinkin' song," says Lister, "and he said, 'Don't worry 'bout it, Big un, I got you covered. I got one that's hotter'n a pistol.'" One other published Hank Williams song, "I Can't Escape from You," had hinted at his problem with alcohol ("A jug of wine to numb my mind"), but the song he gave to Lister, "There's a Tear in My Beer," was an unambiguous celebration of getting plastered ("I'm gonna keep drinkin' until I'm petrified.... I'm gonna keep drinkin' 'til I can't move a toe.... I'm gonna keep drinkin' 'til I can't even think"). Hank cut a demo on the night before the session, right after he'd finished prerecording some radio shows. It had a singalong chorus like the best drinking songs, and was perhaps the strongest song he'd farmed out. He knew he couldn't risk cutting it himself, but Ken Nelson saw the potential and agreed to record it.

After the session, Lister threw the demo acetate, which had no markings on it, into a box of records at his house. At some point between Christmas and New Year, he reconciled himself to the inevitable and moved back to San Antonio. Hank was more or less off the road by then, and his troupe had disbanded. The acetate went back to San Antonio with the Listers and sat out in their yard under a tarp for a few years before being moved up to the loft where, as Lister says, it's hot enough to fry eggs in July. It was discovered during the mid-1980s when Lister was cleaning house. By then, Lister's son did occasional gun work for Hank Jr., and the next time Junior came to San Antonio, Lister presented him with the acetate. "Here's one they ain't never heard your daddy do," he told him. Hank Jr. took the acetate back to Nashville and, in September 1988, overdubbed himself onto it — a thirty-nine-year-old man duetting with his twenty-eight-year-old father. "There's a Tear in My Beer" finally became a hit, helped in no small measure by a video that defied any jaw not to drop. It merged footage of father and son in a dream sequence. Hank Jr. was shot against a neutral backing and was superimposed onto high-grade performance footage of his father. Video engineers slowed down the footage of Hank Sr. to match the tempo of "There's a Tear in My Beer," then new lip movements were "pasted on" from an actor lip-synching the song. Junior was then superimposed over the four thousand frames that made up the forty-six seconds of "duet" footage. The result sent chills up Hank Jr.'s spine — and many others' besides. Hank Jr. gave Bill Lister a percentage of the record's revenue, brought him to Nashville to appear on TNN, and awarded him a gold record. It was a sweet moment for Lister, who had exited the business in the midfifties, concluding that no one cared about six-foot-seven-inch singing cowboys anymore.

The last good year for the ol' Drifting Cowboy was capped that fall when Hank, Bill Lister, the Drifting Cowboys, and Minnie Pearl took part in the Hadacol Caravan. For the first time since 1943, Hank was to play in a medicine show, but he wasn't going to bump around the boondocks playing off the back of a flatbed truck; he was to travel first-class in a fleet of Pullman cars keeping company with the country's biggest stars and a troupe of dancing girls. He was to play to hundreds of thousands of people over the course of six weeks. It was to be the last and greatest medicine show.

The more you earn, the less you learn
To relax-ez vous
Dean Martin, "Relaxez Vous"

THE HADDY-COLE BOUNCE

*H*ANK had been surrounded all his professional life by snake-oil salesmen who used more or less unregulated airtime to sell everything from absolution to job lots of live chicks shipped by mail. He acquired a little arsenal of come-ons and self-deprecating jokes that he would trot out when he was in the business of selling something. "Friends," he would often say, concluding his pitch, "I don't need the money, but the folks I owe it to need it awful bad."

Good as Hank was, Senator Dudley J. LeBlanc could make him and most other salesmen look like rank amateurs. Dudley Joseph LeBlanc was born in Youngsville, Louisiana, on August 16, 1894, and claimed to trace his ancestry back to René LeBlanc in Longfellow's *Evangeline*. He grew up speaking nothing but French, and never lost his Cajun accent. LeBlanc was fiercely proud of his heritage and eventually published a book on Acadian culture. After graduating from Southwestern Louisiana Institute, he became a salesman for a shoe company, working the same patch in north Louisiana as Huey P. Long. LeBlanc and Long were both formidable salesmen, and came to mistrust, then detest each other as only rival salesmen can.

After World War I, LeBlanc got his introduction to selling patent medicines when he represented Wine of Cardui, fetchingly called a "woman's tonic." His first brush with politics came in 1924 when he stood as a candidate for the state legislature in Vermilion Parish, and won. This was at a time when the hot issues of the day included care of

Confederate veterans. In 1932, he stood for governor, but lost. LeBlanc then concentrated on his own patent medicines, starting with Happy Day Headache Powder, a concoction that, in common with most of his remedies, contained a stiff dose of laxative.

In 1942, after another unsuccessful stab at the governorship and the Public Service Commission, LeBlanc fell ill with beriberi, and was cured with vitamin B_1 compounds. With the unquenchable enthusiasm of the autodidact, he set out to learn everything he could about vitamins, and then began distilling his own compound in the family barn. It was a mixture of vitamins, minerals, honey and — not least — 12 percent alcohol. It was dubbed HADACOL, a rough acronym from HAppy DAy CO., topped off with an *L* for LeBlanc. Its alcohol content was roughly the same as wine, but at $3.50 it was four times as expensive and immeasurably more foul-tasting so that people would believe it was doing them some good. With many dry counties still in the South, Hadacol was the closest to a nip that many folk out on the rural routes could get — from a bottle with a label on it, at least.

Hadacol went on the market in 1945 after LeBlanc had tested it on his cattle, himself, and his neighbors. Sales were static for a while as he rekindled his political ambitions, becoming a state senator in 1948. During this second stint in politics, he was instrumental in helping to pass the Old Age Pension bill, then used his newfound credibility among older citizens to sell them Hadacol. LeBlanc more or less introduced saturation advertising to the South. His newspaper ads were rife with testimonials. "I have been suffering from nervousness, weak spells, lack of energy, and never felt like working," wrote Mrs. L. E. Mitchell from Wadsworth, Texas, in March 1949. "After taking Hadacol, I am doing my work better than I have in years. I don't have weak spells; I eat well; and I sleep like a log. My little girl didn't eat very much. After taking Hadacol, she eats two helpings every meal. We just can't praise it enough. I just wish more people knew how wonderful Hadacol is." Others claimed to be cured of cancer, epilepsy, heart trouble, strokes, and tuberculosis, and LeBlanc published their claims until the Federal Trade Commission stepped in. The advertisements concluded that the good senator "has served his people in public life faithfully and well. In private life, he brings you a service which is appreciated by suffering humanity — HADACOL." At first, the advertising was designed to devour pretax profits, but it quickly began to assume a life of its own.

Early in 1949, LeBlanc hooked up with Murray Nash, then head of Mercury Records' southern division. "I asked LeBlanc what was in Hadacol," said Nash, "and he told me there was enough alcohol to make people feel good and enough laxative for a good movement." Nash's commercial antennae began twitching, and he cut two Hadacol paeans — one for the country market, Bill Nettles' "Hadacol Boogie," which charted in June 1949, and another for the rhythm and blues market, Professor Longhair's "Hadacol Bounce." The publicity generated by "Hadacol Boogie" convinced LeBlanc that country music was an effective medium for promoting his product, so he was primed when Mack Hedrick of WSM approached him with the idea of sponsoring Hank Williams' *Health and Happiness* shows in October 1949. Even then, Hank was just a bit player on LeBlanc's stage. In 1950, LeBlanc spent more than one million dollars a month on advertising, making him the nation's second-largest advertiser after Coca-Cola. His enterprise grew to the point that Hadacol was shipped by a wholly owned fleet of trucks from the plants in Lafayette, where the employees were now dressed in white starched uniforms to simulate a lab environment (a far cry from the barn in which Hadacol had been concocted). Sales were astronomical at the peak of the operation in 1950 and 1951.

LeBlanc always said that the 4 S's of salesmanship were Saturation, Sincerity, Simplicity, and Showmanship, and with the last in mind, he staged the Hadacol Caravan. Murray Nash said that he gave LeBlanc the idea based upon a hillbilly jamboree he had organized in Tampa; LeBlanc insisted that the idea came to him at 4:30 one morning in Abbeville, Louisiana. The first Hadacol Caravan ran in August 1950. Hank Williams wasn't aboard; the headliners were Roy Acuff, Connie Boswell, Burns and Allen, Chico Marx, and Mickey Rooney. Researcher Floyd Martin Clay described how LeBlanc skillfully used the Caravan to promote Hadacol in areas where he hadn't secured distribution. He bought heavy advertising on radio in the form of a contest: a well-known song was played and the audience was invited to send in a card with the title. If they were correct, they got a voucher for a free bottle of Hadacol. Of course, Hadacol was nowhere to be found, but druggists were now getting a steady stream of requests for it and pestering the jobbers to carry it. Then the advertising for the Caravan kicked in, with admission restricted to those carrying Hadacol box tops. By this point, the Hadacol trucks were waiting outside the city limits, and the jobbers were begging for the product.

The 1951 Caravan was the largest show of its kind ever staged. The mainstay of the bill was to be Hank Williams, backed by Minnie Pearl, comedian Candy Candido, emcee Emil Perra, juggler Lee Marks, a house band led by Tony Martin, a troupe of dancers, and twelve clowns. Other star attractions were to be added at various points along the route. Cesar Romero was on the first seven dates. Jack Benny and Rochester, Milton Berle, Bob Hope, Jimmy Durante, Rudy Vallee, Carmen Miranda, Dick Haymes, and Jack Dempsey were all conscripted for one or two dates. Admission was one Hadacol box top for children, two for adults. There were prizes for the kids and "reserved seating for coloreds." Most shows were preceded by a parade.

By this point, LeBlanc had a hidden agenda: he wanted to sell Hadacol, and he wanted to use the publicity generated by the Caravan as a base to launch another stab at the Louisiana governorship. His photo loomed larger than any other in his advertisements, and he made an appearance on every show. He knew that demand had peaked, and he knew that the Food and Drug Administration, the American Medical Association, and the Liquor Control Board were sniffing around. More than that, LeBlanc's ruinous advertising budget meant that the corporation lost two million dollars during the second quarter of 1951 alone. With low cunning, he used the second Caravan as a smokescreen to disguise the true financial picture and snare potential buyers.

Inevitably, the Caravan began in Lafayette. Hank and Bill Lister went into the senator's office before the tour started. They noted the shelf full of Old Forester whiskey with a subscript on the label that read, "Bottled Especially for Sen. Dudley J. LeBlanc, Lafayette, Louisiana." Hank and Bill Lister were impressed. A shelf full of premium whiskey with "Bottled Especially for Hank Williams" on the label was alternately Hank's darkest nightmare and his fondest dream.

The Caravan was scheduled to run from August 14 to October 2, although it had been agreed that Hank and Minnie Pearl would miss the Saturday night shows so that they could fly back to Nashville to meet their *Opry* commitments. LeBlanc had spared no expense in mounting the shows. He budgeted $500,000 for talent and another $750,000 for promotion. A fleet of fifteen Pullman cars was leased, and arrangements were made to transfer the fleet from one railroad company's engines to another as the show made its way across eighteen states. Fine food was laid on for the performers, laundry facilities had been prearranged, and the logistics of setting up and tearing down had been rehearsed with military precision.

For most of the performers, this was their first contact with Hank Williams and his audience. The dancers had been recruited from an agency in Los Angeles; they'd never heard of Hank, but by the end they were standing in the wings every night as he performed. The reception even surprised Hank. He knew he was the king of the honky-tonks, but now he had stadium crowds eating out of his hand, and legit entertainers working as his supporting acts. Even the Drifting Cowboys were surprised. They had always thought of themselves as working a lowly rung of the entertainment ladder; now they recognized the magnitude of Hank's stardom. The chorus girls, used to most stars' frosty hauteur, were also surprised at Hank's willingness to do the shake 'n' howdy. He would sign autographs for hours. No one was turned away.

One week into the tour, the show touched down in Montgomery. Braxton Schuffert remembers getting a call from Hank's mother asking him to meet Hank on the Hadacol train, which was parked down at the railroad yard:

> He was sittin' there, and he had the seat in front of him pushed forward and he was sitting with his boots up on the other seat. I set down beside him. I said, "Hank, how you doin' boy?" He said, "I'm doing no good at all." I said, "What's the matter?" I seen them movie stars walking by outside the window. "All them pretty movie stars on this train, Hank." He said, "I don't have nothin' to do with them. They think they're better than I am."

Then Hank got to what was probably the true cause of his foul mood. "He pulled out a pink check about six inches long and three inches high," said Braxton. "It was for something like seventy-five hundred dollars. He said, 'Ever'body on this train has got one of these.'" The paychecks had bounced.

Hank and Minnie Pearl eventually forced the issue of payment by threatening not to return from Nashville unless they were paid, and for a few weeks LeBlanc managed to juggle enough funds into the payroll account to keep everyone happy. From Montgomery, the show moved into Georgia. Walter McNeil drove Lilly to the show in Columbus so that she could savor Hank's triumph once more. Then the Caravan swung up through the Carolinas and into Virginia. After the show in Roanoke on Friday, August 31, Hank flew back to Nashville for the *Opry* and to sign the papers for his spread in Williamson County. The new toy did little to mollify Audrey, who had spent her life trying to get off the farm.

Band members recall that Hank often came back from his weekend furloughs distraught and angry, hinting broadly that all was not well on Franklin Road. There were rumors that Audrey was keeping company with other men, and those rumors gnawed at Hank, despite the fact that he was trying hard to start an affair with one of the dancing girls. He used his failing marriage as an excuse for coming on to her, giving the impression that he wanted to get involved. He took her shopping, bought her some cowboy boots, and squired her to clubs, but she wouldn't succumb.

"When we got to Louisville, Kentucky," said Big Bill Lister, "Dick Haymes said to his wife, 'Well, we're finally getting out of the sticks — the hillbillies won't be tearing them up now.' What he didn't know was that Louisville was a second home to a lot of *Opry* acts; somebody played there every Sunday afternoon on the way to somewhere." Bob Hope joined the show for two appearances in Louisville and Cincinnati. Hank had been closing the show up to that point, but LeBlanc asked him to take second billing and Hank agreed. To make things as difficult as possible for Hope, Hank reached back for something extra and took encore after encore. "That crowd wasn't gonna turn him loose," says Lister, "and LeBlanc was trying to introduce Bob Hope over all this hollerin' and clappin'. They got the crowd quieted down, and somewhere in his wardrobe Bob Hope had this old hat that he'd used in *Paleface,* and he wore that and just stood there, and when the place quieted down he said, 'Just call me Hank Hope.'" When he came off, Hope found LeBlanc and told him that he wouldn't follow Hank Williams again. Hank could afford to smile inwardly, but — being Hank — he probably smiled outwardly as well because a triumph was for nothing if not to be savored. When LeBlanc told him he was topping the bill, Hank said, "That's fine. Just pay me what you're paying Hope."

Lister and everyone else in Hank's entourage had less charitable memories of Milton Berle, who appeared on the show in St. Louis. Uncle

Miltie, Lister recalls, had offered to emcee the entire show in addition to performing his usual schtick:

> He had an ego big as all outdoors, and when Dick Haymes was doing "Old Man River," Milton Berle had a red bandanna around his head and stood out behind Dick Haymes and just ruined the man's act. Nobody deserves that. Uncle Miltie had already been out and done his thing and now he was ruining everybody else's act. I told Hank, "If that joker comes out doing that when we're out there, he's really gonna mess things up. If he wants a good laugh, I'm gonna get this ol' guitar and crown him with it." Hank said, "If you do, I'll buy you any guitar you want," but the word circulated around and Milton's manager got him plumb offstage somewhere.

On Friday, September 14, the movable feast touched down in Wichita, Kansas, for a show designed to coincide with the Frontier Days Rodeo festival. A second show was laid on in the early hours to accommodate those who had just gotten off work at the aircraft plant. Hank and Minnie Pearl flew back to Nashville later that night and rejoined the troupe in Oklahoma City on Sunday. Flying back to Oklahoma City with Minnie and her husband, Henry Cannon, Hank asked Henry to pull his guitar out of the baggage when they stopped to refuel, then wrote a song called "Heart of a Devil, Face of a Saint." Clearly, not a happy weekend.

Over that same weekend, Dudley LeBlanc had sold Hadacol to the Tobey Maltz Company in New York. He announced the sale in Dallas on Monday, September 17, just before the show scheduled for the Cotton Bowl. "The next morning we were having breakfast," remembered Bill Lister, "and Hank asked the senator, 'What did you sell Hadacol for?' He meant, 'Why did you sell it?' but the senator leaned across the table and said, 'Eight and a half million dollars,' and our jaws just dropped to the floor." Jaws dropped again when the performers were handed their final paychecks and tried to cash them. Once again, LeBlanc hadn't juggled enough money into his account to cover payroll.

The caravan, so huge and unwieldy, was torn down in the space of hours. Everyone said their hurried good-byes. Some of the chorus line, who had been living for free on the train and sending their ninety-dollar paychecks back home, ended up in Juarez and had to ride a cattle car back to Los Angeles. Hank flew back to Nashville, and flew Don Helms and Sammy Pruett to Lafayette to pick up the limos. He gave Jerry Rivers and Howard Watts train tickets back to Nashville.

In fact, LeBlanc saw no more than $250,000 for Hadacol. Payments of half a million dollars a month from future profits were called for but weren't made because there were no future profits — only liens, overdue bills, returned shipments, and FTC and Liquor Control Board suits. LeBlanc exculpated himself neatly by saying, "If you sell a cow and the cow dies, you can't do anything to a man for that." He'd sidestepped some potentially damaging fallout, but was tagged as a loser and once again failed in his 1952 bid to become governor. Hadacol was officially declared bankrupt at the height of the campaign.

The tour was supposed to have ended back in Baton Rouge on October 2. Hank had also scheduled a date in Biloxi on October 3 and had committed to perform at the Mississippi-Louisiana Exposition in Vicksburg, Mississippi, on the same day. No one now remembers how he filled the two vacant weeks at the end of the tour, but when he played the *Opry* on October 6 he told the audience that he was "entertaining at home next week for the first time in nine weeks," suggesting that he had filled in the dates at short notice.

On the weekend after the wheels came off the Hadacol Caravan, Hank was photographed backstage at the *Opry* signing a motion-picture contract. His uneasy dance with the legit entertainment world that had started when Tony Bennett covered "Cold, Cold Heart" was now acquiring an unstoppable momentum. The attention left Hank profoundly uneasy. Frank Walker had come down from New York for the MGM Pictures signing. He, Wesley Rose, and Jim Denny circled predatorily around their meal ticket, cigars in hand, as Hank committed himself to a deal for what the local paper called "top quality motion pics." Walker made a point of telling the press that this was the first time anyone had ever been signed to do motion pictures without a screen test or audition. Hank had a keener sense of his limitations than his handlers, and had never cared to capitalize on the link between MGM Records and MGM Pictures. He was happier telling people that the picture division was courting him, all the while keeping them at bay. Inevitably and inexorably, though, the pressure grew. Hank probably read in *Billboard* that his fellow MGM Records act, Billy Eckstine, had been signed to *Skirts*

Away, and all of his heroes, like Roy Acuff, Ernest Tubb, Jimmie Davis, and particularly Gene Autry, had made motion pictures. Even so, Hank had reservations.

Basic economics weighed on Hank's mind as he rebuffed MGM. He could make more money on the road than if he were tied up week after week in Hollywood. Soon after he arrived at the *Opry* he had put his band on salary rather than a per-gig fee, which assured him of having his pickers on call, but also meant that he was committed to paying them regardless of whether they worked. A deeper concern was Hank's sure knowledge that he was getting out of his depth, but in holding out, he only dug a deeper hole for himself. When the offer was tabled, MGM Pictures not only offered to forego screen tests but guaranteed to place him right away in costar billing roles. *Billboard* reported that the movies would "not [be] in the horse opera category," and that Joe Pasternak of MGM had already offered Hank a costarring role in an upcoming Esther Williams movie, *Peg o' My Heart.* He was offered a four-year deal, and no picture was to take more than four weeks of his time. The salary guarantee was between three thousand and five thousand dollars a week, with a ten-thousand-dollar guarantee per picture. Tellingly, at the signing ceremony, Hank wasn't smiling. He knew he didn't belong in *Peg o' My Heart.*

Hank still wasn't smiling when he went to meet Pasternak in California. Pasternak asked him to stand up and turn around, and the hair rose on the back of his neck. "He said it was like he was for sale," said Don Helms afterward. The motion-picture deal also meant that Hank had to wear toupees again. The remaining hair on the crown of his head was shaved off yet again, and he went for several fittings. In Pasternak's office, Jim Denny, himself the owner of a lot of hair that nature hadn't given him, told Hank to take his hat off. Pasternak saw the toupee and asked Hank if he had any hair. "Hell, yes," he said, "I got a dresser drawer full of it." Hank left with some scripts for his consideration.

A few weeks later, the legit entertainment world beckoned again. CBS-TV offered a spot on *The Perry Como Show* for Wednesday, November 14. He would have to stay a week in New York for rehearsals. Bill Lister, who rode up with Hank, said:

> Perry Como was just like he was on television. Relaxed, a real likable guy. We spent most of our time shooting pool. They had

one scene where they had a pool table. While the McGuire Sisters and everybody else on the show was getting all their timing down to just a gnat's hair, Perry Como, Hank, Sammy Pruett, and myself would all shoot pool. That show was sponsored by Chesterfield, and it had a little jingle that Perry Como sang, and he wanted Hank to join him and do it with him, but Hank couldn't get it. Finally, Hank said, "Well, we'll just have to give up on that." And when we got out of New York City a ways, driving along, Hank kind of chuckled to himself, and he said, "I didn't come all the way from south Alabama to sing a commercial."

On the following week's show, Como donned a cowboy hat, sang "Hey, Good Lookin'," then apologized to Hank.

Hank felt as out of place in New York as he had in Hollywood. He was always the first to feel condescension and reacted to it with a mixture of truculence and boorishness. "If you don't like folk music," he once told an interviewer, "stay away from my shows. I can't stand classical music, but I don't tell the world about it."

During rehearsals for the Como show, Hank took time out to do an interview at *Billboard* in which he explained how careful he was to space his releases properly, and follow what he called a "jump tune" with a blues or ballad. The piece also mentioned that Hank was scheduled to do a spot on Ed Sullivan's *Talk of the Town,* although, as far as we know, he never appeared. His rancor toward Milton Berle was still bubbling near the surface, though. He told the *Billboard* columnist that he had been offered a spot on Berle's television show but had turned it down. "The last time I worked with him, there like to have been a killing," he said with a frankness that must have surprised the columnist.

On November 9, possibly anticipating a flood of orders from Como viewers, MGM issued Hank's first album, *Hank Williams Sings.* It was released in three formats: ten-inch LP; four 78s packaged in an album; or four 45s in an album. It was axiomatic that country LPs didn't sell, and the notion of the single as a trailer for the hugely more profitable album was still more than ten years away. Rose used Hank's first album as a dump site for oddball tracks that hadn't sold elsewhere. With the exception of "Wedding Bells," the tracks were the dogs of Hank's catalog, like "I've Just Told Mama Goodbye," "Wealth Won't Save Your Soul," and

"Six More Miles." Rose's thinking in recycling these oldies but not-so-goodies was paraphrased by *Billboard*: "The release of an album [of eight new sides], they feel, would spread jockey and juke plays too thinly instead of getting the concentrated push on the single record."

For Hank, the contrast between the tawdry glamor of network television out of New York and the mundane grind of personal appearances in the South was made all the more apparent by the fact that a week before the Como show he was appearing at the Wagon Wheel Club between Opelika and Auburn, Alabama. Hank almost certainly felt more at home at the Wagon Wheel than in New York or Hollywood, but if he found any incongruity playing the Wagon Wheel one week and Como's show the next, he didn't talk about it. But Hank didn't talk about anything substantive very much, anyway.

One month after the Como show, and just a few days before a scheduled operation on his back, Hank returned to the Castle studio to cut the last of the five hugely prolific recording sessions he'd done in 1951. It would also be the last session to feature all of the Drifting Cowboys. Nothing new was on the menu. The oldest song was "Let's Turn Back the Years," a plea for reconciliation that had first appeared in one of Hank's WSFA songbooks in 1946. Its words now rang truer than ever. Several verses had been omitted from the 1946 draft, including one that Hank couldn't quite bring himself to sing:

> *You have been so faithful, darling*
> *Waiting for me all these years,*
> *And if you'll forget the vows I've broken,*
> *I'll try to pay you for all your tears.*

Finally, Hank got a releasable cut of "Honky Tonk Blues," a song that dated back almost as far as "Let's Turn Back the Years." He had first tried it at the August 1947 session that had yielded "Fly Trouble." He'd taken another stab at it in March 1949, and yet another in June 1950. Rose might have held it back because the title was easily confused with "Honky Tonkin'," but the flurry of activity around "Honky Tonkin'" in 1948 and again in 1950 had died away, and Rose now felt confident scheduling "Honky Tonk Blues" as Hank's first release for 1952. The version that hit the streets didn't contain all the lyrics on his original demo; the next-to-last verse in which Maw and Paw are "really gonna lay down the law" was missing, emphasizing in a way that Hank himself never made it back from the honky-tonks to pappy's farm. On release in February 1952, "Honky Tonk Blues" was coupled with "I'm Sorry for You, My Friend," the song Lefty Frizzell said Hank had written for him.

As 1951 was drawing to a close, Hank Williams needed repair. Two and a half years of almost constant travel, sleep deprivation, and unrelenting pressure had taken their toll on his body and mind. The drinking bouts were becoming increasingly frequent. The lower five vertebrae of his back ached constantly. The brace wasn't working. And now Hank's career seemed to be controlling him rather than vice versa. If he felt guilty about his binges, as he almost certainly did, he covered it up by refusing to acknowledge that there was a problem. When he was drunk or in the process of getting drunk, he was in no condition to discuss his alcoholism, and when he was sober he pulled rank on his band and cut short any discussion. "I'd say to him, 'That's when you really showed your butt,'" said Don Helms, "and he'd say, 'I don't wanna talk 'bout it.'"

At some point in 1951 Hank was sent, or committed himself, to a sanatorium in Louisville, Kentucky, which was supposed to specialize in treatment of alcoholics. There, he was told essentially what he wanted to hear: he wasn't an alcoholic because he went days, weeks, sometimes months without drinking. An alcoholic couldn't do that. Therefore, Hank was a spree drinker. Hank almost certainly knew in his heart that he wasn't a spree drinker, and knew how much strength it took on a daily basis to wrestle down his craving for alcohol. "He got so bitter about alcohol," said Ernest Tubb, one of the few Hank opened up to about his problem because it was one that Tubb shared:

> He hated drinking, and he wanted to take this cure. You'd take this medicine, and you had to carry a letter in your pocket. If you're taking this medicine [and] you take a drink, if you don't get to a hospital quick enough it'll kill you. He asked me if he should do it, take this cure. I told him, "This you have to decide, 'cause if I advise you to do it and you get off some place late at night and you fall off the wagon, and start drinking you could wind up dead and I'd feel responsible." He knew he was an alcoholic. Then it dawned on him.

Unlike Lefty Frizzell, characterized by his drinking buddies as a happy drunk, Hank was a miserable drunk. He became surly and contrary. "He was a pain, a real pain," said Don Helms. "If you wanted to leave, he wanted to wait; if you wanted to wait, he wanted to leave." Hank's problem was aggravated by a low tolerance for alcohol. Helms and Rivers agree that Hank probably drank less than just about anyone else on the *Opry*, but he drank in binges and his low tolerance quickly put him out of commission. A few drinks and he was a foaming-at-the-mouth, under-the-table drunk. When he was drunk, his natural bluntness turned into boorishness. His band members knew all the little telltale signs, like the strange wave from the wings when they were warming up the crowd. Said Jerry Rivers,

> We'd all just wilt 'cause we knew then he was drinking. One time in St. Joseph, Missouri, we were onstage picking and he came to the wings and we knew right away he was drinking. He came on, swung into "Move It on Over," did the verse with "Remember pup before you whine," and then Don did a solo, then he sung the same verse and Jerry took a solo. Then he did "I'm a Long Gone Daddy," which is basically the same tune, and he came out of the break singing "Remember pup before you whine." We'd rather he didn't show. It was just such a letdown to us.

Most of those who knew Hank have a pet theory about his drinking. He drank because of back pain, because of Audrey, because of career pressures, to gain attention — the list was long. Wesley Rose had a complex theory that centered around blood sugar levels, which was probably state-of-the-art thinking about alcoholism that month. Hank drank. It was a behavior he had acquired in his youth — before Audrey, before his back gave him much trouble, before his career took him over. It was a behavior to which he turned at moments both predictable and unpredictable. It was a behavior that took him over and acquired its own momentum as his personal and professional problems mounted. More than anything else, it was a release from whatever ailed him at the time. "I'm gonna keep drinkin' 'til I can't even think," he'd written in "Tear in My Beer," and he was true to every word.

Hank and Fred Rose had discussed Hank's problem many times. Rose approached it from the standpoint of a recovered alcoholic, but was unsuccessful in persuading Hank to tackle his alcoholism with a renewed spiritual awakening. Joining an organization like Alcoholics Anonymous was also out of the question for Hank, partly because of his intensely private nature, but mostly because it would have been an acknowlegment that he had a problem. This left palliative professional help when he was on a binge, which was essentially limited to deprivation, a good meal when he stood a chance of keeping it down, a few vitamins, and a big bill.

With most tours lasting just a few days between *Opry* commitments, Hank was usually brought home if he was drinking, and Audrey would, with good reason, refuse to let him in the house. Jim Denny would ask the band to take him to a sanatorium attached to the hospital in Madison, just north of Nashville. The sanatorium had some outbuildings with bars on the windows that it used for drying out alcoholics. The band would pull up in front of the sanatorium and Hank wouldn't have a clear idea of where he was. Someone would say, "Come on, Hank, let's get out," and he would see where they were and say, "Oh no, oh no, I ain't goin' in there. It's that damn hut." The attendants would have to come and get him, and he would stare daggers at the band as if he had been betrayed. "Seems to me," said Helms, "that everyone would disappear round about that time," but Helms lived close by and had known Hank the longest, so he would come to visit after a couple of days, and he'd bring candy bars and books. Usually, by the third day Hank would say, "Reckon they're gonna let us outta here?" Helms would think to himself, "Hoss, *we* ain't in here."

On another occasion in late 1951, Hank was committed to St. Margaret's hospital in Montgomery. His cousin Walter McNeil came to see him there and found a desperately unhappy man. As was often the case when he was coming off a drunk, Hank was paranoid and surly, and, some thought, occasionally suicidal. "O'Neil," he said ("O'Neil McNeil" was Lilly's nickname for Walter Jr.), "I wish I was back at WSFA making twelve dollars a week. At least then if someone come to see me, I'd know they was coming to see *me*. Now I reckon they just want something from me."

Wondering what Audrey was doing while he was out on the road contributed to Hank's broodiness and general upset. He saw the band members happy to get off the road and get home to their wives and families. He would go home and perhaps not find Audrey there at all. If she was there, they'd probably have a fight. As early as 1950, coming in off the road, he had told the guys that he knew they were all looking forward to going back home. Meantime, he said, he was going to Acuff-Rose to pick up a check for two thousand dollars, go home, give Audrey half of it, then spend the rest of the night fighting with her over the other half. Now he couldn't even joke about it. It just wasn't funny anymore.

Still, Hank loved Audrey, and he loved Randall Hank. A WSM engineer remembered that Hank had once left Nashville in a hurry and got halfway to Jackson before realizing that he hadn't said good-bye to Hank Jr., so he drove all the way back. Another time, Ernest Tubb remembered that he, Hank, and Minnie Pearl were playing the Tri-State Fair in Amarillo, Texas. "Hank had bought every stuffed bear, dog, and he had that Cadillac so loaded the boys said, 'Where we gonna sit?' I said, 'Hank, that kid ain't big enough to play with them,' 'cause Hank had a stuffed dog as big as a man, but he worshipped that boy. Never knew a man worshiped a child like that. He just couldn't buy enough things for Bocephus." In Hank's ideal world, little Hank was the centerpiece of the family that prayed together and stayed together. In that same dream, Audrey was baking a pie as he walked in the door.

The paradox of Hank Williams was that he was easygoing on the outside, yet tense and querulous inside. He pretended that he'd just ridden into town on a mule, yet had a lively intelligence combined with what Minnie Pearl described as a "woods-animal distrust" of anyone who appeared to have any more learning than he did. He wanted to be the drifting cowboy, herding the dark clouds out of the sky and keeping the heavens blue, yet was prone to depression. He saw his own dalliances as one of the perks of the job, yet was infuriated and aggrieved by Audrey's infidelities, perhaps because they were often conducted in full view of his peers.

Through his music, his fans sensed the chasm between Hank's onstage demeanor and his private disquiet, and that in turn accounted for part of his appeal. There was a huge gulf between the way he introduced the songs on radio or onstage and the song itself. The introduction was straight out of hillbilly vaudeville; the songs were from Hank Williams' heart of darkness. When the spotlight was switched off, or the red recording light went off, and the people had gone home, Hank was left with Hiram Williams, who was wretched company for himself. "When he walked on the stage," said Audrey later, "it was the only time Hank was ever really sure of himself. It was shyness and lonesomeness."

Hank tried to get one aspect of his life under control when he finally surrendered up his back to a team of surgeons led by Dr. Ben Fowler and Dr. George Carpenter at the Vanderbilt Medical Center. This was a major step for Hank, who had a country person's pathological fear of big-city doctors. As early as March 31, 1951, *Billboard* had reported that he had a spine disorder and was expected to take six weeks off for surgery. At the time he signed his motion picture deal, he talked about working fewer shows to concentrate on songwriting (Bing Crosby was mentioned as a possible client), but as ever the bottom line was that Hank couldn't keep his band on salary if they didn't work.

A hunting accident finally forced Hank into the hospital. Jerry Rivers had gone hunting with him, and Hank's dog had treed a large groundhog in a stump. The groundhog put up a fight, and Hank and Jerry began running to save the dog. Rivers jumped a gully, carrying a heavy double-barreled shotgun, and beat off the groundhog. Then he looked around for Hank, but couldn't see him.

Hank was on his back in the gully. His face was pale and he was wracked with pain. He had lost his balance jumping the ditch and had fallen four or five feet onto his back. His first step was to check into St. Jude's in Montgomery, where he felt more at home, but the doctors there referred him to the Vanderbilt Medical Center. As he told the story later, Hank went to the doctors and said, "Cure me or kill me, Doc. I can't go on like this."

Before the surgery, Hank had agreed to work Connie B. Gay's New Year's Eve bash. Gay booked theaters in Washington, Baltimore, Toledo, Raleigh, Spartanburg, and Charleston, West Virginia. In conjunction with Jim Denny, he had arranged to bring in virtually every artist working on the *Opry* to fill those venues. Denny and Gay had worked together since 1947, and Gay held the *Opry* franchise for the D.C. area. This was to be their biggest joint venture. It's likely that Denny had a personal stake in the financial outcome of the shows in addition to his professional stake. Hank was to be the headliner, and they planned to "bicycle" him (that is, have him play two locations) in Baltimore and Washington. Booking Hank was a calculated risk for Denny, who was as aware of his condition as anyone, but it was a risk that he was apparently willing to take. Hank had a history of showing up stone cold sober when he absolutely had to, and Denny might have planned to ensure his sobriety by assigning a minder.

Hank didn't make the shows, but not because he was drinking. The operation was less than a total success, and Hank aggravated his condition by insisting upon being moved home on Christmas Eve. Audrey got upset at him for ignoring the doctors' instructions and Hank threw a chair at her, which worsened his condition and necessitated another trip back to Vanderbilt. The house was thick with tension over Christmas, deeply at odds with the cheery family Christmas card Hank and Audrey circulated. Guns were waved and insults traded. Audrey's sister Lynette came up from Banks to spend the week between Christmas and New Year's, and she later said that Hank couldn't understand why he was in so much pain after the operation. Audrey would occasionally disappear in the evening, topping up Hank's jealousy, but he could only rail against it because he was in such pain. It was all he could do to move from the bedroom to the bathroom.

Hank's mood worsened when he realized that he would have to pre-record apologies to the Washington and Baltimore audiences. In effect, he was being asked to prove he wasn't drunk. His voice was sad and muted. Here in part is what he said:

On December the thirteenth, I had to have an operation that I'd been putting off for about a year. I had to have it because it finally got to where I couldn't even walk on one leg hardly. . . . But when he started the operation, when the doctor got into my back he found a lot wrong that he hadn't anticipated before, so naturally he had to go ahead and fix it all. I had what you call a spine fusion. I had two ruptured disks in my back. The first and second vetebrae was no good, it was just deformed or broken when I was a child, or wore out or something. He said he thought I'd rode a few too many hundred thousand miles in these automobiles. So he went ahead and fixed it, so after I came to, after the anesthetic wore off he told me it'd be impossible for me to be out of here before the first of February.

So then me and Mister Denny at the station here, we tried to talk him into letting me take an airplane with a stretcher in it, and fly up to Washington and take an ambulance from there to Baltimore, but he wouldn't go along with it, so he just finally said no.

Denny arranged for Jimmie Davis to take Hank's place, then arranged for Audrey to sing with the Drifting Cowboys and play Hank's message for the fans. It wasn't an easy trip for her. On Saturday, December 29, Audrey alleged that Hank physically attacked her. She moved herself and the kids to the Garretts, a family that had sold Hank a pony for Lycrecia. Then on Sunday afternoon she came back home to pack for the shows.

> There were three elderly women [that] came back home with me so I could get some clothes and fly to Washington. I just wanted to slip in and out. We were just easin' around, and I knew he was there and very edgy, and as we were leaving the gun shot four times. I could hardly walk. I was scared to death. Thinking back, I don't know if he was shooting at me, or wanting me to think that he was shooting at himself. Anyway, I went on to Washington, and New Year's Eve night I called him and said, "Hank, I'll never live with you another day."

Johnnie and Jack and Kitty Wells were in town that Christmas. They came to see Hank to ask for his help in getting them back on the *Opry*, and they arrived to find the screen door riddled with bullet holes and one of Hank's guitars smashed to pieces out on the patio. According to Johnnie Wright, Hank had just found out about Audrey's latest affair. He told Johnnie, "That busted my heart." The troubles, according to Wright, had started when Audrey had said she was going out to buy Hank Jr. a Christmas present and had come back with nothing. Hank suspected that she had been fooling around and exploded.

During the divorce proceedings, Audrey reiterated the story that Hank had shot at her, but Hank vigorously denied it. Wright's confirmation notwithstanding, the shotgun blasts were in keeping with Hank's frame of mind at the time. They were also in keeping with his wayward use of firearms when he was drunk, angry, or in acute pain. And that night he was drunk and angry and in acute pain. The year-end issue of *Billboard* showed that "Cold, Cold Heart" was the top country song of the year and was number thirteen in the year-end tally of the pop charts, but that was no comfort at all.

Hank and Irene as infants.
(COURTESY OF LEILA GRIFFIN)

Lon Williams, gentleman farmer.
(COURTESY OF LEILA GRIFFIN)

The Skippers and McNeils, circa 1925. Lilly is on the far left, with her hands on Hank, next to her brother-in-law, Walter McNeil. In the front row, Hank's cousin J. C. McNeil is fifth from the right; his sister, Irene, is third from the right; his cousin Bernice McNeil is second from the right; and his cousin Marie McNeil is at the far right. (COURTESY OF THE CITY OF GEORGIANA)

Hank, Lilly, Irene, and J. C. McNeil in front of the W. T. Smith log train. (AUTHOR'S COLLECTION)

Georgiana, Alabama. (COURTESY OF THE CITY OF GEORGIANA)

Hank in Montgomery, circa 1940.
(AUTHOR'S COLLECTION)

Hank and Pee Wee Moultrie.
(COURTESY OF PEE WEE MOULTRIE)

Hank and Audrey with Lilly and her third husband, J. C. Bozard.
(AUTHOR'S COLLECTION)

Hank's cousin Marie. (COURTESY OF LEWIS FITZGERALD)

Hank with Lewis "Butch" Fitzgerald. (COURTESY OF LEWIS FITZGERALD)

Stars of WSFA. Left to right top: Sammy Pruett, Hank, unknown, Audrey, Jimmy Webster. Bottom: Lum York. (COURTESY OF LUM YORK)

Fred Rose and Roy Acuff. (*GRAND OLE OPRY* ARCHIVE)

The trade advertisement for Hank's first record. (COLIN ESCOTT)

Hank with Henry Clay, manager of KWKH, Shreveport. (COLIN ESCOTT)

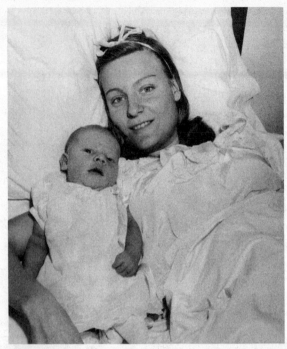

Audrey shortly after giving birth to Hank Jr. (MENASCO)

Friends and nemeses. From left: Jimmie Davis, cowriter of "Lonesome Whistle"; Hank's first manager, Oscar Davis; his first hero, Roy Acuff; West Coast promoter Foreman Phillips. (COLIN ESCOTT)

Hank with Frank Walker, president of MGM Records. (COLIN ESCOTT)

Hank and Lilly at the Montgomery Homecoming. (COLIN ESCOTT)

Hank's Montgomery Homecoming. (COURTESY OF JETT WILLIAMS)

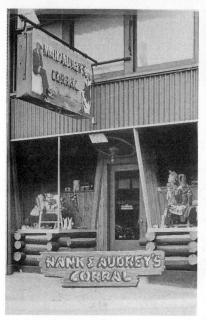

Hank and Audrey's Corral.
(COLIN ESCOTT)

Hank on the *Grand Ole Opry*. (TSLA / ESCOTT)

Mother's Best li'l ol' boys. From left: Cedric Rainwater, emcee Cousin Louie
Buck, Sammy Pruett, Hank, Jerry Rivers, Don Helms. (COLIN ESCOTT)

Shake 'n' howdy in Dallas with young fan Darwin Dunn. (COURTESY OF DAVID DENNARD)

Backstage at the *Opry*. (GRAND OLE OPRY ARCHIVES)

Whistlin' dixie. From left at rear: Hank, Jerry Rivers, Sammy Pruett, Cedric Rainwater, Don Helms. Front: Minnie Pearl. (GRAND OLE OPRY ARCHIVES)

Staged arrest in Texas. (ESTATE OF HONEY WILDS)

With *Opry* costars Jamup and Honey. (ESTATE OF HONEY WILDS)

Greenville Homecoming. Hank is in the front seat with Butch Fitzgerald; Lilly is in the backseat. Lon Williams and Hank's uncle Robert are standing beside the car, in which Hank would die some twenty-one weeks later. (*GREENVILLE ADVOCATE*)

On the West Coast with songwriter Johnny Pusateri, April 1952. (ADAH)

The drinks are on me. Hank with promoter Dub Allbritten, standing. (GLENN SUTTON)

Billie Jean. (ADAH)

"A picture from the past came slowly stealing. . . ." Billie Jean. (COLIN ESCOTT)

Hank marries Billie Jean, New Orleans, October 19, 1952. (MENASCO)

Toby Marshall. (*DAILY OKLAHOMAN*)

The last prescription
(*DAILY OKLAHOMAN*)

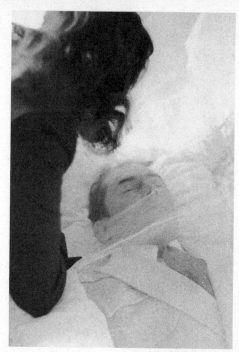

Billie Jean bids farewell.
(AUTHOR'S COLLECTION)

Charles Carr, the driver from Hank's last ride, comforts Marie at the funeral.
(AUTHOR'S COLLECTION)

Irene and Lilly in Hank's former bedroom. (ADAH)

Lilly, Audrey, and Hank Jr. look over the letters of condolence. (ADAH)

Audrey on the town with Jerry Lee and Linda Gail Lewis. (AUTHOR'S COLLECTION)

Chapter

13

• •

"A GOOD TIME ALL THE TIME"

• • • • • • • • • • • • • • • • • •

*P*RESUMABLY, it was at Audrey's request that Hank moved out of the family home on January 3, 1952. His first stop was the Andrew Jackson Hotel. Don Helms visited him there. He told Don that he didn't think he'd be going back this time — and how right he was. His next stop was Lilly's boardinghouse. While he was there, he sent word to Lon asking him to come pick him up. Lon drove in from McWilliams, but just as he was parking he saw Hank being carried out of the boardinghouse on a stretcher, bound for St. Jude's Hospital. Lon followed the ambulance, and when he got to the hospital he was told that Hank was unconscious. One of the doctors took Lon aside and told him that Hank had overdosed and would have to stay in the hospital until what he called "the dope" had been flushed from his system. Lilly said she couldn't understand it; Hank had only had two beers and two aspirins all day. On January 13, Hank made a five-hundred-dollar donation to St. Jude's. Perhaps that was the day he was released back into Lilly's care.

The dope in Hank's system was probably heavy-duty prescription painkillers taken in nonprescription doses. Hank had become increasingly reliant upon painkillers as his back pain worsened through 1951. He would go to see several doctors, obtain multiple prescriptions, then take more than the prescribed dose. "It says, 'Take one every four hours,'" he would say. "Maybe I ought to take four every hour; that's four times as good, ain't it?" It would have been sixteen times as good if the logic held water, but overmedication only raised Hank's tolerance of painkillers so that he needed increasingly large doses, all the while increasing the chance of an overdose.

At some point in January 1952, Hank moved into a house that Ray Price rented at 2718 Westwood Avenue in Nashville. Hank took the downstairs, and Price moved upstairs. Price had come to Nashville from Dallas during the early fall of 1951, and had met Hank backstage at the Opry's *Friday Night Frolics* show. They liked each other at once, and Hank took Price to a show date in Evansville, Indiana, right after the Saturday night *Opry*. On the way, they wrote a song, "Weary Blues from Waitin'," that Hank would copyright as his and Ray would record in October. It was one of the most affecting songs that Hank had a hand in writing.

> Through tears I watch young lovers as they go strolling by
> For all the things that might have been, I hang my head
> and cry.

"Hank called me about two weeks later and wanted to know if he could do it," said Price. "I was trying to get started, and I said, 'Hank, I need it real bad.' He said, 'Well, you go on and use it then. If you don't, I want to do it.'"

On January 10, Audrey initiated divorce proceedings. Her Bill of Complaint was filed that day, but its list of grudges went back to the early days in Montgomery. She alleged that Hank's conduct toward her there had embarrassed and humiliated her to the extent that she insisted that they relocate, explaining how they came to move to Shreveport. They weren't completely happy in Shreveport, she said, because of what she termed Hank's "continued misconduct," but she conceded that they did enjoy "some degree of happiness" there. It wasn't until the spring of 1951, though, that Hank's conduct became what Audrey called "intolerable." "While he had been inconsiderate, and even cruel at times," she alleged, "he then became most abusive, cursing [me] without provocation, and striking [me] on numerous occasions." Audrey then gave her version of the events surrounding New Year's, concluded that "cohabitation was unsafe and improper," and demanded that Hank disclose all of his income, then provide separate maintenance for her as well as child support for Hank Jr.

Gradually, statements came through from Acuff-Rose and MGM concerning Hank's income. It seems that on top of the thirty-two thousand dollars Acuff-Rose had paid Hank in 1951, another twenty-two thousand was awaiting payment. Acuff-Rose noted, though, that some of the money might have to go to Dixie Music after the resolution of the lawsuit over "Cold, Cold Heart." Acuff-Rose had paid Hank on the understanding that they could reclaim the funds if the judgment went against them. From that point, though, "Cold, Cold Heart" funds remained frozen until 1955; by then another thirty-two thousand dollars (equivalent to two million records) had accumulated in escrow. The result of the suit wasn't made public, but on January 3, 1955, Dixie Music was paid just twenty-five hundred dollars in damages and, ten days later, was awarded court costs of five thousand dollars. With that, the case was closed.

MGM stated that between September 1, 1951, and December 31, 1951, Hank had earned $10,754 in domestic royalties and roughly $1,900 in overseas royalties, and that additional royalties covering the period from year-end to February 28, 1952, had yet to be calculated. MGM's deposition also confirmed Hank's contractual obligation to make movies, something the company denied after his death.

Predictably, WSM stated that Hank was in the hole to the station to the tune of five hundred dollars, largely because of unpaid commissions on shows that had used the *Opry* name.

Hank told a New York reporter that he played to around fifteen thousand people a night in 1951, but that was probably a maximum attendance rather than an average attendance. Even so, there's no doubt that he was stuffing several thousand dollars into his valise every night. With radio sponsorship money added in, together with back-pocket money from selling songbooks and photos, Hank had clearly exceeded his declared 1950 income of $92,000, and had almost certainly grossed well over $100,000 in 1951, perhaps as much as the $150,000 he told the *Wall Street Journal* he would earn that year.

After the depositions came Hank's cross-complaint against Audrey. He tried to hold himself up as a model of financial probity while contending that Audrey had indulged in "every extravagance she could possibly stretch his income to cover." He complained of her "insatiable hunger for clothes, jewelry, automobiles, and luxuries far beyond their economic status in life." His cross-complaint was, in essence, a Hank Williams song rendered in a voice that was an incongruous blend of his own and his lawyer's.

The first shot across Audrey's bow was a predictable one:

> The first years of . . . married life were troublesome, because of the inattention of [Audrey] to her home and husband. . . . [She] refused to appreciate the obligations of married life, denying her attentions and affections to her home and husband, insisting that she too was an entertainer and singer of ability, continuously insisting that the defendant include her on his programs . . . despite the fact that she had neither voice nor musical ability.

Hank went on to say that he had lost many jobs during his early years in the business because Audrey had insisted upon being included in the act. She had, he said, been evicted from studios and other places of entertainment because of her fits of rage when her ambitions were denied.

Next, Hank accused Audrey of "extravagant living and carousing . . . such as to keep [his] nose to the grindstone continuously to keep the bills paid." She had, he said, "no interest or disposition to [stay] at home . . . but has always insisted upon traveling about, acting independent and free of all marital restraint, seeking and having everything she wanted, and a good time all the time." Audrey hadn't spent one full day with Hank Jr. since his birth, contended Hank, unless she couldn't get someone to stay with him. "As a matter of fact," he added, "[our] only child refers to its nurse as 'Mama.'" In return for all Hank's efforts to provide for Audrey, he said that she continually referred to him as a " 'son of a bitch' . . . and many other names too vile and vulgar to [mention here]."

Then came the parting shots. First, Hank claimed to have evidence of Audrey's adultery with a highway patrolman while he was on the Hadacol Caravan, and he went on to claim that she'd had an affair with a car salesman. Next, Hank went into detail about Audrey's detestation of Lilly. She had "condemned and castigated him for showing any love or affection for her," he said, adding that Audrey had ordered Lilly out of Vanderbilt on the day after the spinal operation. Finally, Hank confirmed that Audrey had become pregnant around September 1950 but had had an abortion performed at home that had led to an infection, which in turn required treatment at St. Thomas' Hospital. In the cross-complaint Hank spoke of his humiliation and grief when he heard what Audrey had done. Hank's cross-complaint was a document that was, by turns, sad and bitter. Unrealistically, his cross-complaint concluded with a request for custody of Hank Jr.

Both sides of the action speak of a dead weight of hurt. It's hard to tell if Hank still loved Audrey, but it's clear that she no longer loved him. The divorce proceedings acquired their own momentum, and Audrey seemed set upon her course this time. She would have found it difficult to stop, even if she had been inclined to do so. Hank knew that he had failed and, according to those close to him, still hoped from time to time for a reconciliation. Audrey claimed that she was divorcing Hank for the good of the children. "I had these two children," she told Dorothy Horstman in 1973, "and I said, 'These children have to have a mother.' I could see they wasn't going to have a father. He was so far gone that they just got nervous when he walked in the door." Lycrecia later remembered that she'd only seen Hank drunk a couple of times, but the tension in the house when Hank was there must have been unbearable for most of 1951. There's a haunting photograph that has appeared in several television documentaries in which Hank and Audrey are standing outside their house, turning away from each other. Audrey is covering her eyes as if in tears, while Hank looks down and away. Knowing the state of their relationship during this late stage, it seems as though someone has captured one of their arguments. It's just as likely, though, that Hank Jr. and Lycrecia were playing hide-and-seek, and that Hank and Audrey were covering their eyes or averting their gaze while the kids scuttled off to hide.

When he signed his cross-complaint on March 5, Hank claimed not to have worked since the operation, which was almost true. He'd taken the Drifting Cowboys off salary, telling them that he would call them for dates and hope that they were available. Sammy Pruett was the first to take full-time employment elsewhere, when he joined Carl Smith's Tunesmiths. Almost since joining Hank, Pruett had felt stymied keeping the tic-toc rhythm, with so few opportunities for soloing. Don Helms, Jerry Rivers, and Howard Watts tried to keep themselves available for Hank, but Pruett didn't work a day with him after his operation. The other

Drifting Cowboys worked with Ray Price more than anyone else. They wanted to be on call for Hank, but knew that it limited their chances of employment elsewhere because no one wanted to hire band members who were likely to disappear as soon as Hank Williams decided he was ready to put the Cowboys back together.

Hank's first road trip after his hospitalization was in late January, and it was a disaster. He missed a show in Norfolk, Virginia, but was brought into Richmond, Virginia, on January 29 for a two-night stand. Only Don Helms and Howard Watts were available, and local pickers were recruited to round out the band. Ray Price and Johnnie and Jack were also on the show. The troupe was booked into a hotel, and Hank had a minder assigned to him. With the low cunning that he summoned up when he was desperate, he called down to room service for tomato juice. When that was delivered, he told the waiter that his legs were hurting and he needed some rubbing alcohol. Room service brought it up. Hank mixed the rubbing alcohol with the tomato juice, drank it, then began vomiting violently. Just before showtime he was allowed a beer to settle his stomach, but he was still in no shape to perform.

In a review for the *Richmond Times-Despatch* the following day, Edith Lindeman's headline read: "Hank Williams Hillbilly Show Is Different: Star Makes Impression of Unexpected Kind." She went on to describe how Ray Price opened the show, then brought on a clearly inebriated Hank Williams. According to Price, Hank was sitting in the wings, motioning him to do one song after another. Price didn't have that many songs in his repertoire, but he wanted to give Hank time to straighten up. Price recalled,

> This went on for about thirty minutes. Finally, I said, "Folks, now, Hank's had a serious back operation and he's really not feeling too well so you'll all have to forgive him, and here he is, ladies and gentlemen, Hank Williams." And Hank come moping out there, and the newspaper said his legs certainly wasn't holding him erect. He had problems remembering his first song and staying in key, and quit after one song.

The emcee said that anyone who wanted a refund would get one, but the promoter, who was reported to be "ill at home," had already had the proceeds brought to him, and there was nothing left for refunds.

During the intermission, Hank's minder walked him around out in the frigid night air, forcing a sandwich and some coffee down him. Then Hank went back out to face the crowd. "I wish I was in as good a shape as you are," he said. "Hank Williams is a lot of things, but he ain't a liar. If they's a doctor in the house I'll show him I've been in the hospital for eight weeks . . . and if you ain't nice to me, I'll turn around and walk right off." Ray Price, seeing that Hank was about to drop his pants onstage, came running out, and grabbed the microphone. "We all love you, Hank, don't we, folks?" he said, and tried to hustle Hank offstage. Hank headed for his limo. No autographs. No shake 'n' howdy. There had been other nights like that, but this time there was a newspaper reporter on hand. The following night, Hank was hungover and vengeful. He dedicated a song to a "gracious lady writer" and swung right into "Mind Your Own Business." It was a moment to savor: shame followed by swift redemption in song. If only all the large and small humiliations could have been reversed so deftly.

The following day, they were in Charleston, South Carolina. Price had to sub for Hank there. The next night, they worked a show date in Macon, Georgia, and then Hank disappeared. "God only knows where he went," said Price.

> I think he went to the coast. Some banker called Jim Denny and said, "We have a man down here that says he's Hank Williams and wants to cash a check." Jim said, "What does he look like?'"And he told him. And Jim said, "Well, that's Hank all right." Hank's driver was with him. We called him Brains. Jim spoke to him. He was real mad. He said, "You get that check cashed, and when you get to the ocean, don't stop, just drive on out in the damn ocean."

By now word was spreading that getting to see Hank Williams was a hit-or-miss affair. Johnnie Wright reckons that Hank's average had slipped from its best — around .850 — to .500. Sober, no one had more respect for his fans than Hank, but when he was drunk, yet still believing he was able to perform, he was obtuse and would respond rudely to hecklers. "Someone git a shovel and cover that up," he would say, or "Hey, pal, we got a surprise for you. After the show, we gonna git yore momma and yore poppa up here, and git 'em married." Mostly, though, if Hank was drinking, he was too drunk to stand, much less play, but even then he attracted his apologists, much as George Jones later would. If someone said Hank was drunk, someone else would say, "Hell, he had a right to be."

On April 3, Hank and Audrey's lawyers arrived at a tentative property settlement and arrangements for the custody of Hank Jr. In the preamble, buried among the "whereas's" and "hereto's," was a sentence noting that the parties couldn't agree upon a divorce, intimating that Hank was still opposed to it and that Audrey would have to go to court to obtain it. Ray Price remembers that in one set of discussions with the lawyer, Hank more or less agreed to Audrey's terms, despite the fact that his lawyer considered them punitive. This, according to Price, was because Hank wanted to show his continued love for Audrey and his regret over what had happened. Perhaps in acceding to her demands he would achieve that. Price also remembers that Hank would call Audrey almost every day, and that she would hang up on him.

Predictably, the care of Hank Jr. was entrusted to Audrey, with the provision that Hank could have Hank Jr. reside with him for three months during the summer of 1953. Audrey got the house on Franklin Road, including all the fixtures, as well as her 1951 Cadillac convertible and one thousand dollars in cash. Hank also agreed to pay her attorney's fees. According to court documents, $13,559 was still owing on the house, and Audrey assumed that debt, together with a $706 note on the Cadillac. But she got one-half of all Hank's future royalties with a binding obligation upon MGM and Acuff-Rose to remit them directly to her. If Audrey ever remarried, her claim upon the royalties would end and Hank's only obligation would be a maintenance payment of $300 a month for Hank Jr. until he was twenty-one. Hank got Hank and Audrey's Corral, a marginal business at the best of times, and the farm in Williamson County with its derelict house and $45,000 mortgage. Hank would keep all of his road income, presumably because Audrey knew most of the ways he could hide it from her.

In retrospect, it was a fabulous settlement for Audrey, but at the time, she was so skeptical that she built in a provision for Hank to remit extra funds to her if her earnings from half of his royalties dropped below certain thresholds. Audrey would never remarry — not, as she was fond of saying, because no love could ever match what she and Hank had shared, but because she couldn't bear for her half of the oil well to gush in someone else's backyard. She didn't retire to a life of quiet contemplation, but all suitors knew her ground rule on marriage.

If Hank was indeed still besotted with Audrey, it didn't stop him from taking a new girlfriend, Bobbie Jett. Ray Price remembers Bobbie accompanying Hank on the disastrous January tour, and some claim that she was with him in Montgomery earlier in the month, so it is very likely that Hank knew her before he separated from Audrey. Bobbie had lived a life every bit as troubled as Hank's. She came from a prominent Nashville family, but her mother had lit out for California shortly after Bobbie was born, leaving Bobbie in the care of her grandmother. Born on October 5, 1922, Bobbie was slightly less than a year older than Hank. After the war she too had gone to California, where she later claimed to have married movie star Monte Hale. Married or not (likely not), she returned to Nashville with a child, Jo, in 1949, and was working as a secretary when Hank met her. Hank was not alone in fancying Bobbie; Decca Records' Paul Cohen was beguiled by her, as were several others.

By the time the blossoms began appearing along Natchez Trace, Hank was starting to think about work again. On March 22, 1952, he was on the *Grand Ole Opry,* quite possibly for the first time that year. Immediately after the show, Hank and an *Opry* troupe flew to New York for a March 26 appearance on the *Kate Smith Evening Hour.* The following weekend, he was back on the *Opry* and working on shows for WSM. In early April, he left for a tour of California that probably started in Fresno on April 9.

On April 13, Hank was interviewed by jazz journalist Ralph J. Gleason, who later cofounded *Rolling Stone* but was writing for the *San Francisco Chronicle* at the time. Gleason caught up with Hank at the Leamington Hotel in Oakland. Gleason was surprised by the number of pills Hank had about his person, and by the fact that the pills constituted most of his breakfast. Hank talked about his background and about "folk" music in much the same terms as he had in Charleston earlier that year. He professed to like the petulant, melodramatic style of Johnnie Ray, and he told Gleason that he could never sing songs like "Mairzy Doats" or "Rag Mop" because he couldn't relate to the lyrics. Harping on one of his favorite themes, he said, "A song ain't nuthin' in the world but a story with music to it. . . . I've been offered some of the biggest songs to sing and turned 'em down. There ain't *nobody* can pick songs."

Gleason was sufficiently intrigued to catch Hank in person that night at the San Pablo Hall. According to his account, the hall was a one-story white building. You parked in the mud, and inside the door there was a long room with a bandstand at one end and a bar in an annex at one side. Hank "had that *thing*," wrote Gleason. "He made them scream when he sang. There were lots of those blondes you see at C&W affairs [with] the kind of hair that mother never had and nature never grew . . . guys looking barbershop neat but still with a touch of dust on them." Hank appeared a little stoned between sets, didn't remember Gleason from that morning, and was hanging out with a crowd of whiskey drinkers. But here at least, in a northern California beer hall, Hank was on his home turf. He was playing to exiled southerners and Okies, most of whom had come out to work in the munitions factories during the war. He understood them, and they understood him when he sang about getting back to pappy's farm. They both knew it would never happen.

On April 16, Hank was feted by MGM Records distributors in Los Angeles and received an award. The following day, Hank and Wesley Rose went to see Dore Schary at MGM Pictures. Hank had been stalling since he'd signed the movie contract in September 1951, but now he could stall no longer. Things got off to a bad start when he wouldn't take off his hat as he entered Dore Schary's office. Schary was one of MGM Pictures' production chiefs, and had what Rose later called a pompous and condescending manner. Hank had been drinking. He put his boots up on Schary's desk, pulled his hat down over his eyes and answered all questions in monosyllables and grunts. Some said he made anti-Semitic remarks, too. Wesley's accountant's soul couldn't comprehend this. When they got outside, he asked Hank for an explanation of his conduct. "You see this kid here," said Hank, gesturing to a black shoe-shine boy, "this kid is more of a man than that guy in the office will ever be."

Hank, whose inferiority complex often manifested itself in truculence, developed lightning antipathy toward anyone who was even ever so slightly condescending toward him. It's possible that a chance remark from Schary brought all his resentment of the business end of the entertainment business from a simmer to a boil. It's equally likely that Hank had already determined that he wasn't going to make movies for MGM or anyone so he might as well put on an act for his own amusement. He had been given the script to a Jane Powell and Farley Granger movie called *Small Town Girl,* which was to start shooting right away, but the bulk and complexity of the script probably intimidated him to the point that he felt hopelessly out of his depth. He masked his fear with boorishness because the ol' drifting cowboy couldn't appear to be intimidated. Hank wasn't the borderline illiterate that he has been made out to be — and sometimes made himself out to be — but bypassing minor roles and going straight to headlining was like going from college ball to the major leagues. Few were suited to such a transition; Hank wasn't.

The following day, Hank resumed his California trek, touring cities populated by Oklahoma, Texas, and Arkansas émigrés. He was in Los Angeles at Tex Williams' Riverside Rancho, and in Bakersfield and Oakland before flying back to New York for the second *Kate Smith Evening Hour* on April 23. Three days later, he was advertised as the headliner of an *Opry* show at Boston's Symphony Hall, but no one remembers him appearing. From April 29 until May 2, he was on an *Opry* package in southeastern Texas. He swung from there into Ontario for a short Canadian tour in early May, trying to expunge the memories of the 1951 tour. Then he went to Texas, followed by Las Vegas. And then, on May 22, MGM Pictures wrote to him, requesting that he show up for work on June 16. Hank had already decided that he wouldn't.

A little snapshot of the risks involved in booking Hank comes from Sergeant F. D. McMurry of the Beaumont, Texas, police department. In an attempt to raise funds, the Beaumont Police Benefit Association arranged for an *Opry* troupe led by Hank, Ernest Tubb, and Minnie Pearl to play there on April 29 as part of the swing along the Gulf coast. They arrived in Henry Cannon's Beechcraft. Warning McMurry about Hank, Jim Denny had said, "If you take care of him, he's yours." Someone in the cast advised McMurry to keep watch over Hank to ensure that he remained sober until after the show. McMurry took the task upon himself, and like Gleason, he was amazed at the number and variety of pills that he took. "He had pills in his hat band, his guitar, pills everyplace," said McMurry, who'd never seen anything like it.

The troupe arrived in the morning, and McMurry escorted them around to do some PR at the local stations, then took Hank out to his mother-in-law's house for a meal. "Ol' Hank sure did enjoy that," said McMurry. "He said he didn't get meals like that often. He stretched out on the couch, kicked his boots off. We took the pressure off of him."

Hank made the show that night at the Municipal Auditorium, and everyone loved him. It was a good night. He was still in fine form in Ontario a week later, showing off his operation scars and talking positively.

Starting May 16 for two weeks, Hank was supposed to play Vegas. Roy Acuff, who had done *everything* first, had tried to bring hillbilly music there without much success. Hank was booked into the Last Frontier's Ramona Room, where he played second fiddle to an old vaudevillian, Willie Shore. Hank and a supporting *Opry* troupe were booked in connection with a western theme month, Helldorado, run by the Frontier and some other venues. No one had told the bookers that although Hank dressed like a western singing star and led a band called the Drifting Cowboys, he wasn't a western act, and wasn't likely to go over much better than Acuff.

Hank had hired Don Helms and Jerry Rivers for the trip, and the three of them drove out together. "The closer we got to Vegas, the more nervous he became," said Helms. "We got there and checked in and the next day he was wiped out." Jim Denny told Don and Jerry to hire two minders to watch Hank in alternating twelve-hour shifts. He was sober by show time, but with more reason to drink than on any recent trip. Hank felt ridiculed and out of place. As he peeked through the curtains, he knew it wasn't going to work. Music in Vegas had a very specific function: it was supposed to lull sensibilities and provide a backdrop for dining and gambling. Some performers were born to play Vegas; some weren't. The unsettling emotionalism in Hank Williams' music was precisely what Vegas did not want. His five-piece band sounded thin, and his crowd wasn't there. There was a room full of suits, ties, and dinner dresses. Those who had come especially to see him bought an overpriced fifty-cent Coke and nursed it until the end of the show, then left without staying to drink and gamble. Hank no more belonged there than Sammy Davis Jr. belonged at the Wagon Wheel in Opelika, Alabama. It was reported that none of Hank's records were on the jukebox at the Last Frontier, so he ordered a jukebox from a local jobber, filled it with his own records, and hauled it to the showroom. "This one's got some good records on it," he said.

On the morning of May 23, Hank was awakened with a phone call from the Last Frontier's booker. He was being canceled after one week, and comedian Ed Wynn was drafted in at short notice to take his place. "I could see a sigh of relief come over him," said Helms. On the way out of town, they checked out Rex Allen's show at the Thunderbird Lounge. Hank started drinking there, and he drank all the way back to Nashville. Don and Jerry drove in alternating shifts. Four years later, Vegas provided Elvis Presley with the first serious debacle of his career. It was a town without pity for those who didn't understand it.

Hank now presented bookers with an acute dilemma. He was one of the biggest draws in country music, but the odds on his showing up sober or showing up at all were now no better than even. There was only one reason that Fred Rose, Jim Denny, MGM, and all other interested parties didn't give up on him: he never struck out in the studio. "Baby, We're Really in Love" was in the charts for fifteen weeks starting in December 1951, and it was followed in March 1952 by "Honky Tonk Blues," which peaked at number two and stayed twelve weeks on the charts. "Honky Tonk Blues" was followed in May by "Half As Much," which also peaked at number two and stayed around for four months. "Cold, Cold Heart" was still on the charts as 1952 dawned, and "Hey, Good Lookin'" had yet to drop from heavy rotation. The streak was alive.

On June 13, Hank went into the studio for a late morning session — his first for six months. He'd put off recording, holding out for a cash payment. With Sammy Pruett gone, Fred Rose contracted Chet Atkins for the session. Howard Watts was also unavailable, and Charles "Indian" Wright of the Willis Brothers / Oklahoma Wranglers band was drafted in to play bass. Wright had played on Hank's very first session for Sterling almost five years earlier. There were four songs on the menu; the first was Marcel Joseph's "Window Shopping." Joseph was a French Jew who'd settled in New York in 1914; he developed a fascination with country music after hearing it on a New Jersey station. He wrote hundreds of songs, but "Window Shopping" was his only hit. By day, he was an illustrator at the *Journal American*. "Window Shopping" was just one verse and a chorus, and Rose obviously coached Hank on his diction because "window" was not "winn-der."

Joseph was a fortunate man because "Window Shopping" got a free ride on the flip side of the next song recorded that day, "Jambalaya (on the Bayou)." Hank had worked on the song with singer-pianist Moon Mullican, who wasn't a Cajun but had worked the eastern Texas and Gulf Coast honky-tonks since the 1930s. In a letter to Fred Rose just after the session, Hank directed that Mullican surreptitiously receive

25 percent of song's publishing royalties. The ostensible reason was that Mullican was to record it, but that doesn't ring true. If everyone who recorded a Hank Williams song got 25 percent of it, there would have been nothing left. It's likelier that Mullican wrote at least some of the song. Mullican, though, was under contract to King Records and its publishing division, Lois Music; Rose paid him surreptitiously so that he wouldn't have to split the music publishing with King. Mullican was trying hard to get off King, even conscripting Jim Denny to intercede on his behalf, but no one got out from under a King Records contract.

Most cajun songs are interbred, and the melody of "Jambalaya" came from Chuck Guillory's 1946 recording of "Gran' Texas." It's hard to know if Mullican's recording of "Jambalaya" was made before or after Hank's, but it's quite different from Hank's record, suggesting that either Fred Rose or Hank tinkered with the song after Mullican was through with it. Hank had already shown a passing familiarity with cajun culture on "Bayou Pon-Pon," a song he'd written with Jimmie Davis, and there's a sheet among his effects in which he phonetically transcribed the names of cajun foods. He loved the cajun areas of Louisiana because the cajuns offered a view of life that he desperately wished for himself. "He loved the carefree life [down there]," said Jerry Rivers. "He longed for it because he was not ever a carefree person. He took everything seriously." He even seemed to take "Jambalaya" seriously; his performance is dour and completely without sparkle. On live shows, Hank would deliver the song with some panache, but the record sounds enervated.

"Jambalaya" proved to be the Hank Williams song that crossed all musical boundaries to the point that it is no longer a country song. Fats Domino had a hit with it, John Fogerty had a hit with it, and every cajun and zydeco band is obliged to play it whether they want to or not. Its success is probably due to the fact that it *isn't* really a cajun song. Ethnic music is usually unpalatable for a mass market unless it is diluted in some way (Harry Belafonte's calypsos, Paul Simon's *Graceland* . . . the list is endless). The broader audience related to "Jambayala" in a way that it could never relate to a true cajun two-step led by an asthmatic accordion and sung in patois.

The third item on the menu that morning was "Settin' the Woods on Fire." Like "Hey, Good Lookin'," it pointed unerringly toward rockabilly. Although it sounded for all the world like a Hank Williams song, it was written by Fred Rose and an elderly New Yorker, Ed G. Nelson Sr., the writer of "In a Shady Nook by a Babbling Brook" and "When a Yankee Doodle Learns to Parlez-Vous Francais." Nelson had written with Rose back in the mid-1930s and had been partly responsible for his conversion to Christian Science, but where the pair acquired the vocabulary of "Settin' the Woods on Fire" is anybody's guess. Once again, Hank sounded curiously lifeless.

The fourth song on the slate was "I'll Never Get Out of This World Alive." Too much has been made of its significance. It *wasn't* number one on the day he died, although it shot to number one in the wake of his death. Were it not for the coincidence that it was on the market when he died, it would have been seen for no more than what it was: a novelty song, like "Howlin' at the Moon" or "Mind Your Own Business." The addition of Fred Rose to the composer credit suggests that Rose had to contribute more than usual. In fact, this was the only Hank Williams session in which there were no songs that were solely his own work.

It was a lackluster session in every way, and Hank's physical appearance made a deep impression on Chet Atkins. "We recorded 'I'll Never Get Out of This World Alive,'" he told Alanna Nash, "[and] after each take, he'd sit down in a chair. I remember thinking, 'Hoss, you're not just jivin',' because he was so weak that all he could do was just sing a few lines, and then just fall in the chair." Atkins may have been exaggerating a little. Hank probably sat down to ease his back, but he certainly wasn't in peak form that day.

By now, Frank Walker was sick of seeing Mitch Miller scoop Hank's songs and transform them into pop hits, so he gave "Window Shopping" to one of his hottest properties, band leader Art Mooney, who recorded it on July 21. Walker then gave "Settin' the Woods on Fire" to Fran Warren, whose version was released the same day as Hank's, but he neglected "Jambalaya," which Mitch Miller eagerly picked up and recorded with Jo Stafford. Miller also persuaded Stafford to duet with Frankie Laine on "Settin' the Woods on Fire." Once again, Miller got the hits; "Settin' the Woods on Fire" went to number twenty-one on the pop charts, and "Jambalaya" went all the way to number two. And if Hank's version of "Jambalaya" made only a passing nod toward cajun music, Stafford's record didn't make the connection at all; it was sung incongruously to a mambo rhythm. They were *that* clueless.

Right after the session, on June 16, Hank was due to report for work at MGM Pictures, but on June 17, MGM wrote to Hank in care of Fred

Rose notifying him that "for good and sufficient cause, your employment . . . is terminated." Presumably, Hank never showed up. As far as we know, he barely worked at all in June. There was probably an appearance in El Paso with Minnie Pearl, and for many years Minnie told the same story with slight variations, usually referring to Hank as "ill" or "sick" rather than drunk. On an MGM Records documentary she said,

> The boys were worried that Hank was ill and unable to perform. They kinda insisted that he perform, and it made me unhappy. Then I walked backstage, and they were bringing him up the steps, and the look he had on his face was of such implication that I never will forget it. He said, "Minnie, I can't work. I can't work, Minnie. Tell 'em." I had no authority. They went ahead, and he worked and it was bad. A. V. Bamford told me to stay with him between shows. He said, "He may listen to you. You may be able to keep him from getting any worse than he is." Maxine Bamford and Hank and me and someone else drove around with him. This was between shows, and we were trying to keep him from getting anything else that would make him get in worse shape than he was. We started singing. He was all hunkered down, looking out of the side of the car singing. He was singing, "I Saw the Light," then he stopped and he turned around, and his face broke up and he said, "Minnie, I don't see no light. There ain't no light."

Hank's self-defeating conduct stemmed in part from his perception that he was being marketed as a commodity. He was sent here and there to fly the flag for country music in general and the *Grand Ole Opry* in particular. The comfort and joy he'd once drawn from checking the charts diminished now that he came to see himself as commodified. Never especially forthcoming, he withdrew all the more now that Audrey was gone, but still needed the constant distraction of people around him. On a night when he found himself home alone on Natchez Trace, he would phone all around the country trying to find Ray Price or someone else to talk to. Fame seems to carry with it an inability to be alone, or to be yourself without an audience, and the Hank Williams who encountered himself on Natchez Trace didn't like the company he found.

What makes the evidence of Hank's dissolution almost unbelievable is that he could still exercise restraint over his drinking when he absolutely had to. The *Kate Smith Evening Hour* appearances show a rivetingly on-form performer. Hank was intent, focused, and every inch the star. He stared at the cameras during his performance of "Cold, Cold Heart" with a cockiness and self-confidence that bordered on arrogance. His dark Indian eyes were burning and utterly alive in the moment. The rhinestones on his jacket glistened in the television lights, and the fringe swayed in time with the music. When he dueted with Anita Carter on "I Can't Help It (if I'm Still in Love with You)," she seemed terribly in awe of him, perhaps even in love with him. Smith herself was patronizing. Struggling hard to find something to say, she mentioned the *Opry*'s "nice" dancing and "good, wholesome" entertainment. It's hard to know how many people saw Hank and the *Opry* troupe. The *Kate Smith Evening Hour* on NBC ran only from September 1951 to June 1952; it went head-to-head with Arthur Godfrey, and lost.

It wasn't coincidental that Kate Smith was on NBC-TV and the *Grand Ole Opry* was on NBC radio. The *Opry* management wanted to market the show nationwide via television, and to be first in the race to bring country music to network television. As a result, it was playing its aces, like Hank Williams, and calling in favors with the network. By the spring of 1952, there were fifteen country music television shows in Los Angeles alone, and western swing star Tex Williams was trying to find a network that would syndicate his *Roundup Time at the Riverside Rancho* show. The *Opry* didn't want to lose the initiative to Tex Williams or anyone else, so it brought in the heavy guns.

WSM, which owned the *Opry,* had done as NBC had urged: secured channel space and picked up NBC's television shows. WSM-TV had started in September 1950, but, like almost every television station, it was losing money because few people had sets, and, unlike WSM radio, WSM-TV's signal barely reached the Kentucky state line. WSM-TV had a hillbilly show, *Tennessee Jamboree,* but the viewership was pitifully small. The *Opry* needed a network platform if it was to beat out the competition from California and elsewhere, and, with that in mind, Denny had not only arranged to showcase his acts on Kate Smith, but also made an agreement to rotate the *Opry* cast through the Astor Hotel's rooftop ballroom. The Roof was one of the top venues in New York, and the *Opry* was committed to providing a house band and a featured artist every week for sixteen weeks. With the prestige accruing from the Roof and The *Kate Smith Evening Hour,* Denny believed that a network television offer was a foregone conclusion.

Country music, and the *Opry* in particular, was beginning its eternal quest for prime time. The timing seemed right: the "folk boom" was on everybody's lips, Eddy Arnold was to be the summer replacement for Perry Como, Roy Acuff was to go on the cover of *Newsweek* in August, and Hank Williams had songs dotted over two charts. Even so, the plan failed. The Astor roof engagement was canceled by mutual consent after four weeks, and Hank, who had been scheduled to close the series with a grand finale on September 13, didn't get to play. In fact, by September 13, his last appearance on the *Grand Ole Opry* was already a fairly distant memory.

As 1952 wore on, Hank was increasingly past caring what the *Opry's* plans were, and whether or not he figured in them. Most of those who worked with him that year talk of his rapid disintegration, but the truth is a little more complex. He had been drinking and screwing up since the late 1930s, and his back had been troubling him for almost as long. His marriage and his other personal relationships had never been stable. The patterns that troubled everyone in 1952 had always been there; now they were magnified. The ever present problems were exacerbated by the fact that his career was entering uncharted territory. Three years earlier, Hank had been playing schoolhouses in Louisiana and eastern Texas; now he was expected to headline in New York and Vegas, act in motion pictures, perform on network television, and write songs that Bing Crosby could sing. Nothing prepared him for this, and, unlike Elvis Presley, who left the hillbilly market a few years later, Hank had no one like Presley's Colonel Parker to at least give the semblance of knowing what to do. His reaction was to withdraw. "You could see Hank's concern for his career decline," says Don Helms. "He'd often say, 'Aw, to hell with it.' It reached a point where he didn't really care." A year or two earlier, he had been almost desperately eager to keep his hit streak alive; as soon as one record was out and in the charts, he was itching to repeat, or do even better than he had done before. Now those around him sensed that he didn't care as much, and sometimes seemed not to care at all.

*The most chilling look is the look
of an ambition realized.*

Gordon Burn, "Alma Cogan"

● ●

BILLIE JEAN

● ● ● ● ● ● ● ● ● ● ● ● ● ● ● ● ● ● ● ●

O N July 10, 1952, Hank and Audrey Williams, who had been married by the Bible, were divorced by the law. The following day, Hank cut "You Win Again." It was another quintessential Hank moment, one in which art and life appeared to be indivisible.

It might have been no more than coincidence, but, in the absence of hard evidence to the contrary, the songs cut the day after Hank's divorce seem like pages torn from his diary. It took just two hours after lunch on July 11 for Hank to record four songs: two to be issued under his name, and two as Luke the Drifter. The first, "You Win Again," is among the most perfectly realized recordings in country music. Its theme of betrayal had grown old years before Hank tackled it, but, drawing from his bottomless well of resentment, he gave it a freshness bordering on topicality. Apparently, Hank's first draft was titled "I Lose Again," but it was reversed at Rose's insistence. Having just signed the divorce papers, lines like "You have no heart, you have no shame / You take true love and give the blame" must have been viscerally real for him. He certainly sang as if they were. Hank's use of common English, tightened and focused by Fred Rose, was now the standard for country song craft: terse, resonant, exact.

The up-tempo song, "I Won't Be Home No More," worked the same theme from a more belligerent perspective. Hank seemed to have one finger raised at Audrey, rather than pointed accusingly at her. Even though it's supposed to be a lighthearted song, Hank seems vindictive, even spiteful.

Then it was Luke the Drifter's turn. Fred Rose had found a song he thought suitable: Bonnie Dodd's "Be Careful of Stones That You Throw." Dodd was a steel guitar player who had been recording on and off since 1937. She had written Tex Ritter's 1945 hit "You Will Have to Pay," and had worked a spell with him. Little Jimmy Dickens had recorded "Be Careful of Stones That You Throw" in October 1949, but it hadn't done much business, so Rose probably wanted to find another home for it. Another cautionary tale, it was the story of a hypocritical neighbor saved by the "bad girl" down the street. Even cutting a song that wasn't his own, Hank seemed to be drawing parallels to his own life. The tide of criticism was mounting, but "unless you've made no mistakes in your life," he seemed to be saying to the detractors now ranged against him, "be careful of stones that you throw." Rose saw the song as the top side of the next Luke the Drifter single, but with hindsight it paled in comparison with the other side.

"Please Make Up Your Mind," also known as "Why Don't You Make Up Your Mind?" was the most rivetingly vengeful song Hank ever wrote or recorded. Over a slow blues backing and with bleak humor, Hank cataloged his grievances against Audrey: her tantrums, her attempts to belittle him, her ungovernable temper.

> *If a poor little rabbit had you on his side*
> *Every hound in the county would haul off and hide*

The rough draft revealed an even more direct shot:

> *Whoever said women was the weaker sex*
> *Baby never had you on his neck*

The next-to-last line of every verse was "The good Lord only knows what I go through," and Audrey's feelings as she heard it can only be guessed at. Not until Bob Dylan's "Positively Fourth Street" was there a song so bitter and demeaning. "Why Don't You Make Up Your Mind?" had been written at least five or six months before the separation. Hank recorded it as a laconic talking blues, but Little Jimmy Dickens had recorded it in July 1951 as an up-tempo song. Dickens' version was called "I Wish You Didn't Love Me So Much," and was scheduled for release, then canceled at the last minute. It was issued in Canada, probably because someone forgot to tell the Canadian branch to pull the plug. Hank's version omits one of the couplets given to Dickens:

> The preacher man said, "For better or worse"
> But lately I've been lookin' for that big black hearse.

It's tempting to read Hank's intimation of his own mortality into his omission of those lines; he had twenty-five weeks to live. No one touched the song again until 1968 when Hank Jr., who then empathized almost as deeply with the lyrics as his father had once done, recorded it for his *Luke the Drifter Jr.* album (one of the last stops on a long, sorry journey that saw Audrey try to make Junior's career into a movable tribute to his father).

One of the songs Hank had hoped to record in July was "Back Street Affair." During the presession discussions, Hank had pitched the idea to Rose, but Rose balked, partly because he sincerely believed that type of song didn't belong on a country record, and partly because he didn't own the publishing. Hank had sung it on one of his early morning radio shows, and Webb Pierce, who was in town to guest on the *Opry,* had heard it. Pierce collared Hank after the *Opry.* He said, "Hank, I sure like your new record, that 'Back Street Affair,'" and Hank said, "It ain't my new record. Fred Rose won't let me record it. Too risky. I think anyone's got guts enough to record it has got themselves a number one hit." Suggestive songs brought Rose's puritanical streak to the surface. He had immutable ideas about what was, and wasn't, a "Song for Home Folks." Writing to Tillman Franks a few years earlier, he had dismissed a song Tillman was pitching as a poor man's "Slippin' Around." "The folks who buy real country records do not like 'Slippin' Around'," he wrote. Several million others did, though. Billy Wallace, the writer of "Back Street Affair," already had it out, but Webb Pierce recorded it on July 9, two days before Hank's session. It gave Pierce, then the *Hayride*'s top act, his third number one hit in a row, a track record just long enough to ensure that, within a few weeks, he earned an invitation to join the *Opry.* His acquisition showed that the *Opry* was still bringing in any artist who might act as a focal point for a rival jamboree.

MGM put the Luke the Drifter single into production immediately, scheduling it for release on August 29. "You Win Again" was slotted onto the flip side of "Settin' the Woods on Fire" and was released two weeks later. Like most of Hank's flip sides, "You Win Again" got a little play, but only enough to get it onto the charts for one week. The first hit with the song went to the black pop singer Tommy Edwards, best known for "It's All in the Game." Edwards cut it for MGM on August 12, one month before Hank's version was released. Frank Walker had Edwards' record rolling off the presses on the same day as Hank's. It climbed to number thirteen in the pop charts in the fall of 1952, but didn't become a country hit until country deejays found it on the flip side of Jerry Lee Lewis' "Great Balls of Fire" in 1958. It didn't become a hit in its own right until Charley Pride recorded it in 1980. By then it was already a standard.

Hank still seemed to be in good shape the day after the recording session. He introduced "Jambalaya" on the *Opry* on July 12. "I got a brand-new song ain't never been aired," he told Red Foley. "Ain't never been aired?" said Foley, playing the straight man. "No, and it might need airin'," said Hank. Foley said he had the song title in front of him and couldn't pronounce it. "It's Jam-bal-eye-oo on the By-oo," said Hank, as the band kicked it off. A month later, it was on the charts, and by September 6 it was number one, where it remained until December.

Hank didn't hold up for long. Ray Price says that the divorce was a watershed in Hank's life, and it was the last straw for Price himself. After Hank spent several days drinking relentlessly, Price called Jim Denny and Don Helms, asking what he should do. "Jim Denny said, 'Take him over to the doctor. The doctor's gonna give him a shot and knock him out, then I want you all to take him to Madison where they'll dry him out.' Don Helms and I, we took him to the doctor and he knocked him out all right, and we carried him out, and he woke up just as we was taking him into that place. He sat up and said, 'Oh, hell no, not this time, you're not gonna get me this time.' But we put him in there anyway." Both Helms and Price thought that Hank would literally drink himself to death if they didn't intervene. Hank ordered Price to move out of the house, and Price did just that, probably with some relief. He found another place, and called Mac McGee, who ran Hank and Audrey's Corral, to verify that he was taking none of Hank's possessions. As he was loading the truck, Hank drove up wearing his hospital robe, chauffered by someone from the hospital. He said, "You know I didn't mean it, Ray. You don't have to go," but Price went anyway. He told Hank he couldn't take it anymore.

After bottoming out, Hank turned himself around once again. Afraid of being alone, he brought a rotating cast of pickers and hangers-on into the house. The party continued, Hank often sitting in the middle of the floor scribbling away on his notepad. By the time the divorce was finalized, it seems as though Bobbie Jett was out of the picture, but Hank had met another woman who came to love him and tried to help him.

Billie Jean Jones was born on June 6, 1933, on a farm twenty miles out of Shreveport. "I knew when I was five years old draggin' a cotton sack, if I ever got off that son of a bitch, I'd never be back," she says. Soon after the Second World War, her father became a policeman in Bossier City, Louisiana, and it was there that Billie Jean grew up with her two brothers, Alton and Sonny.

Hank Williams drove by the Jones' house on Modica Street every day in early 1949. Billie Jean says that she told her mother she was going to marry him, but when she married that year it was to Harrison Eshliman, a corporal in the air force police. Eshliman worked alongside Billie Jean's father, and she became his wife on her sixteenth birthday, June 6, 1949, just as Hank was leaving Shreveport. She became pregnant during her first week of marriage without ever really understanding how, and her first daughter, Jeri Lynn, was born on March 11, 1950. By the time Jeri Lynn was born, Eshliman was history, and by 1951, Mrs. Jones was baby-sitting while Billie Jean stepped out. With long, flaming ginger hair, Billie Jean was, as she says herself, "something to behold." The party crowd seemed to gravitate to her.

Early in 1951, Billie Jean started dating Webb Pierce's understudy, Faron Young. At that point, Young was just about to quit Pierce's band and strike out on his own. In June 1952, he received a summons to Nashville to guest on the *Opry*. Billie Jean rode up with him. "He was wild as a bear cat," she says. "Oh God! He knew he could sing and he was about halfway wise, but nothing could ever have worked out between us. I was dating him and about a hundred others, but my dad cosigned a note on a car to get us up there. I was just gonna go up and back."

The night before Faron Young came to Nashville, he was on a show date in Memphis with Hank Snow. Jerry Rivers worked the date with Snow, and remembered Faron squiring Billie Jean around backstage. Early the following morning, Rivers and Helms were at WSM to work with Hank when Faron walked in. Rivers asked him where Billie Jean was, and Faron told him that she was asleep in the car outside. As Faron played his first guest spot on the *Opry*, Billie Jean sat in the glassed-in visitors' box. She was wearing an off-the-shoulder dress, black and figure-hugging, with white lace at the top. It caught the wandering eye of the show's star, Hank Williams. Billie Jean recalls:

> He saw me and hunkered down, and looked at me through the glass. He came in, sat down beside me. Just sat there and looked at me. I tried to ignore him. Finally, he said, "Girl, who you up here with?" I said, "Faron Young." He said, "Is that the kid that's guesting up here from Shreveport?" I said, "Yes sir." About that time, Minnie Pearl came up to the glass, and he motioned to her, he said, "Minnie, find Faron Young, tell him ol' Hank wants to see him." So here comes Faron. Hank said, "Faron, you gonna marry this girl?" Faron said, "No-o-o, Hank. She's too mean and too fast. She's got too many boyfriends, I can't keep up with her.'" Hank said, "Well, if you ain't gonna marry her, ol' Hank's gonna marry her." He said, 'Faron, go out there. You see that ol' black-haired gal in the front row with the red dress on. She flew down here from Pennsylvania to see me. After we get through working tonight, let's you and me go out 'n' party. That gal, she's gonna be your gal, and Billie's gonna be my gal."

With the *Opry* in his sights, Faron Young had no intention of crossing the show's star. Billie Jean continues:

> When they got through that night, we went out to Faron's convertible. [Hank] said, "Boy, you drive." He told his girlfriend to sit in the front seat with Faron. We got out to some joint; I said I had a headache and I wasn't going in. He said, "Faron, you go in and have a good time. I'm gonna stay out here and talk with Billie." We moved up to the front seat. Me on the right-hand side with the door open, and him crouched down outside. We started shooting the bull about him living on the same street as me in Bossier. He was telling me about his problems with Audrey and so on. After a while, he said, "Why don't we go in, listen to the music and drink some coffee." I said, "Okay, if you'll drink coffee," 'cause I'd already heard about his clowning. I didn't care if he was King Farouk, because I was Queen Farouk.

Faron Young later insisted that any notions he might have had of another fling with Billie Jean were dispelled when Hank pulled a gun on him. Billie took a room in a girls' boardinghouse on Shelby Avenue. "It cost ten dollars a week," she says, "but I was sending money back to Louisiana to look after my kid and I needed the trolley fare. Hank looked so funny walking across my floor, 'cause it was on an angle, but I wouldn't let him pay my rent. He had hundred-dollar bills falling out of his pocket." She transferred from the Shreveport phone company to the Nashville phone company.

In testimony given in conjunction with a 1975 lawsuit over copyright renewals, Faron Young omitted the incident with the gun, concentrating instead on the good times. WSM had given him a fifteen-minute show at 5:00 a.m., so he took a room at Mom Upchurch's boardinghouse, one floor above Carl Smith. Hank would pick him up and they'd go bowling at Melrose Lanes. Young remembered one day in particular:

> One time, he said, "Boy, drive me down to Ernest Tubb's Record Shop. I wanna buy somethin'." I always jumped at the chance because I got to drive his Cadillac convertible. We headed down Broadway to the record shop, and I heard a squeaking noise. I said, "Hank, this car's got a squeak somewhere." He said, "Yeah, boy, but don't you wish you had a car that squeaked like that?" We got down to the record shop and there wasn't any place to park. He said, "Well, shoot, put it up in the door." I said, "C'mon, Hank, where should I park?" "I told you, boy, put it up in the door." That's where I parked it. Right in E.T.'s doorway."

It seems as though Hank gave Faron Young much more than a chance to drive his Cadillac. In March 1952, Young signed with Capitol Records, but his first three singles went nowhere. Apparently, Hank gave him a song he'd written, "Goin' Steady," and Faron recorded it on October 12, 1952. The song was credited to Faron Young, not Hank Williams, so it could have been ceded to Faron in a trade. The trade might even have been for Billie Jean. It became Faron's breakthrough hit, and the only song Hank ever pitched that became a hit for someone else. The evidence that Hank wrote it is sketchy, but compelling. There's a song manuscript of "Goin' Steady" in Hank's handwriting among his papers at Acuff-Rose, and, as Faron's record wasn't released until a few weeks after Hank's death, it's very unlikely that Hank would have heard it on the radio. It also sounds like a Hank Williams song. Faron Young wasn't a songwriter. His name appears on many songs, but usually as a cowriter, and his "cowriters" almost invariably insist that Faron didn't write anything; he just offered to record the song in return for half of the composer credit. In March 1953 (when "Goin' Steady" was high in the charts), Hank's attorney, Robert Stewart, corresponded with Hank's sister, Irene, about the song. "I understand from Audrey this morning," he wrote, "that he [Fred Rose] is not attaching the royalties on 'Goin' Steady' in spite of definite information sent him as to Hank's authorship." Stewart, though, didn't specify what that information was.

Within weeks of Billie Jean's arrival in Nashville, Hank asked her to marry him. They hired a driver and went to Shreveport to visit her parents in early August; Hank dictated thirteen songs along the way. "He looked over to me in the car," she said, "and he told me, 'I can say one thing, baby, I could never be ashamed of you.' Like he had been of Audrey. He said, 'That'd be a good idea for a song. Write this down for ol' Hank, baby.' He'd call 'em off as fast as I could write." They told Billie Jean's parents that they would marry as soon as her divorce became effective.

As they neared Nashville on the return trip, Hank bought five pounds of fish and was planning to have the driver cook it up that night, but when they pulled up in front of the house, they found the plate glass in the front door smashed in. A woman's red shoes were on the doormat and her luggage was in the hall. One of Hank's old flames had moved in. He ordered her out, then they started wrestling with each other. Billie Jean and the driver stood, mouths agape, as Hank and the ex-girlfriend tussled in the hallway. Billie told the driver to take her back to her apartment. Hank climbed in beside Billie Jean. Then, incredibly, the girlfriend got in too.

"We loaded up the car, got to my apartment," said Billie. "I got out, took off up the path, and Hank came in with me. I was mad. He said he was gonna get rid of that broad but it was gonna take a club. I told him, 'That's it, I'm gone. I'm history. I ain't puttin' up with this crap no more.' It was like wolves chasing him. The rest of that week, I packed. He got rid of that sucker and came back over. I said, 'I'm going back to Louisiana. This is wrong and I don't want any part of it.'" A few days later, she was gone.

Hank was now in a serious mess. According to Billie Jean, Audrey was refusing him access to Hank Jr., and Bobbie Jett had reappeared, heavy with what she insisted was his child. After Billie Jean left, Hank appears to have plummeted downward yet again. He missed show dates and radio commitments, and the only two out-of-town show dates that he's known to have played in July were at Sunset Park in West Grove, Pennsylvania. One of the shows was taped, and Hank was on top of his game, telling jokes and sounding as good as he ever did. Still, WSM would not allow this state of affairs to continue, and everything came to a head during the second week in August. At some point during that week, Jim Denny and Carl Smith visited Hank at his house, and Denny told Hank that WSM's management was demanding that he be dismissed. Denny asked for one more chance, and told Hank that he absolutely had to be at the *Opry* on August 9 and at an *Opry*-sponsored show the following day.

August the ninth arrived, and Hank didn't. Ray Price says that Hank showed up drunk at an *Opry*-sponsored show in Reading, Pennsylvania, the following day, and the park owners raised hell with the *Opry*. Jim Denny couldn't go back on his ultimatum. The *Opry* was a brand, and Hank was ruining its reputation. WSM's program director, Jack Stapp, once took whatever credit was to be had for canning Hank, but it appears fairly certain that, on August 11, Jim Denny picked up the phone and fired him. "It was the toughest thing I ever had to do in my life," he said later. Ernest Tubb said he was hanging around WSM that day. In Tubb's recollection it was Friday that Hank was fired, although newspaper reports indicate that it was Monday. This was how Tubb remembered the events unfolding:

> I heard Jim on the telephone. He said, "Hank, that's it. You gotta prove to me. You call me in December, and I'll let you know about coming back to the *Opry* next year." When Jim hung up the telephone, he had tears in his eyes. He said, "I had to do it. I had to let Hank go." When I was in the parking lot, I ran into [National Life chairman] Mr. [Edwin] Craig. He knew, and he said, "What do you think, Ernest?" I said, "Well, I hate it, but I saw tears in Jim's eyes, and I know it was the hardest thing he ever had to do. He told me he was going to try and get Hank to straighten up." Mr. Craig said, "I'm sure Jim means well, but it may work the other way. It may kill him." I was feeling the same way.

Johnnie Wright claims that he was sitting with Hank at the moment the phone rang. According to Wright, the scene played out with far less sentimentality:

Jim Denny told him he was going to have to let him go. Hank said, "You cain't fire me 'cause I already quit." He had a check coming, about three hundred dollars. Jim asked Hank if anyone was there with him, and Hank said, "Johnnie Wright's here." He said, "Tell Johnnie I want to talk to him." I got on the phone and Jim said, "Johnnie, he's got a check up here. You come by and pick it up." My brother-in-law had a Chrysler limousine, and Hank had his trailer with "Drifting Cowboys" written on the side. We put all his belongings in the trailer and his reclining chair in the back of the limousine, and put him in the reclining chair.

Don Helms heard the news and, just as Hank was leaving with Johnnie Wright, he came over to Hank's house to return a shotgun and a watch that he'd been holding. Helms' wife was with him; they had all been friends since 1944. "I told Hazel," says Helms, "Hank Williams won't live six months." Hank was drinking as he and Wright drove away. According to Wright, their first stop was at WSM:

Roy Acuff and Owen Bradley was in Jim Denny's office. Roy said, "Have you got Hank out there?" I said, "Yeah." Owen said, "Let's go out and see him, Roy." They went out and I picked up his check. Then we took off to Montgomery. We went out on Broadway, and there was a liquor store out there at Sixteenth and Broad, and Hank said, "Johnnie, pull in there and get me some whiskey." So I pulled in and got him a fifth and cashed his three-hundred-dollar check. The guy that owned the liquor store said, "Is Hank out there?" I said, "Yeah," so the guy came out and spoke to him. We took him to his mother's house. We pulled his clothes off, put him to bed, and talked to his mother 'til he woke up. Hank acted like he didn't care that he'd been canned.

Part of Hank's act was bravado, but he may have felt that he had out-grown the *Opry,* and that he now was of greater value to the show than it was to him. Eddy Arnold had quit the *Opry* and was doing well, and Red Foley would soon quit. The *Opry* tied up its entire cast at paltry wages on potentially the most lucrative night of the week. Instead of walking away from a Saturday night show date with several thousand dollars stuffed in his case, he was flying to Nashville at his own expense to work for little more than exposure that he now thought he didn't need. During their conversation, Hank had mouthed off to Denny about the number of records he had on the charts, but from Denny's perspective it didn't mat-ter anymore. The irony of Hank Williams' relationship with the *Opry* is that some *Opry* stars were on the show for forty, fifty, or even sixty years, but Hank Williams remains the star associated in most people's minds with the *Grand Ole Opry,* despite the fact that he was on the show for only three years.

Johnnie Wright was due to work a show with Hank, a Greenville Homecoming organized by the Rotary Club. It was scheduled for August 15, four days after the firing. Hank had to get himself straight and he had to get a car to squire himself through town because he had literally lost his tan Cadillac Coupe de Ville. He bought a four-month-old 1952 powder-blue Cadillac convertible coupe. The first owner was a serviceman at Fort Bragg, North Carolina, named Homer Cooper, who'd bought it for $5,083. Hank paid $3,818 with the help of a loan from the Third National Bank.

The Greenville Homecoming didn't pack quite the punch of the Montgomery Homecoming in July the previous year. Greenville was a smaller city, and Hank had only lived there two years. Still, there were two shows at Greenville Stadium and a parade preceding the afternoon show. In the photographs, Hank has an ugly contusion above his lip, suggesting that he'd recently been in a fight. One strong possibility is that the welt came from a beating Lilly had administered after Hank had returned home fired and drunk. Apart from that, Hank seemed to bounce back yet again. In all, eighty-five hundred people turned out to honor him, including his father and his uncle Robert. Marie's son, Butch, rode in the car. Hank looked for Tee-Tot and acknowledged him publicly, but apparently no one knew that Tee-Tot had been in a pauper's grave since 1939.

After the Homecoming, Hank went back to Lilly's boardinghouse. The word in the local paper was that he was suffering from blood poisoning from an infected wound, and was lying low as he regrouped. On the *Opry* it was announced that Hank was sick, although his dismissal had been made public by the Nashville papers on August 14. Hank finally located his other car in Philadelphia, and arranged for it to be driven to Nashville. He and one of his WSFA band members, Shorty Seals, drove up to collect it. Hank now had one ex-wife, one ex-fiancée, one pregnant girlfriend, two cars, no band, no show dates, and far too much time on his hands. The pregnant girlfriend, Bobbie Jett, joined him in Montgomery. Hank appears to have gotten back with her right after Billie Jean left town.

Lilly phoned Bob McKinnon, a deejay in Alexander City, Alabama, and asked him to take Hank out to the country for a few days. Hank was introducing Bobbie Jett around town as "Bobbie Blue," and telling people that she was his nurse. McKinnon had a cousin who was married to an automobile dealer named Darwin Dobbs, who owned a nicely appointed lodge out on a part of Lake Martin known as Kowaliga Bay. Originally, Kowaliga was the name of a creek that ran into the Tallapoosa River, and when the river was dammed to make Lake Martin, the locals started calling the area where the creek had been Kowaliga Bay. A legend goes that the Creek Indians are supposed to have had a settlement there called "Kia-leach-shi" (headdress) because they made headdresses there.

Hank, Bobbie, and Bob McKinnon got to Dobbs' lodge early on the afternoon of Sunday, August 17. McKinnon left around 4:00 p.m. for Alexander City. Hank was sober and looking forward to some rest. Around midnight, McKinnon was awakened by a call from the police department. Hank was no longer at the lodge nor sober. He was in the Alexander City jail. "I believe he was more or less having DTs," said Chief Winfred Patterson. "He was running up and down the hall [of the Russell Hotel] yelling that someone was whupping old ladies and he was going to stop them." After he was arrested, the chief said that Hank was no trouble. Hank told the chief that he'd been in some worse jails, some better.

Bob McKinnon went to get Bobbie at the Russell Hotel, came down to the jail, made Hank's bail, and got him released. No charges were laid. It has long been supposed that a photograph of Hank, shirtless and disheveled, was taken as he exited the jail that morning. He had the cornered-animal look that he had when coming off a spree. It was a harrowing photo, but probably taken on the occasion of an earlier arrest in Alexander City. That time he had threatened to buy the town.

McKinnon took Hank and Bobbie to another motel, and left Hank to sleep it off. He then took Bobbie back up to the lake to get some of her things. McKinnon heard her vomiting in the bathroom and she told him that she was pregnant. On the way back, she explained what had happened the previous day. Hank had been playing with some kids on a bridge and he'd waded out into the lake. Some people from Red Hill had seen him, found out he was Hank Williams, and produced a five-gallon jug of corn liquor. And so the party began.

The following afternoon, McKinnon went to get Hank and Bobbie. Hank was dreadfully hungover. He only remembered going to jail. "I got me in," he said to McKinnon. "Who got me out?" McKinnon told him what had happened. He drove Hank and Bobbie to Frank "Country" Duncan's house, then back out to Kowaliga. Duncan and a black valet were to stay with Hank for a few days, but Hank was restless. The following day, he appeared at the radio station where McKinnon worked and asked to go to the bank. Lilly had specifically told McKinnon, "No banks," but, as Hank had said for as long as he could remember, "What momma don't know won't hurt her."

McKinnon took Hank to the First National Bank in Alexander City, and Hank arranged to get some money wired in from somewhere. Bobbie asked him what he wanted the money for, and Hank said he wanted to get some clothes. Bobbie said, "Hank, what're you gonna do with clothes? We've got clothes scattered all the way from San Diego, California, to Portland, Maine." But Hank bought clothes anyway. He also bought some tires from Darwin Dobbs' dealership to repay him for the loan of the lodge. While the tires were being changed, Lilly drove up with Detective Louis King. She gave McKinnon some antialcoholic medication, had words with Hank, then drove back to Montgomery.

That night Hank, Bobbie, McKinnon, and a party of locals went back to Kowaliga. When it was time to send out for drinks someone suggested Whitley's near Montgomery. Hank said, "No, I might run into Momma. I don't want to chance it." So they went to a bootlegger in Kellyton instead. On the way there and back Hank started pounding out a wardance rhythm on the dashboard and chanting "Kowaliga, Kowaliga."

Hank worked on his song that night and told McKinnon to phone Fred Rose the following morning. He wanted Rose to get what he called an "arr-plane" down to Montgomery so that they could polish the song. Hank stayed at the cabin for several days, worked on "Kaw-Liga" and several more songs, including "Your Cheatin' Heart" and one called "Lonesomest Time of the Day." Bobbie Jett, meanwhile, returned to Nashville and took a room at a hotel with her daughter, Jo. At some point, Hank and his cousin Marie Glenn drove up to see her, but Marie never said what transpired between them.

Rose didn't get an airplane to Montgomery, but he drove down with Murray Nash. They drove overnight from Nashville and were in Montgomery by eight o'clock the following morning, just as Lilly was serving breakfast to her boarders. She went and roused Hank, and Hank produced the three songs he had written. "I needed to get some things into the post office," said Nash, "and Fred said Hank should go with me to the post office and he'd work on the songs. By the time we came back, Fred had refashioned 'Kowaliga' into 'Kaw-Liga' and made it into a song about a dimestore Indian." If nowhere else, the hand of Fred Rose was apparent in the way "Kaw-Liga" starts in a minor key and modulates to a major key on the bridge. Murray Nash had brought a little home recorder, and Hank's demos of both songs survived. Hank clearly had trouble with the minor key in "Kaw-Liga" and, at one point, stops in exasperation. "Shit," he says. By the third take, he'd mastered the song. "Purr ol' Kaw-Liga," he sang, just as he'd sung "Purr wicked soul" on his first session.

Talking to the local paper a few weeks later, Lilly recalled Hank and Fred Rose sitting in her front room, talking and writing songs until late into the night. "Sometimes," she said, "I woke up and heard the prettiest song I ever heard. They'd already put it on tape and recorded it and they were playing it back. It's so pretty, it made my hair stand on end." Coyly, she added, "It's called . . . well, I better not say." She might have been among the first to hear "Your Cheatin' Heart."

Fred Rose had a plan to get Hank's career back on track. Rose had plenty of other irons in the fire, but Hank Williams was his ace. Aside from anything else, Hank was doing what Acuff had originally done — drawing other writers to the company. Then there was the income that Hank single-handedly generated for the company. Between January and June 1952, Acuff-Rose had a total of 89 copyrights recorded; Hank's records and the cover versions they attracted made the biggest single contribution to that tally. To put those 89 copyrights into perspective, the top popular music publishing group, Robbins Music, which represented hundreds of standards, had 156 copyrights recorded during the same period.

Rose wanted to get Hank back on the *Louisiana Hayride,* and Hank's remaining trump, "Jambalaya," gave him just enough leverage. It had already sold two hundred thousand copies when Rose started talking to KWKH, so many copies in fact that MGM had to lay on a Saturday shift at the plant to cope with the demand. The success of "Jambalaya" pushed the official tally of Hank's record sales to more than ten million in a shade over five years, and on September 12, MGM released his second album. Once again, it was issued in three formats (10-inch LP, or four 45s or 78s packaged in an album), and it was called *Moanin' the Blues.* And once again, Rose used the LP as little more than an excuse to offload some back catalog, in this case songs with "Blues" in the title.

For its part, KWKH needed Hank Williams or someone like him. KWKH's owners, the Ewing family, owned another station, KTHS, in Hot Springs, Arkansas. KTHS had just been alloted a fifty-thousand-watt clear channel, and twenty other stations were picking up the *Hayride* on transcription, while CBS was talking about picking up part of the show for networking. The only cloud in the sky was that the *Hayride* had just lost two of its major stars, Webb Pierce and Faron Young. Only Slim Whitman remained. Sick, sober, or sorry, Hank Williams seemed just the ticket, and the negotiations started that would send him back to Shreveport. Reports in the *Shreveport Times* stated that he signed a three-year contract. The deal was announced on August 30, 1952.

On September 8, 1952, Hank cut one of his last remaining ties to Nashville when he sold his farm in Williamson County in what amounted to a fire sale. He got $28,500 — less than half of what he had paid for it. A little earlier, he sold Hank and Audrey's Corral and $50,000 or $60,000 worth of inventory and fixtures to the manager, Mac McGee, for $4,000. To compound the loss, he paid off the $12,000 in accounts payable to leave McGee with a clean slate. McGee ran the store until April 1953, when it folded.

Hank Williams wanted out of Nashville at any price.

*It's a great separation my friends have caused me
By bearing the spite my favor has won,
It's a great separation, likewise a vexation
And they shall be sorry for what they have done.*

"Adieu to Bon County" (unknown)

· ·

"I'M SO TIRED OF IT ALL"

· ·

"Boy, thank you, Horace, thank you a lot. Boy, sure feels good to be home, y'know."

"Been 'bout two years since you've been home, boy."

WITH that exchange, Hank Williams was back on the *Louisiana Hayride*. It had been a shade over three years since he had left with his heart full of hope. He was brought back on September 13 for a teaser, and after Horace Logan's introduction, he sang "Jambalaya," "Lovesick Blues," "Honky Tonk Blues," and the as-yet-unrecorded "I Could Never Be Ashamed of You." The crowd clapped and stomped, and wouldn't let him off the stage for twenty minutes. He promised to be back to play and sing every week.

Just before Hank left for Shreveport, he called Billie Jean. "Baby," he said, "this is ol' Hank." Billie Jean was taken off guard. "I do believe we've got a date October nineteenth," he said. It was the date they had planned to marry, after her divorce from Harrison Eshliman had become final. "Well," she said, "we *had* a date."

"Listen," he said, "in a coupla days, ol' Hank's gonna be down. I'm movin' to Shreveport. I want you to find me a place." And a few days later, as Billie Jean recalled it, Hank drove in. Marie Glenn, though, said that he flew while she and Clyde Perdue drove his cars. Perdue had staged the Greenville Homecoming and was now Hank's personal manager. Born in April 1914 in Farmersville, Alabama, some twenty-five miles outside Greenville, Perdue was an Air Corps veteran who had returned to Greenville after the Second World War, first as an express clerk and then as a theater manager. Neither occupation had groomed him to be Hank Williams' manager.

Everything Hank owned from his three and a half years at the top of his profession was in those two vehicles. Billie's brother, Sonny Jones, found him a room in an apartment hotel, and, as Hank drove around the streets he knew so well, greeting a few old cronies from the first go-round, no one came away with the impression that he thought he'd been demoted. He was upbeat, or, as he would say, spry, still insisting that he had quit the *Opry.*

"He called me from an Italian restaurant downtown, Tony Sansone's on Spring Street," said Horace Logan. "He said, 'Come on down, I want you to meet my French girl.' I went down, walked in, and there was Billie Jean. I said, 'Billie Jean, where in hell have you been?' Hank said, 'You know my French girl?' I said, 'She's not French — she's Irish as can be.'"

Settled back in Shreveport, Hank tried to reassemble his old band. He called Felton Pruett, his steel guitar player from the first time around, but Pruett had had enough Hank Williams for one lifetime. "He got real perturbed at me for not going back with him," said Pruett. "He was pretty strong with me. He had Billie Jean with him and he was treating her bad, cussin' at her, and I thought, 'Hell, I don't need none of this.'" Although he tried, Hank never succeeded in putting a band together. When he toured, he sometimes used Red Sovine's band, which included pianist Floyd Cramer, steel guitarist Jimmy Day, and guitarist Tommy Bishop; sometimes he used the house band at the clubs. Like Chuck Berry, Hank figured that everyone knew his songs, so he wouldn't even bother to rehearse his pick-up bands. At show time, he would kick off every song with a chord. "Gear of C, boys," he'd say. He'd telegraph the last verse by lifting his foot.

Hank managed to get Oscar Davis to rejoin him for a while. Perhaps with Oscar, he thought, it would be just like 1949 all over again. Hank found him in Vancouver, Canada, and persuaded him to come down to Shreveport. "He was living in a horrible, horrible motel," said Oscar.

"Sparsely furnished. An old kitchen table and junk all around. He wanted me to meet Billie, so every night we had to go out and sit and drink." It's possible that Oscar arrived from Canada with an Australian singer he was managing, Tex Morton. When Morton signed with Columbia Records in 1952, Davis was listed on the contract as his manager, and they'd reportedly worked together in Canada. Morton later told friends in Australia that Davis asked him to hypnotize Hank into giving up alcohol.

Commercially, this would be life lived at a lower level than Hank had known it for several years. Oscar Davis notified *Billboard* that he expected Hank to tour every second week and spend the other week songwriting. It was a gauge of Hank's unreliability that his record of "Jambalaya" was atop the country charts and Jo Stafford's pop cover version was in the top ten, yet he and the song everyone wanted to hear were confined to smaller halls and beer joints around Shreveport. The emphasis on songwriting might have represented much more than an attempt to slow down, though. In terms of record sales, Hank was already a falling star. "Jambalaya" was number one, but his income from record sales had slipped from $22,574 in 1950, to $20,224 in 1951, down to $13,869 in 1952. Meanwhile, his Acuff-Rose income had risen from $18,040 in 1950, to $32,632 in 1951, and jumped to $55,044 in 1952 as the revenue from the pop cover versions kicked in.

Immediately after arriving back in Shreveport, Hank went out on a short tour, accompanied by Billie Jean and Clyde Perdue. On September 17, they went to San Antonio, where they visited the Alamo. That night, Hank played Charlie Walker's club, the Barn. Walker later scored several big hits, chiefly "Pick Me Up on Your Way Down." Doug Sahm, then eleven years old, was in the audience. Already something of a child prodigy, he was brought up onstage to sit on Hank's lap and play "Steel Guitar Rag." "His breath stank of whiskey," said Doug, "and there wasn't nothin' left to him. His knees were sharp. Poked right into me." Hank was in a good mood that night, though. He was celebrating his twenty-ninth birthday, and Charlie Walker had arranged a private party after the show. Walker ordered a cake with the musical notes of "Jambalaya" around the circumference, and "Happy Birthday Hank from All Your Friends" in the center. The cake was hidden behind the piano, then brought out at the end of the set. Hank was so moved that tears streamed down his face.

Hank and Billie Jean went to change after the show while Walker stood guard over the door. Suddenly, a three-hundred-pound oil field worker appeared and demanded to see Hank. He pushed Walker aside and burst into the room. Walker called his bouncers, but the intruder broke free and sent the cake flying to the floor. Billie Jean's brothers were with Hank. One of them, Sonny, had frizzy hair, and Hank called him "Niggerhead." "Git him, Niggerhead," said Hank, and Sonny flew across the table and floored the guy. As he went down, Hank kicked him several times with his pointy-toed boots, and left. It was a bizarre coda to what would be his last birthday.

Three days later, Hank made his official return to the *Louisiana Hayride.* He had hassled with KWKH general manager Henry Clay, insisting that he wasn't going to work for scale, and Clay had agreed to pay him around two hundred dollars a show instead of the usual eighteen. Horace Logan insists that Hank was tied to the show with a one-year contract on which the *Hayride* could exercise two additional one-year options.

On Tuesday, September 23, Hank flew back to Nashville for a recording session. The two songs he had finished in Montgomery with Fred Rose, "Kaw-Liga" and "Your Cheatin' Heart," were on the slate together with the song he'd written for Billie Jean, "I Could Never Be Ashamed of You." To round out the session, Fred Rose contributed perhaps the best song he ever presented to Hank, "Take These Chains from My Heart." It was one of the very few Fred Rose songs that sounded somewhat similar to a Hank Williams song.

If Hank was in terminal decline, it wasn't obvious from this session. Most of those present remember him in better shape than the last couple of times he had recorded. The problems, such as they were, stemmed from the fact that Bobbie Jett had got wind of the fact that Hank was recording and appeared at the studio. Billie Jean was there as well as Paul Cohen, who had been one of Bobbie Jett's suitors. Hank was denying everything to Billie Jean. After the session, Hank and Billie went for dinner with Wesley and Fred Rose at Bozeman's Restaurant on Murfreesboro Road.

Under the circumstances, it's surprising that anything was cut, and even more surprising that the session was, in many ways, one of Hank's best and most productive. It was also his last. Most singers hope to hang their careers on one or two classics; Hank cut four classics between 1:30 and 3:40 on the afternoon of September 23, 1952, including "Your Cheatin' Heart," the song that would become as much his anthem in death as "Lovesick Blues" had been in life. "Your Cheatin' Heart" is the song that — for all intents and purposes — defines country music. Hank's performance of the song underscores its scalding bitterness. Billie Jean says that Hank wrote the song on their drive to Louisiana in August, and insists that it was aimed at Miss Audrey. If so, Hank might have appreciated the irony that Audrey collected copiously off a song that was, in virtually every respect, a character assassination of her. "You'll toss around and call my name. . . . You'll walk the floor the way I do" were prophecies truer than Hank could ever have hoped or imagined. Perhaps unable to come to terms with the implications of the song, Audrey eventually tried to believe that Hank had written it about himself. "You or no one else would ever believe this," she said late in life, setting up her listeners for the required leap of faith. "Hank wrote ['Your Cheatin' Heart'] immediately after he and I had just separated, and he wrote [the] song about himself, hoping that I would think that he thought I might have been cheating."

"Kaw-Liga" needed a drummer, so Fred Rose brought in a big band musician, Farris Coursey, who'd played brushes on "Moanin' the Blues." Drummers were still prohibited on the *Opry* stage, but Coursey was the drummer in WSM's dance band, and provided the Indian wardance rhythm that Rose wanted. At the close, "Kaw-Liga" was faded — the first and only Hank Williams recording to end in a fade, now the industry norm. The lesson of "Jambalaya" had been that a novelty song with a faintly ethnic twist was a hot prospect, and that's what Hank and Fred Rose had crafted on "Kaw-Liga." Hank left the session with an acetate of the song, and when he played it for people he told them that it would be his biggest record yet. No one doubted him.

The first song from the September 23 session to hit the stores was "I Could Never Be Ashamed of You." Rose slotted it onto the flip side of "I'll Never Get Out of This World Alive" for November 21 release. After Frank Walker got the session tapes, he distributed the songs among his pop acts. "Your Cheatin' Heart" went to Joni James, "Kaw-Liga" to Bill Farrell, and "Take These Chains from My Heart" to Tommy Edwards. After Mitch Miller got advance acetates from Fred Rose, he gave "Your Cheatin' Heart" to Frankie Laine. Both Laine's and Joni James' version cracked the pop top ten in 1953. Dolores Gray's Decca recording of "Kaw-Liga" got up to number twenty-three on the pop charts in May 1953.

Two days after the session, Billie Jean finally filed for divorce from

Harrison Eshliman, then accompanied Hank on a tour of Georgia and South Carolina with her old flame, Faron Young, on the bill. Generally, though, Oscar Davis booked short tours with *Hayride* acts. The *Hayride* still didn't have anything comparable to the *Opry*'s Artist Service Bureau, but that was just as well because the *Hayride* would have done what the *Opry* had done: flung Hank from coast to coast, using him as a standard bearer for the show. Fred Rose was clearly hoping that the shock of being exiled from Nashville together with the less demanding schedule would be sufficient to make Hank shape up. The thought also probably occured to him that if Hank screwed up, it would be in front of only a few hundred people somewhere in eastern Texas.

As it was, the biggest show that Hank played after he returned to the *Hayride* was his own wedding. Oscar Davis came up with the notion of a public pay-per-view marriage in New Orleans on Sunday, October 19. "We had most of our meetings at a saloon in Bossier City," Davis recalled during 1975 trial testimony. "No one had any money, and they were worried about what they would do for money. I suggested a public wedding onstage in New Orleans, and I made arrangements with Ed Pendergrass at WBOK." Davis presold tickets at prices ranging from $1.00 to $2.80. Around fourteen thousand people would see Hank married at the Municipal Auditorium at a three o'clock "rehearsal" and again at seven. It appears as though no one from Nashville was invited, except Audrey. If Lilly was invited, she didn't attend.

The last unresolved item of business from Nashville was an ex-girlfriend now six months pregnant. During the week before the wedding, Billie Jean went to New Orleans to do advance publicity for the wedding. Hank worked show dates in and around Oklahoma City on October 13 and 14, and then, on October 15, flew back to Montgomery to sign a document that provided for Bobbie Jett and her child. In the first sentence of the agreement, it was stated that "Hank Williams may be the father of said child," and the document went on to note that Hank would provide for Bobbie Jett's room and board in Montgomery, that he would pay all doctor bills and hospital bills, and that, thirty days after the birth of the child, he would provide a one-way plane ticket from Montgomery to anywhere in California that Bobbie designated.

The child was to be placed in the care of Lilly and Bill Stone for two years, and during that time Hank was to pay for a nurse. The agreement then stated that "both the father [and here Hank was referred to as the father, not the possible father], Hank Williams, and Bobbie Jett shall have the right to visit said child." Then, beginning on the child's third birthday, Hank was to assume custody of the child until his or her fifth birthday. At that point, custody was to be shared; Hank would have custody during school months, and Bobbie Jett would have custody during the summer. On two other instances in the agreement, Hank was referred to as the father, although, contradictorily, the agreement concluded with the notation that the "paternity of said child is in doubt" and emphasized that paternity was not to be construed as admitted by the fact that Hank had entered into the agreement. It strains credibility, though, to believe that Hank would have entered into such complex custody arrangements for a child he did not truly believe to be his own.

For her part, Billie Jean contends that Hank signed the agreement partly at the urging of his mother and partly to get Bobbie Jett off their backs. "Every gig he played, she'd pop up," she said. "Here she is fixing to drop somebody's kid." Billie also contends that Hank was incapable of siring a child in March or April when Bobbie Jett's child was conceived, because when she met him in July he was still incapable of having sex as a result of his operation. "It was on his mind," she says, "but, as my momma always said, 'If it can't get up, it can't get out.'" But if, as Billie Jean says, Hank was impotent when she met him in July or August, it was probably because of the alcohol and pills he had been taking rather than the operation.

On the trip back to Montgomery, Hank ran into his old bass player, Lum York. Lum was working with Lefty Frizzell and was resting up in town for a few days. Lilly tracked him down at the radio station and tried to get him to change Hank's mind about marrying Billie Jean. Lum told her he was having no part of it, but she said that as Hank was just around the corner in the barber shop, Lum should go look him up anyway. Lum recalled their conversation:

> He was in the chair when I got there, so I went into the little coffee shop near the barber, and he come in and said, "Do you wanna go work for me?" I said, "Hank, how much you gonna pay me?" He said, "I'll pay you seventy-five a week." I said, "Hank, I'm making more than that." He said, "Aw, that's the way it is with Frizzell and them guys, they want to pay you all they make." I said, "Well, I'm satisfied where I'm working." He

said, "How 'bout catchin' a plane with me and goin' to Shreveport?" I said, "Naw, I'm staying around here a coupla days." I
never did talk to him 'bout marryin' Billie Jean. I figured he was
a grown man.

On October 17, two days after signing the agreement with Bobbie
Jett, Hank was back in Shreveport. Billie Jean was back from New
Orleans and went to court that day with her father. Judge Louis Lyons of
Bossier City represented her. Billie was told that her decree would be
granted on October 28, some ten days after she planned to marry. Either
she didn't understand the implication of what she was told, or she
decided to ignore it. Hank wasn't with her, and it's unclear what, if anything, she told him. When the court reconvened on the twenty-eighth,
the news of Hank and Billie's marriage was public, and Judge Bolin
asked her attorney, Louis Lyons, if he'd seen the newspaper reports.
Lyons said that he hadn't, and Bolin said that he would grant the decree
on the understanding that Lyons would contact Billie Jean, to inform her
that she should marry again, as the public marriage was invalid. Lyons
said he would probably perform the ceremony himself and collect
another fee.

It's hard to know exactly what Hank was doing on October 17. Billie
Jean says that Audrey flew to Shreveport, trying to convince him to
return to her by threatening that he would never see their son again.
They met in a hotel room, and Hank emerged with a welt on his fore-
head, the result, says Billie Jean, of Audrey hitting him. A welt is clearly
visible in the wedding photos, although its provenance has never been
established. In a 1975 trial over copyright renewals, one of Hank's
Hayride costars, Paul Howard, remembered seeing Hank on October 18
and remarking on his scratched-up appearance.

"What tiger bit you?" Howard asked.

"Audrey and my mother has been down here," Hank replied. "I
don't know what they're going to do in New Orleans."

The hours before the ceremony were very tense. Billie Jean had been
told that she wasn't divorced, and now Audrey had thrown an unexpected curve into the plans, telling Hank that she would disrupt the ceremony. Part of the reason Hank had agreed to a public ceremony was to
spite her, and that now looked likely to backfire. Hank asked Paul
Howard if he knew of a justice of the peace who could marry them

before they left for New Orleans. Howard said he could probably arrange it. After the *Hayride* finished on Saturday, October 18, Hank and Billie drove out to Minden, Louisiana, with Paul and Marie Howard. They arrived around 1:00 a.m. Howard knew a local justice of the peace, P. E. Burton, who was willing to marry them that late and that quickly. Then if Audrey tried to disrupt the ceremony, Hank and Billie could wave a marriage certificate proving that they were already married.

Both Hank and Billie Jean seemed to believe that Audrey was still in town, and took measures to avoid her following them. Billie Jean later testified:

> We borrowed my brother's car, because we were afraid to take Hank's car because she could have been hanging around outside. My brother's car was a 1950 Ford, [and he] never put more than a dollar's worth of gas in it ever, and on the way back we ran out of gas. So Hank got out and started flagging a ride. So here are the witnesses, Mr. and Mrs. Howard, and Hank and myself. He had on a white cowboy uniform made by Nudie in Hollywood. I'd spilled my purse and makeup out on the car seat. My rouge was spilled and Hank sat down in it, and his whole rear end was red. Here he is out hitchhiking late at night. This fellow stopped and we piled in the car. He took us all the way home. Hank asked the fellow to spend the night with us. I said, "You don't want to do that. Not on our wedding night." We were already stuck with [Clyde Perdue in a] two-bedroom apartment. The fellow driving the car realized it wasn't the thing to do.

Oscar Davis had chartered a plane from Shreveport to New Orleans that was due to leave at 7:00 a.m., but it was nearly eight o'clock before it took off. Hank and Billie Jean flew down with one of the *Hayride*'s upcoming stars, Billy Walker. In testimony twenty years later, Walker remembered that Billie Jean was very agitated on the flight down. He remembered her saying, "What are we going to do if he [the first husband] shows up?" Hank then said, "We're going to do it until it takes." Walker might have been confusing two issues under discussion that day. The first was that Billie Jean might have been informed that she could not marry until October 28, leading Hank to say "We're going to do it until it takes." And, in all likelihood, it wasn't the possibility of Billie's first husband turning up that perturbed Hank and Billie so much as the possibility that Hank's first wife might show up.

Oscar Davis had arranged for a limousine to meet Hank in New Orleans and for a police escort to take them to the auditorium. Local merchants had donated Billie Jean's trousseau, as well as furniture and appliances for the new apartment. Hank started drinking as soon as he got to the auditorium. The Minden marriage created a problem when the minister found out about it, and naturally refused to marry a couple who were already married. Oscar Davis scouted around and found the Reverend L. R. Shelton of the First Baptist Church of Algiers to perform the ceremony.

Meanwhile, a convoy of *Hayride* cast members arrived in New Orleans to perform at the prewedding shows. They had driven down overnight. Hank wasn't scheduled to sing, but there was a concert featuring Tommy and Goldie Hill, Billy Walker, and some local acts. Just as Walker started to sing his hit of the day, "Anything Your Heart Desires," Hank came onstage, pulling Billie Jean. Walker stopped cold and looked at him in disbelief. Hank took the microphone and said, "When ol' Hank comes to git married, he wants to git married."

There was a white carpet down the aisle, and Billie Jean had arranged for her sisters-in-law to act as bridesmaids. The daughter of a local radio station owner was the flower girl, and the mayor of New Orleans was among the invited guests. It was a three-ring circus — a fitting end to Hank's association with the old vaudevillian, Oscar Davis. Billie insists that Davis took the lion's share of the proceeds, although his accounts were later subpoenaed, proving that Hank and Billie Jean shared the proceeds with him.

In an oral history deposition given to the Country Music Foundation, Davis insisted that even on the morning of the ceremony Hank was hoping that Audrey would come and stop it, but the photos tell a different story. They capture a few moments of undeniable tenderness between Hank and his new bride. The marriage was more than an impetuous act to spite Audrey. Billie had the glow of health and beauty that attracted Hank; she also had the fiestiness that simultaneously attracted and repelled him. For his part, Hank had a stray-cat quality that made women want to take him in and nourish him with food and affection, but like most alcoholics, he would soon abuse that love, frustrate it, and ultimately alienate it. Billie Jean looked radiant that day, and Hank indeed looked younger than he had in years, despite his thinning hair. He hadn't left his old problems behind, though. His back hurt terribly, and he self-medicated himself from the crates of champagne that Davis had arranged for the guests backstage. After the wedding, Hank and Billie were supposed to fly to Cuba for their honeymoon, but the backache blues and the champagne got to him and he passed out in his room at the Jung Hotel after his third "I do" in two days.

Hank had put on thirty pounds, something that has usually been ascribed to the edema common in heart disease or drug abuse. Billie Jean, though, is adamant that Hank's weight gain was due to the fact that he was eating decently for the first time in years. They'd go on squirrel hunts, she says, then skin and eat the squirrels, and Billie's mother would feed him syrup and biscuits. One of Hank's *Hayride* costars, Claude King, remembers Billie Jean trying to take care of Hank. "She'd order for him [in restaurants] and got him to eat more," he said. "She just looked after him." Shortly after he arrived in Shreveport, it's likely that Hank did indeed gain some weight, but in several photos from the last months of his life, he seems unnaturally bloated, and his fellow performers say that some weeks he would be gaunt and other weeks puffy. The systems were starting to break down.

Hank and Billie lived with Billie's parents for a few days, then moved into a new development at 1346 Shamrock in Bossier City that Sonny Jones was managing for his father-in-law. It was sparsely furnished by the standards of Franklin Road. No carpet, no Oriental furniture, no grotesque paintings, no chandeliers. Hank didn't appear to mind, and Billie Jean didn't miss what she'd never had. She made a concerted effort to give Hank much of the affection she felt he'd lacked. She and her brothers also tried to help Hank manage his alcoholism. Quickly and inevitably, disillusion set in, but Hank and Billie Jean had their honeymoon. "He had never been held," she says. "I knew this. I was wise for my years. I knew I had to be a lover and a mother to him. We wrestled, had picnics. I gave him a childhood. I wouldn't wear shoes in a hotel lobby. He loved my simplicity. We held hands, and I'd sit on his lap. I wore short-shorts and T-shirts tied up in the front. I was a virgin in a lot of ways." When Hank saw Paul Howard a few weeks after the wedding, he told him, "Billie is the best thing that ever happened to me. I was way down and she brought me up out of the ditch." It wasn't long, though, before Billie Jean began to realize that Hank's street called straight never ran for more than a few blocks, and that his problems couldn't be licked.

Sometimes Billie Jean accompanied Hank on the road; sometimes not. Her enthusiasm for the task she had undertaken almost certainly waned as she came to appreciate the nature of Hank's addictions and the extent of his physical problems. The back pain was always there, robbing him of sleep and peace of mind. Sometimes his legs would buckle underneath him. People thought he was drunk, but his legs would simply give way. It's hard to know how much Hank understood of what was happening to him. If the doctors at Vanderbilt had given him a bleak prognosis, he wasn't admitting it to his young wife. Whenever Billie Jean asked him about his back pain he would just say, "Damned ol' horse threw me, babe," and dismiss the issue.

It wasn't until Hank arrived in Shreveport that he began to exhibit the first signs of heart disease. Red Sovine was one to whom Hank complained of chest pains. Just as he was leaving the *Hayride* in 1949, Hank had installed Sovine as a replacement Syrup Sopper on KWKH, and Sovine was still there when Hank returned. Shortly before the marriage, Hank told him that the chest pains were so bad he sometimes couldn't sleep and couldn't get his breath at night. "We were going off to Oklahoma," says Sovine, "and he put both hands on his chest and he says, 'It feels like it's gonna bust, like it's gonna tear open. I couldn't hardly breathe last night.'" When Billie and her brothers took Hank to dry out at the North Louisiana Sanatorium on October 31, he complained of chest pains that worsened when he breathed deeply.

The incontinence associated with spina bifida also began to manifest itself. Almost every night Hank would urinate on himself regardless of whether he had been drinking, and even when he was awake he had only marginal control of his bladder. "When he told you he had to go, if you were driving, you had better stop the car," says Billie Jean. "He'd say, 'Stop this thing or I'll flood the sucker.'" He would occasionally defecate on himself, too. At the same time, the combination of pills, alcohol, and general dissipation had rendered him almost impotent. "He was doin' good if he could get it up," Billie said.

Nothing in Billie Jean's life had prepared her for this. Her brothers tried to act as minders, and sometimes worked as Hank's opening act as well, but as Hank had proved throughout his life, he could outsmart anyone when he really needed a drink. He reacquired a taste for beer, perhaps because it enabled him to take in some alcohol without falling over drunk. Billie tried to keep him from drinking before a show, but on one occasion she remembered coming back to their hotel room after she'd been out shopping, and finding Hank on his hands and knees, digging under a chair. "He jumped up like I was an army sergeant and saluted. He said, 'Hot damn, baby, I was just lookin' for my shoes.' Sonny's eyes was this big, and I said, 'You've got your damn shoes on, Hank.' I looked under there, and there was two cases of beer. I took that beer and one by one I opened them and washed 'em down the drain. He said, 'Baby, just leave ol' Hank a couple. Just a couple.'"

Billie Jean and her brothers were out of their depth. They didn't understand the nature and complexity of Hank's physical disorders, and although they had been around spree drinkers all their lives, they had never been around a serious alcoholic like Hank. Billie tried to bring compassion to the problem, but inevitably it defeated her. "Nobody ever trusted him and left him alone," she says. "That takes your manhood away. Sometimes you just had to let him do what he wanted to do. [Then] he'd say, 'Ol' Hank ain't never gonna drink no more, baby.'" It was the same promise he had made repeatedly to Audrey, but he was less capable of keeping it now than he ever had been.

Billie knew that Hank was going to drink, and tried to at least keep him sober until show time. "Before a performance, I said, 'You go out there and put on a good show. You can't have no beer before the show, but I'll have two of the coldest ones you ever had waiting on the side of the stage.' He'd say, 'Hot damn, boys, let's pick.' That sucker, man, he'd put on a good show." Like every alcoholic, Hank would keep to his deals for a little while, holding out a glimmer of hope to those around him, then he'd dash it. It was a pattern that had frustrated Audrey to the point where she had given up, it had frustrated Lilly for fifteen years, and it quickly frustrated Billie Jean.

Still, there were moments when everything was good. Everywhere they went together, Hank would introduce Billie from the stage. Billie was winsomely shy, but the tenderness and affection apparent in the wedding photos was still there. They went on picnics and drove down to Lafayette to visit Dudley J. LeBlanc. Hank reckoned that LeBlanc still owed him the best part of ten thousand dollars from the Hadacol debacle, so, when he and the senator were out drinking on the lake, Hank stripped LeBlanc's boat of everything he could take home with him.

Hank's problems in Shreveport were exacerbated by the one man he saw as his savior. When Hank had gone to Oklahoma City in mid-

October, shortly before flying to Montgomery to sign the agreement with Bobbie Jett, he'd worked a show at the Trianon Ballroom with the *Hayride* cast. That day, he told Red Sovine about his chest pains, then started drinking. The booker called someone who was supposed to be a doctor who specialized in treating alcoholics. His name was Horace Raphol "Toby" Marshall. According to Billie Jean, Hank went to Oklahoma City with three thousand dollars and returned with three hundred. He told her he had spent the rest of the money for "treatment." He thought he had finally found a medical person who had walked a mile in his shoes.

The treatment that Hank had received from Marshall in Oklahoma City was chloral hydrate, a new drug in Hank's pharmacopoeia, even though it had been introduced in 1860. It was a powerful sedative (classed at the time as a "hypnotic sedative") and antianxiety drug that had briefly become notorious in Oklahoma City three years earlier when it had been used to sedate a leopard that had gotten loose from the Oklahoma City zoo. Leapy the Leopard had been sighted around town, and some meat laced with chloral hydrate was left for him. Leapy ate it and died soon afterward from a collapsed lung, unable to shake off the effects of the drug. Further evidence of the drug's potency came from Billie Jean, who later testified that she had taken Hank's usual dosage, four tablets, one night. "They made me groggy and crazy as a bat," she said in testimony in 1953. "I vomited for two hours and after that felt as if I was in a drunken stupor."

Chloral hydrate was a harmful, potentially lethal, drug when combined with any central nervous system depressant, such as alcohol. It was, in fact, the drug customarily used for making Mickey Finns. The combination of chloral hydrate and alcohol had been the means by which British poet Dante Gabriel Rossetti had offed himself in 1882. Chloral hydrate was not to be prescribed for anyone with heart disease, which Hank now had, and it was strictly advised not to exceed the stated dose, which Hank always did. Various manufacturers produced the drug under different names and specified that a warning be placed on the bottle saying "Overdosage May Be Fatal." If the drug didn't produce a calming or sedative effect, patients were specifically warned not to take more. If Hank was searching for something that would numb every part of his body — perhaps for good — chloral hydrate was it.

Toby Marshall remains a shadowy figure despite the recent discovery of correspondence and an unpublished manuscript. "I think you better list me for the record as a pathological, constitutional liar," he said at one of his trials. Even his date of birth has never been established. The date he gave to the prison system, March 20, 1910, has been questioned. Marshall's first taste of life behind bars came in 1938, when he spent one year in San Quentin for armed robbery. After release, he became by his own admission an alcoholic. He had drinks stashed in all corners of his house and would drink on the way home from work, he said. In what he called an act of desperation, he offered himself up as a guinea pig to a Yale University study of alcoholism, and claimed to be on his way there when he got into a card game in Miami, Oklahoma, lost all his money, and was arrested for passing a forged check for five hundred dollars. He entered McAlester Penitentiary in what he called "an alcoholic-barbiturate-Seconal-bromide haze interposed with flashes of hallucinations," a self-diagnosis that Hank could relate to even if he didn't understand it.

Marshall was jailed on October 15, 1950, and paroled on October 8, 1951. After his release, he told a 1953 inquiry that he devoted himself "as unselfishly as possible to helping others as I could." Armed with a diploma from the "Chicago University of Applied Sciences and Arts," which he had bought from a traveling salesman at a filling station for a fee variously reported at twenty-five or thirty-five dollars, Marshall set himself up as a therapist for alcoholics. At first, he prescribed drugs through a qualified physician, C. W. Lemon, and when Lemon was asked in March 1953 what had brought him to Marshall, he replied simply, "I got drunk." Later, with a forged certificate from a board of medical examiners, Marshall had some prescription pads of his own printed up. Marshall, though, was not without insight into the needs of an alcoholic. "A drunk," he said in jail, "as anyone knows, is most disagreeable to live with. Most wives won't do it. I made myself available to families who needed me, and often spent twenty-four to thirty-six hours at a time giving the alcoholic the attention that his family wouldn't. I'd sit there beside his bed, in a hotel room or at home, for hours. I'd be there when he woke, and I'd talk with him. I'd show him he was wanted." This was the best news Hank Williams had received from the medical profession. Most of the doctors he had seen couldn't approach his alcoholism with anything like the empathy that Marshall could. The only recovered alcoholic Hank knew well was Fred Rose, and Hank couldn't find the strength that Rose had drawn from religion. Marshall offered sympathy, compassion, and hope of a cure. Hank engaged him as his personal physician at three hundred dollars a week, yet another expense that necessitated constant touring.

Hank might have hoped for a fresh start in Shreveport, but the old patterns soon reappeared. When he was sober, he was riveting onstage; when drunk, he was boorish and occasionally lucky not to be lynched. He even turned up drunk for some of the *Hayride* shows. Horace Logan would announce him, and Hank would stand in the wings shaking his head, denying that he was Hank Williams. On a bus ride to a *Hayride* remote show in Brownwood, Texas, he wore out his welcome. "He decided he'd sing," said Logan. "Kitty Wells was there, my wife was there, the Rowley Trio and other women, and Hank was singing,

> *The dirty drawers that Maggie wore*
> *They was torn and they was split*
> *You could see where she had shit.*

"I said, 'Hank, shut up!' He'd apologize later."

In November, Hank headlined a package show composed of Claude King, Tommy Hill, Goldie Hill, and Red Sovine. Billie Jean went with them, and Hank introduced her as his new bride at every show. He had his guitar beside him in the touring sedan, and would sing for hour upon hour, then sing some more in the dressing room. "One night," said Claude King, "we had an off night. I think it was in Beaumont. We'd stopped at some little place to get a drink and he wanted to get a beer. There was a guy in there playing a piano and singing, so we spent the whole night there. Hank singing, playing the piano, and singing with this guy. There wasn't anybody in there when we first stopped by, but when we left it was packed. I guess word got out Hank Williams was there." In diners along the way, he'd punch up Tommy Edwards' record of "You Win Again" on the jukebox and play it repeatedly. When he had a little audience backstage, he'd talk about how Bob Hope couldn't follow him on the Hadacol Caravan.

The best dates that Clyde Perdue could get were now in smaller towns like Homer, Louisiana, and Orange, Texas. "He'd start a trip," said Claude King, "and he'd say, 'I ain't gonna drink a drop,' then his back would get worse and worse and he'd get right back into the drinking. He and I were the same age exactly, yet to me he was an old man." (When

Tillman Franks managed Claude King in the 1960s, he knocked ten years off King's age, telling fan magazines that he was born in 1933; in fact, King was seven months older than Hank.)

In Opelousas, Louisiana, everyone in the audience demanded their money back after Hank showed up drunk, and when light broke the following morning, there was a crowd around the hotel. Claude King went and brought Hank's Cadillac round to a trade entrance, intending to make a dash for the county line. Hank needed a cigarette, though, and walked blithely out of the hotel carrying his valise. He saw the crowd and sat down on the sidewalk in his white western suit. He opened the case and dollar bills started blowing in the wind. Everybody started laughing, picking up the money, and Hank left promising to come back and do a make-good.

On another night in Lafayette, Hank weaved up to the microphone. "You all paid to see ol' Hank, didn't ya?" he said. The crowd started roaring. Hank set down his guitar, said, "Well, you seen him." And he walked off. Perhaps his attitude stemmed in part from the fact that he had records in the top ten, yet he was playing the high school gym in Lafayette, the type of gig he had worked so hard to escape. The interceding four years had ruined his health and wrecked his marriage, and now he was broke and back where he'd started. Money mattered most to Hank because it betokened success, and now, when he stuffed the takings into his valise at the close of a show, he knew it contained a fraction of what it did a year earlier.

Claude King's record "She Knows Why" had just been released by Los Angeles–based Specialty Records. Hank liked Claude and told him that he wanted to change it to "You Know Why" and record it at his next session. Specialty was an R&B label started by Art Rupe, who'd been one of the partners in Sterling Records. Hank called Rupe from somewhere on the road, offering ten thousand dollars for Claude's contract, but Rupe told him that he was hanging on to it. "We were going to get coffee one morning," said Claude. "There's another guy with us, and we went over and was having a cup of coffee, and I guess Hank just felt like talking. He said he liked my singing and thought that I had a great future in the music business. This other guy said, 'What about me, Hank?' Hank said, 'No, to be honest with you, you need to go back to doing whatever you was doing.' And this guy was Tommy Hill." Hank was dead right. Claude King was a natural singer, even though it would take another ten years before he topped the charts with "Wolverton Mountain." Tommy Hill made several more records (a couple of them for Fred Rose's Hickory Records) but eventually became a songwriter, producer, and record label owner.

The tour ended badly. Hank's back hurt terribly. Claude King remembers:

> I was driving, and he was down on the floorboard in the back. Billie Jean was in the backseat and he was down on the floorboard and he was crying, his back was hurting him so bad. He wanted me to drive faster, to try to hurry up and get to Shreveport. It was nighttime, and we was going along pretty fast and all of a sudden we came over this hill, and there was a whole herd of cows going across the highway. I couldn't stop, but kind of zigzagged amongst them and didn't hit any of them. It still didn't faze him. He wanted to get back to the doctor 'cause his back was killing him.

In late November, Hank made a tour of Florida and Georgia for A. V. Bamford, then worked some dates in Georgia. Bamford assembled the supporting cast, which included Ray Edenton, later the premier rhythm guitarist in Nashville, and Radio Dot and Smokey (Swan). The trip had a rough start. Hank and Billie flew to Pensacola on a chartered airplane piloted by James Hutchins of Perry Sanders Aircraft. Hutchins later testified that Billie Jean told Hank that she was pregnant. Hank was overjoyed and vowed to remain sober. As he and Billie flew over the Gulf of Mexico, Hank took the controls for a while, but the plane began running low on fuel while they were still over water. It was touch and go whether they would make it to Pensacola, and Billie panicked. The next morning in the hotel, she awoke in a pool of blood. She had either miscarried or the shock had started her period. Hank was sent out to buy Kotex, but he stopped off in the hotel bar and it was several hours before he reappeared.

On Tuesday, November 18, Hank visited his sister Irene in Jacksonville. As he left, Irene says she was convinced that she would never see her brother again. If that was indeed her premonition, it was correct.

Hank was more or less sober for the entire trip, and talking positively, but during a 1975 trial, Hank's cousin Marie Glenn mentioned that Hank had a heart attack in Florida. As usual, she didn't elaborate. Bamford also remembered Hank complaining of chest pains, but was sufficiently encouraged by his performance to offer him two engagements,

New Year's Eve in Charleston, West Virginia, and New Year's Day in Canton, Ohio. Hank accepted.

Later on that road trip, Hank took Billie Jean to see Pappy McCormick in Pensacola. They went out to the Diamond Horseshoe; Pappy Neal played steel guitar, Hank sang a few songs — and got jealous when he saw Billie Jean with another man on the dance floor. That night, Hank and Billie stayed at the San Carlos Hotel, where Hank had holed up ten years earlier when he was drinking and trying to escape from Lilly. Memories were everywhere. He asked McCormick to come to Shreveport to lead his band in January; it was an almost blanket invitation he extended to his old pals. McCormick said he would.

The Nashville deejays convention was on Friday, November 21, and Hank was scheduled to attend, but it's unclear if he did. Two days later, he was in Montgomery with Billie Jean and Sonny Jones. It was, in all likelihood, the first time that Billie had met her new mother-in-law, and the occasion did not go well. Lilly had already bought an adjoining house and converted it into a rooming house, and was now asking Hank for money to buy yet another house. Billie Jean says that she vetoed the deal, thereby earning Lilly's undying enmity. Wesley Rose later said that he and his father drove to Montgomery to meet Hank and prepare for another recording session. Wesley insists that Fred told Hank that he would be back on the *Opry* in February, but there is no corroboration of this. Back in Shreveport, Hank went on a tear, and was committed once again to the North Louisiana Sanatorium.

The early days of December 1952 remain a blank. Perhaps Hank was still in the sanatorium; perhaps he worked a short tour. On Saturday, December 6, he worked the *Big D Jamboree* in Dallas, then played a few dates along the Mississippi gulf. Back in Shreveport on December 10, he had a big fight with Billie Jean. She took him back to the North Louisiana Sanatorium on December 11, but he got out early in the afternoon and found his way downtown and resumed his binge. At 4:30, he was arrested after a complaint from a restaurant owner about a "drunk in front of my place." The arresting officer said that Hank had insisted that he shouldn't have to go to jail, but he was hauled off on charges of being drunk and disorderly. He was dressed that afternoon in a blue serge suit and a green hat with a big feather, and he was carrying a .38 revolver. Billie Jean and Sonny came to get him out of jail at 9:45 in the evening and took him back to the North Louisiana Sanatorium.

Two days later, December 13, Hank played the *Louisiana Hayride*. Right after the show, he and his personal retinue, together with Tommy and Goldie Hill and Billy Walker, started out for Houston to begin a one-week swing through eastern Texas. Hank had hired a cowboy singer, Al Rogers, to work the first few dates with him, and Charlie Adams, who recorded for 4-Star Records, was scheduled to work a few dates. Billie Jean had probably had enough Hank Williams for a while, and opted to stay home.

Hank was due to play Cook's Hoedown club on Sunday night. Tommy and Goldie Hill were going on to San Antonio and arranged to drop Hank at the Rice Hotel. On the way down, they heard a strange groan from the back and they saw Hank slumped forward, his head between his legs. He had stopped breathing. "He turned black," said Tommy. "Goldie hollered at me, 'Hank can't get his breath.' He was just smothering himself. Goldie was just screaming. I stopped the car, pulled him out, and started hauling him around on my shoulders. We got to Houston about daylight Sunday. I pulled into the Rice Hotel, asked for four porters and a stretcher, and got Hank up to his room. He wouldn't go to no doctor." Toby Marshall wrote a letter to Lilly from the Rice Hotel detailing Hank's condition. Lilly was sufficiently concerned to fly to Texas to meet the tour in San Antonio.

Cook's Hoedown was sold out by Sunday night, but Hank was nowhere to be seen. Around five in the afternoon, Cook phoned the booker, Warren Stark, in Austin and told him to get his ass down to Houston and find Hank. Stark told Cook that he couldn't get down to Houston in time to find Hank, but they should check the jail, then the hotels. They eventually found Hank at the Rice, got some of Toby Marshall's shots in him, and hauled him onstage.

Sergeant F. D. McMurry, who had booked Hank into the police benefit show in Beaumont at the end of September, was in the audience. "They booed him off," said McMurry. "I met him backstage. He said, 'Man, they're killin' me, they killin' me. They're workin' me to death.' He was all hopped up on those durn things. I said, 'Hank, they booed you offstage. Let's get you straight.' I put four cups of coffee in him, and he tried it again and they booed him off again. It just broke my heart." According to Marshall, Hank played two of his three scheduled sets. Some distant cousins of Hank's were there that night. He was suffering ungodly back pain, they said, and drinking heavily. They tried to get him to rest up at their house, but he insisted that he had to carry on. Hank called Billie Jean and told her that he had never been sicker. Marshall was giving him shots every hour, she said.

Tommy Hill saw the lethal combination of barbiturates and alcohol with which Hank was dosing himself. He also saw how Perdue and Marshall had worked out a procedure that would enable their meal ticket to make the show, but at a terrible cost. Hank was allowed a few beers after he woke up, then Marshall injected him with a drug that made him vomit up the beer. Then they would pour black coffee down him, hand him some Dexedrine tablets and point him toward the stage. After the show, he'd be allowed some more beers and put back to bed with some downers.

Hank was scheduled to work in Victoria on Monday, San Antonio on Tuesday, Dallas on Wednesday, Snook on Thursday, and Austin on Friday. On Monday, he overdosed or had a heart attack, and couldn't make the show in Victoria. Marshall noted only that he was "too goofed up" to perform, so the troupe moved on to San Antonio. Hank called Big Bill Lister's house, but Big Bill was out working a show date. He then called Ernest Tubb, although Tubb never mentioned the substance of their talk. Still in a mood to talk, he called Jimmie Rodgers' widow, Carrie, who lived nearby, and poured his heart out to her. He said his "last marriage" (presumably to Billie Jean) hadn't worked out, and he said, "Mrs. Rodgers, I'd like to be one of your boys." He told her that he'd come out to see her the next day, but never called back. Writing to Ernest Tubb a few weeks later, Mrs. Rodgers said, "The circumstances were so similar to Jimmie in many ways." Tubb had been one of her "boys," in that she'd taken a deep, unselfish interest in his career. Perhaps Hank felt in need of that kind of mentor.

To ease the strain on his back, Hank arranged to fly into Dallas with Toby Marshall while Clyde Perdue stayed behind to pick up Lilly. Shortly before they landed, Marshall told Hank that Lilly was joining them, and said later that Hank was very unhappy about it. The Wednesday night show in Dallas was scheduled for the Sportatorium. Hank ran into Ray Price on the street outside the stadium. Price's version of "Don't Let the Stars Get in Your Eyes" was showing up in several markets, and Hank started singing it as he walked toward him. Price invited Hank to spend Christmas with himself and his mother, but Hank said he wasn't certain what he was doing. They agreed to meet in Ohio right after their New Year's dates. Whenever he met someone in the business, particularly someone from Nashville, Hank tried to be upbeat. "I'll be back with you before you know it," he told Price. After the show at the Sportatorium, Hank, Toby Marshall, and Warren Stark went out to see Bob Wills play. That day, Hank received an Air Express package from Acuff-Rose with a check for four thousand dollars.

Hank and Warren Stark drove from Dallas to Austin, then Stark drove Hank to his Thursday night gig at a small theater in Snook, Texas. Marshall said that Hank "did okay" in both Dallas and Snook. The last date on the tour was on Friday, December 19, at Stark's Skyline Club in Austin. Lilly sat with Stark during the show and asked him to take over Hank's bookings after Christmas. Stark said he would. On the drive to Snook, Stark had been griping to Hank about showing up drunk, and Hank had told him what he told everyone else. People hadn't come to see him, he said — knowing it to be false. The crowd had just showed up for a night out, and if anyone wanted their money back they should get it back and he'd make it good to the promoter. Stark told him he couldn't do business like that.

Hank had first appeared at the Skyline as a young *Hayride* hopeful. Horace Logan had called in a few favors to get him on the bill. Four years later, he was a pitiful sight. He was disheveled, his nose ran constantly from a cold or flu he couldn't shake, and he was sweating profusely. He'd lost all pride in his appearance, and, from what was unsaid as much as what was said, he gave the impression that he simply didn't care anymore.

His show was no sad last hurrah, though. Without much advertising, the Starks had sold out the date, then oversold it. Usually, the Skyline's maximum capacity was around eight hundred, but people were lining the walls and the Starks were hoping that the fire marshal wasn't one of them. Tommy Hill remembered the show vividly:

> I went out and did a fiddle tune, then I brought Charlie Adams on, and Charlie did two tunes and Hank asked me to get him off. I didn't know why. He said, "It's time to get Goldie on." I put Goldie on, and he just wanted Goldie to sing two songs, and then I brought Billy Walker out, and Billy did four songs, then Hank said he wanted him off. Then Hank wanted to go on. The show started at eight o'clock, so now it was about nine, and Hank would usually do thirty or forty-five minutes, but that

night he was still singing at one o'clock. He did not quit. He put on one of the best shows I ever saw. He didn't falter a bit. He done some songs over and over. Me and Goldie have talked about it since. He sung everything he knew, even a bunch of gospel songs.

Hank did two sets, backed by Tommy Hill, steel guitarist Jimmy Day, and the Skyline house band led by Leon Carter, a distant relative of the Carter Family. After the first set, Hank went back into the office to get some shots, then did another set. He was running a high temperature; sweat was running off his fingers onto the floor. Right after the show, refusing to check into a hotel, he began the long haul back to Shreveport. Paul Howard's wife, Marie, remembered that immediately after arriving back in Shreveport Hank went to the Highland Hospital to be treated for pneumonia.

On Saturday morning, Lilly went to see Horace Logan and told him that Hank was missing the *Hayride* that night because he was sick and she was taking him back to Montgomery. "I never gave him a release," insists Logan, "because he had a three-year contract, but I gave him a leave of absence on the proviso that he would only make [the] personal appearances that A. V. Bamford had booked for him. Hank also agreed to fly in for the *Hayride,* because I was paying him two hundred a week, and he could afford to fly in on that easy — and bring Billie Jean with him." Later in court testimony, Logan said, "He was ill. Very obviously physically ill. I gave him indefinite leave."

Once again, it's hard to know if Hank saw his departure from the *Hayride* in exactly the same terms as Logan. As he and Billie packed their belongings, closed out their apartment, and got in the car, they left contradictory messages behind. Hank told Billy Walker that he was going to the Caribbean to take a cure, and that he was going to divorce Billie Jean, go back to Nashville and bring Billy with him. But if Hank had intended to split from Billie Jean, he had an ideal opportunity when he went to Montgomery; as it was, she went with him. On the other hand, Hank had left Austin telling Warren Stark that he would be back in Shreveport and that Stark would act as his booking agent.

In truth, Hank probably didn't have a concerted plan of action. He was running out of goals faster than he was running out of future.

My dear old mammy's waiting
With arms outretched so wide
Before the sun goes down again
I'll be right by her side
I can wait no longer for the sun to shine
'Til I get back to my mammy
And that Alabama home of mine

"That Alabama Home of Mine" (unknown)

• •

MIDNIGHT

• • • • • • • • • • • • • • • • • •

*H*ANK Williams was back in his old room, the front downstairs bedroom of Lilly's boardinghouse. His life had come full circle. He'd started in Montgomery, left for Shreveport with his heart full of hope, gone on to Nashville in triumph, then returned in disgrace to Shreveport, and finally come back to his mother's boardinghouse in Montgomery.

Hank was sick. He told friends who came to call that he had the "Asiatic" flu, but he'd had it for several weeks, and couldn't seem to shake it. Toby Marshall had prescribed antibiotics but they hadn't worked, and now Hank's back hurt terribly from the long haul through eastern Texas and back to Alabama. On December 21, Lilly phoned Marshall, who wired a prescription for twenty-four capsules of chloral hydrate the following day. Billie Jean had it delivered by Walgreens, and the prescription was refilled again within the week.

Clyde Perdue was let go as Hank's two-car convoy swept through Greenville. "I told Hank all the time," said Billie, "'You don't need him. He don't book you. The agents are calling you. If you decide to play, you can call the agents and they'll book you.'" So now Hank was without a manager or a band, and with just one firm commitment for the new year, other than the two dates for A. V. Bamford on New Year's Eve and New Year's Day. When Brack Schuffert came to visit, Hank told him that he was booked solid until May, but Hank was spinning tales wherever he went, always trying to maintain the impression that everything was rosy.

Braxton was still working at Hormel Meats, and Freddy Beach's wife, Irella, worked there too in the baking room. They invited Hank to the Christmas party, but he was too sick. "I went up to get him," said Braxton. "He was lying in bed with his clothes on. He was sick in bed and Doctor Stokes had come out. He had a fever. Doctor Stokes tried to get him in the hospital, but he wouldn't go."

Bobbie Jett was somewhere in town, just days away from giving birth. Her daughter, Jo, was with her. It's possible that Bobbie was in Lilly's other boardinghouse, next door to the main house, but Marie Glenn's son, Butch, insists that she was elsewhere. Lilly later told Audrey that Hank was walking around singing the current Jo Stafford hit "Keep It a Secret," and it's clear why he was drawn to the song. If Bobbie was next door, Billie Jean probably didn't know it, but just being confined with Lilly and Marie Glenn was enough like purgatory. Billie Jean and Lilly had been on bad terms since Billie had vetoed Lilly's demand for enough money to purchase yet another boardinghouse. Marie was spookily silent.

Then, as Christmas neared, Hank's thoughts kept drifting back to Nashville and his young son, now three and a half years old. In all likelihood, Hank hadn't seen Hank Jr. since the session in September or the deejays convention in November. Perhaps it had been longer than that. He and Billie had a fight after he bought Hank Jr. a toy and sent it to him. Back in the room he thought he'd left forever four and a half years earlier, he must have wondered if his life could have been more of a mess.

By Christmas Eve, Hank had rallied a little and went to southern Alabama to show off Billie Jean to his kin. Taft and Erleen Skipper lived in a tiny settlement called Advance, and Hank sat outside with Taft in the wan December sunlight. Billie Jean made a deep impression on the Skippers; she was not only strikingly beautiful, but also willing to pitch in and help with the cooking and the washing-up. The Skippers held this up in stark contrast with Audrey, who wouldn't get out of the car unless it was to sit on the porch.

Hank and Taft walked to the pond and down to Ernest Manning's store. "We were going back to the house," he said, "and he got short-winded and he says, 'Taft, I believe I picked up asthma somewhere,' and he kinda felt toward his heart. We got up to the store and sat down and he said, 'That kinda makes me short-winded. I gotta get out and get a little more exercise.'" Hank showed Taft the Acuff-Rose check for four thousand dollars, and told him it was all the money he had in the world.

Hank and Billie Jean joined the Skippers that evening at the East Chapman Baptist Church. Some in the congregation asked Hank to sing, but he thought his songs were inappropriate and refused. Later, though, he played the Skippers the acetate of a song he said he'd just written called "The Log Train." Set in Chapman, it was in traditional ballad form, starting with "If you will listen, a song I will sing . . ." It was a predictably skimpy account of Lon's days as an engineer, but Hank had recorded it at the KWKH studio on December 3 and probably thought that the folks back home would like it.

Hank and Billie Jean stayed overnight with the Skippers, and then, on Christmas morning, drove to McWilliams to see Lon, Ola, and Leila. The only phone in McWilliams was at the railroad depot, so Hank couldn't call ahead, and when he got there he found that Lon and his family had gone to Selma for Christmas. Hank scratched out a note on a plain piece of paper and left a cigarette lighter for Lon and a gift-wrapped five-pound box of candy for Leila and Ola. The missed visit deeply affected Lon. He hung on to the wrapping paper for years, and refused to leave the house in case someone was coming to see him whom he would never see again.

Hank went to see nearly everyone he knew in that part of Alabama, including the proprietor of the Journey's End Inn, where he'd played early in his career. He sang "The Log Train" for several of them, then drove on to see Lon's sister, his aunt Bertha, in Pine Apple and had Christmas supper with her and her family before driving back to Montgomery. On December 27, Hank and Billie Jean went to see the Blue and Gray football game at Crempton Bowl, but their seats were high in the stands and caught the wind; Hank felt chilled. Taft Skipper and his niece Mary were there too; they offered Hank their seats lower down out of the wind, but Hank refused, and he and Billie left before the end of the first half and went back to Lilly's.

The last two full days in Montgomery, December 28 and 29, were not good. Billie Jean faced unrelenting hostility from Lilly and Marie Glenn. The idea of a protracted stay in Montgomery with those two was more than she could bear. Marie saw a lot, and said a little. In 1946, she'd divorced Conrad Fitzgerald, the ostensible father of her son, born three years earlier. The following year, she reportedly married one of

Lilly's boarders, Norris Glenn. But later that year, Glenn deserted from the army, deserted Marie, and disappeared to South America. Marie gave that story in court testimony, although her son, Butch, states that Marie did not in fact marry Norris Glenn, despite taking his name.

Marie was listening when Billie Jean's father phoned to say that he'd received word that Hank and Billie were not legally married. Several heated arguments followed, and Lilly and Marie overheard Hank yelling at Billie Jean. Perhaps Billie threatened to leave, because Marie remembered Hank saying that it didn't matter what she did because they weren't legally married anyway. Lilly squirreled away that piece of information; it would prove to be very useful in the days and weeks ahead.

On Sunday, December 28, Hank gave a performance for 130 members and guests of American Federation of Musicians' local 479 in Montgomery at their eighth annual party. It was held that year at the Elite Café to benefit a member who had been stricken with polio. Hank and Billie Jean tucked into their steaks. Two days later, the *Alabama Journal* reported, "Another star of the show the musicians put on for themselves was a thin, tired-looking ex–country boy with a guitar. He got up and sang (or howled) a number of his tunes that started out to be hillbilly and ended up as pop numbers, played and sung by every band in the land. The boy who once worked here for eleven dollars a week in the Depression sung 'Jumbalaya,' [*sic*] 'Cold, Cold Heart,' 'You Win Again,' and 'Lovesick Blues.' There was thunderous applause as he went back to his steak. He was, of course, Hank Williams."

Several days later, the president of the Montgomery local of the AFM, Tom Hewlett, elaborated on what would be Hank Williams' last show:

> To the average modern musician, frequently called "jazzmen," and also the serious musician, often called "squares" or "long-hair," folk music or hillbilly music is not to their taste. When Hank Williams played and sang to us at the Musicians Party, December 28, all of us, including the above two groups, were there. We listened attentively as if attending a concert by Benny Goodman or hearing the cultivated voice of some operatic star. We forgot our talent, our technical skill, and musical training and truly enjoyed every note.

Hank had planned to fly to Charleston, then probably ride on to Canton with Bamford or one of the other performers, but the weather reports from up north were bad. "That was the hardest I ever saw him fight to get to a gig," said Billie Jean, "'cause it was usually no problem for him to say, 'Ol' Hank just don't want to go. I'll catch you later.'" Billie Jean says that she'd planned to ride with him, but now that he was forced to drive she decided to go back to Shreveport for New Year's and meet Hank in Nashville on January 3. He'd said, "Hey, baby, let's us move to Nashville and buy one of them big houses." He told her that he had a piece of land picked out near Carl Smith's ranch in Williamson County, but it was probably another pipe dream. He'd just sold his place in Williamson County a couple of months earlier.

Hank told Marie Glenn that he'd be back in Montgomery in four days, and he told Lilly the same thing. He'd also signed the agreement to adopt Bobbie Jett's child, so he probably wanted to be there for the birth, or at least see the child. In a letter that Hank's sister, Irene, wrote to her attorney some fifteen years later, she recalled some of what Lilly and Marie had told her of those last days in Montgomery. Irene and Lilly always insisted that Billie left before Hank, although Billie is equally insistent that she saw him off. Irene wrote:

> Billie left Hank in Montgomery on December the twenty-ninth or thirtieth. They had a real loud argument the night before in which she told him that she had found out that they were not legally married and she was going back to Shreveport. . . . The next morning she packed her trunk and addressed the mailing stickers to herself in Shreveport and asked that Railway Express be called and have them ship the trunk on to her. Lawrence Peirce [photographer Laurens Pierce] photographed the trunk and the labels after the funeral and we shipped the trunk on to her.

There's no doubt that Hank and Billie fought in Montgomery; they fought everywhere, just as Hank and Audrey had done. The tension went from simmer to boil several times as Hank continued his pattern of messing up whenever he had a chance. Irella Beach recalled seeing Hank and Billie at a bar. "Hank was up on the counter dancin' or something," she says, "and he hit Billie Jean in the face 'cause she was trying to get him to quit [it]. He was sloppy drunk, and she took off home. She said, 'Ain't no man gonna beat on me,' and she left."

Like almost everything to do with Hank Williams, his relationship with Billie Jean has been seen through the wrong end of the telescope. Hindsight tells us that Hank was country music's greatest star, and thus a prize for any woman, but things must have looked very different to Billie Jean in December 1952. Hank looked like a falling star hanging on by a thread. Even if he kept his hit streak intact, he had a very uncertain future as a performing artist. It's hard to know if Billie Jean reached the end of her tether during the ten days in Montgomery, or whether she intended to rejoin Hank after the New Year's dates. "We wondered how Billie Jean could put up with him at all," said Horace Logan. "Falling down drunk, throwing up drunk, throwing up on himself." Billie had more reason to walk out on Hank than he had reason to put her on a plane back home. She was just nineteen years old; Hank was only twenty-nine but had the physical attributes of a man more than twice that age. Was this what Billie Jean wanted from life? In later interviews, she insisted that it was, but disillusion was probably setting in.

Billie Jean and Audrey would soon stake out their official positions. Billie's position was that she would meet Hank in Nashville on January 3. Audrey insisted that Hank called over Christmas and asked if he could come back, and she said he could. Had she forgotten everything that she had spelled out in such petulant detail in her divorce petition just months earlier? Did Hank call after an argument with Billie Jean? Did he even call at all?

At some point on December 28, Lilly wired Toby Marshall, telling him that Hank was capable of making the trip by himself. Sitting in a drugstore in Oklahoma City, waiting for prescriptions that he shouldn't have written to be filled, Marshall scratched out a two-page letter to Hank. His concern for Hank's well-being seemed unaffected, explaining why Hank and Lilly put such trust in him. "There is only thing I ask, Hank," Marshall wrote, "and this you morally owe to yourself, me, and your public. If [triple-underlined] you run into trouble, call me. Don't for Heaven's sake let the pattern run too long or get too deep before you holler. And there is nothing wrong with an old boy asking for help when he is sick. And no matter where you are or what the circumstances may be, I'll manage to get there. And you know I can help you."

Marshall mentioned a show slated for February 22 in Oklahoma

City, booked by Venita Cravens. "She is writing to you regarding 5 or 6 auditorium dates here for February," wrote Marshall. "This is the sort of thing you need, rather than beer joints or honky tonks, to get you back on top where you belong. . . . If you are going back to the *Opry,* you need some top flight bookings to help things along." The clear implication of Marshall's letter is that the only promise Hank had received from the *Grand Ole Opry* was that they *might* consider taking him back if he straightened himself out. After Hank's death, Wesley Rose and the *Opry* management stated that Hank was scheduled to return to the *Opry* on February 3, 1953, but that was clearly not the case.

On December 29, Hank started to make arrangements for the long haul to West Virginia. First he asked Braxton Schuffert to drive him, but Brack had to be back at work at Hormel. Hank asked several other friends, but they all had commitments. Finally, he went down to the Lee Street Taxi company. The owner, Daniel Pitts Carr, had a son, Charles, who was a freshman at Auburn University and was home for the holiday. Charles was seventeen years old and had driven Hank before. Hank thought that he drove a bit recklessly, but he was starting to look like the only person who could take the time off.

"Dad was a friend of Hank's," Charles Carr told the *Atlanta Journal-Constitution,* "and tried to look out after him in the tough times. He was there talking with Dad and Hank asked me if I'd be interested in making the trip." Carr was eventually paid four hundred dollars for his work, but it's hard to know if this was what Hank had promised, or if it represented an additional payment. It was a lot of money for four days' work in 1952. Hank's guarantee for the shows was probably around two thousand dollars.

Billie Jean's insistence that she was with Hank on his last night in Montgomery, December 29–30, is borne out by Charles Carr, who remembers that on the morning they left she wanted to go along, but Hank wouldn't let her. "He was shadowboxing all that last night," says Billie:

> He went down to the chapel [at St. Jude's Hospital], and he said, "Ol' Hank needs to straighten up some things with the Man." I'd say, "Hank, what in the world is the matter with you?" He'd say, "Every time I close my eyes, I see Jesus coming down the road." He couldn't even sleep in bed then, the pain was so bad. When he left he was looking at me kinda funny. I said, "Hank,

are you sick?" He said, "No babe, ol' Hank just wants to look at you one more time."

Marie Glenn also remembered Hank visiting St. Jude's. He wanted the sisters to pray with him, she said. Hank then came into Marie's room and gave her forty dollars to take care of the taxi fare and other expenses connected with the birth of Bobbie Jett's child. He was pretty certain the child would be delivered before he returned. He stood in the doorway of Marie's room and said to her, "Ol' Hank ain't gonna be with you another Christmas. I'm closer to the Lord than I ever been in my life."

Charles Carr came to the boardinghouse around 11:30 on the morning of December 30. Hank loaded his guitars, stage outfits, songbooks, photos, and records into the trunk. This meant that he couldn't make use of the customizing job he'd had done to the rear seat. When the trunk was empty, the seat could be folded back to make a bed. Hank was wearing his blue suede shoes, a white felt hat, a blue serge suit, and navy blue overcoat. Immediately after they left, Hank asked Carr to go back to the boarding-house so that he could change into his white cowboy boots. Then they stopped at one of the local radio stations, probably WSFA, and Hank let himself be talked into going to a highway contractors convention in the same hotel. Hank stayed awhile and almost certainly had a few drinks. The next stop was Dr. Stokes' office. He prepaid Stokes to deliver Bobbie's baby and asked for a shot of morphine to quiet his back on the long haul, but Stokes smelled liquor on Hank's breath and wouldn't give him one. Hank went down to see Dr. Black, who injected him and sent him on his way.

Between four and five o'clock, Hank and Charles Carr stopped at the Hollywood Drive-in on Bell Street. The Hollywood was a take-out stand that sold beer, sandwiches, and coffee, and Hank saw Leo Hudson's car parked outside. Hudson was a member of the Montgomery local of the American Federation of Musicians, and had helped organize the Sunday night party. Hank got into Hudson's car and told him how much he'd enjoyed the party, then asked Hudson to drive him to Ohio. "Charles is a good boy," said Hank, "but I don't trust his driving like I trust yours." Hudson said he couldn't help. He was on his way to a gig in Selma. Hank picked up a six-pack of Falstaff beer and left Montgomery heading north on Highway 31 toward Birmingham. It was raining and unseasonably cold.

At 4:30 p.m. that day, just before Hank left Montgomery, Lilly phoned Toby Marshall. She told him that Hank had recently undergone a "highly upsetting emotional incident that had caused him to resume his drinking." She asked Marshall to go to Charleston, West Virginia, and minister to him, then go on to Canton and return with him to Montgomery. "I accepted the assignment without reservation," said Marshall in a memo he wrote a year later from his prison cell in Oklahoma.

Around the time that Marshall left Oklahoma City, promoter A. V. Bamford left Nashville for Charleston. He had assembled a bill for the two shows that, in addition to Hank, included the comedy team of Homer and Jethro and local star Hawkshaw Hawkins. The supporting acts were Autry Inman (who had written "I Cried Again," a song Hank performed during his last weeks in Nashville); Bill Monroe's fiddle player, Red Taylor; as well as "Jack and Daniel" (Autry Inman and future pop star Floyd Robinson); and the Webb Sisters, one of whom was married to bass player Buddy Killen. It was an all-star revue, but the posters made it clear that Hank was the headliner.

Hank wouldn't bring a band, but he had hired Don Helms for the two dates. Presumably the other supporting acts would double as the house band. Red Taylor would play fiddle, Floyd Robinson would play electric guitar, Autry Inman would play rhythm guitar, and Buddy Killen would play bass. Bamford sweetened the deal for Killen by offering to buy a new set of tires for his '51 Pontiac.

Hank and Charles Carr didn't get very far on December 30. Contradicting what Lilly told Toby Marshall, Carr remembers Hank in good spirits, singing a few songs along the way. They stopped in Birmingham and tried to get a room at the city's premier hotel, the Tutwiler, but Carr, who had pulled a U-turn and parked illegally near the hotel, was pulled over by the police. Hank told Carr to remind the officer who he was driving for, but that didn't seem to carry as much clout in Birmingham as it did in Montgomery, and Carr was told to move along. They drove on to the Redmont and took two rooms there instead. Within thirty minutes of checking into the Redmont, three women had invited themselves into Hank's room. He asked one of them where she was from. She said, "Heaven." "Well," Hank said, "in that case, you're the very reason I'm goin' to hell." The women eventually left, and Carr ordered two meals from room service.

Early the following morning, Hank headed northeast, and got a haircut, shave, boot-shine, and breakfast in Fort Payne. He drew a small crowd and enjoyed the attention. Charles Carr says that Hank bought a bottle of bonded bourbon, but Fort Payne was in a dry county, so it's likelier that Hank visited a bootlegger. Sitting in the front seat, he asked his young driver what he thought of "Jambalaya." Carr said he didn't much care for it because it seemed a little nonsensical. "That's 'cause you don't understand French," said Hank. Carr told him he'd studied French in school. Hank just said, "Awww." Then he started singing a few songs; the last that Carr remembers was Red Foley's hit "Midnight." "Red would like that," said Hank.

By now, Hank realized that he was running late, but he stopped in Chattanooga for some lunch. Hank played Tony Bennett's "Cold, Cold Heart" on the jukebox and left a fifty-dollar tip. It was snowing when they set out for Knoxville, and by the time they arrived, around 1:00 p.m., Hank realized that the only way he could cover the 315 miles to Charleston was by plane. The first show was scheduled for 8:00 p.m. and the second for 10:30.

The 3:30 flight would put Hank into Charleston with time to spare, but now there were one or two hours to kill in Knoxville. Hank told Carr to phone Cas Walker at WROL and promised to make an appearance on Walker's noontime *Dinner Bell* show. Walker, who died in September 1998 at age ninety-six, had a long career in the Knoxville music scene, but couldn't remember much about that day. He said only that Williams "never showed up, and it was probably because he was not feeling well." So how did Hank fill those hours? Murray Nash says that a nurse at St. Mary's Hospital remembered Hank coming in to get a shot from his "usual" doctor in Knoxville, who was at the hospital to deliver a baby. Perhaps he went there.

For some reason, Hank took Charles Carr with him on the plane. It would have made more sense for Carr to drive on to Charleston so that Hank would have transportation for the ongoing trip to Canton and back to Montgomery or Nashville. This became a moot point when, ninety minutes or so into the flight, the airplane turned around because of bad weather, arriving back in Knoxville a few minutes before 6:00.

Carr booked Hank and himself into the toniest hotel in Knoxville, the Andrew Johnson, at 7:08. The assistant manager, Dan McCrary, didn't see Hank and noted later that Carr appeared nervous. Hank had been sipping from the bottle of bourbon, although Carr insists that Hank didn't drink on the plane. Two porters carried him up to his room. Carr ordered two steaks, but Hank couldn't eat very much because he'd developed hiccups. He lay on the bed fully clothed, and later fell onto the floor.

Charles Carr phoned Lilly to tell her where they were, and possibly to relay his concerns about Hank. Lilly phoned Toby Marshall, who had arrived in Charleston and was waiting for Hank with Clyde Perdue. Although no longer Hank's manager, Perdue had booked these dates and wanted to be on hand to collect his percentage. Marshall phoned Charles Carr, and on his instructions, Carr called down to the front desk for a doctor because Hank's hiccups were now sending his body into mild convulsions. Dr. Paul H. Cardwell came to see him. Cardwell lived and worked about three blocks away, and later described Hank as "very drunk." He administered two shots of morphine mixed with vitamin B_{12} for hiccups, then apparently declared Hank fit for travel. Someone at the front desk of the Andrew Jackson notified Marshall that Hank could leave, and Marshall phoned Charles Carr, ordering him to go at once. He probably thought that he needed some time to get Hank in shape to perform, and didn't want Hank to manipulate Carr into bringing more liquor to the room. Marshall had been in touch with A. V. Bamford and had been told that the Charleston show had been canceled, so he ordered Carr to drive straight to Canton.

Up in Charleston, the musicians arrived to find the theater closed up. Don Helms drove in just in time to see someone locking the doors. Floyd Robinson called earlier from Minnesota and was told that the shows would probably be canceled, so he didn't even leave. Buddy Killen and the Webb Sisters skidded off the road several times en route to Charleston, and arrived just in time for the show, only to see the musicians milling around on the sidewalk. Bamford had sold around three thousand dollars' worth of advance tickets to the show that would now have to be refunded; he'd hired a full program of artists who would have to be paid their guarantees; and he would lose his deposit on the Municipal Auditorium. If Hank showed up drunk in Canton, he would be doubly out of pocket, so he probably brought pressure to bear on Marshall to get Hank to Canton in shape to perform. He and the other musicians bundled up and headed for Canton. The Canton matinee was scheduled for 3:00 p.m. on January 1. More than four thousand tickets had been sold at $2.50 apiece.

On Marshall's instructions, two porters put Hank into a wheelchair, bundled him into the back seat of his car, and laid his overcoat and a blanket on him. Hotel manager Dan McCrary told Marshall that Hank appeared to be very groggy. It was 10:45 p.m. when Carr set off from Knoxville on the Rutledge Pike. Marshall later said that he and McCrary arranged for a relief driver because Carr had been driving since early that morning, but Carr denies this. An hour out of Knoxville, Carr was stopped near Blaine, Tennessee, by patrolman Swann H. Kitts, who was from Roy Acuff and Carl Smith's hometown, Maynardville. Carr had pulled out to pass and had almost hit Kitts' patrol car head-on. Kitts turned around and chased Carr, pulling him over around 11:30. Kitts noted that there was a serviceman sitting with Carr in the front seat, although this could have been a taxi driver in uniform. The mystery codriver has never come forward.

It is from Kitts' after-the-fact investigation that we have some knowledge of Hank's last hours. "I seen him back there and I asked the driver about him — if anything was wrong," said Kitts. "The driver said, 'No, he's been drinking a beer and the doctor gave him a sedative.' I remember I said, 'He's not dead, is he?'" Carr replied that he wasn't, but Kitts later voiced his doubts. Kitts was a rookie (he'd joined the Tennessee Highway Patrol in 1950), but he was driving with a sixteen-year veteran, Grainger County sheriff J. N. Antrican, and it's unlikely that Antrican would have let the suspicion that Carr was transporting a corpse pass so easily. Carr asked the patrolmen not to wake Hank, and followed the patrol car into Rutledge, Tennessee. He was arraigned before Justice of the Peace Olin H. Marshall, tried, convicted, and fined twenty-five dollars with costs. Carr says that he paid the fine out of his own pocket, intending to get the money back off Hank.

It was 1:00 a.m. when Carr left Rutledge and carried on with his eerie journey. He was now a very apprehensive and nervous young man, tired to the point where his mind was reeling. What had seemed like a dream job that would pay next semester's tuition had turned sickeningly wrong, and would haunt him the rest of his life. By the time they reached Bristol on the Tennessee-Virginia line, Carr had been traveling for almost twenty hours. He turned north on Highway 19, going a short distance through Virginia before crossing into West Virginia at Bluefield.

Around 4:30 a.m., Carr pulled into a gas station, filled up, and asked about hiring a relief driver. Someone directed him to the Doughboy Lunch Restaurant. Carr later said that Hank got out in Bluefield to stretch his legs, but didn't go into the restaurant. This is possible, but it seems inconsistent with Hank's condition in Knoxville. Carr also told investigating officers that Hank tried to get a morphine shot in Bluefield, but either couldn't find a doctor or couldn't find one who would administer it. If true, Hank might have gobbled the remainder of the chloral hydrate tablets that Dr. Cardwell had noticed in Knoxville.

Waitress Hazel Wells said that Hank Williams came into the Doughboy Lunch Restaurant, identified himself, and asked for another driver, but it seems likelier that Carr came in, told the waitress that he was driving for Hank Williams, and asked for another driver. Hazel Wells says she pointed to Don Surface, a thirty-seven-year-old driver for the Bluefield Cab Company, seated in one of the booths. The two men had a brief conversation, and, after Surface extracted a promise of extra money for the return bus fare, he took over the wheel for the drive through the mountains. One of the few things that anyone remembers Surface saying about this ride was that he didn't speak to Hank. Perhaps the chloral hydrate tablets had taken effect, or perhaps it was already midnight for Hank Williams.

Carr says he and Surface stopped for a sandwich and beer in Princeton, West Virginia, and insists, less plausibly, that he paid off Surface at some point in West Virginia. Surface died in April 1965 without being interviewed, but newspaper reports place him at the wheel as the car neared Oak Hill, West Virginia, around 6:30 a.m. on January 1, 1953. Carr and Surface told the authorities in Oak Hill that they'd found Hank dead when they'd pulled over to get gas and coffee outside Oak Hill, and it was later assumed that they'd stopped at the Skyline Drive-in, a small cinder block restaurant south of Oak Hill. Once again, this seems unlikely because the Skyline was closed on New Year's Day, and Carr remembered a sign saying that they were six miles from Oak Hill, while the Skyline is just three miles out. Carr and Surface had probably stopped a little further south in the small town of Mount Pleasant, and it was probably there that Carr first suspected that something was wrong. He noticed Hank's blanket and coat had fallen off. Hank was lying on his back, his arms crossed in a V on his chest. Carr pulled the blanket over Hank's hand, then noticed that the hand was stiff, and he sprang back.

He went inside a restaurant, where he remembered seeing a potbellied stove in the corner. An older man came out with him. "I think you got a problem," the man said.

According to the police account from Oak Hill, Carr and Surface pulled into the Burdette's Pure Oil station and asked Burdette for directions to the hospital. Carr asked Burdette to call ahead to the police station. Officer Orris Stamey was on duty, and he called deputy sheriff Howard Janney. "It was about seven, seven thirty in the morning," said Janney. He told Carr to stay at the gas station, and drove down to find Carr and Surface standing beside the car. "I looked in the back and I knew he was dead, so I escorted the car to the hospital." Janney later told researcher Brian Turpen that Hank was still lukewarm to the touch, but that rigor mortis had set in on the arm.

At Oak Hill Hospital, two orderlies picked up Hank by his armpits and his feet and carried him into Emergency. An Italian intern, Dr. Diego Nunnari, pronounced him dead around 7:00 a.m. on January 1, 1953. Carr says that he went into the hospital lobby and phoned his father. Then he says he phoned Lilly, who didn't seem overly surprised. "Don't let anything happen to the car," she told him.

Several questions remain unanswered. Where exactly did Hank die? Did he live to see 1953? Charles Carr said that he last spoke to Hank in Bristol, Tennessee, then changed his mind, saying that it was in Bluefield. He says that Hank got out and walked around the car in Bluefield, and the waitress, Hazel Wells, says that Hank came into the Doughboy Lunch restaurant. The problem with both accounts is that rigor mortis had set in seventy-one miles up the road. Rigor mortis usually begins in the face, and is inhibited by cold. Hank's car was a convertible and would thus have been very cold that night, so if rigor mortis was afflicting his arms between 6:00 and 7:00 a.m., he had probably been dead awhile. Swann Kitts concluded after the fact that Hank had died in Knoxville, but researcher Brian Turpen has concluded that Hank *was* still alive in Bluefield and surmises that his death probably occured between 5:30 and 6:45 a.m. Hank's light body mass, says Turpen, would have meant that rigor mortis could set in quite quickly. Oak Hill police officer Howard Janney asked Dr. Nunnari how long Hank had been dead, and Nunnari said two to four hours.

A strange twist in the tale came from Dr. Leo Killorn, a Canadian intern working the New Year's overnight shift at Beckley Hospital, West

Virginia, fifteen miles down the road from Oak Hill. Killorn claimed that Carr drove up to the hospital and asked him to come take a look at a man in the back seat. Killorn said that the fact that the driver told him it was Hank Williams caused him to remember the incident. He told the driver that Hank was most assuredly dead but there was no coroner on staff that morning so he should drive on to Oak Hill. Killorn returned to practice in the Canadian maritimes, and was not an attention-seeking man, which makes it hard to totally dismiss his story. Carr, though, has always unequivocally denied it.

Carr and Surface were nervous enough to invite suspicion that foul play had been involved in Hank's death; that suspicion was reinforced by a welt on Hank's head. The local magistrate in Oak Hill, Virgil F. Lyons, called the Fayette County prosecutor, Howard W. Carson, and decided that there should be an inquest. Hank's body was taken from the hospital to the Tyree Funeral Home. By 1:00 p.m., Lyons and Carson had impaneled a group of six local citizens, and they were led upstairs at the funeral home. Hank's body was under a sheet, and the six jury members looked at it for about fifteen minutes. They all remarked how emaciated and unhealthy looking it was, and they noted the needle marks on the arms. A pathologist from Beckley hospital, Dr. Ivan Malinin, was brought in to conduct it. Fayette County coroner J. B. Thompson was there, together with Howard Janney, Orris Stamey, and West Virginia state troopers William Seal and Ted Anderson. Joe Tyree's assistant, Jim Alexander, was also there and took blood from the body. A corked bottle of blood together with a package of some internal organs was handed to trooper Ted Anderson, with the instruction that it should be taken to Charleston for analysis. Anderson looked at the bottle, turned green, and walked into the broom closet.

The autopsy was quite thorough for 1953, although Dr. Malinin didn't test for drugs. He found hemorrhages on the tongue, which would be consistent with an unconscious death, and found that Hank had been severely beaten and kicked in the groin recently, something that no one remembered doing in the tributes that were about to flood out. He stated that "death resulted due to insufficiency of right ventricle of heart due to the high position of the diaphragm with following external edema of the brain, congestive hyperemia of all the parenchymatous organs and paralysis of the respiratory center with asphyxia (punctate hemorrhages)." Several of Malinin's findings were consistent with alcoholic cardiomyopathy, but the key issue seemed to be Hank's position in the car, which led to a high diaphragm, combined with the respiratory system depressants that he'd taken (alcohol, chloral hydrate, and morphine). The combination of his traveling position, his drug intake, and his already weakened heart probably killed him. The respiratory depression he'd suffered en route to Houston ten days earlier would probably have had the same outcome if Tommy and Goldie Hill had not got him out of the car and walked him around.

Hank was embalmed in Oak Hill. The embalmer had extreme difficulty locating Hank's veins; excessive administration of intravenous drugs had collapsed them. The jury reconvened, reviewed the autopsy, and decided that there had been no evidence of foul play. The official cause of death was listed as heart failure, aggravated by acute alcoholism. The jury entered its verdict on January 10, 1953. By then, Hank Williams had been in the ground six days.

Darkling I listen; and for many a time
I have been half in love with easeful death
Called him soft names in many a muséd rhyme
To take into the air my quiet breath;
Now more than ever it seems rich to die
To cease upon the midnight with no pain.

John Keats, "Song"

• •

WUTHERING DEPTHS

• •

*T*HERE'S no way to describe how it feels when they tell you," says Billie Jean. "There was a person-to-person call to my dad from [West] Virginia. I thought Hank was in some kind of trouble. My daddy said, 'Oh Lord,' and asked the driver some questions, then hung up. I was sitting up by that point. He held me and said that Hank was dead, and I was screaming and crying. I said, 'Don't let them touch him. He often pretends he's asleep.' I thought they were going to bury him alive."

Billie had flown in from Montgomery on New Year's Eve, and was asleep by the time her father, Captain John A. Jones, arrived home from his afternoon shift with the Bossier City police department. The call from West Virginia came before daylight. Now there was a race to Hank's remains.

Charles Carr had already phoned Lilly to give her the news. At 7:01 a.m., Lilly sent a telegram to Irene, "Come at once. Hank is dead," then called her attorney, Robert Stewart, who made arrangements to charter a plane from Montgomery Aviation to take her and Daniel Carr to West Virginia. They landed at Beckley, and drove on to Oak Hill in a taxi. Lilly's first stop was the police station, where she was briefed on the situation. Clearly prepared by Robert Stewart, she'd brought along papers identifying herself as the next of kin.

Billie Jean, together with her father and brother, took commercial flights from Shreveport to Birmingham, Alabama, and from Birmingham on to Charlotte. They arrived late on New Year's Day and met Lilly and Daniel Carr the following morning. Lilly had chosen the suit in which

Hank was to be buried and the casket in which he was to be carried back to Montgomery. She had also taken possession of his jewelry and other items from the car.

On hearing of Hank's death, Toby Marshall caught a Greyhound bus to Charleston, then got a ride to Oak Hill. He should have been worried because his "patient" had died, but he seems to have convinced himself that he really was a doctor, and was preparing his final bill of $736.39.

Charles Carr was taken to the police station for questioning, then released. Joe Tyree put him up in the employees' quarters of his funeral home, and then in the afternoon of January 1, Carr went to the house of magistrate Virgil Lyons. Television was still a novelty, so he watched some football games on Lyons' TV. After his father and Lilly arrived, they all took rooms at the Hotel Hill in Oak Hill. Don Surface was questioned and let go, but was asked to stay around Oak Hill for a day or so. He had some friends and relatives nearby, so he stayed with them. Then, on being told he was free to leave, he caught a bus back to Bluefield. The car was impounded in a bay at Burdette's Pure Oil station, then moved to N&W Motors, the local Ford dealership, where it was cleaned out by one of Burdette's employees. Beer cans littered the floor, and among them was one verse of a song. It might have been written on an earlier trip, but, in light of the circumstances around its discovery, it seemed a final valentine to Audrey or Billlie Jean. A shoe or boot print stained the bottom left-hand corner, and the handwriting was almost illegible.

> *We met, we lived*
> *And dear we loved*
> *Then came that fatal day*
> *The love that felt so dear fades fast away*
> *Tonight we both are all alone*
> *And here's all that I can say*
> *I love you still and always will*
> *But that's the price we have to pay*

One item missing from the car was Hank's felt hat, apparently stolen by Pete Burdette. An alcoholic, Burdette had contracted jungle rot, a fungal disease that attacks skin tissue, while serving in Asia during the war. His hair fell out after he started wearing Hank's hat, and it was assumed locally to be a curse. Burdette later killed himself around the back of his filling station, and the hat continued to change hands. A pearl-handled gun was also taken. Lilly, who had fought hard for every one of her possessions, developed an obsession with the car and its contents, and according to Carr, phoned him every few weeks until she died inquiring about various items she was convinced Hank had taken with him.

Lilly, Daniel Carr, Charles Carr, and Toby Marshall drove back to Montgomery in Hank's car. Daniel drove most of the way, although Charles relieved him occasionally. They probably drove through the night of January 2–3, because Irene remembers them pulling up around breakfast time on January 3. The hearse was just in front of them.

Audrey had spent New Year's Eve with A. V. Bamford's wife, Maxine, at the tony Plantation Club in Nashville. Maxine pointedly remembered that Audrey said nothing about Hank coming back to Nashville, or to her. Bamford had sucked up his losses on the Charleston show, then driven to Canton late on New Year's Eve. He checked into the hotel where he'd arranged to meet Hank, then went to bed. Don Helms and Autry Inman drove to Canton a few hours behind him, checking into the hotel around 5:00 a.m. "Bam got up early," said Helms, "and Autry and I got up and went down to the auditorium. Bam met me at the dressing room door. He said, 'Brace yourself: Hank died on the way here.'"

The Canton show was staged by a local company, Harry Lashinsky and Lew Platt's LCL Presentations. Platt (who later managed rock 'n' roll deejay Alan Freed) and Lashinsky decided that the show should go on. Hank would have wanted it that way, they were sure. One of Platt's associates found Eddie Wayne, a singing deejay on WCUE, Akron, to fill out the program, and the remainder of the cast was there. Everyone on the show gathered backstage before the matinee. Akron deejay Cliff Rodgers from WHKK went out and took the microphone to make the announcement: "Ladies and gentlemen," he said, "I've been in show business almost twenty years, and I've been called upon to do many difficult things in front of an audience, but today I'm about to perform the most difficult task I have ever done." Rodgers heard some laughter from somewhere in the crowd. "This morning on his way to Canton to do this show, Hank Williams died in his car." There were a few more laughs from people who thought it was a joke of some kind. "Ladies and gentlemen," continued Rodgers, "this is no joke. Hank Williams is dead."

Backstage, the cast could hear some weeping. Some of the cast was crying too. A single spotlight was directed at the empty stage as the band, still behind the curtain, played "I Saw the Light." A few people in the audience sang along. Then the curtain was opened and the show went on. Hawkshaw Hawkins gave the performance of his life, possibly sensing that there was an opening at the top. Within the year, he would be in Nashville, but ten years later he perished in the plane crash that took the lives of Patsy Cline and Cowboy Copas.

There are a few strange codas to the Canton show. Southwest of Canton, in Dayton, Ohio, there was a *Grand Ole Opry* show slated for January 1, 1953, and several in and around Dayton swear that Hank Williams was scheduled to appear, although this seems highly unlikely in light of the fact that he was no longer a member of the *Opry*. Surviving advertisements show a lineup that included Carl Smith and the Carter Sisters, although it's just possible that Hank was slated to appear before his dismissal. At some point in the 1960s, Jim Denny's family acquired control of the Hatch Show Print company, found some Hank Williams plates, and faked a poster for the Canton show. According to Denny's poster, Hank was a *Grand Ole Opry* artist at the last, and the fake poster is still widely circulated, typifying the culture of misinformation that bedevils Hank Williams. Then, in 1964, when Audrey was managing Hank Jr., she scheduled a promotional tour to coincide with his first record. The first show was on January 1, 1964; the location, of course, was Canton. Eleven years later, the story was to be continued. That same year, the execrable biopic *Your Cheatin' Heart* premiered. In it, Audrey placed herself backstage in Canton for the fateful 1953 New Year's Day show. She stood stoically, fighting back tears. "You have no heart," Hank had once sung, "you have no shame."

Joe Tyree and his assistant Alex Childers had set out for Montgomery with Hank's remains at 4:00 p.m. on Friday, January 2. They'd taken turns at the wheel, driving nonstop. "It was raining all the way down," said Tyree, "and when we got into Alabama and we'd pull into a filling station and they'd see the West Virginia plates, they'd want to know if we was carrying Hank back. They'd start peeping in the windows."

Hank's body arrived back in Montgomery at 7:00 a.m. on Saturday, January 3. The funeral was scheduled for the following afternoon. A. V. Bamford had flown from Canton to Nashville, then driven down to Montgomery with Audrey to organize the funeral. Before leaving Montgomery, Lilly had called Leaborne Eads, who'd helped her promote some of Hank's shows back in the late 1930s and early '40s. Eads worked for the Henley Monument company, and sang with the Henley Harmony Boys on one of Hank's old WSFA spots. Lilly was very calm, Eads remembered, and gave the impression that she'd half expected Hank's death. While she was away, Eads made arrangements for Dr. Henry Lyon to preach the funeral service and for Reverend Talmadge Smith to assist. He also secured a burial plot in Oakwood Cemetery Annex, next to the grave of Irene's first child. On Lilly's instructions, Eads ordered a top-of-the-line Wilbert Continental copper-lined hermetically sealable casket from Atlanta. The original plan had been for a church service, but it soon became apparent that no church could accommodate all those who wanted to attend. Robert Stewart's idea was to rent Crempton Bowl, but the weather looked unpromising, so either Stewart or Bamford persuaded the city of Montgomery to make the Municipal Auditorium available. The police and fire department would then escort the cortege on its way to Oakwood Annex. Bamford chartered a plane to bring the *Grand Ole Opry* cast down for the funeral program. No one seemed to question why *Opry* rather than *Louisiana Hayride* artists were invited.

Billie Jean and her father and brother flew from West Virginia back to Shreveport, then returned to Montgomery late on Friday, January 2. They were staying at the boardinghouse when Lilly arrived early the following morning. Lilly immediately hid the car.

Irene had flown in. She wrote to her attorney, Robert Stewart:

> The morning Mother returned, Billie refused to speak to her. Mother went into her bedroom and sat down on the bed. Billie came out of the bedroom where she had spent the night, picked up the telephone which was on the wall in the hall and placed a long-distance call to her attorney in Shreveport. Her words to him were, "Get up here. This old gray-haired bitch is trying to steal all of Hank's stuff from me." She hung up the telephone and returned to her room. Mother told me that if I did not get her out of the house, she would kill her.

Lilly and Audrey, discovering a commonality of interest they'd never had while Hank was alive, began looking for a sheaf of lyrics as if they were maps to buried treasure. They found them in the bedroom that Hank and Billie Jean had shared. Lilly grabbed them while Billie was in the bathroom, and handed them to Bamford, who put them in the trunk of his car. Bamford then handed them to Fred Rose when he appeared the following day. Nobody realized that without Hank singing them, the scribblings were fool's gold.

Lilly then sat with Irene, blaming Billie for the concussion marks on Hank's head. Irene later wrote:

Mother told me that Billie did not like the suit that had been put on Hank at the funeral home in West Virginia. She [Lilly] wanted me to take [Billie] to a men's shop on Dexter Avenue where Hank traded and pick out a new suit and tie. I went into the bathroom where Billie, her father and brother were talking as she finished putting on her makeup. I told her what my mother had said and told her I would be ready in a few minutes to go with her. Her words were, "This is your mother's show. Let her run it." My words, "This is no show, this is my brother's funeral." By this time I was so mad, guess I could have killed her myself. I just said, "Billie, I have tried to love you and treat you good because I figured Hank loved you or he would not have married you, but let me say something to you here and now. . . . I will go through this funeral by your side. I will go with you to pick out the suit and tie. I realize that you think you are the meanest woman alive, but honey you have now met on [sic] much meaner than you. Now come on, we have a job to do. When it is over, don't ever cross my path again." At this time, my mother comes into the bathroom and starts for Billie. I made her go back to her room, took Billie by the arm, very calmly walked out the front door with she and her father and brother, went to the clothing shop where she again changed her mind. Hank was buried in the suit that was picked out in the first place.

Billie's mother arrived from Shreveport and it was decided that they would be more comfortable in a hotel. The night before the funeral, Doctor Toby Marshall showed up. Billie comes strolling in, in of all things, red slacks, going from one group of people to another telling them what the ole gray-haired bitch has done to her or was trying to do to her cars and possessions. Billie and Doctor Marshall got into a pretty good discussion, and he told her very frankly what he thought about her attire and her conduct.

On Saturday evening, Lon Williams hitched a ride to Montgomery. He had five dollars in his pocket when he arrived at the boardinghouse. Hank was lying in state by then, and Braxton Schuffert was on the door screening entrants. Lon told Braxton that he wanted some flowers, so Braxton took him to Rosemont Gardens, where everyone was working late preparing floral arrangements. "I got Hank Williams' daddy out here with me, and he wants y'all to make him a bouquet of flowers for his son," said Braxton. "They let us in. The old man said, 'I'm a poor man. I just want a five-dollar bouquet of flowers for my son.' They made him a big bouquet. His voice right then was just like Hank's."

By this point it was clear that Hank hadn't left a will, so, in the normal course of events, Lon would have been the administrator of his estate. Hank's lawyer, Robert Stewart, notified him of this and Lon apparently agreed to be the administrator or executor, but Lilly confronted him and told him that she would fight a lawsuit in hell before she would see him have it. He said he'd fought her on earth all these years and when he died he hoped to be rid of her, and she could take it. He hired a lawyer but eventually relinquished all claims. There are many crowd photos from the funeral, but Lon is not among the official mourners.

On Sunday morning, lines formed once more outside the boardinghouse to view the body. "In comes a couple of Hank's friends bringing Myrna Fay [Myrna Faye Kelley], the Indian girl that fainted at the funeral," wrote Irene to attorney Robert Stewart in 1972:

> She goes over to the coffin and starts screaming. Billie comes up and says "Francis." She thinks she is Francis Williams from WSM [Irene means Frances Williams Preston, later president of BMI]. Billie says, "Thank you for forwarding our mail to us in Shreveport." Turns one upshook Indian. "I am not Francis. I'm not anybody you ever heard of, I am just a person that loved Hank with all my heart, not a tramp like you that married him for his money." By this time I have come out of shock and I am breaking up a fistfight between the two of them over Hank's coffin. By some miracle I was able to get Myrna Fay out the front door, Billie calmed down, and return to my mother who was trying to keep Audrey [and] Audrey's family and various other people from hearing what was going on.

In a 1969 letter connected with Billie Jean's subsequent lawsuit, Robert Stewart also remembered her getting into a fistfight with "some Indian girl" at the casket.

On Sunday afternoon, January 4, 1953, Hank was buried. Crowds estimated at between 15,000 and 20,000 were outside the city auditorium; 2,750 were inside. The balcony was set aside for black mourners, of whom there were around two hundred. The casket was brought in at 1:00 p.m. and opened at 1:15. Hundreds filed past. The Drifting Cowboys, now reunited, stood by in a guard of honor. The casket was framed by two guitar-shaped floral arrangements, one with silver strings. Two purple lamps glowed in the background. A tiny white Bible was placed in Hank's frozen hand. Backstage, Roy Acuff was attempting to organize the musical program. In addition to the *Opry* artists, there was a Montgomery-area black gospel quartet, the Southwind Singers, and a white quartet, the Statesmen, who would later sing at Elvis' funeral. "Roy Acuff was in charge," said the Statesmen's lead tenor, Jake Hess, "and he asked us to sing 'I Saw the Light.' That was before gospel singers knew that song, and he was upset when we said no. He cussed us out, but couldn't do much because Hank's mother had invited us."

At 2:30, the doors were closed. "My friends," said Dr. Lyon, "as we begin this service this afternoon, Ernest Tubb will bring us closer to the Lord as he sings 'Beyond the Sunset.'" The Southwind Singers (possibly the only black quartet to perform at a prominent white funeral in Alabama prior to the civil rights era) sang "My Record Will Be There" before Dr. Lyon read from the Bible. Lyon had told Bamford that he needed half an hour, but Bamford had told him that he had only ten minutes. Roy Acuff made a confused announcement before leading the singing on "I Saw the Light." Other *Opry* performers there that day included Jimmy Dickens, Carl Smith, Lew Childre, Webb Pierce, Bill Monroe, Ray Price, June Carter, and Johnnie and Jack, as well as Eddie Hill from WSM's on-air staff. Tears were on their faces, but the task was harder yet for Don Helms, who led the Drifting Cowboys. "It was the eeriest thing I ever had to do in my life," he says. "I had to stand up there and play with Hank's coffin right below me. I can never explain how I felt playing his songs for somebody else the way I played for him with him laying in his coffin."

Billie Jean was seated in the front row, uncomfortably close to Audrey, before deciding to move her family one row back. "Everybody ignored me," she said. "Money begets money. They thought they were gonna have all the money. When Hank was alive it was a different story. None of them crossed him. Ernest Tubb, who was pretty close to Hank when he was alive, wouldn't speak to me. He looked at me kinda stupid. I stopped to speak to him, and he looked at me like he didn't even know me."

After Talmadge Smith led the congregation in prayer, Dr. Lyon introduced Red Foley, who came forward to sing "Peace in the Valley." Foley said later that Hank had made him promise he would sing it at his funeral should he go first and Red remain. Foley's normally rich and measured baritone was cracking by the time he finished. Then Lyon gave a final, lengthy eulogy, saying that Hank's true eulogy was in his music. At Lilly's request, the Statesmen Quartet sang "Precious Memories" before the final benediction. The cortege then moved slowly toward Oakwood Cemetery.

Horace Logan had flown to Montgomery with Felton Pruett, *Hayride* guitarist Dobber Johnson, and a few others. "Acuff was talking about 'Hank's friends from the *Grand Ole Opry* . . . ,'" said Logan. "Jim Denny sat in front of me. He turned around and said to me, 'Logan, if Hank could raise up in his coffin, he'd look up toward the stage and say, "I told you dumb sons of bitches I could draw more dead than you could alive."'"

At the grave site, Lyon gave a rosebud to the survivors as they threw handfuls of earth on Hank's coffin. Fred Rose was one of the honorary pallbearers. Talking to reporters after the funeral, he was refreshingly down to earth. "Whatever people say about Hank, he never hurt anybody but himself," he said. "He was his own worst enemy . . . but one thing he had — and all his friends recognized it — was loyalty. I don't give a hang whether he drank or not, I appreciate the fact he was loyal. . . . [If someone tried to bribe him away], he'd say, 'I started with Rose and I'll stay with Rose.'" Rose also threatened to sue anyone who duplicated recordings of the funeral. With so much litigation to follow, it was altogether fitting that the first threat of legal action was made as the earth was covering the coffin.

Everyone then went their separate ways. Audrey, Randall Hank, and Lycrecia returned to Nashville with A. V. Bamford; Lilly went back to the boardinghouse, and Irene joined her for a few days before returning home. Toby Marshall went back to his "practice" in Oklahoma City. Billie Jean and her family caught the Greyhound back to Shreveport, although attorney

Robert Stewart later remembered her coming up to him after the funeral, "telling me that if I didn't have them seven Cadillacs ready for her to take back to Shreveport, her brothers would personally stomp my God-damn teeth down my throat." Irene remembered the parting in slightly warmer tones. "Billie and her father came back to the house, said goodbye," she wrote later. "I promised to send her things on to her the following week. Her father thanked me for being able to keep a fairly cool head. His words were, 'But for you, child, there would have been a killing here.'"

It typified the ambiguity of Hank's life that his last journey wasn't quite his last. On January 17, 1953, his casket was dug up and moved. The Oakwood Annex housed Free French and British airmen who had been killed during training, and their remains were now disinterred and returned to their relatives. It was a gruesome job because they hadn't been buried in caskets, nor always in one piece. The remains of those who had no relatives were consolidated, leaving a large plot that the cemetery owner, John Hart, sold to Lilly.

On the afternoon of January 16, 1953, Leaborne Eads and a crew dug a new grave for Hank in what would become the family plot, and then, in the middle of the night, they moved Hank to the new site. Some passersby after midnight saw the lamps flickering and the coffin being moved, and the rumor quickly started that Hank had been taken from his casket, his boots stolen, and his body pickled. Eads, though, insists that the casket wasn't opened.

A monument in Vermont granite now sits atop several tons of poured concrete. Beneath that impregnable tomb lies the ol' Drifting Cowboy, almost certainly looking, according to Eads, exactly as he did on January 4, 1953, when the lid was closed on him. Perhaps the skin would have pinched a little around his nose, says Eads, adding with the undertaker's ghoulish detachment that the eyes might have popped open as well. One or both of the black, riveting Indian eyes that burned so intensely for twenty-nine years may now stare lifelessly into eternity. For the reverse of the monument, Audrey wrote a mawkish poem that scans about as well as she sang.

Within a week of Hank's burial, Audrey began rewriting history. That task, together with her adventures in the music business, would consume the remainder of her days. "I knew he would never hurt me or anyone else," she said, all evidence, especially her own, to the contrary. "The dream was good, it was true. . . . The heights of joy could not be told or even imagined of the happiness I [knew] as his wife. . . . Everything I ever wanted or could desire I found in Hank Williams." Hank might have wished for those flowers while he was living, but he might have stomped on them too. Audrey was the first of many who found Hank more lovable dead. In a letter to Irene dated February 24, 1953, she sounded a slightly more realistic note. "I believe Hank's love for me is what destroyed him," she said, "and there wasn't too much I could do about it. That's what makes it so bad. I was helpless. If I was weak like he was, the same thing would happen to me."

In Nashville, Hank Williams was welcomed back in death to preside beatifically over country music. The *Opry* was as anxious to reclaim him in death as it had been to cast him out in life, but as Jerry Byrd, who had played steel guitar on "Lovesick Blues," remembers, his canonization didn't go unchallenged in private:

> There was a bunch of us in the hallway at WSM on January 1. George Morgan, Ken Marvin, Jim Denny, and me. Jim Denny said, "We'll never see his like again." I said, "I hope not." Everybody looked at me like I'd blasphemed, and I said, "You're trying to put a halo on him that won't fit." He had a great chance and he blew it. He did as much to hurt country music as he did to help it — doing shows drunk as hell and insulting the audience. Everyone forgets that. They have short memories.

George Morgan, who had been the butt of some of Hank's arrogance, broke the awkward silence. "I'm with Byrd," he said.

Out on Long Island, Frank Walker composed a letter to Hank addressed "c/o Songwriter's Paradise." Walker started by saying that he always enjoyed writing to Hank on New Year's Day, although the only letter anyone ever found was a curt reply to Audrey, who had called inquiring where the year-end royalty statements were. "An hour or so ago," Walker wrote, "I received a phone call from Nashville. It was a rather sad call too for it told me that you had died early this morning. . . . I think HE wanted to have you just a bit closer to HIM. Nashville's pretty far away, so HE just sent word this morning, Hank, that HE wanted you with HIM. . . . You'll be writing for the greatest singers too, the Angels, they're so wonderful — I know they'll want you to join them."

Then a voice borne on a sepulchral breeze spoke to Walker: "When the plant reopens tomorrow," it said, "take records by all other artists off the presses, lay on an extra shift, and press only Hank Williams records; this is the opportunity of your lifetime." Walker didn't go to Nashville; instead, he heeded the voice and reaped the rewards. "Honestly," he'd said in his letter, "I'm not too unhappy for I must rejoice with you at the tremendous opportunity you will have to do good for others." How true those words would become. Walker's folly was that to the end of his stewardship at MGM in 1958, he would sign average, occasionally above-average, country singers, believing them to be the next Hank Williams.

Two months after Toby Marshall arrived back in Oklahoma City, he was unmasked. His wife, Fay, died in mysterious circumstances on March 4, 1953, and Hank Williams' name was found among a list of "patients." An investigation was launched, and lots of damaging innuendo was heard, but in the end Marshall could be indicted for nothing more serious than parole violation. Before he was arrested, he contacted Billie Jean once again for payment, intimating that he knew things that could prove very valuable to her in the legal battles ahead. Then, while serving out his time, he wrote a 222-page book detailing much that Hank Williams told him during their sessions. Marshall's manuscript surfaced recently but has never been released. Its thesis is that Hank Williams committed suicide. "It occurs to me," Marshall said during testimony in March 1953,

> that perhaps Hank got to mulling things over in his mind, and having a very persuasive personality he might have just talked the doctor in Knoxville out of enough stuff [barbiturates] to kick himself off. . . . He had been on a rapid decline. Most of his bookings were of the honky-tonk beer-joint variety which he simply hated. If he came to this conclusion [suicide], he still had enough prestige as a star to make a first-class production out of it. Six months from now, he might have been playing for nickels and dimes on skid row.

Marshall is the only person to have raised the specter of suicide, but his opinion cannot be discounted because he was as close to Hank as anyone during those last weeks, perhaps even closer than Billie Jean. Many around Hank would have ruled out the notion of suicide, insisting that he had everything to live for — which, in a sense, he did. Even so, the world must have looked very different to Hank Williams when he was coming off a drunk, reeling from ceaseless back pain, soaked in his own urine, the taste of vomit still in his mouth, facing the prospect of a three-hundred-mile haul to the next beer joint, always knowing that midnight was approaching.

"He wanted to destroy the Hank Williams that was making the money that fair-weather friends and relatives were getting," said Marshall. "Although he had a multiplicity of personal problems, basically he was a very lonely person, and couldn't stand being alone. . . . He had a host of fair-weather friends, most of whom were parasites, who fawned on him, played up to him, and kept him supplied with liquor." Several of those who worked with Hank during his last year lend credence to Marshall's theory. Don Helms says that he sometimes dreaded coming into Hank's hotel room for fear that the window would be open and Hank would be gone. Whether he jumped on that final trip will forever be conjecture, though. Setting out, he seemed determined to show his Nashville costars that he could arrive on time and put on a hell of a show, but we'll never know the thoughts that beset him on that long, final ride.

Hank had lost the focus that had driven him in 1949. One moment he felt suicidal; the next he wanted to reclaim his position at the top in Nashville. One moment he wanted to jettison Billie Jean and return to Audrey; the next he wanted to stay with Billie. He left so many contradictory messages behind him. He had lost the centeredness that had helped him achieve his success, and this too is hard to believe, because so few years separated the intently focused Hank Williams of late 1949 from the bruised, buffeted, and directionless Hank Williams of late 1952. There are enough questions around that last journey and the events that followed to suggest that a secret was buried with him, but the problem with conspiracy theories is that Hank Williams would almost certainly have been dead within weeks or months anyway. He was in such poor shape.

Bobbie Jett was a name on nobody's lips during the lying-in-state, the funeral, or its immediate aftermath. Two days after Hank was buried, she gave birth to a daughter named Antha (Bobbie's mother's name) Belle (her grandmother's name) Jett. A lonely confinement was followed by a lonely delivery. She was the only mother giving birth that day in St. Margaret's Hospital. Under the influence of painkillers, she began singing Hank's songs. A week or so later, she checked herself out, picked up Jo, and left Antha Belle with Lilly and Marie Glenn.

On January 28, Lilly attended a hearing at the Montgomery County Department of Public Welfare. She stated that the child had been left at her house when she had gone back to Butler County, and she told the public welfare officers that the child was Hank's and she would be willing to adopt her because "this was what her son would want her to do, and he once commented that he did feel that Miss Jett was not a suitable person to take care of the child." According to the report, Lilly seemed quite devoted to the baby, and wanted to keep her because she would help her feel closer to Hank. Lilly, though, had been diagnosed with heart disease, and her fitness to adopt was questioned. Meanwhile, Bobbie Jett was back in Nashville, caring for her grandmother, and cooking and cleaning for several other family members. At no time did she consider taking Antha Belle.

Three days later, Irene wrote to Robert Stewart, "Please talk my mother into never bringing Bobbie into this mess no matter what. Yea Gods, if all of the scandall [sic] that could be dug up ever was, I would feel like changing my name." Robert Stewart was equally opposed to Lilly's adopting the child. "I am making as few suggestions as possible," he wrote to Irene on March 16, 1953, "other than to say that I feel it [the child] should be turned over to the Welfare Department or to the Sisters in the event that Bobbie will not take care of it." Four days later, Irene replied to Stewart, mentioning that she'd had a letter from Bobbie Jett that morning in which Bobbie told her that she was going to Montgomery the following week to sign the papers allowing Lilly to adopt the child.

All the while, Irene was making it clear that she would never assume responsibility for the baby (referred to by both Irene and Robert Stewart as "it"), despite the fact that she'd told social workers that she would. In another letter to Robert Stewart dated April 6, 1953, she made her position clear: "Tee [Irene's husband, John T. Smith] says that if she [Lilly] adopts it and then can't take care of it, he is not going to let me take it. Keep this under your hat, mabey [sic] it will never be necessary for me to have the child at all. I feel that the poor child would have a better chance in life if it were adopted by someone that would never know its origin at all."

Lilly went ahead with the adoption, and the child became Cathy (a name Lilly picked from her favorite book, *Wuthering Heights*) Yvone (from "Jambalaya") Stone. Lilly was still married to Bill Stone, but would divorce him in April 1954 — one legal action of many that year. Lilly took another lover, named Slim Stern, while Stone moved in with Marie and Butch in the boardinghouse next door.

In the absence of a will, Hank's estate was the subject of contention. Audrey's share was clear, but the thought that Billie Jean would share the other half with Hank Jr. prompted Audrey and Lilly to become strange bedfellows. Some might say that they had a case; they had gone up and down with Hank Williams for nine and twenty-nine years, respectively, whereas Billie Jean had been in the picture for only three months. Very quickly, Audrey and Lilly played their trump. Lilly remembered the overheard conversation in which Billie Jean had told Hank that they weren't legally married (presumably, Audrey forgot that her 1944 marriage to Hank hadn't been legal either, for exactly the same reason).

"If it was left to Audrey and me, we could work this thing [the estate] out on friendly terms," said Billie Jean, striking an unusually conciliatory note a week after Hank died. "I don't want to fight over Hank's estate. He wouldn't have wanted it that way." But big money was at stake, and very soon Hank's presumed wishes were irrelevant.

Lilly and Audrey developed a plan: first they would prove that Hank and Billie Jean were not legally married, then they'd try to blacken Billie's reputation. On February 24, Audrey wrote to Irene: "I'm leaving early Thursday morning to check on this Billie. . . . I may also go to Ft. Jackson, S.C. to check to see Farron [sic] Young." The following month, Lilly went to Nashville because three of Billie Jean's former coworkers at the telephone company apparently had information that they wanted to share, but wouldn't give to Audrey. Meanwhile, Irene, Lilly, and Audrey were still following up leads on Billie's first husband, Harrison Eshliman. Their anger rose as Faron Young's "Goin' Steady" (a song that Hank almost certainly wrote) began climbing the charts. Irene wrote bitterly to Robert Stewart, "This Johnny Horton that [Billie] goes out with will probably be the next one to come out with one of Hank's songs." Irene clearly thought that Billie had made off with a stash of songs and was feeding them to her friends.

"I had youth, but no knowledge," Billie concluded. Two weeks after Hank's death, Paul Howard had called her. Howard was the bandleader who had arranged Hank and Billie's first marriage. "He asked me if I could sing, and I said I'd been singing all my life in churches, and at the officers' club. Paul said, 'G-o-o-o-d, because I'm fixing to make us a lot of money.' We rented a costume and took a picture of me with a hat on. We were making two thousand dollars or more a night not counting pictures. We could have sold as many pictures as we had. I was sending money home every day." At the same time, Audrey put together an all-girl band, the Drifting Cowgirls, and Bamford began booking her out on show dates.

For several months there were two "Mrs. Hank Williams" on the road, invoking Hank's memory and singing his songs. Sometimes they played at competing parks. "One time up in Missouri," said Billie Jean, "Audrey was playing thirteen miles down the road. I said over the loudspeaker, 'If you guys hurry up, you go on down the road you can catch my husband's ex-wife down there.' I used to pull crap like that all the time." It was a situation that couldn't last.

On August 19, 1953, Billie Jean signed an agreement with Audrey and the estate in which she relinquished all rights to Hank's estate and to any future income from it, and agreed not to perform as "Mrs. Hank Williams." She and her attorney had been persuaded that the chance of income beyond 1953 was "slight and speculative," and that she would be better off taking a one-time settlement instead of fighting a protracted legal battle. The agreement was very specific, right down to requiring Billie Jean to divulge the location of Hank's Tennessee walking horse, Highlight Merry Boy. She was also required to deliver the saddle along with three pieces of luggage left in Shreveport. In exchange, she received thirty thousand dollars. Her lawyers, she says, took ten thousand, and the remainder barely paid off the debt load of her next husband, Johnny Horton, whom she married one month later, on September 26, 1953. Horton made Hank look like a model of fiscal probity.

Audrey's divorce settlement had given her half of Hank's royalty income, leaving him the other half and all performance income. In death, of course, royalties made up almost all of the posthumous income. Half went to Audrey, and with Billie Jean out of the picture, the other half went to the estate, administered by Lilly on behalf of Hank Jr. No one foresaw what would happen to the value of Hank's estate. Billie Jean didn't foresee it when she signed the agreement, but neither did those who would profit from it.

"Kaw-Liga" became the best-selling country record of 1953, and the flip side, "Your Cheatin' Heart," also became a top-seller. Joni James' cover version of "Your Cheatin' Heart" reached number two on the pop charts, and Frankie Laine's version wasn't far behind it. The next single,

"Take These Chains from My Heart," also reached number one. Hank's entire catalog began moving in unprecedented quantities. Two albums were on the shelves by March, *Memorial Album* and *Hank Williams as Luke the Drifter* (the secret not a secret anymore). Within ten weeks of his death, Hank had as many albums on the market as he did all the years he lived; hundreds more would follow. The oil well that Hank Williams became in death was starting to gush. In 1952, his MGM royalties had been $13,869 and his Acuff-Rose royalties had been $55,044; in 1953, they had been $60,636 and $72,762, respectively.

Lilly opened a shrine to Hank in his old bedroom and wrote a booklet, *Life Story of Our Hank Williams,* that she sold over the radio. She attended events in honor of her son and corresponded ceaselessly with her lawyer, Robert Stewart. Marie Glenn took on the raising of Cathy Yvone, but fell out with Lilly in 1954. For most of that year, they didn't talk. The years of ceaseless work eventually took their toll on Lilly, and she died in her sleep on February 26, 1955. Her maid called Marie and told her that she couldn't get Lilly up. Marie went next door and found Lilly slumped across the bed.

Irene became the executor of the estate and thus the Alabama guardian of Hank Jr., but wouldn't adopt Cathy, who was put up for re-adoption later in 1955. Marie made one last-ditch attempt to save Cathy from adoption. She tracked down Bobbie Jett, then living in California, and told her that Cathy would be put up for adoption if Bobbie didn't reclaim her. Bobbie told Marie that she'd remarried and that her new husband didn't know about Cathy, and she could therefore do nothing. Bobbie had married a man named John Tippins, and had six more children with him. Apparently, Pappy Neal McCormick visited Marie and offered to adopt the child, but Marie told him that they didn't want anyone to have the child who "knowed anything about Hank."

In a meeting with the Department of Public Welfare, Robert Stewart gave an indication of Irene's thinking on the matter. Irene would be in Montgomery for Hank Williams Day parades and the like, said Stewart, and "she could just hear the tongues wagging now when Cathy would ride down the street." Lilly had divorced Bill Stone in April 1954, but he was still the adoptive father and was called upon to sign the papers necessary to put Cathy up for readoption. Social services reported that he cried that day. He was still living at Marie's boardinghouse, as was Cathy, so if they cared for Cathy as much as they said, it seems strange that they apparently made no effort to prevent her being put up for adoption.

In March 1955, Cathy went to Mr. and Mrs. J. H. Cook in Pine Level, Alabama, and then, in February 1956, to a middle-aged couple, Wayne and Mary Louise Deupree in Mobile. She became Cathy Louise Deupree. Irene wrote to Robert Stewart in January 1956 from her new home in Dallas and asked, "Has the baby been adopted?" The following month, a payment of $2,281.14 was made to a lawyer from Lilly's estate with the instruction that it be paid to Cathy Stone / Deupree when she reached the age of twenty-one.

After the boardinghouses had been sold and all of Lilly's debts paid, just $6,504.38 remained in her estate. It wasn't much to show for a terribly hard life. Lilly left nothing to Marie Glenn, but Irene gave her sufficient furnishings to start her own boardinghouse on North Decatur Street. Several more moves followed. In 1958, Marie married Ed Harvell, who had lived for years in Lilly's boardinghouse, sharing the room next to Hank's on the ground floor (Marie's son, Butch, says that Marie and Ed were never married, although Marie took his name, and was buried as Marie Harvell).

Immediately upon Lilly's death, Audrey sought to have Irene removed as administrator of the estate. Irene not only refused to give up the job, for which she received 2.5 percent of Hank's income, but also hung on to a large number of his artifacts. She justified her actions by saying that Audrey had squandered her half of Hank's income, and would squander the other half if she were administering it. The Alabama estate had borne the total cost of all the judgments against Hank as well as the total cost of the settlement with Billie Jean. Audrey doggedly refused to share anything but the income.

Fred Rose died three months before Lilly, on December 1, 1954. He had been much more than Hank's music publisher and record producer; he had been his mentor and his quality-control department. In the last photos of him, some of them taken with Lilly and Audrey, he looked gaunt and sick, but still fearsomely intense. He'd developed heart disease, and had once suffered a heart attack in the recording studio, but his Christian Science beliefs prevented him from seeing a doctor. After his death, Wesley Rose assumed control. The accountant began to fancy himself a music man, but he could never have sat with Hank, as his father had done, helping him polish those diamonds in the rough. Even less could Wesley have helped Hank weather the upset triggered by rock 'n' roll. Seven months after Fred Rose died, an Elvis Presley record nudged its way onto the country charts, heralding the revolution. The hard and fast borders between pop, country, and R&B began to dissolve, and rock 'n' roll emerged. In perhaps the most ludicrous statement he ever made, Wesley Rose said that if Hank had lived "I don't think we would have had a rock era." His contention was that rock 'n' roll filled the void left by Hank's death.

Every one of Hank's contemporaries had to come to terms with rock 'n' roll. Webb Pierce, Hank Snow, Carl Smith, Faron Young, Red Foley, and Eddy Arnold saw their careers take a precipitous nosedive in the mid- to late 1950s. Only Ray Price went from strength to strength as he finally escaped Hank's long shadow to forge his own style. As rock 'n' roll erupted and everyone was wondering what would happen next, Price took country music back to the barrooms, cutting classic beer hall shuffles, like "Crazy Arms" and "My Shoes Keep Walking Back to You." Price was the only one from that generation to see his career surge during the birth of rock 'n' roll by making music true to country music's roots.

Hank Williams was elected to the Rock 'n' Roll Hall of Fame in 1987, but scarcely belonged there. His music was for adults, whereas rock 'n' roll was for, by, and about teenagers. The exaggeration and over-statement of rock 'n' roll had no place in his music, and its sledgehammer beat was the opposite of the Drifting Cowboys' sweet, mellow swing. Had he lived, there would have been no place for Hank Williams in rock 'n' roll or in Nashville. His thinning hair, his incorrigibly rural ways, and his "Pitchers from Life's Other Side" were the antithesis of nearly everything recorded in Nashville from 1955 onward.

With the exception of Ray Price, the new era's most successful artists, like Jim Reeves, Johnny Cash, and Marty Robbins, blurred the line between pop and country, whereas Hank's music always needed to be reinterpreted for the mass audience. Some of his records, like "Hey, Good Lookin'" or "Settin' the Woods on Fire," almost prefigured rock 'n' roll's giddiness, but Hank himself was inalienably country.

Rhythm 'n' blues singer Wynonie Harris had much of what became rock 'n' roll swagger on his late 1940s and early '50s hits like "Good Rockin' Tonight," but that didn't help him score one hit after rock 'n' roll erupted. He was too old and too black. Hank was probably too old and too hillbilly, but by dying prematurely, he avoided the indignity of having to answer the question of what he would have done. For its part, MGM tried to imagine the sound by grafting drums, electric guitar, and piano solos onto his records and bathing the results in echo, beginning a long, sorry history of reinventing Hank's music according to the season.

As early as 1955, the ongoing success of Hank's catalog was surprising everyone. The emerging LP market was a godsend. MGM could endlessly repackage Hank's recordings, and Acuff-Rose could pitch his songs to other artists as LP filler. When Hank had signed his contract renewal with MGM in 1951, the LP royalty rate was artificially low, and the estate renegotiated the rate to the standard 5 percent, but not without squawking from Frank Walker. On October 20, 1955, Walker wrote to the estate: "We in the record business know that interest pretty much ceases in a record artist the day after his funeral," he said. "The flowers dry very quickly, so do eyes, and so do royalties." Walker reminded the estate that, in his view, the ongoing success was because of his ceaseless work. With Acuff-Rose's assistance, he had at least overcome the problem that Hank left so few recordings. Aside from "Kaw-Liga" / "Your Cheatin' Heart," just five studio recordings remained unissued, and two of those were hymns that Audrey rendered unlistenable. Acuff-Rose retrieved vocal-guitar demos for overdub. The Drifting Cowboys were still around Nashville, most of them working with Ray Price, and the results of their overdub sessions were surprisingly convincing. A few of the overdubs, notably "Weary Blues from Waitin'," became hits.

Then, in 1955, MGM acquired the Johnnie Fair Syrup shows. Between January and May 1949, Hank had prerecorded early morning radio shows for Johnnie Fair, and many of the shows survived on acetate. An engineer at KWKH reportedly found them and sold them to Leonard Chess, boss of Chess Records. Chess realized that he couldn't issue them and sold them on to MGM. With few hits of his own at the time, Hank had generally performed other artists' songs, and did so without a band. The results were artlessly affecting. At the dawn of the rock 'n' roll era, MGM began issuing these very spare vocal-guitar recordings as singles, and they sold respectably well. The faux folk ballad "At the First Fall of Snow" was released in September 1955 and had sold thirty thousand copies by the end of February 1956.

Hank's royalty income, which had peaked in 1953 at $132,000, was still at a very healthy $74,000 in 1958, despite the fact that his singles were no longer hitting the charts. In 1959 and 1960, MGM overdubbed the Johnnie Fair shows for LP release, and by 1960 the royalties once again topped $130,000. In 1961, the *Health and Happiness* shows were acquired, providing the basis for a couple of spurious live albums. Then, in 1962, Ray Charles included two of Hank's songs on his chart-topping *Modern Sounds in Country and Western Music,* and Hank's Acuff-Rose royalties jumped from $45,626 in 1961 to $71,049 the following year.

Acuff-Rose had become hugely successful by 1960, managing and publishing the Everly Brothers and Roy Orbison, but Hank Williams was still the jewel of the catalog, and Wesley Rose wanted to preserve it at all costs. As early as 1960, Rose began to talk to the Alabama estate about copyright renewal. Copyright law back then stated that copyrights must be renewed every twenty-eight years. At the time of renewal, the copyright can be reassigned to another music publisher, and that prospect had Wesley Rose running scared. Hank Jr. would reach the age of majority in 1970, and might well reassign his father's copyrights when they began coming up for renewal in 1974.

With that in mind, Wesley Rose offered a deal to Irene, who was still Hank Jr.'s guardian in Alabama and executor of the estate. The estate would receive a one-time, nonrecoupable payment of twenty-five thousand dollars and Irene would receive a one-time, nonrecoupable payment of five thousand dollars. In return, the estate preagreed to renew the copyrights with Acuff-Rose. The ostensible reason for this was that the long-debated movie was on the point of being made, and Acuff-Rose needed to know that they had the copyrights for another term in order to offer synchronization rights.

The estate had a reason for wanting to get the matter resolved, too. In a handwritten memo to himself, Irene's attorney, Robert Stewart, said, "Renewal rights vest in the twenty-eighth year in both legitimate and illegitimate children." In other words, the problem of Cathy that they thought they'd solved in 1956 might come back to haunt them. In fact, Acuff-Rose almost ensured that it would. Acuff-Rose's attorney, Maury Smith, didn't have an especially good case when Audrey sued to gain control of the entire estate and have the renewal deal reversed. Trying to explain why Acuff-Rose had paid so little for the renewal rights, Smith mentioned Hank's October 1952 contract with Bobbie Jett and stated that the child covered by that agreement might come forth with a claim that would diminish the value of the rights under discussion. In a December 1966 decision, an Alabama judge left the administration of the estate with Irene, and refused permission for the renewal deal to be undone. At some point, an attorney contacted Cathy's adoptive parents, probably asking if they wanted to pursue a claim on her behalf. They said that they didn't, not realizing the amount of money at stake.

The lawsuit proved that Audrey had spent everything that she'd taken in from Hank's estate, and that there was nothing left for Hank Jr. There wasn't much more left in Alabama. In 1968, Irene settled sixty thousand dollars in bills that Junior and Audrey had run up. By then, the estate's total earnings since Hank's death were in excess of $1.6 million. Half of that amount had gone to Audrey, and she had spent it all, and of the remaining $830,000, just $203,592 was left. Irene, meanwhile, was turning to other sources of income, and in July 1969 was arrested at the U.S.-Mexican border with seven million dollars' worth of cocaine concealed under the rear seat of her Cadillac. Her next few years were spent in a federal penitentiary in West Virginia, quite close to where Hank was pronounced dead. After her incarceration, the Alabama guardianship was taken over by Robert Stewart. In 1979, Irene wrote one of the last of many letters to Stewart on the occasion of Jay Caress' biography of Hank Williams. Stewart replied, "When it comes to airing the real facts about the Williams family, just think what you and I together could tell." Neither, though, ever told. Stewart died in January 1985, and Irene died impoverished and alone in Dallas on March 24, 1995. In an act of great magnanimity, Hank Jr. sang "I Saw the Light" at her funeral. Shortly before she died, she sold a storage locker full of Hank's stage outfits, photos, contracts, and ephemera to country star Marty Stuart for thirty thousand dollars.

While Irene was in jail, her father, Lon, died. The only person to remain above the squabbles with a modicum of dignity, he had continued to live in McWilliams, Alabama. He ran a store for a while, fixed fences and spliced cable, and told stories that sometimes stretched credibility. He died at age seventy-eight, on October 22, 1970, and wasn't buried in the same Williams family plot as Hank and Lilly, but in another family plot that bore his name.

In 1974, Hank Williams' copyrights, which no one thought would be worth anything past the end of 1954, started coming up for renewal. By then Billie Jean was a widow once more. Johnny Horton had died in a car wreck on November 5, 1960. His last paying gig had been at the Skyline Club in Austin, the site of Hank's last paying gig.

By the early 1960s, Billie Jean realized the enormity of the mistake she'd made in settling for thirty thousand dollars. She sued first over the manner of her portrayal in MGM's biopic, *Your Cheatin' Heart,* but a United States district court in Atlanta determined that although she and Hank *had* been legally married, the movie hadn't maliciously defamed her, and so damages were not payable. Billie Jean then took the decision that she and Hank had been legally married and sued for half of the copyright renewals. Someone, quite possibly a music business entrepreneur named Ernest D. Brookings, put the word in her ear that she hadn't signed away the renewals because she couldn't have signed away what she didn't have. On October 9, 1968, she gave Brookings permission to shop her as-yet-unproven claim on the renewals. On May 28, 1969, Brookings assigned them to Acuff-Rose's archrival, Hill & Range, which in turn funded her lawsuit on the understanding that they would handle her share of the music publishing should she win. The case came to trial in March 1975, and judgment in Billie Jean's favor was rendered on October 22 of that year.

On November 4, 1975, Audrey died, ostensibly of heart failure. She had lived her last years in a pharmaceutical and alcoholic daze as if in fulfillment of the prophecy Hank had made: "You'll walk the floor the way I do. . . ." A year before her death, she'd held a garage sale. Local news media reported it as if she were selling off Hank's possessions, but in fact she was selling off the detritus of her own life at hugely inflated prices, charging two dollars admission. She sat out front, a sadly diminished figure, looking much older than her fifty-one years. Seated in front of a huge cardboard cutout of Hank, she hid behind oversized dark glasses, and had extreme difficulty getting up.

On January 6, 1974, Cathy Yvone Stone turned twenty-one. The twenty-two hundred dollars left to her in the settlement of Lilly's estate hadn't been placed in an interest-bearing account, but the return on it would be greater than anyone could have imagined. Days before she turned twenty-one, Cathy's adoptive mother told her about a Dickensian inheritance awaiting her, and hinted that her birth father might have been none other than Hank Williams, but Cathy's visit to the Montgomery County Courthouse to pick up the check yielded no further clues. Three months later, on April 17, 1974, Bobbie Jett died in California, leaving only the vaguest intimations that she had once been involved with Hank Williams.

Just two days before Bobbie's death, attorney Richard Frank had written to fellow attorney Robert Stewart in connection with Billie Jean's lawsuit. "I am much afraid," Frank wrote, "that if Baby Jett has personally come up with a lawyer to get the money from Mrs. Stone, her ancestry may well be reasonably obvious to her, and further trouble may ensue."

Further trouble did ensue. Until 1980, Cathy made only desultory efforts to uncover the truth about her parentage. She found Marie Glenn (by then Marie Harvell), who was overjoyed to see her again but remained guarded on several big issues, and she found Bobbie's surviving children in California. Then, in September 1984, Cathy went to see an investigative attorney, Keith Adkinson, who was sufficiently intrigued by her case to take it on. Adkinson discovered the October 1952 agreement between Hank and Bobbie, and, in July 1985, Cathy went public with her allegation that fraud had been committed. Over Hank Jr.'s strenuous objections, the Alabama Supreme Court eventually recognized her claim, reopened Hank's estate, and awarded her a proportionate share together with some of his effects. By then, she'd married Keith Adkinson and become Jett Williams.

Marie's son, Butch, saw all that his former playmate went through in order to establish her share of the estate, and wondered if it was a price he was willing to pay. Marie died on January 17, 1991, without ever quite telling him who his father was, but there had been enough gossip for him to see a lawyer. Depositions were taken, although Butch is guarded about the advice he was given as a result. At some point, though, he decided that he would take it no further. His wide, thin-lipped mouth is much as Hank's was, and he has the same dark, deep-set Indian eyes. He also began losing hair in his twenties, just as Hank had. He lives in a poor area of Montgomery, and his protestations that he needs no more than he has do not ring entirely true, but he understands the financial and emotional cost of challenging for a share of the estate. "I don't see the sense of fighting a battle, to lose it all even if I was to win," he says.

Hank Williams Jr., meanwhile, became a star in his own right. For all the hits, now numbering around one hundred, perhaps his greatest achievement is that he at least partly escaped his father's long shadow. While the offspring of other country stars such as Marty Robbins, Conway Twitty, and Buck Owens were unable to sustain music careers, "Junior" went from strength to strength.

Audrey planned Junior's career as a tribute to his father, thereby stoking the legend upon which her livelihood depended. Signed to his father's record label, MGM, in December 1963, Junior's first public appearance as a recording artist was, as noted, in Canton. Before he was out of his teens, Junior was touring with his father's band members, singing his father's songs for his father's label, adding music to some of the lyrics Bamford and Lilly had grabbed from Hank's bedroom, and recording some faked-up father-son duets. He even recorded narrations as Luke the Drifter Jr. As an act of fealty, it worked, but as music for the late '60s, it did not. Turnout at the shows was good; record sales were generally poor. There were just two top five country hits during Junior's first four years as a recording artist; the first was his father's "Long Gone Lonesome Blues" and the other was a self-deprecatory tribute, "Standing in the Shadows" ("I know that I'm not great / Some folks say I imitate").

"At first," Junior told interviewer John Eskow, "I thought it was the greatest thing in the world — a ghost of this man that everyone loved. They think I'm daddy. Mother's smilin', money's rolling in, seemed ideal." By 1970, it seemed less so, and Junior's distress only mounted as MGM edged him away from the tribute act toward country-pop. His first number one hit, "All for the Love of Sunshine," was every bit as vacuous as its title. "Pain," wrote Junior in his autobiography, *Living Proof,* "is walking out on stage two nights out of three, with your insides knotted all into a ball, and singing songs to a crowd who didn't appreciate if you lived or died."

As the outlaw movement coalesced around Waylon Jennings and Willie Nelson, Junior bought into its anti-Nashville stance and rock 'n' roll attitude. He became the outlaw with the private income. Although bracketed with Waylon 'n' Willie, he felt a closer spiritual kinship with southern rock bands like Lynyrd Skynyrd and the Marshall Tucker Band, and, in a series of albums culminating with *Hank Williams, Jr. & Friends,* declared his independence. He wrested himself free of his mother, free of Nashville, and free of MGM and all that it entailed.

But then, on August 8, 1975, just as . . . *and Friends* was being readied for release, Junior fell down a mountainside in Montana while on a hunting trip. The injuries were horrific; parts of his face were literally scraped away. There was a long layoff and his appearance was forever transformed. When he reemerged, it was on Warner Bros., then Elektra Records, but by this point he was confident in his new direction. Ironically, though, his first major hit in more than five years came with yet another examination of his legacy, "Family Tradition." The follow-up, "Whiskey Bent and Hell Bound," began to establish the Hank Williams Jr. persona. He'd stared down death on the mountainside, and now he was going to live each day as if it were his last. His music was swaggering, unapologetically sexist, hugely self-referential — and very successful. Of his thirty hits during the '80s, seven of them peaked at number one. "All My Rowdy Friends Are Coming Over Tonight" was adopted as the theme of ABC-TV's *Monday Night Football.*

Junior's musicality came to the fore on a chart-topping revival of Fats Waller's "Ain't Misbehavin'" and on occasional album cuts, but it was the defiant bubba-ness of songs like "Good Friends, Good Whiskey, Good Lovin'" (his last top ten country hit to date) or "Naked Women and Beer" (his duet with rap rocker Kid Rock) that his audience wanted.

"Hey," he said, "we don't all live in New York or Los Angeles."

The copyrights on Hank's songs, which had come up for their first twenty-eight-year renewal starting in 1974, came up again beginning in 2002. By this point, the business interests representing Hank's legacy had undergone some changes. Wesley Rose began suffering the onset of Alzheimer's disease in the early 1980s, and sold Acuff-Rose to Gaylord Broadcasting in 1985. Two years earlier, Gaylord had bought the *Grand Ole Opry* and WSM, but by August 2002 Gaylord was hemorrhaging money, and it offloaded Acuff-Rose, by then one of the few profitable parts of its business, to the Sony corporation for $157 million. Hank Jr. reclaimed his share of the publishing from Sony/Acuff-Rose, but left the administration of songs with them. Shortly before the sale to Sony, Acuff-Rose also made a deal with Billie Jean to purchase her share outright for an undisclosed amount.

Hank's records no longer appeared on MGM because MGM Records no longer existed. In April 1972, the German record company Polydor had bought the MGM record catalog without rights to the logo, so Hank's records began appearing first on Polydor, then on Mercury. In May 1998, Polydor was gobbled up by the Universal Music Group. Universal was the descendant of Decca Records, the label that had tried and failed to acquire Hank in 1947.

Even Hank's old house has gone. In 1984, part of it was moved to Music Row, although there were rumors to the effect that very little of it was actually moved. In May the following year, the house or a replica of it became a poorly stocked museum hosted by Audrey's daughter, Lycrecia. The museum closed in 1988, and the house changed hands several times before Reba McEntire's company, Starstruck Entertainment, bought the property in May 1998 and brought in a backhoe. Hank's old farm in Williamson County was eventually acquired by Tim McGraw and Faith Hill, who applied to have the antebellum farmhouse torn down.

Hank Williams' story deserved to end with a ringing, plangent E chord, and perhaps a flash of lonesome blue falsetto, but instead it continues to the drone of lawyers fighting their little fights. The lawsuits will continue as long as Hank's posthumous income makes it worthwhile for anyone to pay two hundred dollars or more an hour — in other words, into the foreseeable future. His songs now accompany television commercials and have been reinterpreted across the musical spectrum, from the British punk acts to jazz divas like Cassandra Wilson and Norah Jones. Hank's songs, in fact, are almost everywhere. As the records grow smaller, Hank Williams grows bigger.

Anyone who dies as young as Hank invites endless "what if" speculation. It has been an item of faith in country music circles that Hank would have had a rosy future if only he had lived. The reality might have been a little different. It's doubtful that he could have saved himself even if he had rested up in Shreveport or Montgomery, concentrated on songwriting, and just made the short tours that he once intended. Too many of his self-destructive behaviors were hardwired. The spinal pain was irremediable, and the physical damage already done to his heart and perhaps his liver and other organs was irreversible. "He didn't have a chance," concluded Oscar Davis, who had seen the contrast between the Hank Williams of early 1949 and the Hank Williams of late 1952. "[but] I think he died happy [because] he proved to the world he was somebody." It is far from certain whether that was as much a consolation to Hank at the last as Davis thought.

The circumstances that combined to make Hank the most powerfully iconic figure in country music will never come again. No one will cut three or four classics in an afternoon session again; no one will redefine the vocabulary of the music in the way that he did. No one will be allowed to mess up in the way that he did, either. The stakes are too high, and professional help would have been foisted upon him. The specialness in Hank Williams would then have ebbed away because the compelling nature of his records stemmed in great measure from the fact that he held too much inside. Just how much was bottled up in Hank Williams is made clear by the vocal-guitar demos, most of which were probably recorded on home disc cutters or primitive tape decks. Hank probably thought that no more than two or three people would ever hear them, yet he sang as if his entire life and career hung upon his performance.

If Hank had started his career a few years earlier, he would have lived and died in almost total obscurity because the social and market conditions that brought about the wider acceptance of hillbilly music weren't in place, and the country was mired deep in the Depression. If he had lived a few years longer, he would have become an embarassment to the changing face of country music — too hillbilly by half. But, in arriving when he did and dying when and how he did, he became a prophet with honor.

The final paradox is that Hank Williams left no journals, almost no letters, and no extended interviews, and the people who knew him best have to admit that on some level they didn't know him at all. Yet, for all the ambiguity and unknowableness, Hank Williams appears almost desperately real to us through his music. He escaped the shame of seeing his drunks and dalliances splashed over the tabloids, but left a life diarized in verses sung with such riveting conviction that we feel as though we know him well. At his best, he froze a moment or a feeling in terms simple enough to register instantly yet meaningful enough to listen to forever. No one in any field of popular music can hope to do more.

It's impossible not to feel that Hank Williams' "heart" songs, with their sense of unshakable solitariness, define his music and, in all likelihood, the man himself. He had his triumphs — many, many of them. He could grin his shiteating grin, slap the table, shout "Hot damn!" when someone who once hadn't given him the time of day, or had once called him a damn drunk to his face, was almost coerced into recording one of his songs or booking him, but the moment of victory inevitably passed and he was left with Hiram Williams. Sometimes Hiram was good company, but too often he was not. There's a romantic notion that the writer or poet calms his troubled soul by reducing it to rhyme, but as Hank Williams pulled off his boots and eased himself gingerly onto his bed, the little verses he had scratched out in his untutored spidery handwriting almost certainly offered him no relief at all.

DISSOLVE TO BLACK — HANK IN HOLLYWOOD

A movie based on the life of Hank Williams was, and is, such a logical idea that it's surprising it has only been done once, and done badly. The arc of Hank's career lends itself naturally to a movie treatment, even if the unhappy ending doesn't. His life played out over a short time frame, and the songs are plentiful and well known.

The movie of Hank's life was in discussion almost from the moment of his death, and the ties between MGM Records and MGM Pictures meant that Hank's original recordings could be used for the soundtrack if MGM Pictures was prepared to forgive and forget. Shortly after the estate paid off Billie Jean, Audrey asked A. V. Bamford to go to Hollywood on her behalf and shop for a deal. In a letter to Lilly's attorney, Robert Stewart, on September 24, 1953, Bamford explained why he was hawking a proposal around Hollywood without consulting anyone in Montgomery. It was Bamford's opinion, "based on many years in show business . . . , that this picture should be released not later than the end of 1954." Like nearly everyone else, Bamford believed that Hank would be forgotten within a year, at best two years.

On November 19, Bamford returned to Hollywood, this time with Audrey. He'd lined up an appointment with Kenneth MacKenna at MGM Pictures. MacKenna, born Leo Mielziner, had been a bit actor in the 1920s and 1930s before moving into production. He later returned to acting, starring in *Judgment at Nuremberg* before his death in 1962. Talking to

MacKenna, Bamford tried to squeeze a percentage of the profits from MGM, but the company held firm in offering twenty thousand dollars for the rights to Hank's life and another twenty thousand for the rights to the music. Bamford went around to Universal, Gene Autry Productions, and Republic Pictures, all of whom expressed an interest in making the movie. Returning to Nashville, he told everyone that he was in favor of holding out for fifty thousand up front and a percentage of the gross, but he was bluffing. MGM Records, which controlled Hank's voice, and Acuff-Rose, which controlled most of the songs, would decide who made the movie. Bamford was irrelevant.

Lilly took Fred Rose's advice and sided with MGM. On April 8, 1954, MGM Pictures wrote to Lilly, mentioning that a screenplay was already under consideration. "We would agree not to refer to the divorce of Hiriam 'Hank' Williams, or to his second wife," they said. The family would be paid two thousand dollars to option the story, and an additional eighteen thousand in the event that the movie was actually made. The check for the option arrived in November 1954. Fifty percent went to the estate, 25 percent to Audrey, 20 percent to Lilly, and 5 percent to Irene.

A script, dated September 2, 1954, went out to the estate for consideration. It was written by Guy Trosper, a forty-three-year-old westerner and Hollywood journeyman. Two years later, Trosper wrote *Jailhouse Rock* for Elvis Presley, and, shortly before his death in 1963, wrote three hit movies, *One-Eyed Jacks, Birdman of Alcatraz* (which he also produced), and *The Spy Who Came In from the Cold*. MGM assigned Hungarian-born producer Joe Pasternak to the Hank Williams project. Pasternak had worked on *The Great Caruso* in 1951 with the troubled and troublesome Mario Lanza, and would later produce several Presley movies.

The hand of Audrey Williams seems evident in Trosper's treatment. In the first draft, Audrey worked for a radio station: "She sings, acts as emcee, promotes, hands out publicity, etc." Hank enters a talent contest, and she is immediately consumed with such belief in him that she quits her job. "All he needs," she says to herself, "is some encouragement." Ernest Tubb offers to hire her, and Audrey is torn. "It's a wistful scene," wrote Trosper, "with Audrey hoping that Hank won't let her go, and Hank wanting her to say she doesn't want to." Of course, she stays. They go to see Fred Rose, but Rose doesn't think Hank has what it takes as a singer. But wait! Over in the corner, there's a stranger who'd like to take a listen to the tape. It's Frank Walker! "The music starts as we . . . DISSOLVE TO: Records pouring out of a pressing machine. A montage shows the number reaching the chart."

In one of the few scenes to make it to the final version, Hank attacks Walker in a drunken stupor, then goes to see him in the hospital to give him a wristwatch. Trosper's original draft concluded with Hank performing on nationwide television from New York:

> He and Audrey leave the theatre building from which the show was telecast. Hank has a quart bottle in his hand. As they pass a garbage can, he drops it in. Audrey asks him why he didn't break it. Hank looks down at the bottle and bids it goodbye. Somebody else might need it, he says. DISSOLVE: Dawn finds them in the rolling hills headed for home. As we watch, the big Cadillac is going away from us. It becomes smaller and smaller, and then disappears. THE END.

No death, no puking, no second wife. It had so little to do with Hank Williams that MGM could have renamed the characters and made it anyway.

Realizing that it might be tough getting this fanciful rendering past the family, MGM's Kenneth MacKenna came to Montgomery on September 22, 1954, to give a verbal presentation. "Inasmuch as ours is admittedly not a factual account of his life, but is rather a freely fictionalized and romanticized version, it seems proper to present it to you in this way," he wrote beforehand. The meeting didn't go well. Lilly and Irene were outraged, and on October 12, 1954, their attorney, Robert Stewart, advised them to refuse permission for the movie to be made. It's hard to know if they objected to the drinking scenes, or if they wanted to recognize the Hank Williams they knew.

MGM conscripted Frank Walker to calm the waters. Writing to Lilly on October 14, Walker laid it on thickly. "There isn't and never has been any intention to play up any particular weakness in Hank's life, but it is necessary that the facts be portrayed but in such a manner that only good can come from the portrayal. Hank was a grand boy, you and I both know that." Walker added that the producer, Joe Pasternak, had met Hank, and that they were lucky to get him for this movie. Trying to explain the way

Hollywood worked, Walker said that it was necessary "in the writing of the preliminary script to point out all important factors, and then in the final work through acting and picturization, play away from those initial points. That is the intention with this picture, Mrs. Stone." Lilly wasn't buying it.

Some ten years later, Pasternak told Hank's first biographer, Roger M. Williams, that he couldn't find anyone to fill the lead role, but newspaper accounts seem to suggest that he kept trying. In February 1955, there was a report that pop singer Kay Starr would play Audrey, which was not a bad idea because Starr was from Memphis and had grown up with country music. Unlike Audrey, though, she could sing. In May 1956, there were reports that the movie was on the verge of being made with the star of *Seven Brides for Seven Brothers,* Jeff Richards, as Hank and June Allyson as Audrey. All the while, Frank Walker was dangling the carrot of the Hank movie role in front of every country singer he wanted to sign to MGM Records.

Frank Walker left the presidency of MGM Records in 1958, but continued to work for the parent company, Loews, as a consultant, and appears to have been the one to have revived the idea of a Hank Williams movie in 1959. In November that year, it was announced that Paul Gregory, producer of *Night of the Hunter* and *The Naked and the Dead,* was at the helm, and trying to get Steve McQueen for the title role. But then the project landed in the lap of the legendary "King of the Quickies," Sam Katzman.

The hugely prolific Katzman had produced Tim McCoy Westerns during the 1930s, then ground out East Side Kids movies for Monogram. His life was a whirlwind of Hollywood, Vegas, deals, girls, and incredibly bad movies. In 1956, he produced thirteen movies, although he'd slowed down a little by the time he took over the Williams project in 1963. He put the movie, now titled *Your Cheatin' Heart,* into production immediately after wrapping up one of Elvis Presley's less creditable ventures, *Kissin' Cousins.* The script was entrusted to Stanford Whitmore, a television scriptwriter who'd worked on *The Fugitive* and later wrote some episodes of *Night Gallery.* Director Gene Nelson also came from television, and would return to the small screen immediately after working with Katzman, first on the execrable *Hootenanny Hoot,* then on *Kissin' Cousins,* and finally on *Your Cheatin' Heart.* He had directed some episodes of *The Andy Griffith Show* and *The Rifleman,* and later worked on *Star Trek.*

Stanford Whitmore delivered his first draft on January 14, 1964, and the movie went into production a few weeks later. Whitmore had done a creditable amount of homework. He tried to interpolate Hank's first song, "WPA Blues," into the script, and his first draft featured Tee-Tot singing an old Joe Turner song, "Jump for Joy." Wesley Rose, of course, objected to Tee-Tot singing a non–Acuff-Rose song, so musical director Fred Karger was conscripted to write a number called "Poppin' That Shine" (Whitmore and Gene Nelson were listed as cowriters). Fred Rose might have smiled because it was curiously similar to the song he'd surrendered in order to get Hank on the *Opry,* "Chattanoogie Shoe Shine Boy."

Hank Williams would be played by George Hamilton, who told reporters that he went to Nashville three times in preparation for the role. Part of the movie was shot inside Audrey's home. "We didn't go for any art in it," Katzman cheerfully admitted to Roger Williams. "We had to exaggerate a lot of spots and make a lot of points that didn't really exist, just to get a story out of it." The finished product was crafted to suit everyone's agenda. Hank was deemed never to have sung a non–Acuff-Rose copyright (thereby writing "Lovesick Blues" out of the story), and Audrey got Hank Jr. to sing the soundtrack, thereby giving his young career a boost. "MGM didn't want that," Audrey told Dorothy Horstman. "There was no way they'd let the boy do the soundtrack. George Hamilton wanted to do it, plus they had some other singers in mind. So I took Hank Jr. in the studio here, and I did a number of his dad's songs with him. I put those under my arm and I went straight to the MGM studios, to the head guy. I said, 'I got something I want you to listen to.' They listened, and they said nobody else could do it." Audrey probably leaned upon Acuff-Rose to deny clearances if Junior didn't get the soundtrack, but the fact remains that Junior did a fine job for a fourteen-year-old. *Time* magazine said that *Your Cheatin' Heart* was a movie "better heard than seen."

The movie premiered in three cities: Montgomery, Nashville, and Atlanta. The world premiere was in Montgomery on November 4, 1964, with Katzman and several cast members in attendance. It was preceded by a concert featuring Johnny Cash, Roy Acuff, Tex Ritter, and Hank Jr.

Two days later, it premiered in Nashville. The deejays convention was in full swing, and MGM lined up a gala guest list that included Ernest Tubb, Roy Acuff, Faron Young, and Pee Wee King. All those who'd known Hank kept their thoughts to themselves as they emerged (and Acuff and Tubb emerged before the end). The movie did good business, especially in the South. It had cost $1.2 million to make, and reportedly grossed more than 10 million during its first go-round. By Katzman's criteria, that was success.

In April 1978, another Hank Williams movie was attempted. Warner Bros. wanted to make it, and assigned Paul Schrader, the writer of *Taxi Driver,* to the project. The script was written, and the call went out for someone to play Hank Williams. If George Hamilton had been an unlikely Hank, then those up for the role in 1978 were even more improbable. Henry Winkler, Robert DeNiro, David Carradine, Jack Nicholson, and Kris Kristofferson were among those considered. The script, though, was so unremittingly dark that Acuff-Rose refused synchronization rights, thereby scuppering the project.

Other Hank Williams movies have been mooted since Schrader's project went down in flames, but four parties with conflicting agendas (Hank Jr., Billie Jean, Acuff-Rose / Sony, and Jett Williams) must sign off on the manner of Hank's portrayal. Thus, benighted as it is, *Your Cheatin' Heart* remains the only Hank Williams movie as of this writing.

HANK WILLIAMS SONGOGRAPHY

*T*HIS listing does not include an almost infinite number of parodies, answer discs, and foreign-language versions set to Hank Williams' melodies (such as "Your Cold, Cold Heart Is Melted Now," "Jam-Bowl Liar," etc.). In addition, songwriters have come forward with songs on which they've assigned half of the composer credit to the Hank Williams estate, based on the unproven assertion that Hank helped write the songs. These have also been omitted.

ALABAMA WALTZ
Contract Date: February 10, 1950. Copyright Date: April 21, 1950.
First Issued Version: Bill Monroe, recorded February 3, 1950. See "I'm Blue,
    I'm Lonesome."

ALL THE LOVE I EVER HAD
Contract Date: Unknown. Copyright Date: 1991.
First Issued Version: Hank Williams' demo, issued 1991.

ALONE AND FORSAKEN
Contract Date: December 11, 1951. Copyright Date: December 5, 1951.
First Issued Version: Bill Darnel, recorded January 16, 1952.

AM I TOO LATE TO SAY I'M SORRY?
Uncopyrighted song, first published in song folio circa 1946.

ANGEL MINE
Unpublished song, dated January 5, 1951.

ANGEL OF DEATH
Contract Date: January 19, 1949. Copyright Date: December 20, 1954.
First Issued Version: Hank Williams' demo, issued 1954.

ARE YOU BUILDING A TEMPLE IN HEAVEN?
Contract Date: November 1, 1947. Copyright Date: January 11, 1951.
First Issued Version: Hank and Audrey Williams (as "A Home in Heaven"),
    recorded March 23, 1951.

ARE YOU LONELY TOO?
Dated January 19, 1947. Music added by Hank Williams Jr. Copyright Date:
    February 13, 1969.
First Issued Version: Hank Williams Jr., recorded November 26, 1968.

ARE YOU WALKIN' AND A TALKIN' FOR THE LORD?
Contract Date: January 22, 1953. Copyright Date: December 2, 1952.
First Issued Version: Wilma Lee and Stoney Cooper, recorded February 17, 1953.

AWAY BEYOND THE SKY
Early version of "Heaven Holds All of My Treasures."

BABY, WE'RE REALLY IN LOVE
Contract Date: October 15, 1951. Copyright Date: October 17, 1951.
First Issued Version: Hank Williams, recorded July 25, 1951 (unissued), and
    August 10, 1951.

BACK ACHE BLUES
Uncopyrighted song, published in song folio circa 1946.

BAYOU PON-PON (Hank Williams and Jimmie Davis)
Contract Date: October 31, 1951. Copyright Date: December 19, 1951.
First Issued Version: Jimmie Davis, recorded October 14, 1951; manuscript,
    possibly in Davis's handwriting, dated July 1951.

A BEAUTIFUL LAND OF ROSES
Uncopyrighted song. No details.

BLUE IS MY HEART
Uncopyrighted song, probably circa February 1947.

THE BLUES COME AROUND
Contract Date: November 1, 1947. Copyright Date: September 7, 1951.
First Issued Version: Hank Williams, recorded November 7, 1947.

BRAND NEW BABY
Uncopyrighted song. No details.

BROKEN DOWN TRAMP
Uncopyrighted song. No details.

BROKEN DREAMS
Uncopyrighted song. No details.

THE BROKEN MARRIAGE
Uncopyrighted song, dated January 19, 1947.

BURY ME BY THE LONELY RIVER (Hank Williams and Mel Foree)
Contract Date: September 27, 1948. Copyright Date: Uncopyrighted.

CAJUN BABY
Probably written 1952. Music added by Hank Williams Jr. Copyright Date:
    April 17, 1969.
First Issued Version: Hank Williams Jr., recorded December 4, 1968.

CALIFORNIA ZEPHYR
Contract Date: July 24, 1953. Copyright Date: December 30, 1955.
First Issued Version: Hank Williams' demo, issued 1956.

Note: On *Mother's Best* (circa January–March 1951), Hank says he wrote it a few
    days earlier.

CALLING YOU
Contract Date: December 7, 1946. Copyright Date: November 30, 1948.
First Issued Version: Hank Williams, recorded December 11, 1946.

CITY OF THE ANGELS (Hank Williams and Beasley Smith)
Contract Date: Unknown. Copyright Date: December 27, 1977.

COLD, COLD HEART
Contract Date: January 2, 1951. Copyright Date: February 16, 1951.
First Issued Version: Hank Williams, recorded December 21, 1950.

COUNTRYFIED
Contract Date: April 24, 1951. Copyright Date: July 25, 1951.
First Issued Version: Big Bill Lister, recorded April 24, 1951.

COWBOYS DON'T CRY
Attributed to Hank Williams. Music added by Mickey Newbury, 1984.
Recorded by Waylon Jennings for television performance (unknown date)
    and by Country Gazette, 1998.

THE DAYS ARE SO LONG
Uncopyrighted song, published in song folio circa 1946.

DEAR BROTHER
Contract Date: January 19, 1949. Copyright Date: June 15, 1949.
First Issued Version: Hank and Audrey Williams, recorded March 1, 1949.

DEAR FRIEND, DON'T WAIT UNTIL TOMORROW
Uncopyrighted song. No details.

DON'T MAKE ME WAIT TOO LONG
Uncopyrighted song. No details.

THE DRIFTWOOD BLUES
Uncopyrighted song. No details.

THE DRUNKARD'S DREAM
Uncopyrighted song, dated November 24, 1947.

DRUNKARD'S PRAYER
Contract Date: July 24, 1953. Copyright Date: Uncopyrighted.

EVERYTHING'S OKAY
Contract Date: April 16, 1951. Copyright Date: April 5, 1950.
First Issued Version: Hank Williams (Luke the Drifter), recorded January 10, 1950.

Note: The first version of this song was sent to Acuff-Rose in 1947.

FACE OF AN ANGEL
Uncopyrighted song. No details.

Note: This might have been the song that Hank wrote during the Hadacol Caravan,
    remembered by Minnie Pearl as "Heart of a Devil, Face of a Saint."

FOOL ABOUT YOU (Ralph C. Hutcheson)

Note: Hank's demo of this song was overdubbed after his death (once with hillbilly backing in 1954 and again with rock 'n' roll backing circa 1956), and copyright was posthumously claimed in his name on July 24, 1953, but the song's composer, Ralph C. Hutcheson, subsequently claimed copyright based on a 1951 recording of the song by the Barker Brothers.

FOOLISH HEART
Uncopyrighted song, circa February 1947.

FOR ME THERE IS NO PLACE
Dated January 8, 1951. Music added by Hank Williams Jr. Copyright Date: April 17, 1969.
First Issued Version: Hank Williams Jr., recorded January 24, 1969.

FOREVER'S A LONG, LONG TIME (Hank Williams and Jimmie Davis)
Contract Date: October 13, 1951. Copyright Date: December 31, 1951.
First Issued Version: Jimmie Davis, recorded October 14, 1951.

Note: A very similar song of same title published in song folio circa 1946.

FRIENDS OF MINE
Uncopyrighted song. No details.

FROM HERE TO THERE
Uncopyrighted song, published in song folio circa 1945.

THE FUNERAL (Lyrics Will Carleton arr. Hank Williams / Music "A House Built on a Rock" Fred Rose)
Contract Date: March 4, 1960. Copyright Date: March 10, 1960.
Recorded by Hank Williams (Luke the Drifter) on January 10, 1950.

Note: Other recorded arrangements of this poem, written circa 1909 by Will Carleton, predate Hank's version.

GO AWAY AND HAVE YOUR CRY
Uncopyrighted song. No details.

GO AWAY AND LET ME DREAM
Uncopyrighted song. No details.

GOD SEES EVERYTHING
Uncopyrighted song, circa 1951.

GOD SO LOVED THIS WICKED WORLD
Uncopyrighted song. No details.

GOIN' STEADY (Faron Young)

Note: Although Faron Young's first hit was credited to himself, there is substantial documentation suggesting that it was in fact a Hank Williams composition.

GRANDAD'S MUSKET
Uncopyrighted song, published in song folio circa 1946.

HADACOL EXPRESS
Uncopyrighted song. No details.

HAVE YOU BROKEN MY HEART? (HOW MANY TIMES?)
Uncopyrighted song. No details.

A HEART FILLED WITH HATE
Uncopyrighted song, written November 24, 1950, rewritten October 9, 1951.

THE HEART THAT ONCE WORSHIPPED YOU
Uncopyrighted song. No details.

HEAVEN HOLDS ALL OF MY TREASURES
Contract Date: Unknown. Copyright Date: 1985.
First Issued Version: Hank Williams' demo, 1984.

THE HEAVENS ARE LONELY TOO
Uncopyrighted song, dated February 19, 1947.

HEAVEN'S CALLING ME (Hank Williams, Vito Pelletieri, and Beasley Smith)
Contract Date: Unknown. Copyright Date: Unknown.

HELP ME UNDERSTAND
Contract Date: September 9, 1950. Copyright Date: October 25, 1950.
First Issued Version: Audrey Williams (Hugh Cherry, narration), recorded
    March 28, 1950.

A HELPLESS BROKEN HEART
Uncopyrighted song, dated January 19, 1947.

HEY, GOOD LOOKIN'
Contract Date: February 6, 1951. Copyright Date: June 20, 1951.
First Issued Version: Hank Williams, recorded March 16, 1951.

THE HILLS OF KOREA
Uncopyrighted song. No details.

A HOME IN HEAVEN
Contract Date: April 14, 1951. Copyright Date: June 8, 1951.
First Issued Version: Hank and Audrey Williams, recorded March 23, 1951.
    See "Are You Building a Temple in Heaven?"

HOMESICK
Dated February 8, 1951. Music added by Hank Williams Jr. Copyright Date:
    April 17, 1969.
First Issued Version: Hank Williams Jr., recorded December 4, 1968.

HONEY, DO YOU LOVE ME, HUH? (Hank Williams and Curley Williams)
Contract Date: September 27, 1948. Copyright Date: August 16, 1950.
First Issued Version: Curley Williams, recorded June 5, 1950.

HONKY TONK BLUES
Contract Date: August 4, 1947. Copyright Date: November 30, 1948.
First Issued Version: Hardrock Gunter, recorded January 19, 1951. Recorded by
    Hank Williams on August 4, 1947 (unissued), March 1, 1949 (unissued),
    June 14, 1950 (unissued), and December 11, 1951.

HONKY TONKIN'
Contract Date: February 14, 1947. Copyright Date: November 16, 1948.
First Issued Version: Hank Williams, recorded August 4, 1947. First published
    with additional verse in song folio circa 1946.

HONKY TONKIN' GRANDMAW
Uncopyrighted song. No details.

HONKY TONKIN' MAMA
Uncopyrighted song dated June 29, 1947.

A HOUSE OF GOLD
Contract Date: December 15, 1948. Copyright Date: April 21, 1950.
First Issued Version: Milton Estes, recorded December 30, 1949.

HOUSE WITHOUT LOVE
Contract Date: August 31, 1949. Copyright Date: November 25, 1949.
First Issued Version: Hank Williams, recorded August 30, 1949.

HOW CAN YOU REFUSE HIM NOW?
Contract Date: April 16, 1951. Copyright Date: December 29, 1950.
First Issued Version: Audrey Williams, recorded March 28, 1950.

HOW MANY TIMES HAVE YOU BROKEN MY HEART?
Uncopyrighted song, dated March 31, 1947.

HOWLIN' AT THE MOON
Contract Date: February 6, 1951. Copyright Date: April 23, 1951.
First Issued Version: Hank Williams, recorded March 16, 1951.

I AIN'T GOT NOTHIN' BUT TIME
Contract Date: June 6, 1951. Copyright Date: August 17, 1954.
First Issued Version: Hank Williams' demo issued 1954.

Note: Song contracts in the Lefty Frizzell estate indicate that this song might
   have been written by, or started by, Lefty.

I AM HAPPY I'VE FOUND YOU
Uncopyrighted song, dated November 22, 1950.

I BID YOU FREE TO GO
Uncopyrighted song, published in song folio circa 1946.

I CAN'T ESCAPE FROM YOU
Contract Date: October 15, 1951. Copyright Date: November 21, 1951.
First Issued Version: Rusty Gabbard, recorded September 30, 1951.

I CAN'T GET YOU OFF OF MY MIND
Contract Date: November 1, 1947. Copyright Date: November 30, 1948.
First Issued Version: Hank Williams, recorded November 6, 1947.

I CAN'T HELP IT (IF I'M STILL IN LOVE WITH YOU)
Contract Date: unknown. Copyright Date: April 23, 1951.
First Issued Version: Hank Williams, recorded March 16, 1951.

I COULD NEVER BE ASHAMED OF YOU
Contract Date: September 8, 1952. Copyright Date: October 31, 1952.
First Issued Version: Hank Williams, recorded September 23, 1952.

I DIDN'T BUILD A HOUSE OF LOVE
Uncopyrighted song. No details.

I DIDN'T CARE WHAT YOU DO
Uncopyrighted song. No details.

I DON'T CARE (IF TOMORROW NEVER COMES)
Contract Date: February 14, 1947. Copyright Date: November 30, 1948.
First Issued Version: Hank Williams, recorded February 13, 1947.

(I HEARD THAT) LONESOME WHISTLE (Hank Davis and Jimmie Davis)
Contract Date: Unknown. Copyright date: 1951.
First Issued Version: Hank Williams, recorded July 25, 1951.

I HOPE YOU SHED A MILLION TEARS
Uncopyrighted song. No details.

I JUST CAN'T SAY GOODBYE (Hank Williams and Jeri Miller)
Uncopyrighted song. No details.

I JUST DIDN'T HAVE THE HEART
Uncopyrighted song. Music added by Hank Williams Jr., 1969.

I JUST DON'T LIKE THIS KIND OF LIVIN'
Contract Date: August 30, 1949. Copyright Date: December 14, 1949.
First Issued Version: Hank Williams, recorded August 30, 1949.

I JUST WISH I COULD FORGET
Uncopyrighted song, published in song folio circa 1946.

I KNOW YOU'RE CRYING TONIGHT
Uncopyrighted song. No details.

I LOST THE ONLY LOVE I KNEW (Hank Williams and Don Helms)
Contract Date: March 4, 1952. Copyright Date: October 31, 1952.
First Issued Version: Ray Price, recorded February 8, 1952.

I LOVED NO ONE BUT YOU
Uncopyrighted song, published in song folio circa 1946.

I NEVER CRY IN MY DREAMS (Hank Williams, Curley Williams, and Mel Foree)
Contract Date: September 27, 1948. Copyright Date: Unknown.

I NEVER WILL FORGET THE DAY YOU SAID GOODBYE
Uncopyrighted song, first published in song folio circa 1946.

I PRAY FOR YOU
Uncopyrighted song. No details.

I SAW THE LIGHT
Contract Date: April 9, 1947. Copyright Date: November 16, 1948.
First Issued Version: Clyde Grubbs, recorded August 13, 1947.

Note: Hank Williams' version was recorded earlier, on April 21, 1947, but Grubbs'
    version was issued first.

I SHOULD HAVE KNOWN YOU'D CHEAT ON ME (Hank Williams and Don Helms)
Uncopyrighted song. No details.

I THANK MY GOD FOR YOU
Uncopyrighted song, dated October 11, 1951.

I TOLD A LIE TO MY HEART
Contract Date: Unknown. Copyright Date: 1984.
Song written November 24, 1947. First Issued Version: Hank Williams' demo, 1984.

I WANT AN OLD-FASHIONED SWEETHEART
Uncopyrighted song. No details.

I WANT YOU NOW
Uncopyrighted song. No details.

I WATCHED MY DREAM WORLD CRUMBLE LIKE CLAY
Contract Date: Unknown. Copyright Date: 1986.
First Issued Version: Hank Williams' demo, issued 1986. First published in song folio
    circa 1946.

I WENT FOR A WALK WITH JESUS
Uncopyrighted song. No details.

I WISH I HAD A DAD
Uncopyrighted song. No details.

I WISH YOU DIDN'T LOVE ME SO MUCH
Contract Date: December 11, 1951. Copyright Date: November 16, 1951.
First Issued Version: Little Jimmy Dickens, recorded July 12, 1951.

Note: Refashioned by Hank into "Please Make Up Your Mind" (see below).

I WON'T BE HOME NO MORE
Contract Date: August 27, 1952. Copyright Date: September 15, 1952.
First Issued Version: Hank Williams, recorded July 11, 1952. Written as
    "You're Just in Time."

I'D STILL WANT YOU
Contract Date: October 15, 1951. Copyright Date: December 5, 1951.
First Issued Version: Hank Williams, recorded July 25, 1951.

IF I DIDN'T LOVE YOU (Hank Williams and Fred Rose)
Contract Date: November 3, 1947. Copyright Date: November 30, 1948.
First Issued Version: Rome Johnson, recorded November 25, 1947.

IF I DON'T LOVE YOU (Hank Williams and Jimmy Dickens)
Contract Date: November 23, 1948. Copyright Date: Unknown.

IF I LOVED A LIAR, I'D HUG YOUR NECK
Uncopyrighted song. No details.

Note: On April 15, 1952, Floyd Tillman recorded a song of this title, credited to
    Jimmie Davis and Marge Tillman. It's unknown if this is the same song.

IF THE ONE YOU WANT DON'T WANT YOU
Uncopyrighted song. No details.

IF YOU'LL BE A BABY (TO ME)
Contract Date: January 22, 1953. Copyright Date: March 25, 1953.
First Issued Version: Red Sovine, recorded September 26, 1952.

I'LL BE A BACHELOR 'TIL I DIE
Contract Date: November 1, 1947. Copyright Date: November 16, 1948.
First Issued Version: Hank Williams, recorded November 7, 1947.

I'LL LOVE YOU 'TIL I DIE
Uncopyrighted song, dated February 20, 1947.

I'LL NEVER GET OUT OF THIS WORLD ALIVE (Hank Williams and Fred Rose)
Contract Date: June 24, 1952. Copyright Date: October 6, 1952.
First Issued Version: Hank Williams, recorded June 13, 1952.

I'LL NEVER GIVE UP HOPE
Uncopyrighted song. No details.

I'LL TAKE THE BLAME
Uncopyrighted song. No details.

I'M A LONG GONE DADDY
Contract Date: November 1, 1947. Copyright Date: August 13, 1948.
First Issued Version: Hank Williams, recorded November 6, 1947.

I'M AMONG THE LIVING DEAD (Hank Williams and Mel Foree)
Contract Date: September 27, 1948. Copyright Date: Unknown.

I'M BLUE, I'M LONESOME (Hank Williams and Bill Monroe)
Contract Date: Unknown. Copyright Date: Unknown.
First Issued Version: Bill Monroe, recorded February 3, 1950.

Note: This was recorded at the same session as "Alabama Waltz" and credited to
    "James B. Smith." It was either a song that Hank Williams and Bill Monroe
    wrote together, or one that Hank ceded to Monroe.

I'M GOING HOME ("When my work here is o'er . . .")
Contract Date: July 24, 1953. Copyright Date: October 31, 1960.
First Issued Version: Hank Williams' demo, issued 1960.

(I'M) GOING HOME ("Standing by the bedside . . .")
Contract Date: Unknown. Copyright Date: 1986.
First Issued Version: Hank Williams' demo, issued 1986.

I'M HEADING BACK TO TENNESSEE (Hank Williams and Don Helms)
Uncopyrighted song. No details.

I'M (JUST) CRYING BECAUSE I CARE (Hank Williams and Beasley Smith)
Contract Date: June 27, 1961. Music added by Hank Williams Jr. Copyright Date:
    April 17, 1969.
First Issued Version: Hank Williams Jr., recorded January 24, 1969.

I'M NOT COMING HOME ANY MORE
Contract Date: Unknown. Copyright Date: 1990.
First Issued Version: Hank Williams, private recording, April 7, 1942.

(I'M PRAYING FOR THE DAY THAT) PEACE WILL COME (Hank Williams and
    Pee Wee King)
Contract Date: Unknown (registered with Library of Congress, December 20, 1943).
    Copyright Date: March 1944.
First Issued Version: Rosco Hankins, recorded 1951.

I'M SO LONESOME I COULD CRY
Contract Date: August 31, 1949. Copyright Date: October 31, 1949.
First Issued Version: Hank Williams, recorded August 31, 1949.

I'M SO TIRED OF IT ALL
Contract Date: Unknown. Copyright Date: March 25, 1970.
Song written June 29, 1947. First Issued Version: Hank Williams Jr., recorded
    January 14, 1970. First Recorded Version: Hank Williams, recorded circa 1947;
    issued 1998.

I'M SORRY FOR YOU, MY FRIEND
Contract Date: October 15, 1951. Copyright Date: December 5, 1951.
First Issued Version: Hank Williams, first recorded August 10, 1951 (unissued).
    Rerecorded December 11, 1951.

IN DEATH HE'S STILL MINE (Hank Williams, Johnnie Wright, and Jack Anglin)
Contract Date: Unknown. Copyright Date: Unknown.

IN MY DREAMS YOU STILL BELONG TO ME
Contract Date: Unknown. Copyright Date: 1986.
First Issued Version: Hank Williams' demo, issued 1986. Published in song folio
   circa 1946.

IS THERE ANY ROOM IN HEAVEN? (Hank Williams and Don Helms)
Contract Date: April 7, 1950. Copyright Date: Unknown.

IS THIS GOODBYE?
Probably written 1951. Music added by Hank Williams Jr. Copyright Date:
   May 23, 1969.
First Issued Version: Hank Williams Jr., recorded January 22, 1969.

IT AIN'T SO (Hank Williams and Babe Fritsch)
Contract Date: January 19, 1949. Copyright Date: Unknown.

IT WORKS ONE WAY OR THE OTHER
Uncopyrighted song. No details.

IT'S A LITTLE BIT LATE TO CRY
Uncopyrighted song. No details.

I'VE BEEN DOWN THAT ROAD BEFORE
Contract Date: June 4, 1951. Copyright Date: July 9, 1951.
First Issued Version: Hank Williams (Luke the Drifter), recorded June 1, 1951.

I'VE FOUND THE ONE FOR ME (Hank Williams and Billie Jones)
Uncopyrighted song. No details.

JAMBALAYA (On the Bayou)
Contract Date: June 24, 1952. Copyright Date: July 28, 1952.
First Issued Version: Hank Williams, recorded June 13, 1952.

Note: A quarter-share of the composer royalties was paid surreptitiously to Moon
   Mullican, who also recorded a slightly different version of the song several
   weeks after Hank.

JESUS DIED FOR ME
Contract Date: February 10, 1950. Copyright Date: March 1, 1950.
First Issued Version: Roy Acuff, recorded December 1949.

JESUS IS CALLING (Hank Williams and Charlie Monroe)
Contract Date: November 10, 1950. Copyright Date: October 3, 1951.
First Issued Version: Charlie Monroe, recorded May 6, 1951.

JESUS REMEMBERED ME
Contract Date: Unknown. Copyright Date: December 7, 1949.
First Issued Version: Hank and Audrey Williams, recorded March 1, 1949.

JUST ME AND MY BROKEN HEART
Contract Date: Unknown. Music added by Hank Williams Jr. Copyright Date: 1969.
First Issued Version: Hank Williams Jr., recorded January 22, 1969.

JUST WAITIN' (Hank Williams and Bob Gazzaway)
Contract Date: October 17, 1949. Copyright Date: February 16, 1951.
First Issued Version: Hank Williams (Luke the Drifter), recorded January 10, 1950.

KATY DONE BARRED THE DOOR (Hank Williams and Hugh Cherry)
Contract Date: November 29, 1950. Copyright Date: Unknown.

Note: Vic McAlpin said that he and Hank wrote a song called "Goodbye Katy, Bar
the Door." If this is the same song, it was credited solely to McAlpin and first
recorded by Orval Prophet, March 21, 1953.

KAW-LIGA (Hank Williams and Fred Rose)
Contract Date: September 9, 1952. Copyright Date: December 2, 1952.
First Issued Version: Hank Williams, recorded September 23, 1952.

LAND OF ROSES
Uncopyrighted song. No details.

THE LAST MESSAGE
Uncopyrighted song, published in song folio circa 1946.

LAST NIGHT I DREAMED OF HEAVEN
Contract Date: July 24, 1953. Copyright Date: October 31, 1960.
First Issued Version: Hank Williams' demo, issued 1960.

(LAST NIGHT) I HEARD YOU CRYING IN YOUR SLEEP
Contract Date: April 9, 1947. Copyright Date: July 16, 1947.
First Issued Version: Hank Williams, recorded April 21, 1947.

LAST NIGHT I STOOD AT HEAVEN'S DOOR
Uncopyrighted song. No details.

LET ME BE YOUR DADDY
Uncopyrighted song. No details.

LET ME LIVE FOR THE LORD
Uncopyrighted song, dated July 1, 1951.

LET NOT THE SUN GO DOWN
Uncopyrighted song. No details.

LET'S TURN BACK THE YEARS
Contract Date: November 7, 1947. Copyright Date: March 3, 1952.
First Issued Version: Hank Williams, recorded December 11, 1951. First published
in song folio circa 1946.

LITTLE BOCEPHUS (Music: COLD, COLD HEART)
Contract Date: June 5, 1954. Copyright Date: October 1955.
First Issued Version: Audrey Williams, recorded July 6, 1955 (unissued).
Rerecorded July 27, 1955.

THE LITTLE HOUSE WE BUILT (JUST O'ER THE HILL) (Hank Williams and
Don Helms)
Contract Date: April 24, 1951. Copyright Date: July 2, 1951.
First Issued Version: Big Bill Lister, recorded April 24, 1951.

THE LOG TRAIN
Contract Date: July 24, 1953. Copyright Date: Unknown.
First Issued Version: Hank Williams' demo, issued 1981.

LONG GONE LONESOME BLUES
Contract Date: February 10, 1950. Copyright Date: March 1, 1950.
First Issued Version: Hank Williams, recorded January 9, 1950.

LOOKY HERE, SWEET MAMA
Uncopyrighted song. No details.

LOST ON THE RIVER
Contract Date: December 24, 1948. Copyright Date: June 15, 1949.
First Issued Version: Hank and Audrey Williams, recorded December 22, 1948.

THE LOVE THAT FADED
Uncopyrighted song, dated May 2, 1947.

THE LOVELIGHT IS GONE FROM YOUR EYES
Uncopyrighted song. No details.

LOW DOWN BLUES
Contract Date: July 24, 1953. Copyright Date: February 19, 1954.
First Issued Version: Hank Williams' demo, issued 1954.

MAKE HEAVEN YOUR GOAL
Uncopyrighted song. No details.

MANSION FOR YOUR SOUL
Uncopyrighted song, probably circa 1951.

A MANSION ON THE HILL (Hank Williams and Fred Rose)
Contract Date: November 3, 1947. Copyright Date: November 30, 1948.
First Issued Version: Hank Williams, recorded November 7, 1947.

MAY YOU NEVER BE ALONE
Contract Date: March 3, 1949. Copyright Date: November 25, 1949.
First Issued Version: Hank Williams, recorded March 1, 1949. First published in
    song folio circa 1946 as "I Loved No One but You."

ME AND MY BROKEN HEART
Contract Date: June 5, 1951. Copyright Date: August 15, 1951.
First Issued Version: Carl Smith, recorded June 8, 1951.

MEAN OLD BLUES
Attributed to Hank Williams. Music added by Mickey Newbury, circa 1984.

MEN WITH BROKEN HEARTS
Contract Date: January 2, 1951. Copyright Date: February 16, 1951.
First Issued Version: Hank Williams (Luke the Drifter), recorded December 21, 1950.

MESSAGE TO MY MOTHER
Contract Date: July 24, 1953. Copyright Date: May 4, 1955.
First Issued Version: Hank Williams' demo, issued 1955.

MIND YOUR OWN BUSINESS
Contract Date: Unknown. Copyright Date: July 7, 1949.
First Issued Version: Hank Williams, March 1, 1949.

MOANIN' THE BLUES
Contract Date: September 5, 1950. Copyright Date: October 25, 1950.
First Issued Version: Hank Williams, recorded August 31, 1950.

MOTHER IS GONE
Contract Date: July 24, 1953. Copyright Date: May 4, 1955.
First Issued Version: Hank Williams' demo, issued 1955. First published in song
    folio circa 1946.

MOVE IT ON OVER
Contract Date: April 9, 1947. Copyright Date: July 16, 1947.
First Issued Version: Hank Williams, recorded April 21, 1947.

MY BOY'S IN JAIL TONIGHT (Hank Williams and Bob Gazzaway)
Contract Date: August 23, 1951. Copyright Date: Unknown.

MY BUYO BABY
Uncopyrighted song. No details.

MY DARLING BABY GIRL (Hank and Audrey Williams)
Uncopyrighted song, published in song folio circa 1946.

MY HEAD RUN OFF WITH MY HEART
Uncopyrighted song. No details.

MY HEART WON'T LET ME GO
Dated June 29, 1947. Music added by Hank Williams Jr. Copyright Date: May 23, 1969.
First Issued Version: Hank Williams Jr., recorded January 22, 1969.

MY HEART WOULD KNOW
Contract Date: April 14, 1951. Copyright Date: June 25, 1951.
First Issued Version: Hank Williams, recorded March 16, 1951.

MY LOVE FOR YOU (HAS TURNED TO HATE)
Contract Date: February 14, 1947. Copyright Date: November 30, 1948.
First Issued Version: Hank Williams, recorded February 13, 1947.

MY MOMMY
Uncopyrighted song. No details.

MY SON CALLS ANOTHER MAN DADDY (Hank Williams and Jewell House)
Contract Date: March 1, 1949. Copyright Date: November 25, 1949.
First Issued Version: Hank Williams, recorded March 2, 1949 (unreleased) and
    January 9, 1950.

MY SWEET LOVE AIN'T AROUND
Contract Date: November 7, 1947. Copyright Date: February 7, 1948.
First Issued Version: Hank Williams, recorded November 7, 1947.

'NEATH A COLD GRAY TOMB OF STONE (Hank Williams and Mel Foree)
Contract Date: September 27, 1948. Copyright Date: November 25, 1949.
First Issued Version: Charlie Monroe, recorded October 20, 1950.

NEVER AGAIN (WILL I KNOCK AT YOUR DOOR)
Contract Date: December 11, 1946. Copyright Date: November 30, 1948.
First Issued Version: Hank Williams, recorded December 11, 1946.

NEVER BEEN SO LONESOME
Contract Date: July 1, 1949. Copyright Date: July 1950.
First Issued Version: Zeb Turner, recorded October 28, 1949.

NEW WEDDING BELLS
Uncopyrighted song. No details. Possibly not a Hank Williams song.

NO, NOT NOW (Hank Williams, Mel Foree, and Curley Williams)
Contract Date: September 27, 1948. Copyright Date: November 25, 1949.
First Issued Version: Curley Williams, recorded September 11, 1949.

NOBODY'S LONESOME FOR ME
Contract Date: September 5, 1950. Copyright Date: October 25, 1950.
First Issued Version: Hank Williams, recorded August 31, 1950.

OH MAMA, COME HOME
Uncopyrighted song. No details.

THE OLD MAN'S LAST GOODBYE
Uncopyrightod song, datod January 26, 1947.

AN OLD USED TO BE
Uncopyrighted song. No details.

ON THE BANKS OF THE OLD PONTCHARTRAIN (Hank Williams and
    Ramona Vincent)
Contract Date: August 4, 1947. Copyright Date: November 30, 1948.
First Issued Version: Hank Williams, recorded August 4, 1947.

ON THE EVENING TRAIN (Hank and Audrey Williams)
Contract Date: January 6, 1949. Copyright Date: June 29, 1949.
First Issued Version: Molly O'Day, recorded April 4, 1949.

PAN AMERICAN
Contract Date: February. 14, 1947. Copyright Date: March 19, 1948.
First Issued Version: Hank Williams, recorded February 13, 1947.

PEACH PICKIN' PAPA (Hank Williams and Curley Williams)
Contract Date: September 27, 1948. Copyright Date: Unknown.

A PHOTOGRAPH OF YOU
Uncopyrighted song. No details.

PICTURES FROM LIFE'S OTHER SIDE (aka A PICTURE FROM LIFE'S OTHER SIDE)
Contract Date: June 4, 1951. Copyright Date: August 1951.
First Issued Version: Hank Williams (Luke the Drifter), recorded June 1, 1951.

PLEASE MAKE UP YOUR MIND
Contract Date: August 27, 1952. Copyright Date: October 6, 1952.
First Issued Version: Hank Williams (Luke the Drifter), recorded July 11, 1952.

PLEASE MOMMY, BEFORE I GO
Uncopyrighted song. No details.

PRISON OF MEMORIES
Uncopyrighted song, undated.

RAMBLIN' MAN
Contract Date: June 4, 1951. Copyright Date: September 7, 1951.
First Issued Version: Hank Williams (Luke the Drifter), recorded June 1, 1951.

READY TO GO HOME
Contract Date: March 6, 1953. Copyright Date: May 5, 1953.
First Issued Version: Hank Williams' demo, issued 1957.

ROCKIN' CHAIR DADDY (Hank Williams and Braxton Shooford)
Contract Date: February 10, 1950. Copyright Date: May 1950.
First Issued Version: Braxton Shooford, recorded February 8, 1950.

SEARCHING IN VAIN
Uncopyrighted song, probably circa 1951.

THE SERMON ON THE MOUNTAIN
Uncopyrighted song, dated January 8, 1951.

SHE WAS MINE IN LIFE (SHE'S STILL MINE IN DEATH) (Hank Williams,
    Johnnie Wright, and Jim Anglin)
Contract Date: Unknown. Copyright Date: Unknown.

SINCE WE SAID GOODBYE
Uncopyrighted song, dated February 5, 1947.

SING, SING, SING (aka I'M GONNA SING, SING, SING)
Contract Date: unknown. Copyright Date: January 24, 1951.
First Issued Version: Charlie Monroe, recorded October 20, 1950.

SINGING WATERFALL
Contract Date: November 1, 1947. Copyright Date: November 25, 1949.
First Issued Version: Molly O'Day, recorded December 27, 1948.
Note: First published in song folio circa 1946.

SIX MORE MILES (TO THE GRAVEYARD)
Contract Date: November 8, 1946. Copyright Date: November 30, 1948.
First Issued Version: Hank Williams, recorded April 21, 1947.

SOME DAY YOU'LL BE LONESOME TOO
Uncopyrighted song, published in song folio circa 1946.

SOMEBODY'S LONESOME
Dated January 14, 1951. Music added by Hank Williams Jr. Copyright Date:
    February 13, 1969.
First Recorded Version: Hank Williams Jr. (unissued).

A STRANGER IN THE NIGHT (Hank Williams and Bill Morgan)
Contract Date: July 11, 1951. Copyright Date: June 20, 1951.
First Issued Version: George Morgan, recorded April 16, 1951.

TAKE AWAY THOSE LONELY MEMORIES
Uncopyrighted song, published in song folio circa 1943.

A TEARDROP ON A ROSE
Contract Date: February 10, 1950. Copyright Date: May 1950.
First Issued Version: Braxton Shooford, recorded February 8, 1950.

TEARDROPS START WITH EACH NEW DAWN
Uncopyrighted song. No details.

TEARS TODAY, BLUES TOMORROW
Uncopyrighted song. No details.

THANK HEAVEN I STILL HAVE YOU (Hank Williams and Beasley Smith)
Contract Date: April 11, 1961. Copyright Date: Unknown.

THAT LAST LONG RIDE
Uncopyrighted song, dated September 18, 1948.

THEN CAME THAT FATAL DAY
Uncopyrighted song fragment found on the floor of the car in which Hank died.

THERE'LL BE NO TEARDROPS TONIGHT
Contract Date: February 2, 1948. Copyright Date: May 4, 1949.
First Issued Version: Hank Williams, recorded December 22, 1948.

Note: Contract issued to Hank Williams and WCKY deejay Nelson King; subsequent
    contract issued to Hank Williams as sole composer.

THERE'S A NEW LIGHT SHINING IN OUR HOME (Hank and Irene Williams)
Uncopyrighted song written February 1, 1944, published in song folio circa 1946.

THERE'S A NEW LOCK ON THE DOOR
Uncopyrighted song. No details.

THERE'S A TEAR IN MY BEER
Contract Date: September 23, 1952. Copyright Date: September 15, 1952.
First Issued Version: Big Bill Lister, recorded October 26, 1951.

THERE'S NOTHING AS SWEET AS MY BABY
Contract Date: April 16, 1951. Copyright Date: April 11, 1951.
First Issued Version: Carl Smith, recorded January 30, 1951.

THEY CARRIED MY DARLING HOME
Uncopyrighted song. Very possibly the same song as "I'm Among the Living Dead."

THIS AIN'T NO PLACE FOR ME
Uncopyrighted song, dated October 10, 1947.

THIS OLD BEAT-UP HEART OF MINE
Uncopyrighted song. No details.

THOSE HAPPY DAYS THAT USED TO BE
Uncopyrighted song. No details.

'TIL DEATH DO US PART (Hank Williams and Bob Gazzaway)
Contract Date: October 17, 1949. Copyright Date: Unknown.

TIME HAS PROVEN I WAS WRONG (Hank Williams, Curley Williams, and Mel Foree)
Contract Date: September 27, 1948. Copyright Date: Unknown.
First Issued Version: Hank Williams' demo, issued 1998.

TO ME, YOU'LL ALWAYS BE MINE
Uncopyrighted song. No details.

TODAY HAS BEEN A LONESOME DAY
Uncopyrighted song, possibly circa 1951.

TOMORROW MAY NOT COME
Uncopyrighted song, written April 10, 1948.

TOO LATE TO PRAY
Uncopyrighted song, written June 24, 1948.

TROUBLES ON MY WEARY MIND (Hank Williams and Don Helms)
Contract Date: April 7, 1950. Copyright Date: Unknown.

VISION IN THE NIGHT
Uncopyrighted song. No details.

WANTING TO SHOW HOW MUCH I CARED
Uncopyrighted song. No details.

WE ALL GET TROUBLED AND BLUE SOMETIME
Uncopyrighted song. No details.

WEALTH WON'T SAVE YOUR SOUL
Contract Date: Unknown. Copyright Date: November 30, 1948.
First Issued Version: Hank Williams, recorded December 11, 1946.

WEARIN' OUT YOUR WALKIN' SHOES
Contract Date: April 16, 1951. Copyright Date: April 23, 1951.
First Issued Version: Tex Ritter, recorded September 20, 1950.

WEARY BLUES FROM WAITIN'
Contract Date: December 11, 1951. Copyright Date: November 28, 1951.
First Issued Version: Ray Price, recorded October 16, 1951.

WE'RE GETTING CLOSER TO THE GRAVE EACH DAY
Contract Date: July 24, 1953. Copyright Date: April 23, 1957.
First Issued Version: Hank Williams' demo, issued 1957.

WHAT CAN A HEART DO?
Uncopyrighted song, probably circa 1951.

WHAT'S THE USE?
Uncopyrighted song. No details.

WHEN GOD COMES AND GATHERS HIS JEWELS
Contract Date: November 8, 1946. Copyright Date: November 30, 1948.
First Issued Version: Hank Williams, recorded December 11, 1946.

WHEN THE BOOK OF LIFE IS READ
Contract Date: Unknown. Copyright Date: March 3, 1952.
First Issued Version: Jimmie Skinner, recorded January 14, 1952.

WHEN THE WALTZ ENDED
Uncopyrighted song. No details.

WHEN YOU BROKE YOUR VOW
Uncopyrighted song. No details.

WHEN YOU'RE TIRED OF BREAKING OTHERS' HEARTS (Hank Williams and
    Curley Williams)
Contract Date: March 29, 1949. Copyright Date: December 7, 1949.
First Issued Version: Curley Williams, recorded September 15, 1952.

WHERE DO I GO FROM HERE?
Dated January 14, 1951. Music added by Hank Williams Jr. Copyright Date:
    April 17, 1969.
First Issued Version: Hank Williams Jr., recorded January 24, 1969.

WHY DID MOMMY SAY GOODBYE?
Uncopyrighted song. No details.

WHY DID YOU LIE TO ME?
Uncopyrighted song, published in song folio circa 1945.

WHY DON'T YOU LOVE ME? (LIKE YOU USED TO DO)
Contract Date: February 10, 1950. Copyright Date: April 7, 1950.
First Issued Version: Hank Williams, recorded January 9, 1950.

WHY SHOULD I CRY?
Contract Date: February 10, 1950. Copyright Date: May 1950.
First Issued Version: Braxton Shooford, recorded February 8, 1950.

Note: An early version was written May 4, 1947, as "Why Should I Pay, Why Must I
    Cry?" (Hank says on *Mother's Best* that he wrote it in 1941.)

WHY SHOULD WE TRY ANYMORE?
Contract Date: February 10, 1950. Copyright Date: April 7, 1950.
First Issued Version: Hank Williams, recorded January 9, 1950.

WILL GOD WELCOME YOU HOME?
Uncopyrighted song. No details.

WISH I COULD SAY NO TO YOU
Attributed to Hank Williams. Music added by Mickey Newbury, possibly circa 1984.

WON'T YOU PLEASE COME BACK?
Uncopyrighted song, published in song folio, 1946.

WON'T YOU SOMETIMES THINK OF ME?
Contract Date: Unknown. Copyright Date: Unknown. Published in song folio circa 1945.
First Issued Version: Hank Williams' demo, issued 1984.

WPA BLUES
Reportedly the first song Hank wrote, circa 1938.

YESTERDAY MY DREAMS ALL DIED
Uncopyrighted song. No details.

YOU ALWAYS SEEM TO GO THE OTHER WAY
Uncopyrighted song, published in song folio circa 1946.

YOU BETTER KEEP IT ON YOUR MIND (Hank Williams and Vic McAlpin)
Contract Date: July 24, 1953. Copyright Date: February 15, 1954.
First Issued Version: Hank Williams' demo, issued 1954.

YOU BROKE YOUR OWN HEART
Written January 26, 1947. Music added by Hank Williams Jr. Copyright Date:
    June 5, 1969.
First Recorded Version: Hank Williams Jr., January 22, 1969 (unissued).

YOU BROKE YOUR OWN HEART (WHEN YOU TRIED TO BREAK MINE)
Contract Date: 1986. Written at unknown date, circa 1946–1947.
First Issued Version: Hank Williams' demo, issued 1986.

YOU CAN'T TAKE MY MEMORY/MEMORIES OF YOU
Written at unknown date. Music added by Hank Williams Jr. Copyright Date:
    February 13, 1969.
First Issued Version: Hank Williams Jr., recorded November 26, 1968.

YOU HAVE GROWN TO BE A STRANGER TO ME
Uncopyrighted song, dated January 8, 1951.
Possibly adapted by Hank Williams Jr. as "Your Love's Like a Stranger," recorded
    November 26, 1968 (unissued).

YOU KNOW THAT I KNOW
Uncopyrighted song, dated November 24, 1947.

YOU SLAMMED THE DOOR OF LOVE
Uncopyrighted song. No details.

YOU TORE MY HEAVEN DOWN
Uncopyrighted song. No details.

YOU WIN AGAIN
Contract Date: August 27, 1952. Copyright Date: September 3, 1952.
First Issued Version: Hank Williams, recorded July 11, 1952.

YOU'LL (ALWAYS) BE MINE
Uncopyrighted song. No details.

YOU'LL BE THE LONELY ONE (Hank Williams, Curley Williams, and Mel Foree)
Contract Date: September 27, 1948. Copyright Date: Unknown.

YOU'LL LOVE ME AGAIN
Uncopyrighted song, first published in song folio circa 1946.

YOU'LL NEVER AGAIN BE MINE
Uncopyrighted song, written April 21, 1952.

YOUR CHEATIN' HEART
Contract Date: September 8, 1952. Copyright Date: October 31, 1952.
First Issued Version: Hank Williams, recorded September 23, 1952.

YOUR TURN TO CRY
Dated June 29, 1947. Music added by Hank Williams Jr. Copyright Date: May 8, 1969.
First Issued Version: Hank Williams Jr., recorded January 22, 1969.

YOU'RE BARKING UP THE WRONG TREE NOW (Hank Williams and Fred Rose)
Contract Date: November 3, 1947. Copyright Date: January 5, 1949.
First Issued Version: Red Sovine, recorded September 1, 1949.

YOU'RE GONNA CHANGE (OR I'M GONNA LEAVE)
Contract Date: March 3, 1949. Copyright Date: August 5, 1949.
First Issued Version: Hank Williams, recorded March 1–2, 1949.

YOU'RE THROUGH FOOLIN' ME
Uncopyrighted song. No details.

YOU'VE BEEN LONESOME TOO
Uncopyrighted song. No details.

With very special thanks to Bill Whatley and David Mitchell for their research.

Appendix

3

● ●

DISCOGRAPHY

● ● ● ● ● ● ● ● ● ● ● ● ● ● ● ● ● ● ● ●

*T*HE following is a discography of all issued recordings. Unissued recordings made at the same time as issued recordings have usually been noted, but unissued radio performances have not been included, with the exception of the *Mother's Best* shows, which were referenced in the text, and may soon be cleared for release.

The dates and the number of musicians employed on regular studio sessions were logged by Acuff-Rose on behalf of MGM. The exact personnel was researched by Bob Pinson and first published in *The Complete Hank Williams* on Mercury Records. Most nonsession recordings are undated and undatable.

Note the following:

1. Hank Williams sings and plays acoustic guitar unless noted.
2. The composer is Hank Williams unless noted.
3. Many demos were overdubbed, often more than once. A complete schedule of overdub sessions can be found in *The MGM Labels,* a two-volume discography by Michel Ruppli and Ed Novitsky, published by Greenwood Press.
4. Only the first issue has been listed, *unless* the first issue was overdubbed, in which case the issue number cited below is the *first undubbed issue.*
5. The AFRS shows listed below are *Grand Ole Opry* shows transcribed by the Armed Forces Radio Service.

TITLE (COMPOSER[S])	RECORDING NO.

Demos circa 1939–1940.

Pee Wee Moultrie (accordion).

MARIE (Irving Berlin) (instrumental)	Mercury 314536077
HAPPY ROVING COWBOY (Bob Nolan) and RADIO DEMO	Mercury 314536077

Demos circa late 1940–1941.

SAN ANTONIO ROSE (Bob Wills)	Mercury 314536077
FREIGHT TRAIN BLUES (Roy Acuff)	Mercury 314536077

WSFA shows recorded at Highland Bridge Radio and Shoe Shop, Montgomery. Circa April 1942.

Possibly Boots Harris (steel guitar); Lum York (bass).

I'M NOT COMING HOME ANY MORE	Polydor 847194
OLD SHEP (Red Foley)	Unissued
I AIN'T GONNA LOVE YOU ANY MORE (Ernest Tubb)	Mercury 314536077
I'LL NEVER CRY OVER YOU (Unknown)	Unissued
ROCKIN' ALONE IN AN OLD ROCKIN' CHAIR (Bob Miller)	Unissued
AUNT DINAH'S QUILTING PARTY (Trad.)	Unissued
WILL THE CIRCLE BE UNBROKEN (Trad.)	Unissued
THE LAST LETTER (Rex Griffin)	Unissued
JESUS WALKED THAT LONESOME VALLEY (Trad.)	Unissued
BENEATH THAT LONELY MOUND OF CLAY (Roy Acuff)	Unissued
HAPPY ROVIN' COWBOY (Bob Nolan)	Unissued

Demos for Acuff-Rose. July 1946–fall 1948.

I'M GOING HOME (1) ("Standing by the bedside . . .")	Arhoolie EP 548

Note: See 1950 demos for another song with the same title.

I'M GOING HOME (2) ("Standing by the bedside . . .")	Mercury 314536077

Note: With mandolin, Dobro, guitar; dated by Bob Pinson
   to circa 1950.

MOTHER IS GONE (1)	Arhoolie EP 548
MOTHER IS GONE (2)	CMF 07
MOTHER IS GONE (3)	MGM11975
A HOME IN HEAVEN (1)	Arhoolie EP 548
A HOME IN HEAVEN (2)	Mercury 314536077

Note: Version 2 possibly recorded later, per Bob Pinson.
Note: This is the same song (except for one word) as
   "Are You Building a Temple in Heaven?"

ARE YOU BUILDING A TEMPLE IN HEAVEN? (1)	MGM E-3850
ARE YOU BUILDING A TEMPLE IN HEAVEN? (2)	Unissued
IN MY DREAMS YOU STILL BELONG TO ME	Arhoolie EP 548
WON'T YOU SOMETIMES THINK OF ME?	CMF 07
WHY SHOULD I CRY?	CMF 07
YOU BROKE YOUR OWN HEART (1)	CMF 07
YOU BROKE YOUR OWN HEART (2)	Mercury 314536077

Note: Version 2 with unknown band.

I WATCHED MY DREAM WORLD CRUMBLE LIKE CLAY	CMF 07
I TOLD A LIE TO MY HEART	CMF 07
CALLING YOU (1*)	CMF 07

*With Audrey Williams (vocal)

Title (Composer[s])	Recording No.
CALLING YOU (2)	Mercury 314536077
PAN AMERICAN	CMF 07
WEALTH WON'T SAVE YOUR SOUL	CMF 07
SINGING WATERFALL	CMF 07
HONKY TONK BLUES	CMF 06
I'M SO TIRED OF IT ALL	Mercury 314536077

Note: With unknown band.

Session: December 11, 1946: WSM studios, Nashville.

James "Guy" Willis (guitar); Vic Willis (accordion); Charles "Skeeter" Willis (fiddle); Charles "Indian" Wright (bass).

CALLING YOU	Sterling 201
NEVER AGAIN (WILL I KNOCK ON YOUR DOOR)	Sterling 201

Note: On label as "Never Again (Will I Knock at Your Door)."

WEALTH WON'T SAVE YOUR SOUL	Sterling 204
WHEN GOD COMES AND GATHERS HIS JEWELS	Sterling 204

Note: On label as "When God Comes and Fathers His Jewels."

Session: February 13, 1947: probably WSM studio.

Tommy Jackson (fiddle); Dale "Smokey" Lohman (steel guitar); Zeke Turner (electric guitar); Louis Innis (bass).

I DON'T CARE (IF TOMORROW NEVER COMES)	Sterling 208
MY LOVE FOR YOU (HAS TURNED TO HATE)	Sterling 208
HONKY TONKIN'	Sterling 210
PAN AMERICAN	Sterling 210

Session: April 21, 1947: Castle Studio, Nashville.

Tommy Jackson (fiddle); Dale "Smokey" Lohman (steel guitar); Zeke Turner (lead guitar); Louis Innis (rhythm guitar); Brownie Reynolds (bass).

MOVE IT ON OVER	MGM 10033
I SAW THE LIGHT	MGM 10271
(LAST NIGHT) I HEARD YOU CRYING IN YOUR SLEEP	MGM 10033
SIX MORE MILES (TO THE GRAVEYARD)	MGM 10271

Session: August 4, 1947: Castle Studio, Nashville.

L. C. Crysel (fiddle, except "Pontchartrain"); Tommy Jackson (fiddle on "Pontchartrain"); Herman Herron (steel guitar); Sammy Pruett (lead guitar); Slim Thomas (rhythm guitar); Lum York (bass).

FLY TROUBLE (Honey Wilds / Bunny Biggs / Fred Rose)	MGM 10073
HONKY TONK BLUES	Unissued / lost
I'M SATISFIED WITH YOU (Fred Rose)	MGM 11768
ON THE BANKS OF THE OLD PONTCHARTRAIN (Hank Williams / Ramona Vincent)	MGM 10073

Session: November 6, 1947: Castle Studio, Nashville.

Robert "Chubby" Wise (fiddle); Jerry Byrd (steel guitar); Zeke Turner (lead guitar); probably Louis Innis (bass); possibly Fred Rose or Owen Bradley (piano).

ROOTIE TOOTIE (Fred Rose)	MGM 10124

Title (Composer[s])	Recording No.
I CAN'T GET YOU OFF OF MY MIND	MGM 10328
I'M A LONG GONE DADDY	MGM 10212
HONKY TONKIN'	MGM 10171

Session: November 7, 1947: Castle Studio, Nashville.

Same personnel as previous session.

MY SWEET LOVE AIN'T AROUND	MGM 10124
THE BLUES COME AROUND	MGM 10212
A MANSION ON THE HILL (Fred Rose / Hank Williams)	MGM 10328
I'LL BE A BACHELOR 'TIL I DIE	MGM 10171

Session: December 22, 1948: E. T. Herzog Studio, Cincinnati.

Tommy Jackson (fiddle); Jerry Byrd (steel guitar); Clyde Baum (mandolin); Zeke Turner (lead guitar); Louis Innis (rhythm guitar); Willie Thawl (bass); Audrey Williams (duet vocal).

LOST ON THE RIVER*	MGM 10434
THERE'LL BE NO TEARDROPS TONIGHT	MGM 10461
I HEARD MY MOTHER PRAYING FOR ME* (Audrey Williams)	MGM 10813
LOVESICK BLUES (Irving Mills / Cliff Friend)	MGM 10352

*Duet credited on label to "Hank and Audrey."

Shreveport radio recordings. August 1948–May 1949.
Most are probably Johnnie Fair Syrup transcriptions,
KWKH studio, Shreveport, Louisiana.

YOU CAUSED IT ALL BY TELLING LIES (Clyde Moody)	Mercury 314536077
PLEASE DON'T LET ME LOVE YOU (Ralph Jones)	MGM 11928
FADED LOVE AND WINTER ROSES (Fred Rose)	MGM 11928
THERE'S NO ROOM IN MY HEART FOR THE BLUES (Fred Rose / Zeb Turner)	MGM 12244
THE LITTLE PAPER BOY (Johnnie Wright / Jack Anglin)	Polydor 823695
I WISH I HAD A NICKEL (Tommy Sutton / Sammy Barnhart)	MGM 12244
ROCKIN' CHAIR MONEY (Lonnie Glosson / Bill Carlisle)	Mercury 314536077
TENNESSEE BORDER (Jimmie Work)	Mercury 314536077
MY MAIN TRIAL IS YET TO COME (Pee Wee King / J. L. Frank)	Mercury 314536077
THE DEVIL'S TRAIN (Cliff Carlisle / Mel Foree)	MGM E-3850
THE SINGING WATERFALL	MGM 12332
COOL WATER (Bob Nolan)	Mercury 314536077
THE WALTZ OF THE WIND (Fred Rose)	MGM 12535
AT THE FIRST FALL OF SNOW (Lorene Rose)	MGM 12077
DIXIE CANNONBALL (Gene Autry / Vaughn Horton)	Mercury 314536077
I'M FREE AT LAST (Ernest Tubb)	Polydor 825554
LEAVE ME ALONE WITH THE BLUES (Joe Pope)	MGM 12484
IT JUST DON'T MATTER NOW (Ernest Tubb)	Polydor 827531
SWING WIDE YOUR GATE OF LOVE (Hank Thompson)	Mercury 314536077
THE OLD HOME (J. W. Earls)	MGM E-3803
ALONE AND FORSAKEN	MGM 12029
SOMEDAY YOU'LL CALL MY NAME (Jean Branch / Eddie Hill)	MGM 12077
THANK GOD (Fred Rose)	MGM 12127

Title (Composer[s])	Recording No.
BLUE LOVE (IN MY HEART) ("Floyd Jenkins," aka Fred Rose)	MGM 12332
ROLY POLY (Fred Rose)	Mercury 314536077
THE BATTLE OF ARMAGEDDON (Roy Acuff / Odell McLeod)	MGM 12127
WE LIVE IN TWO DIFFERENT WORLDS (Fred Rose)	Mercury 314536077
WAIT FOR THE LIGHT TO SHINE (Fred Rose)	Mercury 314536077
NO ONE WILL EVER KNOW (Fred Rose / Mel Foree)	MGM 12535
WITH TEARS IN MY EYES (Paul Howard)	MGM 12484
ROCK MY CRADLE ONCE AGAIN (Johnny Bond)	Polydor 825548
FIRST YEAR BLUES (Ernest Tubb)	Mercury 314536077
SUNDOWN AND SORROW (Pee Wee King / J. L. Frank)	MGM E-3803

Missing Johnnie Fair Masters.

THE PRODIGAL SON ("Floyd Jenkins," aka Fred Rose)	Unissued / lost
TRAMP ON THE STREET (Grady and Hazel Cole)	Unissued / lost
WE PLANTED ROSES ON OUR DARLING'S GRAVE (Roy Acuff / Odell Macleod)	Unissued / lost

Note: The above three were logged into the MGM vaults in 1955, but have never been released. Versions of "The Prodigal Son" and "Tramp on the Street" were issued later, but derive from the *Health and Happiness* shows.

Shreveport-era song demos.

HEAVEN HOLDS ALL MY TREASURES	CMF 07
LOST ON THE RIVER	CMF 06
A HOUSE OF GOLD (1)	Polydor 833752
A HOUSE OF GOLD (2)	CMF 06
WHEN YOU'RE TIRED OF BREAKING OTHERS' HEARTS (Hank Williams / Curley Williams)	Polydor 833749
'NEATH A COLD GRAY TOMB OF STONE (Hank Williams / Mel Foree)	Polydor 827531

Note: Full band performance, possibly from Shreveport.

NO, NOT NOW (Hank Williams / Curley Williams / Mel Foree)	Polydor (UK) 2391.519

Note: The demo features a fiddle and a second vocalist on the refrain, possibly Curley Williams.

HONEY, DO YOU LOVE ME, HUH? (Hank Williams / Curley Williams)	Mercury 314536077
TIME HAS PROVEN ME WRONG	Mercury 314536077

Radio performance with Johnnie Wright and Kitty Wells, 1948/1949.

DEAR BROTHER	Mercury 314536077

Miscellaneous radio show circa 1948/1949.

DON'T DO IT, DARLING (Zeke Manners)	Mercury 314536077

Title (Composer[s])	Recording No.

Session: March 1, 1949 (7:30–10:30 p.m.): Castle Studio, Nashville.

Dale Potter (fiddle); Don Davis (steel guitar); Zeb Turner (lead guitar); Clyde Baum (mandolin); Jack Shook (rhythm guitar); probably Ernie Newton (bass); Audrey Williams (duet vocal).

DEAR BROTHER*	MGM 10434
JESUS REMEMBERED ME*	MGM 10013
LOST HIGHWAY (Leon Payne)	MGM 10506
MAY YOU NEVER BE ALONE	MGM 10609

*Issued as "Hank and Audrey"

Session: March 1–2, 1949 (11:00 p.m.–2:00 a.m.): Castle Studio, Nashville.

Same personnel as previous session.

HONKY TONK BLUES	Polydor 823695
MIND YOUR OWN BUSINESS	MGM 10461
YOU'RE GONNA CHANGE (OR I'M GONNA LEAVE)	MGM 10506
MY SON CALLS ANOTHER MAN DADDY (Hank Williams / Jewell House)	Polydor 823695

Session: March 20, 1949 (7:30–10:30 p.m.): Castle Studio, Nashville.

Dale Potter (fiddle); Don Davis (steel guitar); Zeb Turner (electric guitar); Jack Shook (rhythm guitar); Velma Williams (bass).

WEDDING BELLS (Claude Boone)	MGM 10401
I'VE JUST TOLD MAMA GOODBYE (Sunshine Slim Sweet / Curley Kinsey)	MGM 10401

Prince Albert Opry, June 18, 1949.

Probably with Red Foley's band.

LOVESICK BLUES (Irving Mills / Cliff Friend)	Mercury 314536077

Prince Albert Opry, November 18, 1949 (on location in Germany).

Probably with Red Foley's band.

MOVE IT ON OVER	Mercury 314536077

Demos probably recorded in Nashville, 1949.

JESUS DIED FOR ME (1)	Polydor 825551
JESUS DIED FOR ME (2)	Mercury 314536077

Note: Version 2 with Audrey Williams.

WE'RE GETTING CLOSER TO THE GRAVE EACH DAY	Polydor 825557
ALABAMA WALTZ	Polydor 825554

Session: August 30, 1949 (2:00–5:30 p.m.): E. T. Herzog Studio, 811 Race Street, Cincinnati, Ohio.

Tommy Jackson (fiddle); Jerry Byrd (steel guitar); Zeke Turner (lead guitar) Louis Innis (rhythm guitar); Ernie Newton (bass).

I'M SO LONESOME I COULD CRY	MGM 10560
A HOUSE WITHOUT LOVE	MGM 10696
I JUST DON'T LIKE THIS KIND OF LIVIN'	MGM 10609
MY BUCKET'S GOT A HOLE IN IT (1) (Clarence Williams)	MGM 10560

Title (Composer[s])	Recording No.

MY BUCKET'S GOT A HOLE IN IT (2) (Clarence Williams)   Mercury 314536077
Note: Version 2 is a vocal / guitar demo version for the band
to learn the song.

Health and Happiness *Shows. WSM studios, October 1949.*

Audrey Williams (vocals, shows 1–4); Jerry Rivers (fiddle);
Don Helms (steel guitar); Bob McNett (lead guitar); possibly
Jack Shook (rhythm guitar); Hillous Butrum (bass).

SHOW 1

HAPPY ROVIN' COWBOY (THEME) (Bob Nolan)	Mercury 314517862
WEDDING BELLS (Claude Boone)	Mercury 314517862
LOVESICK BLUES (Irving Mills / Cliff Friend)	Mercury 314517862
OLD JOE CLARK *(Jerry Rivers solo)* (Trad.)	Mercury 314517862
WHERE THE SOUL OF MAN NEVER DIES (William Golden)	Mercury 314517862
SALLY GOODIN *(Jerry Rivers solo)* (Trad.)	Mercury 314517862

SHOW 2

HAPPY ROVIN' COWBOY (Bob Nolan)	Mercury 314517862
YOU'RE GONNA CHANGE	Mercury 314517862
(THERE'S A) BLUEBIRD ON YOUR WINDOWSILL	
(Audrey solo) (Elizabeth Clarke / Robert Mellin)	Mercury 314517862
FIRE ON THE MOUNTAIN *(Jerry Rivers solo)* (Trad.)	Mercury 314517862
TRAMP ON THE STREET (Grady and Hazel Cole)	Mercury 314517862
SALLY GOODIN *(Jerry Rivers solo)* (Trad.)	Mercury 314517862

SHOW 3

HAPPY ROVIN' COWBOY (Bob Nolan)	Mercury 314517862
I'M A LONG GONE DADDY	Mercury 314517862
I'M TELLING YOU *(Audrey solo)* (Audrey Williams)	Mercury 314517862
BILL CHEATAM *(Jerry Rivers solo)* (Trad.)	Mercury 314517862
WHEN GOD COMES AND GATHERS HIS JEWELS	Mercury 314517862
SALLY GOODIN *(Jerry Rivers solo)* (Trad.)	Mercury 314517862

SHOW 4

HAPPY ROVIN' COWBOY (Bob Nolan)	Mercury 314517862
LOST HIGHWAY (Leon Payne)	Mercury 314517862
I WANT TO LIVE AND LOVE *(Audrey solo)* (Gene Sullivan /	
Wiley Walker)	Mercury 314517862
BILE THEM CABBAGE DOWN *(Jerry Rivers solo)* (Trad.)	Mercury 314517862
I'LL HAVE A NEW BODY (Trad.)	Mercury 314517862
FINGERS ON FIRE *(Bob McNett solo)* (Arthur Smith)	Mercury 314517862
SALLY GOODIN *(Jerry Rivers solo)* (Trad.)	Mercury 314517862

SHOW 5

HAPPY ROVIN' COWBOY (Bob Nolan)	Mercury 314517862
A MANSION ON THE HILL (Hank Williams / Fred Rose)	Polydor 422827531
THERE'LL BE NO TEARDROPS TONIGHT	Mercury 314517862
WAGNER *(Jerry Rivers solo)* (Trad.)	Polydor 422827531
THE PRODIGAL SON ("Floyd Jenkins," aka Fred Rose)	MGM E-3850
SALLY GOODIN *(Jerry Rivers solo)* (Trad.)	Mercury 314517862

TITLE (COMPOSER[S])	RECORDING NO.

SHOW 6

HAPPY ROVIN' COWBOY (Bob Nolan)	Mercury 314517862
PAN AMERICAN	Polydor 422823695
LOVESICK BLUES (Irving Mills / Cliff Friend)	Polydor 422823695
ARKANSAS TRAVELER *(Jerry Rivers solo)* (Trad.)	Mercury 314517862
I SAW THE LIGHT	Polydor 422823095
SALLY GOODIN *(Jerry Rivers solo)* (Trad.)	Mercury 314517862

SHOW 7

HAPPY ROVIN' COWBOY (Bob Nolan)	Mercury 314517862
MIND YOUR OWN BUSINESS	Polydor 422823695
WEDDING BELLS (Claude Boone)	Polydor 422827531
COTTON-EYED JOE *(Jerry Rivers solo)* (Trad.)	Polydor 422827531
I'VE JUST TOLD MAMA GOODBYE (Curley Kinsey / Sunshine Slim Sweet)	Mercury 314517862
SALLY GOODIN *(Jerry Rivers solo)* (Trad.)	Mercury 314517862

SHOW 8

HAPPY ROVIN' COWBOY (Bob Nolan)	Mercury 314517862
I CAN'T GET YOU OFF OF MY MIND	Polydor 422827531
I'M SO LONESOME I COULD CRY	Polydor 422827531
FISHERMAN'S HORNPIPE *(Jerry Rivers solo)* (Trad.)	Mercury 314517862
THY BURDENS ARE GREATER THAN MINE (Pee Wee King / Redd Stewart)	Polydor 422827531
SALLY GOODIN *(Jerry Rivers solo)* (Trad.)	Mercury 314517862

Note: These shows were overdubbed in 1961 and 1962 to form the core of two "live" albums. Occasionally, session masters were used in their place, overdubbed with applause. The issue numbers cited above are the first undubbed issues.

AFRS 103, November 12, 1949.

Unknown band.

YOU'RE GONNA CHANGE (OR I'M GONNA LEAVE)	MGM MG-1-5019

Demos probably recorded 1950.

I'M GOING HOME (1) ("When my work here is o'er . . .")	MGM E-3850
I'M GOING HOME (2) ("When my work here is o'er . . .")	Mercury 314536077
LAST NIGHT I DREAMED OF HEAVEN	Polydor 831633
HOW CAN YOU REFUSE HIM NOW?	Polydor 833749
HELP ME UNDERSTAND	CMF 06
JESUS IS CALLING (Hank Williams / Charles Monroe)	Mercury 314536077
THERE'S NOTHING AS SWEET AS MY BABY	CMF 06
WEARIN' OUT YOUR WALKIN' SHOES (1)	Polydor 833752
WEARIN' OUT YOUR WALKIN' SHOES (2)	Unissued
SING, SING, SING (aka I'M GONNA SING, SING, SING)	Mercury 314536077
MESSAGE TO MY MOTHER	Polydor 831634

Session: January 9, 1950 (2:00–5:00 p.m.): Castle Studio, Nashville.

Jerry Rivers (fiddle); Don Helms (steel guitar); Bob McNett (lead guitar); Jack Shook (rhythm guitar); Ernie Newton (bass).

TITLE (COMPOSER[S])	RECORDING NO.
LONG GONE LONESOME BLUES	MGM 10645
WHY DON'T YOU LOVE ME?	MGM 10696
WHY SHOULD WE TRY ANYMORE?	MGM 10760
MY SON CALLS ANOTHER MAN DADDY	MGM 10645

Session: January 10, 1950 (2:00–5:00 p.m.): Castle Studio, Nashville.

Don Helms (steel guitar); Hillous Butrum (bass); probably Owen
    Bradley or Fred Rose (organ).

TOO MANY PARTIES AND TOO MANY PALS* (Billy Rose / Mort Dixon / Ray Henderson)	MGM 10718
BEYOND THE SUNSET* (Blanche Kerr Brock / Virgil P. Brock / Albert Kennedy Rowswell)	MGM 10630
THE FUNERAL* (Poem: Will Carleton; music: Fred Rose)	MGM 10630
EVERYTHING'S OKAY*	MGM 10718

*Issued under pseudonym "Luke the Drifter — with Musical
    Accompaniment"

AFRS 116, February 18, 1950.

Unknown band.

I JUST DON'T LIKE THIS KIND OF LIVING	MGM MG-1-5019
LOVESICK BLUES (Irving Mills / Cliff Friend)	MGM MG-1-5019

Radio station WSLI, Jackson, Mississippi, February 21, 1950.

Milton Beasley (mandolin); Red Pleasant (rhythm); Junior Stanley
    (lead guitar); Miller Lowther (steel guitar); Wayne "Pedro"
    Stanley (bass); "Farmer Jim" (James Houston Neal, emcee).

LOST HIGHWAY (Lone Payne)	Mercury 314536077
Conversation with Farmer Jim.	
I'M A LONG GONE DADDY	Mercury 314536077
Conversation with Farmer Jim.	
LONG GONE LONESOME BLUES	Mercury 314536077
Conversation with Farmer Jim.	

Audrey Williams session: March 28, 1950: Castle Studio, Nashville.

Same personnel as January 9, 1950, except Audrey Williams (vocal) and
    Hugh Cherry (vocal) on 76048; probably Hank Williams (guitar).

76046 MY TIGHTWAD DADDY (Unknown)	Decca 46264
76047 MODEL T LOVE (Audrey Williams)	Bear Family BFX 15346
76048 HELP ME UNDERSTAND	Decca 46275
76049 HOW CAN YOU REFUSE HIM NOW?	Decca 46275

As above, except Cherry out. April 1, 1950.

76066 WHAT PUT THE PEP IN GRANDMA (Jethro Burns / Mel Foree)	Decca 46233
76067 I LIKE THAT KIND (Audrey Williams)	Decca 46264
76068 HONKY TONKIN'	Decca 46233

AFRS 130, June 10, 1950.

Unknown band.

LONG GONE LONESOME BLUES	MGM MG-1-5019
WHY DON'T YOU LOVE ME?	Mercury 314536077

Title (Composer[s])	Recording No.

Session: June 14, 1950 (12:00–3:30 p.m.): Castle Studio, Nashville.

Same personnel as January 9, 1950, except Sammy Pruett replaces
McNett. Jack Shook possibly replaced by Rusty Gabbard (rhythm
guitar).

THEY'LL NEVER TAKE HER LOVE FROM ME (Leon Payne)	MGM 10760
HONKY TONK BLUES	Unissued / lost

Radio show, August 4, 1950.

With Red Foley, Grady Martin (guitar); others unknown.

THEY'LL NEVER TAKE HER LOVE FROM ME (Leon Payne)	Mercury 314536077

AFRS 139, August 12, 1950.

Unknown band.

WHY DON'T YOU LOVE ME?	MGM MG-1-5019
Dialogue with Minnie Pearl.	*MGM MG-1-5019*
THEY'LL NEVER TAKE HER LOVE FROM ME (Leon Payne)	MGM MG-1-5019
Dialogue with Minnie Pearl.	*MGM MG-1-5019*

Session: August 31, 1950 (2:00–5:00 p.m.): Castle Studio, Nashville.

Jerry Rivers (fiddle); Don Helms (steel guitar); Sammy Pruett
(electric guitar); probably Jack Shook (rhythm guitar); Ernie
Newton or "Cedric Rainwater," aka Howard Watts (bass); Fred
Rose or Owen Bradley (organ); possibly Farris Coursey (drums)
on "Moanin' the Blues."

NOBODY'S LONESOME FOR ME	MGM 10832
MOANIN' THE BLUES	MGM 10832
HELP ME UNDERSTAND*	MGM 10806
NO, NO, JOE* (Fred Rose)	MGM 10806

*Issued under pseudonym "Luke the Drifter — with Musical
Accompaniment"

AFRS (unknown show), probably October 1950.

Unknown band.

MOANIN' THE BLUES	Mercury 314536077

AFRS 151, November 11, 1950.

Unknown band.

MOANIN' THE BLUES	MGM MG-1-5019
NOBODY'S LONESOME FOR ME	MGM MG-1-5019

Unknown location, probably WSM; probably fall 1950 March of Dimes.

Announcer, Ralph Christian.

Spoken pitch by Hank.	ACM 3
MOANIN' THE BLUES	ACM 3
HELP ME UNDERSTAND*	ACM 3
WHEN GOD DIPS HIS LOVE IN MY HEART (Cleavant Derricks)	ACM 3

*With Audrey Williams (vocal)

TITLE (COMPOSER[S])   RECORDING NO.

Session: December 21, 1950 (7:15–9:50 p.m.): Castle Studio, Nashville.

Jerry Rivers (fiddle); Don Helms (steel guitar); Sammy Pruett
  (electric guitar); Chet Atkins (rhythm guitar); Ernie Newton or
  "Cedric Rainwater," aka Howard Watts (bass).

COLD, COLD HEART	MGM 10904
DEAR JOHN (Tex Ritter / Aubrey Gass)	MGM 10904
JUST WAITIN'* (Hank Williams / Bob Gazzaway)	MGM 10932
MEN WITH BROKEN HEARTS*	MGM 10932

*Issued under the pseudonym "Luke the Drifter — with Musical
  Accompaniment"

TITLE (COMPOSER[S])

Shows for Mother's Best Flour and other sponsors: January–March 1951, and possibly other dates.

Jerry Rivers (fiddle); Don Helms (steel guitar); Sammy Pruett (electric
  guitar); "Cedric Rainwater," aka Howard Watts (bass).
Note: Every show opens and closes with a chorus of "Lovesick Blues."
Note: No title was issued legitimately, although a few have appeared
  on bootleg compilations.

SHOW 1-A1

THE BLIND CHILD (Ida B. Mercer)
BLUE STEEL BLUES *(Don Helms solo)* (Ted Daffan)
WHEN GOD DIPS HIS LOVE IN MY HEART (Cleavant Derricks)

1-A2

WHERE THE OLD RED RIVER FLOWS (Jimmie Davis)
MOONLIGHT WATERS *(Don Helms solo)* (Trad.)
HOW CAN YOU REFUSE HIM NOW?

1-B1

MOANIN' THE BLUES
HONKY TONKIN' *(Audrey Williams solo)*
I'LL HAVE A NEW BODY (Unknown)

1-B2

ALABAMA WALTZ
FIRE ON THE MOUNTAIN *(Jerry Rivers solo)* (Trad.)
LORD BUILD ME A CABIN (Unknown)

2-1A

NOBODY'S LONESOME FOR ME
TWIN GUITAR POLKA *(Sammy Pruett and Don Helms solo)* (Unknown)
GATHERING FLOWERS FOR THE MASTER'S BOUQUET (M. D. Baumgardner)
EIGHTH OF JANUARY *(Jerry Rivers solo)* (Trad.)

2-A2

A MANSION ON THE HILL
I LIKE THAT KIND *(Audrey Williams solo)* (Audrey Williams)
HOW CAN YOU REFUSE HIM NOW?

Title (Composer[s])

2-B1

EVERYTHING'S OKAY
WHY SHOULD I CRY *(Audrey Williams solo)*
I HEARD MY MOTHER PRAYING FOR ME *(Hank and Audrey Williams)*

3-A1

MOVE IT ON OVER
I'M SATISFIED WITH LIFE *(Audrey Williams solo)* (Unknown)
I SAW THE LIGHT

3-A2

SEAMAN'S BLUES (Talmadge Tubb / Ernest Tubb)
BLUES IN MY MIND *(Audrey Williams solo)*
SOMETHING GOT A HOLD OF ME *(Hank and Audrey Williams)* (Warren Caplinger)

3-B1

BLUE EYES CRYING IN THE RAIN (Fred Rose)
BONAPARTE'S RETREAT *(Audrey Williams solo)* (Pee Wee King / Redd Stewart)
I'VE JUST TOLD MAMA GOODBYE (Curley Kinsey / Sunshine Slim Sweet)

3-B2

ON THE BANKS OF THE OLD PONTCHARTRAIN (Hank Williams / Ramona Vincent)
BLUE LOVE IN MY HEART *(Audrey Williams solo)* (Fred Rose)
CALLING YOU

4-A1

MY SWEET LOVE AIN'T AROUND
MODEL T LOVE *(Audrey Williams solo)* (Audrey Williams)
WHERE THE SOUL OF MAN NEVER DIES (William M. Golden)

4-A2

PINS AND NEEDLES (IN MY HEART) ("Floyd Jenkins," aka Fred Rose)
FOUR FLUSHER *(Audrey Williams solo)* (Unknown)
I HEARD MY MOTHER PRAYING FOR ME (Audrey Williams)

4-B1

MIND YOUR OWN BUSINESS
I LIKE THAT KIND *(Audrey Williams solo)* (Audrey Williams)
WHEN GOD DIPS HIS LOVE IN MY HEART (Cleavant Derricks)

4-B2

MAY YOU NEVER BE ALONE
MY LOVE FOR YOU *(Audrey Williams solo)*
DEAR BROTHER *(Hank and Audrey Williams)*

5-A1

THEY'LL NEVER TAKE HER LOVE FROM ME (Leon Payne)
(LAST NIGHT) I HEARD YOU CRYING IN YOUR SLEEP *(Audrey Williams solo)*
WAIT FOR THE LIGHT TO SHINE (Fred Rose)
WHISTLIN' RUFUS *(Band only)* (Trad.)

5-A2

COOL WATER (Bob Nolan)
ORANGE BLOSSOM SPECIAL *(Jerry Rivers solo)* (Ervin Rouse)
LONELY TOMBS (J. E. Mainer)

TITLE (COMPOSER[S])

5-B1

I JUST DON'T LIKE THIS KIND OF LIVIN'
YOU DON'T HAVE TO BE A BABY TO CRY *(Audrey Williams solo)*
(Bob Merrill / Terry Shand)
JESUS REMEMBERED ME

5-B2

COLD, COLD HEART
HONKY TONKIN' *(Audrey Williams solo)*
SALLY GOODIN *(Jerry Rivers solo)* (Trad.)
Hank Williams and Louie Buck call square dance.

6-A1

DEAR JOHN (Aubrey Gass / Tex Ritter)
I'M SATISFIED WITH LIFE *(Audrey Williams solo)*
SOMETHING GOT A HOLD OF ME *(Hank and Audrey Williams)* (Warren Caplinger)

6-A2

AT THE FIRST FALL OF SNOW (Lorene Rose)
I LIKE THAT KIND *(Audrey Williams solo)* (Audrey Williams)
WHEN GOD DIPS HIS LOVE IN MY HEART (Cleavant Derricks)

6-B1

WEDDING BELLS (Claude Boone)
MY TIGHTWAD DADDY *(Audrey Williams solo)*
WHERE THE SOUL OF MAN NEVER DIES (William Golden)

6-B2

WHY DON'T YOU LOVE ME?
BLUE LOVE *(Audrey Williams solo)* (Fred Rose)
DEAR BROTHER *(Hank and Audrey Williams)*

7-A1

FADED LOVE AND WINTER ROSES (Fred Rose)
FIRE ON THE MOUNTAIN *(Jerry Rivers solo)* (Trad.)
I HEARD MY SAVIOR CALL (Unknown)

7-A2

JUST WHEN I NEEDED YOU (Johnnie Wright / Jack Anglin / Clyde Baum)
I CAN'T TELL MY HEART THAT *(Johnnie and Jack)* (Johnnie Wright / Jack Anglin / Jim Anglin)
FARTHER ALONG (Rev. W. B. Stevens)

7-B1

MOVE IT ON OVER
DARKTOWN STRUTTERS BALL *(Sammy Pruett solo)* (Shelton Brooks)
THY BURDENS ARE GREATER THAN MINE (Redd Stewart / Pee Wee King)

7-B2

THERE'S NOTHING AS SWEET AS MY BABY
TURKEY IN THE STRAW *(Jerry Rivers solo)* (Trad.)
WAIT FOR THE LIGHT TO SHINE (Fred Rose)

TITLE (COMPOSER[S])

8-A1

I CAN'T HELP IT
PANHANDLE RAG *(Drifting Cowboys)* (Trad.)
GATHERING FLOWERS FOR THE MASTER'S BOUQUET (M. D. Baumgardner)
BILL CHEATAM *(Jerry Rivers solo)* (Trad.)

8-A2

WHERE THE OLD RED RIVER FLOWS (Jimmie Davis)
BLUE STEEL BLUES *(Don Helms solo)* (Ted Daffan)
THIRTY PIECES OF SILVER (Unknown)

8-B1

ON TOP OF OLD SMOKY (Trad.)
COLUMBUS STOCKADE BLUES *(Sammy Pruett solo)* (Jimmie Davis)
THE PRODIGAL SON ("Floyd Jenkins," aka Fred Rose)

8-B2

MAY YOU NEVER BE ALONE
ARKANSAS TRAVELER *(Drifting Cowboys)* (Trad.)
HOW FAR TO LITTLE ROCK (portion)
I'LL HAVE A NEW BODY (Unknown)

9-A1

NEXT SUNDAY DARLING IS MY BIRTHDAY (Syd Nathan / Arthur Q. Smith)
OLD JOE CLARK *(Jerry Rivers solo)* (Trad.)
DECK OF CARDS (T. Texas Tyler)

9-A2

TENNESSEE BORDER (Jimmie Work)
BLUE BONNET RAG *(Don Helms solo)* (Unknown)
DEAR BROTHER
WHISTLIN' RUFUS *(Jerry Rivers solo)* (Trad.)

9-B1

PICTURES FROM LIFE'S OTHER SIDE
SALLY GOODIN *(Jerry Rivers solo)* (Trad.)
SING, SING, SING

9-B2

JUST WAITIN' (Hank Williams / Bob Gazzaway)
PARADISE ISLAND *(Don Helms solo)* (Unknown)
WHEN THE FIRE COMES DOWN FROM HEAVEN (Milton Estes /
    Wally Fowler / Paul Kinsey / Tommy Harrell)

10-A1

MY SWEET LOVE AIN'T AROUND
I CAN'T TELL MY HEART THAT *(Jimmie Skinner solo)* (Jim Anglin /
    Jack Anglin / Johnnie Wright)
WHERE THE SOUL OF MAN NEVER DIES (William Golden)

10-A2

I CAN'T HELP IT
PANHANDLE RAG *(Don Helms solo)* (Unknown)
DRIFTING TOO FAR FROM THE SHORE (Charles E. Moody)

TITLE (COMPOSER[S])

10-B1

JUST WHEN I NEEDED YOU (Jack Anglin / Johnnie Wright / Clyde Baum)
STEEL GUITAR STOMP *(Don Helms solo)* (Unknown)
I'LL FLY AWAY (Albert E. Brumley)

10-B2

COLD, COLD HEART
UNKNOWN FIDDLE TUNE *(Jerry Rivers solo)*
OLD COUNTRY CHURCH (John Whitfield Vaughn)

11-A1

MOANIN' THE BLUES
BLUE STEEL BLUES *(Don Helms solo)* (Ted Daffan)
I DREAMED ABOUT MAMA LAST NIGHT (Fred Rose)

11-A2

I HANG MY HEAD AND CRY (Gene Autry / Fred Rose)
TENNESSEE WAGONER *(Jerry Rivers solo)* (Trad.)
AT THE CROSS (Ralph E. Hudson)

11-B1

I DREAMED ABOUT MAMA LAST NIGHT (Fred Rose)
BLACK MOUNTAIN RAG *(Jerry Rivers solo)* (Trad.)
I HEARD MY SAVIOR CALL (Johnnie Bailes)

11-B2

LOW AND LONELY (Fred Rose)
FOOLISH QUESTIONS *(Big Bill Lister solo)* (Arthur Smith)
STEAL AWAY / THE FUNERAL (Trad.)

12-A1

WHERE THE OLD RED RIVER FLOWS (Jimmie Davis)
ORANGE BLOSSOM SPECIAL *(Jerry Rivers solo)* (Ervin Rouse)
WHERE HE LEADS ME I WILL FOLLOW (E. W. Blandly / J. S. Norris)

12-A2

IF I DIDN'T LOVE YOU *(with recitation by Louie Buck)*
PANHANDLE RAG *(Don Helms solo)* (Trad.)
WAIT FOR THE LIGHT TO SHINE (Fred Rose)

12-B1

I JUST DON'T LIKE THIS KIND OF LIVIN'
TENNESSEE WAGONER *(Jerry Rivers solo)* (Trad.)
THE PALE HORSE AND HIS RIDER (Johnnie Bailes / Ervin Staggs)

12-B2

HEY, GOOD LOOKIN'
ALABAMA JUBILEE *(Jerry Rivers solo)* (Jack Yellen / George Cobb)
SEARCHING FOR A SOLDIER'S GRAVE (Roy Acuff)

13-A1

I'VE BEEN DOWN THAT ROAD BEFORE
LITTLE ANNIE *(Don Helms / Jerry Rivers duet)* (Stephen Foster)
I'VE GOT MY ONE WAY TICKET TO THE SKY (Johnnie and Walter Bailes)

Title (Composer[s])

13-A2

CALIFORNIA ZEPHYR
DOWN YONDER *(Jerry Rivers solo)* (L. Wolfe Gilbert)
SOFTLY AND TENDERLY (Will Thompson)

13-B1

LONESOME WHISTLE (Hank Williams / Jimmie Davis)
ROADSIDE RAG *(Don Helms solo)*
I'M BOUND FOR THE PROMISED LAND (Dr. Samuel Stennett)

13-B2

I CAN'T TELL MY HEART THAT (Jim Anglin / Jack Anglin / Johnnie Wright)
GEORGIA STEEL GUITAR *(Don Helms solo)* (Unknown)
TAKE MY HAND, PRECIOUS LORD (Rev. Thomas A. Dorsey)

14-A1

JUST WAITIN' (Hank Williams / Bob Gazzaway)
EIGHTH OF JANUARY *(Jerry Rivers solo)* (Trad.)
FROM JERUSALEM TO JERICHO (Rev. W. M. Robison)

14-A2

CHEROKEE BOOGIE (Moon Mullican / Chief William Redbird)
COLUMBUS STOCKADE BLUES *(Don Helms solo)* (Jimmie Davis)
BEAUTIFUL HOME (H. W. Elliott / Emmett S. Dean)

14-B1

LONESOME WHISTLE (Hank Williams / Jimmie Davis)
I DON'T LOVE NOBODY *(Jerry Rivers solo)* (Lew Sully)
GREAT JUDGMENT MORNING (Shadduck / Picke)

14-B2

I'LL SAIL MY SHIP ALONE (Henry Bernard / Morry Burns / Syd Nathan / Henry Thurston)
LITTLE ANNIE *(Don Helms / Jerry Rivers duet)* (Stephen Foster)
I'LL HAVE A NEW BODY (Unknown)

15-A1

DEAR JOHN (Aubrey Gass / Tex Ritter)
ROADSIDE RAG *(Don Helms solo)* (Unknown)
I'LL FLY AWAY (Albert E. Brumley)
BONAPARTE'S RETREAT *(Jerry Rivers solo)* (Pee Wee King / Redd Stewart)

15-A2

COLD, COLD HEART
FIRE ON THE MOUNTAIN *(Jerry Rivers solo)* (Trad.)
FARTHER ALONG (Rev. W. B. Stevens)

16-A1 (DEMO FOR AUNT JEMIMA PANCAKES)

WHY DON'T YOU LOVE ME?
SAN ANTONIO ROSE *(Owen Bradley Orchestra)* (Bob Wills)
HONEY, BE MY HONEY BEE *(Beasley Sisters)* (Unknown)
COLD, COLD HEART

TITLE (COMPOSER[S])

SHOW DATED 2/12/51
MOVE IT ON OVER
WALTZ OF THE WIND *(Audrey Williams solo)* (Fred Rose)
I'LL HAVE A NEW BODY (Unknown)

SHOW DATED 2/13/51
FADED LOVE AND WINTER ROSES (Fred Rose)
FOUR FLUSHER *(Audrey Williams solo)* (Unknown)
I SAW THE LIGHT

SHOW DATED 2/21/51
WHY SHOULD WE TRY ANYMORE?
LOW AND LONELY *(Audrey Williams solo)*
JESUS DIED FOR ME

SHOW DATED 2/22/51
LONG GONE LONESOME BLUES
(LAST NIGHT) I HEARD YOU CRYING IN YOUR SLEEP
    (Audrey Williams solo)
LONELY TOMBS (J. E. Mainer)
TURKEY IN THE STRAW *(Jerry Rivers solo)* (Trad.)

SHOW DATED 2/23/51
DEAR JOHN
IF YOU WANT SOME LOVIN' *(Audrey Williams solo)* (Unknown)
I HEARD MY MOTHER PRAYING FOR ME *(Hank and Audrey Williams)*
    (Audrey Williams)

SHOW NUMBERED 146
MIND YOUR OWN BUSINESS
OLD JOE CLARK *(Jerry Rivers solo)* (Trad.)
I DREAMED ABOUT MAMA LAST NIGHT (Fred Rose)

SHOW NUMBERED 147
I'M SO LONESOME I COULD CRY
CORRINE, CORRINA *(Don Helms solo)* (J. W. Williams / Bo Chatman)
I HEARD MY SAVIOR CALLING ME (Unknown)

SHOW NUMBERED 150
MY SWEET LOVE AIN'T AROUND
FIRE ON THE MOUNTAIN *(Jerry Rivers)* (Trad.)
I SAW THE LIGHT

SHOW NUMBERED 151
YOU BLOTTED MY HAPPY SCHOOLDAYS (Edith and Sherman Collins)
ORANGE BLOSSOM SPECIAL *(Jerry Rivers solo)* (Ervin Rouse)
DUST ON THE BIBLE (Johnnie and Walter Bailes)

SHOW NUMBERED 156
HAVE I TOLD YOU LATELY THAT I LOVE YOU (Scotty Wiseman)
SALLY GOODIN *(Jerry Rivers solo; Hank sings a little)*
WHEN THE SAINTS GO MARCHIN' IN (Trad.)

SHOW NUMBERED 157
HEY, GOOD LOOKIN'
SILVER BELL *(Drifting Cowboys)* (Trad.)
SING, SING, SING
TURKEY IN THE STRAW *(Jerry Rivers solo)* (Trad.)

SHOW NUMBERED 158
I CAN'T HELP IT
STAY ALL NIGHT (Bob Wills)
LONELY TOMBS (J. E. Mainer)

UNDATED / UNNUMBERED SHOW
NOBODY'S LONESOME FOR ME
I'LL HAVE A NEW BODY (Unknown)

Demos, probably recorded 1951.

THY BURDENS ARE GREATER THAN MINE (Pee Wee King / Redd Stewart)	MGM 12185
TEN LITTLE NUMBERS (Roy Acuff)	Mercury 314536077
FOOL ABOUT YOU (Ralph C. Hutcheson)	MGM 2391.519 (UK)

Note: This song was copyrighted in Hank Williams' name
in 1962, but was actually written by Ralph C. Hutcheson
and first recorded by the Barker Brothers on Jaybird Records
in 1951.

CALIFORNIA ZEPHYR	Polydor 825554
ANGEL OF DEATH (1)	Mercury 314536077
ANGEL OF DEATH (2)	Polydor 831634
READY TO GO HOME	Polydor 833752
I CAN'T ESCAPE FROM YOU	Polydor 831634
WEARY BLUES FROM WAITIN'	Polydor 825551
WHEN THE BOOK OF LIFE IS READ	Polydor 825557

Demo, possibly recorded October 25, 1951.

THERE'S A TEAR IN MY BEER   Polydor 847194
Note: Hank Williams demo overdubbed with Hank Williams Jr. and
group, 1988, and first issued on Warner Bros. / Curb 7–27584.
Hank Williams' undubbed demo issued on Polydor 847194.

Demo, reportedly recorded October 25, 1951.

YOU KILLED ALL THE LOVE I EVER HAD   Polydor 847194

Session: March 16, 1951 (1:30–5:00 p.m.): Castle Studio, Nashville.

Jerry Rivers (fiddle); Don Helms (steel guitar); Sammy Pruett
(electric guitar); Jack Shook (rhythm guitar); Ernie Newton or
"Cedric Rainwater," aka Howard Watts (bass); Owen Bradley or
Fred Rose (piano).

I CAN'T HELP IT (IF I'M STILL IN LOVE WITH YOU)	MGM 10961
HOWLIN' AT THE MOON	MGM 10961
HEY, GOOD LOOKIN'	MGM 11000
MY HEART WOULD KNOW	MGM 11000

Session: March 23, 1951 (7:00–10:30 p.m.): Castle Studio, Nashville.

Audrey Williams (vocal duet and solo); Jerry Rivers (fiddle);
    Don Helms (steel guitar); Sammy Pruett (electric guitar); Jack
    Shook (rhythm guitar); Ernie Newton or "Cedric Rainwater,"
    aka Howard Watts (bass).

LEAVE US WOMEN ALONE* (Audrey Williams)	MGM 11083
IF YOU SEE MY BABY* (Audrey Williams)	MGM 11083
THE PALE HORSE AND HIS RIDER[†] (Ervin Staggs / Johnny Bailes)	MGM 12394
A HOME IN HEAVEN*	MGM 12394

*Issued as "Audrey Williams"
[†]Issued as "Hank and Audrey"

AFRS 175, May 5, 1951.

Unknown band.

COLD, COLD HEART	MGM MG-1-5019
DEAR JOHN (Aubrey Gass / Tex Ritter)	MGM MG-1-5019

Unknown radio show, probably 1951.

Unknown band.

DEAR JOHN (Aubrey Gass / Tex Ritter)	Forever Music 0409

Session: June 1, 1951 (7:00–10:00 p.m.): Castle Studio, Nashville.

Jerry Rivers (fiddle); Don Helms (steel guitar); Sammy Pruett (electric
    guitar); Jack Shook (rhythm guitar); Ernie Newton or "Cedric
    Rainwater," aka Howard Watts (bass); unknown, possibly Owen
    Bradley (organ).

RAMBLIN' MAN*	MGM 11120
PICTURES FROM LIFE'S OTHER SIDE*	MGM 11120
I'VE BEEN DOWN THAT ROAD BEFORE*	MGM 11017
I DREAMED ABOUT MAMA LAST NIGHT (Fred Rose)	MGM 11017

*Issued under the pseudonym "Luke the Drifter — with Instrumental
    Accompaniment." "Ramblin' Man" reissued under Hank Williams'
    name, MGM 11479 and subsequent issues.

Session: July 25, 1951 (7:15–10:35 p.m.): Castle Studio, Nashville.

Don Helms (steel guitar); Jerry Rivers (fiddle); Sammy Pruett (lead
    guitar); probably Jack Shook (rhythm guitar); "Cedric Rainwater,"
    aka Howard Watts (bass).

I'D STILL WANT YOU	MGM 11100
LONESOME WHISTLE (Hank Williams / Jimmie Davis)	MGM 11054
CRAZY HEART (Fred Rose / Maurice Murray)	MGM 11054
CRAZY HEART (alternate take)	MGM X-1014(EP)
BABY, WE'RE REALLY IN LOVE	Unissued / lost

Session: August 10, 1951 (7:00–10:30 p.m.): Castle Studio, Nashville.

Personnel as on July 25, 1951, except add Fred Rose or Owen Bradley (piano).

I'M SORRY FOR YOU, MY FRIEND	Unissued / lost
HALF AS MUCH (Curley Williams)	MGM 11202
I'D STILL WANT YOU	Polydor 823695
BABY, WE'RE REALLY IN LOVE	MGM 11100

TITLE (COMPOSER[S])	RECORDING NO.

Unknown location, probably WSM studios, possibly September 1951.

RADIO SPOT FOR *HOW TO WRITE FOLK AND*
    WESTERN MUSIC . . .   Mercury 314532601

AFRS 197, September 22, 1951.

Unknown band.
HEY, GOOD LOOKIN'   MG-1–5019

Unknown show, probably 1951.

Unknown band.
I CAN'T ESCAPE FROM YOU   Forever Music 0409

Session: December 11, 1951 (10:00 a.m–12 noon): Castle Studio, Nashville.

Jerry Rivers (fiddle); possibly Sammy Pruett (electric guitar); Don
    Helms (steel guitar); probably Jack Shook (acoustic guitar); Ernie
    Newton or "Cedric Rainwater," aka Howard Watts (bass).
I'M SORRY FOR YOU, MY FRIEND   MGM 11160
HONKY TONK BLUES   MGM 11160
LET'S TURN BACK THE YEARS   MGM 11202

Unknown location, late December 1951.

THE APOLOGY (1)   Polydor 833752
THE APOLOGY (2)   Mercury 314536077

Demos probably recorded 1952.

IF YOU'LL BE A BABY TO ME   Polydor 825557
YOUR CHEATIN' HEART   CMF 06
I COULD NEVER BE ASHAMED OF YOU   Mercury 314536077
KAW-LIGA (and two false starts)   Mercury 314536077
ARE YOU WALKIN' AND A TALKIN' FOR THE LORD? (1)   Mercury 314536077
ARE YOU WALKIN' AND A TALKIN' FOR THE LORD? (2)   Polydor 833749
JAMBALAYA   CMF 06
A TEARDROP ON A ROSE   Polydor 833749
YOU BETTER KEEP IT ON YOUR MIND (Hank Williams /
    Vic McAlpin)   CMF 06
Note: Second vocalist is probably Hank Snow.
LOW DOWN BLUES   Polydor 831633
I AIN'T GOT NOTHIN' BUT TIME   Polydor 825548

AFRS 221, March 22, 1952.

Unknown band.
LET THE SPIRIT DESCEND (J. M. Purdom)   Mercury 314536077
HONKY TONK BLUES   Mercury 314536077

Radio show April 1, 1952.

Unknown band.
ARE YOU WALKIN' AND A TALKIN' FOR THE LORD?   Mercury 314536077

Radio show April 4, 1952.

DRIFTING TOO FAR FROM THE SHORE (Charles Moody)   Mercury 314536077

Title (Composer[s])	Recording No.

AFRS 223, April 5, 1952.

Unknown band.
BABY, WE'RE REALLY IN LOVE   Polydor 827531
THE OLD COUNTRY CHURCH* (John Whitfield Vaughn)   Polydor 825548
*With Little Jimmy Dickens

Kate Smith Evening Hour, April 23, 1952.

Unknown band.
COLD, COLD HEART   Unissued
I CAN'T HELP IT*   Mercury 314536077
*With Anita Carter (duet vocal)

Radio show(s) April 1952.

Unknown band(s).
WILD SIDE OF LIFE (Arlie Carter / William Warren)   Mercury 314536077
I CRIED AGAIN (Autry Inman)   Mercury 314536077

Session: June 13, 1952 (10:00 a.m.–1:00 p.m.): Castle Studio, Nashville.

Jerry Rivers (fiddle); Don Helms (steel guitar.); Chet Atkins
    (electric guitar); probably Jack Shook (rhythm guitar);
    Chuck Wright (bass).
WINDOW SHOPPING (Marcel Joseph)   MGM 11283
JAMBALAYA (ON THE BAYOU)   MGM 11283
SETTIN' THE WOODS ON FIRE (Fred Rose / Ed Nelson)   MGM 11318
I'LL NEVER GET OUT OF THIS WORLD ALIVE (Hank Williams /
    Fred Rose)   MGM 11366

Session: July 11, 1952 (1:45–3:45 p.m.): Castle Studio, Nashville.

Jerry Rivers (fiddle); Don Helms (steel guitar); probably Chet Atkins
    (lead guitar); Harold Bradley (rhythm guitar); probably Ernie
    Newton (bass).
YOU WIN AGAIN   MGM 11318
I WON'T BE HOME NO MORE   MGM 11533
BE CAREFUL OF STONES THAT YOU THROW* (Bonnie Dodd)   MGM 11309
PLEASE MAKE UP YOUR MIND*   MGM 11309
*Issued under pseudonym "Luke the Drifter — with Instrumental
    Accompaniment"

Session: September 23, 1952 (1:30–3:40 p.m.): Castle Studio, Nashville.

Tommy Jackson (fiddle); Don Helms (steel guitar); Chet Atkins (lead
    guitar); Jack Shook (rhythm guitar); Floyd "Lightnin'" Chance
    (bass); Farris Coursey (drums)*.
I COULD NEVER BE ASHAMED OF YOU   MGM 11366
YOUR CHEATIN' HEART   MGM 11416
KAW-LIGA* (Hank Williams / Fred Rose)   MGM 11416
TAKE THESE CHAINS FROM MY HEART (Hy Heath / Fred Rose) MGM 11479

Title (Composer[s])	Recording No.

Demo session, KWKH, December 3, 1952.

THE LOG TRAIN   Time-Life TLCW-01

Undated radio performance.

Audrey Williams (duet vocal).
SOMETHING GOT A HOLD OF ME (Warren Caplinger)   Polydor 831033

SOURCES

GENERAL

Documents

Birth, marriage, and death certificates; divorce proceedings; guardianship accountings and related correspondence for Randall Hank Williams and Cathy Yvone Stone; real estate transaction records: Alabama, Louisiana, Tennessee.
Hatch Show Print records.
R. J. Reynolds *Grand Ole Opry* records.
Library of Congress, song copyright data.
MGM Records recording sheets.
MGM Records contract file.
MGM Records royalty statements.
Acuff-Rose correspondence file.
Acuff-Rose royalty statements.
American Federation of Musicians, membership logs.

Books — General

ASCAP Biographical Dictionary. New York: Bowker & Co., 1980.
Escott, Colin, and Kira Florita. *Hank Williams: Snapshots from the Lost Highway.* New York: DaCapo Press, 2001.
Fowler, Gene, and Bill Crawford. *Border Radio.* New York: Limelight Editions, 1990.
Gentry, Linnell. *History and Encyclopedia of Country, Western, and Gospel Music.* Nashville: Clairmont Corp., 1969.
Hank Williams and His Stars of WSFA. Songbook, 1946.
Kingsbury, Paul, ed. *The Encyclopedia of Country Music.* New York: Oxford University Press, 1998.
Malone, Bill C. *Country Music USA.* Austin: University of Texas Press, 1968.
———. *Singing Cowboys and Musical Mountaineers.* Athens, GA: University of Georgia Press, 1993.
Odom, Mr. and Mrs. Burton. *The Hank Williams Story.* Greenville, AL: Butler County Historical Society, 1974.
Radio Annual. New York: Radio Daily, 1938–1948.
Rivers, Jerry. *From Life to Legend.* Denver, CO: Heather Publications, 1967.

Rockwell, Harry E. *Beneath the Applause.* Privately published, 1973.

Rogers, Arnold, and Bruce Gidoll. *The Life and Times of Hank Williams.* Nashville: Haney-Jones Books, 1993.

Sanjek, Russell, and David Sanjek. *American Popular Music Business in the Twentieth Century.* New York: Oxford University Press, 1991.

Shapiro, Nat. *Popular Music.* 6 vols. New York: Adrian Press, 1964–1973.

Whitburn, Joel. *Top Country Singles.* Menomonee Falls, WI: Record Research, 2001.

Williams, Hank, and Jimmy Rule. *Hank Williams Tells How to Write Folk and Western Music to Sell.* Nashville: Harpeth Publishing, 1951.

Williams, Jett, and Pamela Thomas. *Ain't Nothing As Sweet As My Baby.* New York: Harcourt Brace Jovanovich, 1990.

Williams, Lycrecia, and Dale Vinicur. *Still in Love with You.* Nashville: Rutledge Hill, 1989.

Williams, Roger M. *Sing a Sad Song.* New York: Doubleday, 1970.

CHAPTER 1: THE DRIFTING COWBOY'S DREAM

AUTHOR INTERVIEWS

Leila Griffin, Mrs. M. C. Jarrett, J. C. McNeil, Walter McNeil, Robert Williams, 1989–1993.

Harold Sims, 1996.

Leila Griffin, Lum York, and Walter McNeil reinterviewed, 2003.

SOURCES

Gleason, Ralph. "Hank Williams, Roy Acuff and Then God!!" *Rolling Stone,* June 28, 1969.

Greenville (AL) Advocate, "Hank Williams Buried Sunday," January 8, 1953.

Harp, Alice. Online features about "Tee-Tot": http://www.tokyo-blues.com/Rufus _Tee_Tot_Payne.html; http://www.bluepower.com/news.jsp?contentId=2719.

———. "Rufus Payne Teacher / Mentor / Friend to Hank Williams the Child." *Hank Williams Fanzine* 20.

Hendrix, Vernon. "Father of Famed Singer Lives By the Side of the Road." *Montgomery (AL) Advertiser,* December 24, 1967.

Mason, Red. "From Peanuts to Fame." *Millbrook (AL) Tri-Co News,* August 14, 1969.

McGuire, Colin. "Only People Left Here Are Old Folks." *Montgomery (AL) Advertiser,* March 16, 1969.

Rankin, Alan, and Lilly Stone. *Life Story of Our Hank Williams.* Montgomery, AL: Philbert Publications, 1953.

Smith, Irene Williams. "The Day Hank Williams Lived." *Washington Post,* January 1, 1993.

Williams, Lon. Application for Social Security card, 1941.

———. Undated letter to *Camden (AL) Progressive Era.*

CHAPTER 2: "ROY ACUFF, THEN GOD!"

AUTHOR INTERVIEWS AND CORRESPONDENCE

Leila Griffin, Mrs. M. C. Jarrett, J. C. McNeil, Walter McNeil, Jimmy Adams (principal of Sidney Lanier High School), Freddy Beach, Irella Beach, Leaborne Eads, Boots Harris, Braxton Schuffert, Mrs. Caldwell Stewart, Robert Williams, Paul Dennis, 1989–1993.

Harold Sims, 1996.

Leila Griffin, Braxton Schuffert, Walter McNeil, and Boots Harris reinterviewed, 2003.

Lum York, Billy Walker, Lewis Fitzgerald, Pee Wee Moultrie, 2003.

SOURCES

Compton, Thomas H. Letter to Butler County Historical Society. April 7, 1980.

Gleason, Ralph. "Hank Williams, Roy Acuff and Then God!!" *Rolling Stone,* June 28, 1969.

Greenville (AL) Advocate, "Homecoming for Hank Sunday," July 12, 1951.

Mason, Red. "From Peanuts to Fame." *Millbrook (AL) Tri-Co News,* August 14, 1969.

Montgomery (AL) Advertiser, "'Hezzy,' Hank Williams Partner Dies," September 13, 1970.

Rankin, Alan, and Lilly Stone. *Life Story of Our Hank Williams.* Montgomery, AL: Philbert Publications, 1953.

Smith, Irene Williams. "The Day Hank Williams Lived." *Washington Post,* January 1, 1993.

Sutton, Juanealya. *The Man Behind the Scenes.* Defuniak Springs, FL: privately published, 1987.

Williams, Hank. Application to Alabama Dry Dock and Shipbuilding Company. January 28, 1944.

———. Letter to Lilly Williams, November 18, 1940. Courtesy of Marty Stuart.

———. Radio promotional spot for Homecoming, July 1951.

Williams, Lon. Application for Social Security card, 1941.

———. Undated letter to *Camden (AL) Progressive Era.*

CHAPTER 3: SWEET AUDREY FROM PIKE

AUTHOR INTERVIEWS

Paul Dennis, Don Helms, J. C. McNeil, Walter McNeil, Sebie Smith, Bernice Turner, 1989–1993.

Bernice Turner, Don Helms, Walter McNeil reinterviewed, 2003.

Lewis Fitzgerald, 2003.

SOURCES

Gunter, Hardrock. "A Guitarist's Lighthearted Memoir of Hank Williams." In *Hank Williams, the Legend.* Denver: Heather Enterprises, 1972.

Hall, Wade. *Hell-Bent for Music.* Lexington, KY: University Press of Kentucky, 1996.

Honicker, Bunny. "Rose Applauds Famed Protégé." Undated newspaper clip, ca. 1954.

National Hillbilly News, "Fred Rose: Writer of World's Most Powerful Folk Song Music," December 1946.

Owen, Jim. *Star Stories* (radio documentary). Nashville, 1977.

Pearl, Minnie. Interviewed by Country Music Foundation, undated. Hiram Brooks & Assoc. transcript provided to authors.

Rankin, Alan, and Lilly Stone. *Life Story of Our Hank Williams.* Montgomery, AL: Philbert Publications, 1953.

Rumble, John. "Fred Rose and the Development of the Nashville Music Business." PhD diss., Vanderbilt University, 1980.

Williams, Audrey. Interviewed by Dorothy Horstman, 1973. Courtesy of the estate of Dorothy Horstman.

CHAPTER 4: SONGS FOR HOME FOLKS

AUTHOR INTERVIEWS

Lynn Davis, Don Helms, Murray Nash, R. D. Norred, Joe Pennington, Vic Willis, Lum York, 1989–1993.

SOURCES

Billboard (Acuff-Rose suppl.), "Wesley Rose Chooses Nashville — a Crucial Decision for the World of Music," February 3, 1968.

Daniel, Wayne W. "They Left Them to Die Like a Tramp on the Street." *Bluegrass Unlimited* 20 (August 1985).

Hawkins, Martin, and Colin Escott. *A Shot in the Dark.* Vollersode, Germany: Bear Family Records, 2001.

Howard, Paul. Deposition in *Randall Hank Williams et al. v. Fred Rose Music et al.,* 1975.

Rose, Fred. Foreword to *Hank Williams' Country Hit Parade,* by Hank Williams. Nashville: Acuff-Rose Sales, 1950.

Rumble, John. "Fred Rose and the Development of the Nashville Music Business." PhD diss., Vanderbilt University, 1980.

———. "The Emergence of Nashville as a Recording Center." *Journal of Country Music* (December 1978).

State of New York. Department of State. Certificates of incorporation for Sterling Records (July 27, 1945), Sterling Records Distribution (October 24, 1945), and Juke Box Records Company (October 24, 1945).

Tribe, Ivan. Liner notes to *Molly O'Day.* Vollersode, Germany: Bear Family Records, 1992.

Williams, Audrey. Interviewed by Dorothy Horstman, 1973. Courtesy of the estate of Dorothy Horstman.

Williams, Hank. Interview with *National Hillbilly News,* November–December, 1949.

Willis, Vic. Interviewed by Jack Hurst. "Requiem for a Country Boy." *Nashville Tennessean,* January 2, 1972.

Zolotow, Maurice. "Hillbilly Boom." *Saturday Evening Post,* February 12, 1944.

CHAPTER 5: THE YEAR OF THE LION

AUTHOR INTERVIEWS

Leaborne Eads, Walter McNeil, R. D. Norred, Joe Pennington, Lum York, 1989–1993. Lum York, R. D. Norred reinterviewed, 2003.

SOURCES

"Frank Walker." Obituary in *Billboard,* October 26, 1963.

"Frank Walker, Former MGM Exec, Disk Pioneer Dies." *Music Reporter* (Nashville), October 26, 1963.

"(Last Night) I Heard You Crying in Your Sleep." Lyric sheet, Alabama Department of Archives and History.

Time, "A Platter for the Lion," February 24, 1947.

Turnipseed, Rev. A. S. Undated clip, *Montgomery News.*

Walker, Frank. Deposition in Circuit Court of Montgomery. February 7, 1963.

———. "Music Which Is Distinctively Our Own." *World of Country Music* (*Billboard* Publications, New York), November 1963.

Williams, Audrey. Interviewed by Dorothy Horstman, 1973. Courtesy of the estate of Dorothy Horstman.

CHAPTER 6: *THE HAYRIDE*

AUTHOR INTERVIEWS

Don Helms, Merle Kilgore, Horace Logan, Tillman Franks, 1989–1993. Tillman Franks, Merle Kilgore reinterviewed, 2003.

SOURCES

Foree, Mel. Interviewed by Doug Green. Country Music Foundation Oral History Project. April 30 and July 29, 1974.

Franks, Tillman, and Robert Gentry. *I Was There When It Happened.* Many, LA: Sweet Dreams Publishing, 2000.

Gentry, Robert, ed. *The Louisiana Hayride: The Glory Years — 1948–1960*. Many, LA: Sweet Dreams Publishing, 1998.

Jones-Hall, Lillian, "A Historical Study of Programming Techniques and Practices of KWKH 1922–1950." PhD diss., Louisiana State University at Shreveport, 1982.

Stubbs, Eddie. Liner notes to the Bailes Brothers, *Oh So Many Years*. Vollersode, Germany, Bear Family Records, 2002.

CHAPTER 7: A FEELING CALLED THE BLUES

AUTHOR INTERVIEWS

Claude Boone, Zeke Turner, Jerry Byrd, Lum York, Clent Holmes, Felton Pruett, Bob McNett, Johnnie Wright, Mitchell Torok, Billy Byrd, Billie Jean Horton, Murray Nash, Lum York, 1989–1993.

Clent Holmes, Felton Pruett reinterviewed, 2003.

SOURCES

Bledsoe, Wayne. "Knoxville's Great Lost Songwriter, Arthur Q. Smith." *Knoxville (TN) News Sentinel*, May 12, 1991.

Coffey, Kevin. Booklet text to *Rex Griffin: The Last Letter*. Vollersode, Germany: Bear Family Records, 1996.

Davis, Oscar. Interviewed by Doug Green. Country Music Foundation Oral History Project. July 24, 1974.

Gunter, Hardrock. "A Guitarist's Lighthearted Memoir of Hank Williams." In *Hank Williams, the Legend*. Denver: Heather Enterprises, 1972.

Pearl, Minnie. Interviewed by Country Music Foundation, undated. Hiram Brooks & Assoc. transcript provided to authors.

Roe, Gene L. "Got 'Lovesick Blues'? No, Sir, Not Hank Williams." *National Hillbilly News*, January–February 1950.

Shreveport Times, "Clyde Baum: He Picked Bluegrass Tunes with Hank Williams," July 10, 1980.

Snow, Hank, Jack Ownbey, and Bob Burris. *The Hank Snow Story*. Chicago: University of Illinois Press, 1994.

Southern Star, "Hank Williams Presents Grand Ole Opry Show Here," September 21, 1950.

Williams, Hank. Dialogue recorded at Sunset Park, MD, 1952.

Wolfe, Charles. Booklet text to *Emmett Miller: The Minstrel Man from Georgia*. New York: Sony Music, 1996.

CHAPTER 8: "TONIGHT, LIVE FROM NASHVILLE, TENNESSEE . . ."

AUTHOR INTERVIEWS

Hillous Butrum, Don Helms, Bob McNett, Billy Robinson, Grant Turner, 1989–1993. A. V. Bamford, Irving Waugh, 2003.

SOURCES

Acuff, Roy. Interviewed on *Hank Williams: Reflections by Those Who Loved Him*. MGM Records, 1975.

Cunniff, Albert. "Muscle behind the Music: The Life and Times of Jim Denny." *Journal of Country Music* 11, nos. 1–2 (1986).

Davidson, Bill. "There's Gold in Them Thar Hillbilly Tunes." *Collier's*, July 28, 1951.

Davis, Oscar. Interviewed by Doug Green. Country Music Foundation Oral History Project. July 24, 1974.

Harris, Jack. "Hushpackana: Judge Hay is Back at WSM's Opry." *Rural Radio* (Nashville), November 1938.

Honicker, Bunny. "Rose Applauds Famed Protégé." Undated newspaper clip, ca. 1954.

Montgomery (AL) Advertiser, "Hank Williams Europe Bound," November 9, 1949.

Rumble, John. Liner notes to *Red Foley: Country Music Hall of Fame.* Nashville: MCA Records, 1991.

Rust, Brian. *Jazz and Ragtime Records.* Denver: Mainspring Press, 2002.

Shriver, Jerry. "Hank Williams' Buddy Remembers When." *Pensacola (FL) Journal,* January 1, 1982.

Tubb, Ernest. Interviewed on *Hank Williams: Reflections by Those Who Loved Him.* MGM Records, 1975.

Variety, "Grand Ole Opry Competes with Europe's Own Hillbilly Gasthaus," November 30, 1949.

CHAPTER 9: "HURRIED SOUTHERN TRIPS . . ."

AUTHOR INTERVIEWS

A. V. Bamford, Tillman Franks, Don Helms, Bob McNett, W. B. Nowlin, Braxton Schuffert, 1989–1993.

Braxton Schuffert, Bernice Turner, 2003.

SOURCES

Nashville Banner, "Hillbilly Singing Star Forfeits Fire Bond," April 16, 1950.

Pruett, Sammy. Interviewed by Jim Owen. *Star Stories* (radio documentary). Nashville, 1977.

Smith, Richard D. *Can't You Hear Me Callin': The Life of Bill Monroe.* New York: Little, Brown and Co., 2000.

Vinicur, Dale. Liner notes to Audrey Williams, *Ramblin' Gal.* Vollersode, Germany: Bear Family Records, 1989.

CHAPTER 10: A GOOD YEAR FOR THE ROSES

AUTHOR INTERVIEWS

Jim Boyd, Jimmy Dickens, Bill England, Don Helms, Clent Holmes, Mac McGee, Bob McNett, Mitch Miller, Grant Turner, 1989–1993.

SOURCES

Atkins, Chet. Interview in *Behind Closed Doors* by Alanna Nash. New York: Knopf, 1987.

Clay, John W. Letter to the authors. June 8, 1993.

Cunniff, Albert. "Muscle behind the Music: The Life and Times of Jim Denny." *Journal of Country Music* 11, nos. 1–2 (1986).

Davidson, Bill. "There's Gold in Them Thar Hillbilly Tunes." *Collier's,* July 28, 1951.

Davis, Oscar. Interviewed by Doug Green. Country Music Foundation Oral History Project. July 24, 1974.

McWethy, John. "Hillbilly Tunes Boom." *Wall Street Journal,* October 2, 1951.

Rankin, Allen. "Rankin File." *Montgomery Alabama Journal,* February 4, 1953.

Shriver, Jerry. "Hank Williams' Buddy Remembers When." *Pensacola (FL) Journal,* January 1, 1982.

Van Ness, Clark. d/b/a. *Dixie Music v. Hank Williams, Acuff-Rose, et al.* New York (S. District), December 3, 1951.

Williams, Audrey. Interviewed by Dorothy Horstman, 1973. Courtesy of the estate of Dorothy Horstman.

Williams, Hank. Interviewed in Charleston, SC, March 2, 1951.

CHAPTER 11: FOLK AND WESTERN MUSIC TO SELL
AUTHOR INTERVIEWS
Bill England, Tillman Franks, Don Helms, Billie Jean Horton, Bill Lister, J. C. McNeil,
    Walter McNeil, Braxton Schuffert, 1989–1993.
Bill Lister reinterviewed, 2003.

SOURCES
Bocephus News (Paris, TN), data on "Tear in My Beer" video, spring / summer 1989.
Cooper, Dan. *Lefty Frizzell — the Honky Tonk Life of Country Music's Greatest Singer.*
    Boston: Little, Brown and Co., 1995.
Flippo, Chet. *Your Cheatin' Heart.* New York: Simon & Schuster, 1981.
Frizzell, Lefty. Interview on *Hank Williams: Reflections by Those Who Loved Him.*
    MGM Records, 1975.
Hudgins, Helen. Interviewed by John Rumble in *The Complete Hank Williams.*
    Nashville: Mercury Records, 1999.
Law, Don. Unpublished notebooks, 1950–1967.
Montgomery (AL) Examiner, "Hank Williams Stars in Homecoming Event," July 15, 1951.
Russell, Tony. Liner notes to Jimmie Davis, *You Are My Sunshine* and *Nobody's
    Darlin' but Mine.* Vollersode, Germany: Bear Family Records, 1998.
Williams, Hank. Promotional spots for the Homecoming Show and for *Hank Williams
    Tells How to Write Folk and Western Music to Sell.*
Wolfe, Charles. Liner notes to Lefty Frizzell, *Life's Like Poetry.* Vollersode, Germany:
    Bear Family Records, 1992.

CHAPTER 12: THE HADDY-COLE BOUNCE
AUTHOR INTERVIEWS
Art Celsie, Bill Lister, Frank D. McMurry, J. C. McNeil, Walter McNeil, Murray Nash,
    Braxton Schuffert, Johnnie Wright, 1989–1993.
Bill Lister reinterviewed, 2003.

SOURCES
Angers, Trent. "The Three Faces of Dudley J. LeBlanc." *Acadiana Profile* 6, no. 1
    (1977).
Clay, Floyd Martin. *Coozan Dudley LeBlanc, from Huey Long to Hadacol.* Gretna, LA:
    Pelican Publishing, 1987.
Grand Ole Opry transcription, October 6, 1951.
Hadacol Caravan program and itinerary, 1951.
Pearl, Minnie. Interviewed by Country Music Foundation, undated. Hiram Brooks &
    Assoc. transcript provided to authors.
Tubb, Ernest. Interviewed on *Hank Williams: Reflections by Those Who Loved Him.*
    MGM Records, 1975.
Williams, Audrey. Interviewed by Dorothy Horstman, 1973. Courtesy of the estate
    of Dorothy Horstman.
Williams, Hank. Interview in Charleston, SC, March 3, 1951.
———. Two taped apologies, December 1951.

CHAPTER 13: "A GOOD TIME ALL THE TIME"
AUTHOR INTERVIEWS
Don Helms, 1989–1993.
Ray Price, Jett Williams, 2003.

SOURCES
Atkins, Chet. Interview in *Behind Closed Doors* by Alanna Nash. New York: Knopf: 1987.
Brown, Gordy. "Hank Williams at Symphony Hall, Boston: Fact or Scam?" *Hank Williams Fanzine* 21.
Davidson, Bill. "There's Gold in Them Thar Hillbilly Tunes." *Collier's,* July 28, 1951.
Davis, Oscar. Interviewed by Doug Green. Country Music Foundation Oral History Project. July 24, 1974.
Gleason, Ralph. "Hank Williams, Roy Acuff and Then God!!" *Rolling Stone,* June 28, 1969.
Lucas, Mike. "Hank Williams: The Original Country-Western Superstar Flopped in His Only Las Vegas Strip Appearance." *Las Vegas Sun,* January 2, 1983.
McWethy, John. "Hillbilly Tunes Boom." *Wall Street Journal,* October 2, 1951.
Montgomery (AL) Advertiser, "Hank's First Wife Tells of Ups and Downs of Marriage," January 13, 1953.
———. "Cold, Cold Heart Changeover to Cold, Cold Cash," January 5, 1955.
Newsweek, "Country Music Is Big Business and Nashville Is Its Detroit," August 11, 1952.
Pathfinder, "Country Music Comes to Town," June 1952.
Pearl, Minnie. Interviewed by Country Music Foundation, undated. Hiram Brooks & Assoc. transcript provided to authors.
Stark, Mrs. Warren, and Leon Carter. Interviewed by unknown interviewer. April 1986.
Williams, Hank. Interview in *Country Song Roundup* (Charlton Publications), June 1953.
Williams, Audrey. Interviewed by Dorothy Horstman, 1973. Courtesy of the estate of Dorothy Horstman.

CHAPTER 14: BILLIE JEAN

AUTHOR INTERVIEWS
Tillman Franks, Murray Nash, Johnnie Wright, 1989–1993.
Don Helms, Ray Price, 2003.

SOURCES
Clayton, Frank. "Remembering Hank." *Montgomery Alabama Journal,* February 20, 1971.
Grand Ole Opry transcription. July 12, 1952.
Greenville (AL) Advocate, "Friday Is Hank Williams Day for Greenville, Butler Co.," August 14, 1952.
———. "Hank Williams Is Booked Here," July 17, 1952.
———. "Hank Williams Is Rated No. 1 Goodwill Ambassador . . . ," July 31, 1952.
Kitsinger, Otto. Liner notes to *Webb Pierce: 1951–1958.* Vollersode, Germany: Bear Family Records, 1996.
McKinnon, Bob. "Hank Williams' First Week after the Opry." Unpublished manuscript. Courtesy of the McKinnon estate.
Nashville Tennessean, "WSM Drops Contract for Hank," August 15, 1952.
Rankin, Allen. "Rankin File." *Montgomery (AL) Advertiser,* September 28, 1952.
Rose, Fred. Letter to Tillman Franks. November 11, 1949.
Tubb, Ernest. Interviewed on *Hank Williams: Reflections by Those Who Loved Him.* MGM Records, 1975.
Williams Berlin, Billie Jean. Deposition in Civil Action No. 12,181, *Billie Jean Williams Berlin v. MGM Inc., CBS Inc., Storer Broadcasting Inc.* in the Northern District of Georgia, Atlanta Division. December 13, 1968.

Young, Faron. Testimony in *Randall Hank Williams et al. v. Fred Rose Music et al.* 1975.

———. Interviewed by Biff Collie. The Nashville Network Radio, February 26, 1990.

CHAPTER 15: "I'M SO TIRED OF IT ALL"

AUTHOR INTERVIEWS

Ray Edenton, Tommy Hill, Billie Jean Horton, Claude King, Horace Logan, F. D. McMurry, Felton Pruett, Billy Walker, Lum York, 1989–1993.

Billie Jean Horton, Claude King, Felton Pruett, Billy Walker, Lum York reinterviewed, 2003.

Merle Kilgore, Frank Page, Ray Price, Charlie Walker, 2003.

SOURCES

Cromley, Allan. "Secret of Quack's License Baffles Narcotics Probers." *Oklahoma City Times,* March 25, 1953.

Davis, Oscar. Interviewed by Doug Green. Country Music Foundation Oral History Project. July 24, 1974.

———. Testimony in *Randall Hank Williams et al. v. Fred Rose Music et al.* 1975.

Ene, George. "Walker Questioned Williams Vows." *Nashville Banner,* March 19, 1975.

Glenn, Marie. Testimony in *Randall Hank Williams et al. v. Fred Rose Music et al.* 1975.

Greenville (AL) Advocate, "Clyde Perdue Dies," November 26, 1963.

Howard, Paul. Testimony in *Randall Hank Williams et al. v. Fred Rose Music et al.* 1975.

Hutchins, James. Testimony in *Randall Hank Williams et al. v. Fred Rose Music et al.* 1975.

Mackey, Wayne. "Singer Given Leopard Drug." *Oklahoma City Times,* March 11, 1953.

McKee, Don. "Legality May Be Questioned in Williams' Second Marriage." *Montgomery (AL) Advertiser,* January 9, 1953.

Medley, Robert. "Manuscript in a Black Bag." Unpublished, 1992.

Mobile (AL) Register, "Hank Williams and Wife Said Married Illegally," January 15, 1953.

Oklahoma City Daily Oklahoman, "Dope Witness Parole Revoked," March 13, 1953.

Oklahoma City Times, "Was Singer a Suicide?" March 15, 1953.

Rose, Wesley. Testimony in *Randall Hank Williams et al. v. Fred Rose Music et al.* 1975.

Shreveport (LA) Journal, "Famous Song Composer Is Arrested Here," December 12, 1953.

State of Oklahoma Department of Corrections. Letter to authors re. inmate #58545 and 51646. November 12, 1992.

Stone, Catherine Yvone v. Gulf American Fire & Casualty Co. et al. Supreme Court of Alabama, docket no. 87–269. Cited in *554 Southern Reporter,* 2d series. July 5, 1989.

Taylor, J. Nelson. "Pretty Witness Tells Hillbilly's Bizarre Story." *Oklahoma City Daily Oklahoman,* March 18, 1953.

Turpen, Brian. Unpublished research on Hank Williams' itinerary and on Toby Marshall.

Van Dyke, Bill. "Forged License Cost Him $25, Quack Declares." *Oklahoma City Daily Oklahoman,* March 25, 1953.

Ward, Ed. Liner notes to *Sir Doug's Recording Trip.* London: Edsel Records, 1989.

Williams, Audrey. Interviewed by Dorothy Horstman, 1973. Courtesy of the estate of Dorothy Horstman.

Williams Berlin, Billie Jean. Deposition in Civil Action No. 12,181, *Billie Jean Williams Berlin v. MGM Inc., CBS Inc., Storer Broadcasting Inc.* in the Northern District of Georgia, Atlanta Division. December 13, 1968.

CHAPTER 16: MIDNIGHT

AUTHOR INTERVIEWS

A. V. Bamford, Irella Beach, Charles Carr, Leila Griffin, Marie Glenn Harvell, Billie Jean Horton, Dr. Leo Killorn, Horace Logan, Murray Nash, Braxton Shuffert, Erleen Skipper, Taft Skipper, 1989–1993.
Charles Carr, Billie Jean Horton reinterviewed, 2003.
Lewis Fitzgerald, 2003.

SOURCES

Brown, Ricardo, and Martha Garrett. "Hank Planned to Remarry Her in February, Former Wife Says." *Montgomery Alabama Journal,* January 9, 1953.
Knoxville (TN) Journal, "Mystery Shrouds Death of Singer Hank Williams," January 2, 1953.
Knoxville (TN) News Sentinel, "ET Officer Suspected Williams Wasn't Alive," January 2, 1953.
Marquee Club. Contract with Hank Williams. October 5, 1952.
Marshall, Toby. Letter to Hank Williams. December 28, 1952. Courtesy of Marty Stuart.
McKee, Don. "First Wife Out of Hank's Plans, Widow Declares." *Montgomery (AL) Advertiser,* January 10, 1953.
Montgomery Alabama Journal, "Country Boy Returns," December 29 and 30, 1952.
Morris, Doug. "Hank Williams' Death Still Issue." *Knoxville (TN) Journal,* December 15, 1982.
Nashville Tennessean, "Williams' Death Laid to Heart Condition," January 11, 1953.
Oak Hill Hospital. Hank Williams autopsy. January 1, 1953.
Oak Hill (WV) Fayette Tribune, "Six Man Jury Awaits Autopsy Report . . . ," January 5, 1953.
O'Quin, Beecher. Full-issue article on Donald Surface. *International Traditional Country Music Fan Club* 4, no. 3 (November 1999).
Taylor, J. Nelson. "Pretty Witness Tells Hillbilly's Bizarre Story." *Oklahoma City Daily Oklahoman,* March 18, 1953.
Turpen, Brian. Unpublished research on Hank Williams' death and on Toby Marshall.
Tyree, Joe, et al. Interviews with Vic Gabany. Undated. Oak Hill, WV. Used by permission.
Williams, Susan. "Did Hank Williams Die in Oak Hill?" *Oak Hill (WV) Fayette Tribune,* December 22, 1982.

CHAPTER 17: WUTHERING DEPTHS

AUTHOR INTERVIEWS

A. V. Bamford, Jerry Byrd, Charles Carr, Leaborne Eads, Leila Griffin, Don Helms, Billie Jean Horton, Horace Logan, Braxton Schuffert, 1989–1993.
Charles Carr, Braxton Schuffert, Billie Jean Horton, Leila Griffin reinterviewed, 2003.
Lewis Fitzgerald, 2003.

SOURCES

Azbell, Joe. "Hank's Funeral Is Far Largest in Montgomery's History." *Montgomery (AL) Advertiser,* January 5, 1953.
Canton (OH) Repository, "Hank Williams Dies En Route to Show Here," January 2, 1953.
Davis, Oscar. Interview with Doug Green. Country Music Foundation Oral History Project. July 24, 1974.
Honicker, Bunny. "Rose Applauds Famed Protégé." Undated newspaper clip, ca. 1954.
Horton, Billie Jean. "Fear and Loathing at Hank's Funeral." *Texas Music,* June 1976.

Jones, Eddie. "Thousands at Rites for Hank Williams." *Nashville Banner,* January 5, 1953.

Montgomery Alabama Journal, "Williams Failed to Leave Will," January 6, 1953.

Montgomery (AL) Advertiser, "Williams' Body in New Grave," January 18, 1953.

Oak Hill Hospital. Hank Williams autopsy. January 1, 1953.

Oklahoma City Times, "Was Singer a Suicide?" March 18, 1953.

Rose, Wesley. Interview in "Remembering Hank." *Country Music,* March 1975.

Smith, Irene Williams. Letters to Robert Stewart. April 6, 1953; January 28, 1972; and others. Courtesy of Marty Stuart.

Stewart, Robert. Letter to M. Cook Barwick. May 30, 1969. In Randall Hank Williams guardianship file.

Stone, Catherine Yvone v. Gulf American Fire & Casualty Co. et al. Supreme Court of Alabama, docket no. 87–269. Cited in *554 Southern Reporter,* 2d series. July 5, 1989.

Sullivan, Phil. "Williams Estate Left in Three-Way Triangle." *Nashville Tennessean,* January 9, 1953.

Turpen, Brian. Unpublished research on Hank Williams' death and on Toby Marshall.

Williams, Audrey. Letter to Irene Williams Smith. February 24, 1953. Courtesy of Marty Stuart.

Williams Berlin, Billie Jean. Deposition in Civil Action No. 12,181, *Billie Jean Williams Berlin v. MGM Inc., CBS Inc., Storer Broadcasting Inc.* in the Northern District of Georgia, Atlanta Division. December 13, 1968.

Williams, Hank. Funeral broadcast. Private collection.

Williams, Hank, Jr. *Living Proof.* New York: Dell, 1983.

INDEX